I0887680

AMERICAN CATHOLICS AND THE CHURCH OF TOMORROW

BUILDING CHURCHES FOR THE FUTURE, 1925–1975

AMERICAN CATHOLICS AND THE CHURCH OF TOMORROW

Catherine R. Osborne

UNIVERSITY OF CHICAGO PRESS
CHICAGO AND LONDON

PUBLICATION OF THIS BOOK HAS BEEN AIDED
BY A GRANT FROM THE BEVINGTON FUND

The University of Chicago Press, Chicago 60637
The University of Chicago Press, Ltd., London
© 2018 by The University of Chicago
All rights reserved. No part of this book may be used or reproduced in any manner whatsoever without written permission, except in the case of brief quotations in critical articles and reviews. For more information, contact the University of Chicago Press, 1427 E. 60th St., Chicago, IL 60637.
Published 2018
Printed in the United States of America

27 26 25 24 23 22 21 20 19 18   1 2 3 4 5

ISBN-13: 978-0-226-56102-8 (cloth)
ISBN-13: 978-0-226-56116-5 (e-book)
DOI: https://doi.org/10.7208/chicago/9780226561165.001.0001

Chapter 4 features material adapted from "From Sputnik to Spaceship Earth: American Catholics in the Space Age." *Religion & American Culture* 25, no. 2 (Summer 2015): 218–63.

Chapter 6 features material adapted from "Renovating for the New Liturgy: The Boston College Students' Chapel." *American Catholic Studies* 125, no. 3 (Fall 2014): 93–104.

Library of Congress Cataloging-in-Publication Data

Names: Osborne, Catherine R., 1979– author.
Title: American Catholics and the Church of tomorrow : building churches for the future, 1925–1975 / Catherine R. Osborne.
Description: Chicago : University of Chicago Press, 2018. | Includes bibliographical references and index.
Identifiers: LCCN 2017043826 | ISBN 9780226561028 (cloth : alk. paper) | ISBN 9780226561165 (e-book)
Subjects: LCSH: Catholic church buildings—United States—History—20th century. | Modern movement (Architecture)—United States—History—20th century. | Modernism (Christian theology)—Catholic Church—History—20th century.
Classification: LCC NA5212.5.M63 082 2018 | DDC 726.0973/0904—dc23
LC record available at https://lccn.loc.gov/2017043826

♾ This paper meets the requirements of ANSI/NISO Z39.48–1992 (Permanence of Paper).

For Lee, Paul, and Anna

The future of the Church

We are the people of the future in the land of the future.

Walter Ong, SJ, on American Catholics,
in *Frontiers in American Catholicism*, 1956

Every society faces not merely a succession of *probable* futures, but an array of *possible* futures, and a conflict over *preferable* futures. The management of change is the effort to convert certain possibles into probables, in pursuit of agreed-upon preferables. . . . Change is the process by which the future invades our lives.

Alvin Toffler, *Future Shock*, 1970

CONTENTS

ACKNOWLEDGMENTS

This project has grown significantly in scope over the course of many years. An interest in the Liturgical Arts Society's connections to Bauhaus refugees eventually extended backward into nineteenth-century biology and forward to urban "renewal" and modern corporate transfers, along the way picking up the postwar monastic revival, early LSD use, Pentagon protest liturgies, homespun post–Vatican II chapel renovations, and landmark buildings by many of the twentieth century's signature architects. I can only partially acknowledge my debts to those who have supported me through this long exploration: first and foremost, my mother, a writer who taught me to love looking, and my father, an architect who taught me to love words. My brother Nick and my sister-in-law Mary Kate are wonderful conversation partners on American history and rhetoric. Dorothy Fortenberry and Colin Wambsgans, Heather Weidner and Brian Dudley, Erica and Dan Olson-Bang, Heather DuBois, Chris Cobb and Catherine Pellegrino, Vincent Virga and James McCourt, and Leah Zimmer and Peter Ringenberg have welcomed me into their homes and families. Three parish communities sustained me during these years: St. Joseph of the Holy Family, New York; the Oratory Church of St. Boniface, Brooklyn; and

St. Augustine, South Bend. My special gratitude to the St. Peter Claver Catholic Worker community. Blessings on the work.

Fordham University, Franklin & Marshall College, and the Cushwa Center for the Study of American Catholicism at the University of Notre Dame have all provided travel support, excellent libraries, and, most important, rich communities of friends and colleagues. I am grateful to Swarthmore College for many things, but especially for the training in looking at and writing about art and architecture I received from Michael Cothren, Connie Hungerford, and T. Kaori Kitao. Many friends read various stages of this work, in whole or in part, and all provided thoughtful, affirming, and challenging comments; I especially thank Fran Altvater, Gretchen Buggeln, Pete Cajka, Jennifer Callaghan, Matthew Cressler, Massimo Faggioli, Margaret Grubiak, Katherine Harmon, Christine Firer Hinze, Richard Kieckhefer, Katharine Mahon, Scott MacDougall, Margaret McGuinness, Mark Massa, Brenna Moore, Thomas Rzeznik, John Seitz, Jane Skoljdi, Thomas Tweed, and Benjamin Wurgaft. As usual, James T. Fisher is in a class by himself. Peter Ringenberg, Pete Hlabse, Vincent Virga, and Joel McNary lent expert eyes to the photography. I am infinitely grateful to Timothy Mennel at the University of Chicago Press, whose unflagging support helped this book get written in the first place, and whose precise editing clarified and streamlined the final text. Editorial associate Rachel Kelly, senior manuscript editor Yvonne Zipter, and copyeditor Johanna Rosenbohm helped me navigate many tangled questions around permissions, citations, textual clarity, and production; and I am grateful as well to the design and promotions staff of the press.

Dozens of archivists and librarians went far beyond the basics to suggest possible new sources in their collections, to smooth the path toward seeing restricted files, to secure photos, and to mail me materials that I couldn't see in person. First and foremost, I thank the superb staff of the University of Notre Dame Archives, especially Kevin Cawley, Charles Lamb, Elizabeth Hogan, and Sharon Sumpter. I am also especially grateful for the collaboration of these men and women, who helped me so much, in so many ways: St. Andrew's Abbey: Dominique Guillen, OSB; Arcosanti: Hanne Sue Kirsch and Lissa McCullough; Archdiocese of Baltimore: Tricia Pyne; Boston Redevelopment Authority: Dean Huggins; Cal Poly San Luis Obispo: Laura Sorvetti and Catherine Trujillo; Catholic University of America: William Shepherd; Columbia, Maryland: Barbara Kellner, Robin Emrich, and Jeannette Lichtenwalner; Conception Abbey: Bernard Montgomery, OSB; Diocese of Kansas City: Fr. Michael Coleman; Harvard Graduate School of Design: Ines Zalduendo; Marquette University: Mark Thiel; Mount Angel Abbey: Augustine

DeNoble, OSB; Archdiocese of New York: Kate Feighery; Passionist Historical Archives: Rob Carbonneau, CP; Portsmouth Abbey: Damian Kearney, OSB; Redwoods Abbey: Veronique Gerooms, OSCO; Archdiocese of San Francisco: Jeffrey Burns, Sr. Jude Ristey, PBVM, and Chris Doan; Archdiocese of Seattle: Joshua Zimmerman; Taliesin West: Indira Berndtson; and the staff of the Library of Congress Manuscript Division and of the Archives of American Art (Smithsonian Institution).

Many architects, artists, priests, men and women religious, lay ministers, and parish staff corresponded with me, facilitated my visits, allowed me to take photographs, and frequently gave me a tour, shared a story, or dug up old files from the basement. Some even housed and fed me for a night or three. Their generosity constantly renewed in me the will to produce a study worthy of their work in the Church. Of those who consented to be interviewed, Clovis and Maryann Heimsath, Robert Lawton Jones, Willy Malarcher, Barbara Mills, Ray Pavia, and Patrick Quinn were especially generous with their time, energy, and personal papers. While it is impossible to mention everyone I learned from, I am particularly grateful to these men and women: Annunciation Abbey, Bismarck, North Dakota: Jill Ackerman, Gemma Peters, OSB, Denise Ressler, OSB, and Edith Selzler, OSB; Chapel + Cultural Center, Rensselaer Polytechnic Institute, Troy, New York: Mary Holbritter, Fr. Ed Kacerguis, and Diane Waters; Chapel of the Holy Cross, Sedona, Arizona: Vicki Milner and Fr. Charles Reaume; Christ the King, Seattle, Washington: Fr. Marty Lundberg; Conrad Schmitt Studios, Milwaukee, Wisconsin: Eileen Groger and Heidi Gruenke; Holy Name, Watertown, South Dakota: Fr. John Lantsberger; Our Divine Savior, Chico, California: Mimi Atkins; Portsmouth Abbey, Portsmouth, Rhode Island: Fr. Damian, OSB; Rambusch Decorating Company, New York, New York: Viggo and Katha Grace Rambusch; Resurrection of Our Lord, St. Louis, Missouri: Dominic Dung Anh Nguyen, SVD; St. Ann's, Normandy, Missouri: Fr. Bill Kempf; St. Ann's, Palo Alto, California: Rev. Rob Kemp; St. Bede's Priory, Eau Claire, Wisconsin: Michaela Hedican, OSB; St. Francis Xavier, Kansas City, Missouri: Mary Medellin and John Vowells, SJ; St. James the Less, Jamesburg, New Jersey: Fr. Kevin Duggan; St. John's Abbey, Collegeville, Minnesota: Carla Durand, David Klingeman, OSB, and Alan Reed, OSB; St. John the Evangelist, Hopkins, Minnesota: Fr. Jim Liekhus and Virginia Vonhof; St. Leo's, Pipestone, Minnesota: Susan VanMoorelehem; St. Louis Abbey: Ambrose Bennett, OSB, Timothy Horner, OSB, Bede Price, OSB, and Sixtus Roslevich, OSB; St. Mark's, University of California–Santa Barbara: Fr. John Love; St. Mary's, Sioux Falls, South Dakota: Fr. David Krogman; St. Matthew's, San Mateo, California: Fr. Anthony

McGuire and Jim Walsh; St. Norbert Abbey, De Pere, Wisconsin: Fr. Stephen Rossey, O. Praem., and Judy Turba; St. Peter's, Kirkwood, Missouri: Msgr. Jack Costello; SS. Peter and Paul, Pierre, South Dakota: Fr. Kevin Doyle; St. Philip Neri, Portland, Oregon: Fr. Charlie Brunick; St. Richard's, Jackson, Michigan: Suzan Cox; St. Rita's, Cottage Grove, Minnesota: Maureen O'Kane; St. Thomas Aquinas, St. Paul Park, Minnesota: Fr. Greg Esty; St. Thomas More, Portland, Oregon: Julian Kegg; Wilde Lake Interfaith Center, Columbia, Maryland: Margo Duke.

Alongside those who preserve and share their legacy today, I remember St. John XXIII and all the men and women of the twentieth century who, with great joy and hope, devoted themselves to building the church.

INTRODUCTION

In the fall of 1917 an American Catholic soldier, an interpreter stationed near the French-Belgian border, paid a courtesy call on the cardinal archbishop of Reims. Hearing that the young man hoped to spend time at the École des Beaux-Arts (then the foremost architectural school in the world) after the war, Cardinal Lugon generously escorted him around the cathedral—one of the purest and most beautiful Gothic buildings in France, but recently the victim of a viciously successful German artillery campaign. The two men had to step carefully to avoid workers filling buckets with pieces of stained glass fallen from the shattered windows. Above them, in the crossing, they could see the sky through a yawning hole in the vault.

For the next half century, Maurice Lavanoux recalled this sight as a turning point in his life. "Although I had listened carefully to the lectures on architecture during my evening courses at Columbia," he later wrote, "I was not prepared for the impact this cathedral would have on me when I saw it in all its structural glory and integrity." The artillery fire that had ripped open the vault also revealed the building's engineering genius: the hole, like a cross section cut through a model, allowed Lavanoux to "*see* the construction devised by those medieval master masons—they were not yet then called architects!—and . . . *feel* the sense of positive design in the play of buttress versus vault."[1]

Before his stint as an army interpreter, Lavanoux had worked as an office boy for the New York neomedievalist church architect Gustave Steinback, and after he returned to the United States, he became a draftsman for Maginnis & Walsh of Boston—among the most respected architectural firms of the day and, like Steinback, specialists in neohistoricist design. Yet for the remainder of his long career, Lavanoux used his encounter with Reims Cathedral to explain not his medievalism, but what we would now call his *modernism*. Lavanoux was no radical, but over the course of his forty-year stint as secretary of the Liturgical Arts Society—a New York–based group promoting the "advancement" of the Catholic arts—and editor of its journal *Liturgical Arts*, his stubborn support for the application of modernist design principles to Catholic church architecture proved critical to that movement's success.[2]

Generations of American Catholics had been deeply concerned with the making and maintaining of sacred space, part of what Jay Dolan calls "brick and mortar Catholicism."[3] In the nineteenth and early twentieth centuries, immigrants labored by day on the skyscrapers of metropolis, then volunteered by night to erect parish churches; priests were evaluated and promoted based on their capacity to establish extensive physical plants; bishops like Philadelphia's Dennis Dougherty, nicknamed "God's bricklayer," rested reputations on their records as buyers of land and builders of schools, convents, hospitals, and churches.[4] Yet the tenor of this architectural preoccupation changed dramatically during the mid-twentieth century as laity, clergy, and vowed religious imported the discourse of modern architecture into conversations on sacred space. Their interventions included visual and spatial experiences of buildings, plans, models, photographs, sketches, and exhibitions, as well as journals, books, conferences, catalogs, and ephemera like sermons and dedication programs.[5]

In the long aftermath of the so-called modernist crisis at the turn of the twentieth century, the people I call "Catholic modernists" were sometimes reluctant to claim this terminology for themselves, or carefully distanced the modernism they espoused from problematic "modernistic" art and architecture.[6] Yet as with the Catholic literary modernism recently studied by Una Cadegan, the Church's hierarchy monitored aesthetic conversations less closely than the output of theologians, creating a professional and intellectual space where forbidden ideas about change, growth, and development could reemerge earlier and with greater freedom.[7] Meanwhile, modernists' interest in development frequently saw them not only diagnosing the present, but slipping into futurist forecasting.[8] American Catholic architectural modernists turned away from the maintenance or recovery of past glories and toward speculation about a future that would be different from the present, in ways that might be morally neutral—or even positive.[9] While their predecessors and many of their peers built churches to assert their presence and power, to memorialize and claim their past, or as, in Paula Kane's words, "a 'sign of contradiction' against a rapidly secularizing culture, and to reject . . . the values of modernity," Catholic modernists saw the design of worship space as an opportunity to forecast and to mold a new tomorrow.[10] Their specific spatial and aesthetic goals were diverse, changing dramatically from the 1920s to the 1970s, but the relation they posited between the future of the Catholic Church and of the church building remained stable. In 1966, the Catholic architect and Berkeley professor Patrick Quinn articulated long-standing key questions with a flair typical of the '60s: "Has the church anything to say or contribute, in the most exciting period of man's development, that will help him chart the technopolitan future?" he wondered. "Has the architect or planner anything to offer the church, in its most exciting period, that will help it in its relevant renewal?"[11]

How did Catholic modernists come to believe that churches designed according to modernist architectural principles were essential components of an authentic and strong future for the Church? What separated this group from Steinback or Maginnis & Walsh? More broadly, why did some mid-twentieth-century American architects and their Catholic clients stop building in styles that looked to the Church's glorious past, and begin to build for the present and the future? What did they identify as the needs of the future, and how did they present their case to the Church's hierarchy and to their peers? The answers to these questions have roots deep in the intellectual and social histories of the nineteenth and twentieth centuries, as well as the history of Catholic theology and practice.

In the late 1920s, a handful of American Catholics began to consistently make the case that the Church could only benefit from participating in the architectural developments made possible by a series of engineering breakthroughs and by consistent attention to a set of "basic questions" about the purpose and nature of buildings. In its earlier phases, this argument rested on a mixture of Arts and Crafts ideas, neoscholastic theology as interpreted by the French philosophers Jacques and Raïssa Maritain, and, most of all, the emerging modernist discourse that eventually united designers as heterogeneous as Frank Lloyd Wright, Le Corbusier, Mies van der Rohe, Walter Gropius, Alvar Aalto, and Eero Saarinen. Modernist theories, often divergent in detail, shared one major characteristic: they borrowed the language of biology—and specifically, the language of evolution and adaptation—to suggest that buildings, like plants, animals, and other living things, developed naturally over time in accordance with their environments. The growing cultural authority of progressive evolutionary theories supported Catholic modernists' argument that the present was not and could not be the peak of development and change. Neither was any period from the past, even the revered Middle Ages. Instead, the concept of a fundamentally evolutionary universe kindled these Catholics' ambition for shaping the future, intertwining the local (the formation of a parish community) with the cosmically vast (the redemption of creation).

Over time, rising educational levels exposed more and more American Catholics to evolutionary concepts. With few exceptions, Catholic modernists belonged to a rapidly growing postimmigrant, college-educated demographic. Simultaneously, growing deference to professional authority—a phenomenon peaking in the postwar decades—shaped the interactions of architects and their clerical, religious, and lay clientele.[12] As a result, openness to modernist building theories steadily grew, blossoming in the 1950s and 1960s, the years surrounding the Second Vatican Council. Catholic modernists' ideas illuminate their spiritual lives, theological commitments, and liturgical practices well beyond the narrow confines of church design. Through more general conversations on theology and worship, they claimed the future of churches as vital to a renewed ecclesiology (or theory about the nature of the Church), and as critically connected to a renewed eschatology (the theology of the redemption of creation). The making of worship space, from pedestrian parish churches to storefronts and science fiction confections, came to seem implicated in the salvation of the Church and the cosmos. The theologian Louis Bouyer summed up this position in 1967:

> The places where [we meet for worship], although they are only transitory tabernacles on the way of our pilgrimage toward the heavenly Temple, are to provide as it were the visible frame of the Church, and, insofar, are rightly called 'churches.' They are, here on earth, true houses of God with His people. Their functional adaptation to the making in time of the one true and everlasting Church is a basic expression on earth of what we are to do there which, however imperfect it may be, is a preparation for and even some inauguration of, what we are to do in future eternity.[13]

Ecclesiastical clients who shared Bouyer's exalted vision were not always prepared for the endless decisions and delays that characterize any construction process—what color should be chosen for the wall-to-wall carpeting in the sanctuary? where should the toilets be located? why was the roof leaking only a month after the dedication?—but, in partnership with architects, they gamely forged ahead. Because of this perceived interpenetration of the future of the church building with the future of the Church and indeed, of the cosmos, American Catholic visions of the church buildings of tomorrow intersected with Catholic conversations about the future more generally, as well as with international conversations in both architecture and theology.

EVOLUTION AND THE FUTURE

Interest in the nature and form of the future was hardly new to Catholicism, but its reemergence in the mid-twentieth century represented a major shift in priorities. Catholic spirituality and practice since the Reformation had made use of a rhetoric of the past, of memory, and of a type of faithfulness that modernists came to see as slavish and deadly copying, to be avoided by a living Church looking toward the future.[14] Nineteenth- and twentieth-century intraecclesial struggles over approaches to "modern" thought, including the aftermath of the antimodernist encyclical *Pascendi dominici gregis* (1907), also challenged and delayed attempts by ordained Catholic scholars to adopt an explicitly developmentalist worldview in both scientific and nonscientific contexts.[15]

Despite (or perhaps partly because of) the challenges of two world wars and the threat of nuclear weapons, positive attitudes toward the future began to reappear during the twentieth century. *Pascendi* significantly overstated the degree of organization and coherence among emerging modernist tendencies, but Pope Pius X had correctly identified the underlying idea that eventually reshaped these Catholics' thought: "At the head of what the Modernists teach," he wrote, "is their doctrine of evolution."[16] As priests and laypeople alike increasingly professionally qualified as biologists, physicists, social scientists, architects, and in other areas marginal to the American theological academy, their conversations (including those on liturgy and church design) were caught up in a larger movement. Catholics often saw their professional commitments through the lens of their faith, but many also began to understand that faith in the light of their professional education and experience. These men and women came to see the principles of change, development, and adaptation—in short, of evolution—at the heart of every facet of creation and every human endeavor.[17]

More than any specific scientific argument, the general concept of an evolving, adapting world proved the most powerful legacy of nineteenth-century science, penetrating deeply into Western culture. Evolutionary theory, as Gillian

Beers writes, "has functioned in our culture like a myth in a period of belief, moving effortlessly . . . between metaphor and paradigm, feeding an extraordinary range of disciplines beyond its own original biological field."[18] Naturalists' evolutionary consensus reshaped how intellectuals understood the world, even if they did not agree with Charles Darwin that evolution was fundamentally directionless. In France, for example, the philosopher Henri Bergson developed a distinctive and highly influential theory of reality, positing that a living force, the élan vital, permeated the universe and drove evolution ever upward.[19]

Twentieth-century American Catholics were not immune to this postevolutionary milieu, much as they might have wished they were. Sometimes slowly and haltingly, many Catholics joined their peers in absorbing and valuing the style, language, and the methods of modern science: the routine use of words like *evolution* and *adaptation* to describe nonbiological processes; the positive or neutral valuing of change across time and space; the sensitive observation of the minute details that differentiate one species (or one culture) from the next; and great respect for empiricism and the experimental method, even as applied to religious life. Earlier thinkers who had engaged evolutionary ideas enjoyed a new surge of transatlantic popularity; a 1963 biography of John Henry Newman opened with the observation that "we are still trying to understand the implications of the great theory of evolution, the most fundamental of nineteenth-century discoveries, which alters the whole context of our thought."[20] Meanwhile, Henri Bergson's former students, the Catholic converts Jacques and Raïssa Maritain, elaborated a theory of art and theology according to which visual and verbal forms could be expected to change, even if the truth they expressed remained "certain, unchanging, and eternal." The Maritains brokered a peace accord between Bergson's evolutionary dynamism and Rome's "explicitly static eternalism" that allowed many European and American Catholics to see modernist formal tactics as acceptable for Christian art and architecture.[21] By the mid-1960s, the sometime Catholic Robert Smithson could write, in Bergsonian terminology, that biology had "since the nineteenth century infused in most people's minds an unconscious faith in 'creative evolution.'"[22]

THE PROFESSIONALIZATION OF ARCHITECTURE AND THE BIOLOGICAL PARADIGM

Walter Ong, SJ, spoke for American Catholic modernists in stating that "the reorientation which the modern world demands rests on the fact of evolution—cosmic, organic, and intellectual."[23] But if this biological, evolutionary paradigm was absorbed or "infused" more than chosen, so that a select group of American Catholics came to value "originality" and aesthetic divergence (not qualities often associated with American Catholicism as a whole), how did these ideas become not only available but inescapable for this community, and what larger conditions enabled their success? While modernist architects and artists welcomed theological support from figures like Newman and the Maritains, their commitment to the idea of development derived primarily from their integration into the professional milieu of twentieth-century architecture and art. Catholics took advantage of the high-level professional training offered at MIT, Yale, Princeton, Harvard, IIT, Pratt, Cranbrook, and elsewhere, while art and architectural education at the University of Notre Dame, the Catholic University of America, and St. John's–Collegeville, came to strongly resemble that offered at secular institutions. Years of training, reading (for coursework, for professional development, and for pleasure), and museum-going naturalized a way of thinking about building and decoration that was, however haltingly, shaped by an evolutionary view of the world.

The general expansion of evolutionary thought roughly coincided with the emergence of a new understanding of architects and architecture. In the late nineteenth and early twentieth centuries, architects sought what members of older professions had already: self-regulation (and, concomitantly, the ability to restrict credentialed professionals) and a considerable degree of autonomy founded on societally recognized expertise. These goals became self-reinforcing, as the professionalization of architecture both made possible and depended upon a strengthened institutionalization of schools, credentialing bodies, and professional organizations.[24] Professionalization made ordinary architects more powerful social figures, more protective of their creative prerogative. While at the beginning of the century it was still possible to apprentice into the profession, bachelor's and eventually master's degrees became mandatory as a system of testing and licensing took hold. The formative power of modernized universities increased as students were exposed and held to a coherent set of ideas and practices. Even the few well-known mid-twentieth-century Catholic artists and architects who treated their calling like a religious vocation—for example, Adé Bethune, Frank Kacmarcik, and William Schickel—had considerable secular training and often worked commercially, providing expert consultation for a fee.[25]

When Maurice Lavanoux returned to the United States after his visit to Reims, neohistoricism still dominated professional architecture, especially American church architecture. While medievalists and beaux arts classicists often clashed on philosophy and design, they shared some core beliefs about the nature of architecture, as well as some important practices.[26] Neohistoricists understood architecture as an act of creative and unifying bricolage. Certain historical forms (whether the Corinthian order or the Gothic arch) were permanently valid and normative; architects selected and reassembled these to create harmonious wholes. For churches, in particular, the primary question for neohistoricists was posed by Heinrich Hübsch in 1828: "In what style shall we build?"[27] Which earlier period of church architecture, from Byzantine to Baroque, best conveyed eternal Christian principles? This process foregrounded the selection of historical models and the design of surface elements: facade, ornamentation, wall surfaces. The work often involved the use of "pattern books," architectural catalogues of premade elements, and detailed drawings of plans, elevations, sections, and ornamentation from portfolios and architectural journals. From these study tools and from the observation of buildings, students and practicing architects alike could cull components to assemble into a new building.

Although this paradigm persists today, the men and women who became "Catholic modernists" absorbed—via reading, education, and personal acquaintance with architects and critics—a new set of ideas and discourse about architecture, articulated by both theorists and practitioners, that analogized the history of architecture to the history of biological development. Theorists variously posited that valid architectural forms emerged or "evolved" from the nature of the materials used; the nature of the surrounding environment (other buildings already present, the natural environment, characteristics of society, or some combination); and/or the nature of the specific situation or "problem." Analogizing the building to the body, they believed that plan, volume, and structural elements were more critical than surface, just as what came to seem most important to biologists was the internal structure of plants or animals (bones, circulatory system, ligaments), which gave rise to their surface characteristics. As a result, modernists believed that good architects did not impose forms drawn from imagination or history, but rather drew out already implicit forms, a process often called "evolving a design." They consistently used language borrowed from the life sciences—*living*, *vital*, *organic*, *evolving*, *natural*—to describe both the qualities of individual buildings and architecture as a whole. Looking broadly across the fields of artistic criticism and practice, Oliver A. I. Botar and Isabel Wünsche identify "the privileging of biology as the source for the paradigmatic metaphor of science, society, and aesthetics" as a "constituent element of modernism."[28]

There were many holdouts—some older, some merely uninterested—as schools and journals shifted toward the modernist discourse that constituted the architectural orthodoxy of the mid-twentieth century. But the architects and architecturally literate Catholics who embraced a biological, evolutionary paradigm for Church architecture were profoundly shaped by that orthodoxy and by the professional rhetoric of autonomy and expertise. Modernist discourse provided them with the vocabulary to discuss the ideas and practices that, they insisted, were necessary if the Church were to have a valid architecture; professionalization provided them with a rationale for asserting their own expertise in the face of a sometimes recalcitrant clerical clientele. Like modernist architects and artists as a whole, Catholic modernists did not form an undisputed and easily marked group; rather, individuals participated in loose, overlapping social and professional networks and sometimes navigated profound aesthetic and philosophical disagreements. Yet they shared an orientation toward the future: the revival of Catholic church building, and beyond that, a sometimes hazy yet nevertheless powerful vision of a redeemed world. Believing that truth was truth, they drew on their secular expertise to inflect their approach to Catholicism, and on their reading of Catholic theology and practice to inflect their practice of architecture, art, and criticism.

THE LITURGICAL MOVEMENT AND MODERNIST DESIGN

Why did modernist, future-oriented approaches to Catholic worship space become first thinkable, then viable, in the mid-twentieth century? Support for Catholic modernist architecture grew alongside, and intertwined with, the great theological revival that crested in the Second Vatican Council (1962–1965).[29] Many of Vatican II's signature concerns—the nature of the Church, its relationship to "the modern world," the proper understanding of the Catholic laity and of members of other religions—grew from renewed attention to the implications of the doctrines of creation, incarnation, and redemption. The council also set in motion extensive liturgical changes.[30] Most laypeople experienced the council through these changes, most notably the transition from Latin to "the vernacular" and priests' new position "facing the people" across a main altar shifted toward the congregation, among other changes with significant spatial and architectural dimensions.[31] Yet as earthshaking as these developments were for many churchgoers, theologically and architecturally sophisticated American Catholics understood the council as an invitation to go even further, rethinking such basic principles of church design as the separation between the nave, where the congregation gathered, and the sanctuary, where priests offered Mass.[32]

Disputes about modernist church architecture had been under way for several decades prior to Vatican II. The council did not cause Catholics to develop an evolutionary mindset, but, through its perceived authorization of certain strands of preconciliar thought, allowed their freer expression.[33] Modernist architects had made preconciliar headway by forging an alliance with the so-called liturgical movement, a coalition of clergy and laity dedicated to reforming and renewing the Church's liturgy, especially the central ritual of the Mass.[34] Participation in this movement—originating in Germany and active in the United States from the mid-1920s—distinguished nearly all American Catholics interested in an evolutionary understanding of church architecture.[35] It is impossible to establish simple causality, as some architects became interested in the liturgical movement because it was hospitable to modernist discourse and practice, and some Catholics warmed to modernist architectural theory as a consequence of their exposure to liturgists' ideas. Regardless, the movement provided a forum for the emergence of an evolutionary worldview, particularly as applied to church architecture. And, like the architectural profession, the American liturgical movement had its own institutions where liturgists developed and reinforced shared ideas, including journals, yearly national and regional conventions called "liturgical weeks," and institutes of study at the University of Notre Dame and St. John's Abbey.

Before, during, and after Vatican II, liturgists and modernist designers jointly studied the spaces of Catholic ritual, especially those where the Mass was offered. While many of these spaces were church buildings, others were not; the long-standing Catholic practice of celebrating the Eucharist outside of churches played an important part in conceptualizing the "church of the future" during the mid-twentieth century. Catholics who came into contact with the liturgical movement encountered an expansive sacramental theology that understood the Mass as a way of making God present in the world.[36] Each time a priest called Christ into the elements of bread and wine, he created an eschatological moment in which the whole earth was renewed. The community of laypeople, through their "active participation" in the Mass, also contributed; the Eucharist was more than a personal medicine to be received by sinners (though it was that, too). It was above all an offering by "the whole Christ"—that is, Christ the head with his body the Church, in which "the baptized, the confirmed, the ordained" shared in priesthood.[37] The presence of the Eucharist could make any place holy, and during the twentieth century, Catholics celebrated Mass not only in churches and chapels but in fields, cemeteries, foxholes, airplanes, and living rooms, using tools ranging from chalices and patens of approved precious metals to coffee mugs and paper plates. Memorably, the French Jesuit and evolutionary theorist Pierre Teilhard de Chardin, finding himself in Outer Mongolia "with neither bread, nor wine, nor an altar," invited "the whole creation" to join him in offering the Mass, consecrating the entire world and proclaiming Christ's incarnation in "all matter."[38]

The central importance of the Eucharist made the places where Mass was offered perennial topics of concern for American liturgists, who often turned to one of the most self-consciously forward-thinking of American liturgical institutions, the Liturgical Arts Society (1928–1972).[39] The society—in the person of its indefatigable secretary Maurice Lavanoux, who edited the quarterly *Liturgical Arts* for nearly forty years—acted as a clearinghouse for those interested in, as Lavanoux often put it, "the evolution of art and architecture in our day." Lavanoux fiercely guarded his independence as the sole, and often idiosyncratic, arbiter of *Liturgical Arts*' contents after the resignation of its first editor, Harry Lorin Binsse, in 1937. Nevertheless, he provided an influential venue for architects, artists, and other interested Catholics—one that, despite its low circulation, played a crucial role in introducing new thought to seminarians, clergy, religious, and lay intelligentsia. Lavanoux's cramped midtown office, bursting with slides, photos, and marked-up manuscripts, became an important site for the unfolding revolution in church architecture: "People who were interested in change had a tendency to stop by . . . and talk to him," one friend recalled—a memory corroborated by hundreds of diary entries and letters.[40]

Liturgical Arts bridged the gap between exclusively Catholic publications like *Orate Fratres* (later *Worship*) and *Christian Social Art Quarterly* (later *Catholic Art* and *Good Work*) on the one hand, and the secular architectural press: *Architectural Record*, *Architectural Forum*, and *Progressive Architecture*. Like the former category, *Liturgical Arts* presented itself as a voice in the international Catholic dialogue of clergy, religious, and theologically and liturgically literate laypeople; like the latter, it employed the tools of architectural discourse—drawings, plans, photographs, and "the literary practice of history, theory, and criticism"—to define modernist and futurist aesthetics.[41] Lavanoux often followed his instincts, irritating both readers who would have preferred to see less "modern" work, and those who could not understand why even in the 1970s he published articles on such retrograde topics as the chasuble. But he also maintained close working relationships with more consistent modernist gatekeepers, including theologians like Jacques Maritain and editors like Mildred Schmertz of *Architectural Record*.

Liturgical Arts provided a distinctively American venue for promoting these ideas, even as it closely followed international developments. American Catholic modernists, both architects and liturgists, read European quarterlies like the French *L'art sacré* and (later) the Belgian *L'art d'église*, and were well aware of pioneering modernist church designers ranging from Dominikus Böhm, Rudolf

Schwarz, and Justus Dahinden in Germany to Oscar Nitzchke in Latin America. The international conversations of modernist architectural theory shaped their work. Yet one of the major themes of that theory was the necessity of adaptation to local conditions; evolution made regionalism a constituent component of modernism. While the "international style" prioritized adaptation to time (the twentieth century and its technologies) over place, modernist architects also paid attention to local climate and culture. In the 1950s, as Lavanoux traveled to Europe, Asia, Africa, and Latin America with foundation funding, his reports characterized each locality's specific issues as well as its relationship to the global Church and the international style. Meanwhile, American Catholic modernist architects like Barry Byrne, Clovis Heimsath, and Robert Lawton Jones all had close ties to the community of international modernists. But in their own work they wanted to elaborate a church architecture suitable for America, and deliberately avoided any hint of copying European modernist churches, whether by Schwarz or Le Corbusier.[42] While European theologians and international modernist architects appear throughout, American Catholic liturgists, architects, artists, and critics and their US-based modernist allies are at the center of my story.

THE LITURGICAL MOVEMENT AND THE FUTURE

From its earliest days, the American liturgical movement had an expansive sense of possibility. As the title of Virgil Michel's 1935 article "The Liturgical Movement and the Future" suggests, to be a liturgist was to be concerned with matters far beyond the Church, its rituals, and its buildings; its objective was no less than "bringing all things under the headship of Christ."[43] This brief wedded the minutiae of liturgical celebration, and of church design, to the vast redemptive sweep of the biblical promise. In the heart of the Great Depression, Michel sought the renewal of the social order in the aftermath of an economic catastrophe brought on by an overemphasis on the individual, the material, and the "natural" (as opposed to the supernatural). Later, Cold War concerns pushed Michel's heirs to reemphasize the liturgy's relationship to the redemption of all creation. As Michael Novak wrote in 1967, "the experience which captivates the imagination of our age is the experience of change, the move toward further frontiers, the hope of a human brotherly world civilization."[44]

By the mid-1960s, many American Catholics found themselves in general agreement with a larger cultural discourse about not only the inevitability of change generally, but the special quality of recent change. Twentieth-century technological and communications revolutions seemed comparable to nothing in history except, perhaps, the invention of agriculture.[45] These changes, and the new frontiers beyond them, were not merely dramatically greater in scale; futurists also argued that the rate of change was *accelerating*, in a way that would prove ever more troubling to those unprepared to adapt.[46] These revolutions signaled an approaching crisis: humanity was moving into a future that would be almost unrecognizable. This sense of speeding up permeates Catholic writing of the 1960s, explicitly linked to changes both in the Church and in technology and politics; the literary critic Michael Christopher, for example, argued that "the kind of evolution we are going through today is not new in the Church but it is unprecedented" in its swiftness and visibility.[47]

Artists, architects, and critics shared this broader feeling that, as Maurice Lavanoux wrote in 1962, "centuries ago the tempo of life was in terms of years; today it is in minutes."[48] "The millennium is upon us!" exclaimed a 1969 *Commonweal* ad. "What forms of the church are possible in the future? What will Christians believe in 2000 A.D.? How will they pray and celebrate? Will there still be priests? What will it mean to be 'moral' in the next century? How will the church respond to a world of accelerated technology?"[49] Individual churches, wider technological developments, the theology and bureaucratic organization of the Catholic Church: all were drawn into the maelstrom of change, and each domain seemed to affect the others profoundly. This interpenetration is evident in a 1967 letter from the industrialist William Keady to Archbishop Joseph McGucken of San Francisco:

> We are living in an era not yet completed the Age of Invention and Development. Iron has become steel and then stainless alloys; non-ferrous is copper, then aluminum and new magnesium and more alloys; glass—machine-made—is structural and abundant; newest are the plastics which are flexible or rigid, colored or translucent. In our time, Portland Cement has graduated from foundations to the pre-form, pre-stressed, reinforced and mouldable. What a plethora of media for our modern architects who are now free to design according to our need and their genius! . . . These are times of accelerating change, when new speeds, energies and communicative forces open far and wondrous horizons, times in which Popes John and Paul and the Church Fathers are devotedly examining relations, teachings, and man's spiritual needs for his salvation.[50]

Keady's logic connected the torrential pace of technological development, the openness of the Church to theological change, and the design of San Francisco's new cathedral.

As Christians, Catholics grounded their futurism in the virtue of hope. "It is of the essence of hope," the French theologian Jean Daniélou wrote in April 1960, "to hold a positive attitude with regard to time."[51] The scriptures had "completely reversed all [pagan] values when they gave meaning to time and placed hope in the future."[52] American Catholics took up this challenge, reflecting explicitly on this concept in letters, magazine articles, conference speeches, and in a string of bestselling books like *American Catholics Face the Future*; *The Council and the Future*; *Projections: Shaping an American Theology for the Future*; *The Church Tomorrow*.[53] They joined their fellow "futurologists" both in peering curiously ahead and in boldly attempting to realize the future by experimenting with new ways of life.[54] But they were continually reminded, as by liturgist Louis Bouyer, that "where some men face the future and see only what threatens them, we Christians must find reasons for hope and set about building the new city."[55] The "secular" quest of urban renewal evoked the millennial Jerusalem: "It is in struggling for the present city that the future city is won."[56]

The midcentury debate about worship spaces of the future was, therefore, deeply implicated in eschatology's concurrent restoration to the theological center.[57] Eschatology was, after all, as John Dixon pointed out, "the root tradition of futurism," emerging from "a Judeo-Christian tradition of concern and 'hope for things to come.' "[58] A renewed eschatology—especially prevalent in the American discovery of the theologians Pierre Teilhard de Chardin, SJ, and Harvey Cox, and in the documents of Vatican II—unsettled ideas about the Church's stability and drew evolutionary concepts into the theological mainstream. If the Church was in some sense eternally the same, Catholics began to argue, it might nevertheless evolve dramatically as it reached out toward God's future. So too should the places where the future met the present in the celebration of the Mass.

FIGURE I.1. Church of St. Gregory the Great, Portsmouth Abbey, Portsmouth, Rhode Island (Pietro Belluschi, 1962). Photo: Author.

CHAPTER ONE

THE BIOLOGICAL PARADIGM

> The methodical spirit of science permeates everywhere.
>
> HANS-GEORG GADAMER, *Truth and Method*, 1960

In 1971, the architect Pietro Belluschi reflected on the convictions that had informed his career, illuminating a corpus that can appear to swing violently between raw concrete brutalism and graceful, compact organicism: "The modern architect must gain his insight from the world in which he lives. . . . He will accept and interpret the enormous variety of situations which our age has created, just as nature has evolved the weed and the orchid, the whale and the mouse, the eagle and the hummingbird, from a wonderfully complex but orderly set of things."[1] Guided by this principle, Belluschi had recently designed both a vast concrete-and-glass cathedral in technological, commerce-driven San Francisco, and a more intimate, warmly colored fieldstone-and-laminated-wood structure for a rural abbey church in Portsmouth, Rhode Island (figs. 1.1, 1.2). Although both designs were firmly "modern"—as (he argued) was

FIGURE 1.2. Cathedral of St. Mary of the Assumption, San Francisco, California (Pietro Belluschi with Angus McSweeney and John A. Ryan; consulting engineer, Pier Luigi Nervi, 1964–1970). Photo: E. M. Gill, October 1971, San Francisco History Center, San Francisco Public Library.

demanded by both architecture and reality itself—he maintained their continuity with the great tradition of Catholic architecture, precisely because they adhered to the law of adaptive variation.

Portsmouth's Benedictine monks, meanwhile, actively sought a "distinctly modern church." Only a few decades earlier, however, they had commissioned an elaborate plan for an English Gothic church, cloister, and school complex from Boston's Maginnis & Walsh. Delayed by the Depression and the materials shortages of World War II, by 1952, when the monks were ready to resume building, neo-Gothic buildings no longer seemed plausible. Instead, they engaged Belluschi, dean of the School of Architecture and Planning at MIT, to formulate a master plan for campus and monastery. What had happened, that clients enthusiastic about Maginnis & Walsh in 1928 could hire Belluschi twenty-five years later and even, by the 1980s, demand to know "who in this age of the computer and space shuttle would want a Gothic church?"[2]

Belluschi's explanation of the coherent principles behind his seemingly disparate buildings (and his patrons' acceptance of these principles in both San Francisco and Portsmouth) indicate a thorough acceptance of a paradigm testing architectural practice against scientific knowledge. The analogy of buildings to biology is ancient, yet its implications changed significantly under the pressure of nineteenth-century evolutionary science, producing a modernist architectural theory tied intimately to notions of adaptation and growth. Simultaneously, Catholic ecclesiology also shifted toward organic metaphors. These twin developments, strongly resisted in many quarters of the architectural establishment and the Catholic Church alike, enmeshed evolutionary ecclesiology with proposals for new kinds of worship spaces.

Among both architects and American Catholics, the constituency for a biological paradigm grew dramatically during the twentieth century. During the first half of the century, the vast majority of American Catholic churches were designed in a neohistoricist style: Romanesque, Byzantine, Gothic, or Baroque. Yet discomfort with this practice dated at least to John Henry Newman's comment that the Catholic Church required a "living architecture" for a "living ritual."[3] The emergence of a biological paradigm as a pervasive intellectual structure made it possible for Catholics to understand architecture, the Church, and all reality within an evolutionary framework, and thus to prioritize a "living" future worship space, rather than a "dead" recapitulation of the past. With their adoption of modernism's biological and evolutionary language, a small group began redefining American Catholic architectural standards during the interwar period. In the 1940s and 1950s, as Bauhaus refugees in partnership with disciples of Frank Lloyd Wright came to dominate the architectural profession, Catholic modernists expanded in both number and influence. Collaborations between Catholic clients and modernist architects (Catholic or not) became common, although they did not always result in buildings as successful as Portsmouth's St. Gregory the Great. Regardless, as architects, liturgists, critics, theologians, clients, and other interested clergy, religious, and laypeople mixed in the physical spaces of conferences, classes, and exhibits and in the intellectual spaces of letters, journals, and magazines, they produced a layered argument for modernist churches ultimately dependent on their adoption of biological metaphors.

"ALL THINGS IN NATURE HAVE A FORM THAT TELLS US WHAT THEY ARE": THE BIOLOGICAL PARADIGM IN ARCHITECTURAL THEORY

Art and architectural history emerged as academic disciplines in the late nineteenth century, part of the reorganization and reinvention of universities as modern research institutions.[4] Although the study of the humanities expanded greatly, it was natural history, encompassing biology, geology, and cognate disciplines, that dominated nineteenth-century thought as evidence for "evolution" gained traction. While evolutionary theory was often far from ideologically neutral, its convincing explanations for species diversity and the fossil record powered its expansion into other domains, making it an increasingly inescapable paradigm for university-educated Europeans and Americans. The establishment of architectural history and art history—among the first humanistic disciplines "born of modernism"—during this period virtually ensured that they would turn to the natural sciences for both methodological insight and intellectual validation.[5]

While few early art historians engaged directly with evolutionary theory, many drew on prevalent languages and methods of science, aligning themselves with naturalists' four-step method of "description, the recognition of pattern in the historical record, the creation of mental models or trial narratives to explain those patterns, and the testing of each model to see how well it really [worked] and . . . how broadly it applied."[6] First in Germany and France, then in the United States, self-conscious aspirations to scientific standards embraced method (the collection of specimens and their division into typologies) and institutional organization (the museum, the laboratory, the research university). Specialists began to argue that artwork and buildings should be understood not as isolated pieces, but as examples of "styles," each belonging to its own time and place. Universities established "laboratories" for the study of art and architecture, and practitioners of "scientific connoisseurship" carefully identified forms and techniques that could be labeled and filed into a growing genealogy of art in much the same way that biologists examined and classified specimens found around the globe.[7] Graphic representations of this genealogy—such as Sir Banister Fletcher's 1896 *The Tree of Architecture* (fig. 1.3) and the Princeton medievalist Charles Rufus Morey's 1924 illustration of the evolution of style—made explicit the analogy to evolutionary theories.[8] Some of Morey's students, like the future director of the Museum of Modern Art Alfred Barr, found his taxonomic method "too mechanical," and abandoned medieval art history.[9] But the approach stuck: two decades later, Barr's famous chart *The Development of Abstract Art* evoked the diagram accompanying *On the Origin of Species*.[10] The taxonomic, developmentalist approach to art and architecture had come to dominate the profession.[11]

Architectural theory, aimed at practitioners rather than students of history, began embracing evolutionary concepts simultaneously.[12] Like many later modernists, the most notable early theorist of architectural modernism was closely associated with the study of the Middle Ages. Through his controversial "restorations" of medieval churches and in articles on French Gothic

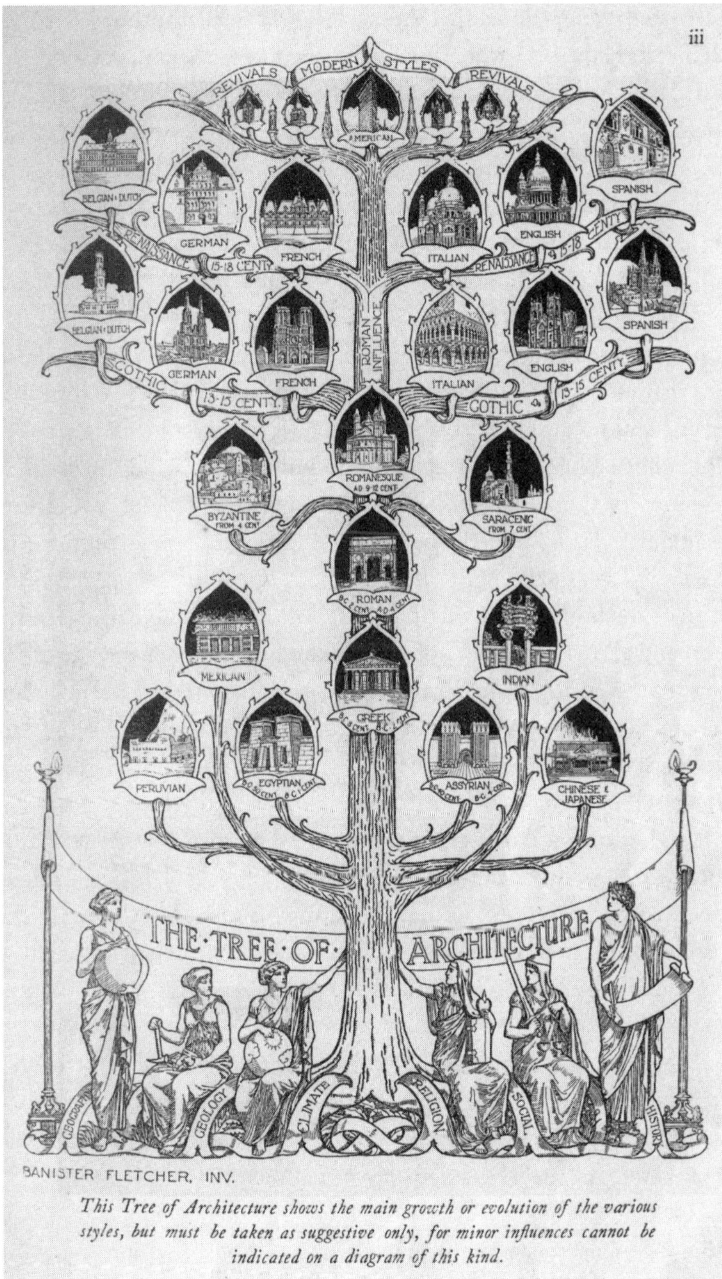

FIGURE 1.3. *The Tree of Architecture*, from *A History of Architecture*, 9th ed. (Sir Banister Fletcher, [1896] 1931). Photo: RIBA111570, RIBA Collections.

architecture, Eugène-Emmanuel Viollet-le-Duc (1814–79) proposed that medieval architects had been rational, scientific, and experimental, the modern men of their day—an assessment subsequently shared by many nineteenth- and twentieth-century historians of medieval art.[13] Viollet-le-Duc claimed that each part of a Gothic building, down to the gargoyles, had served some structural and practical function. As the product of a rational system, he argued, Gothic architecture could be observed and analyzed much as Georges Cuvier and other comparative biologists deduced natural forms through analysis of their underlying structures.[14]

Viollet-le-Duc parlayed this assessment into a general architectural theory, arguing that all good design begins from a rational approach. Thus, the first step in an ideal process is the elaboration of a program outlining a building's functions. The architect then conceives the best possible arrangement of spaces and volumes for those functions. The facade, regarded by most neohistoricists and beaux arts classicists as the most important part of the design, becomes, if not exactly an afterthought, primarily an outgrowth of the rational construction of the building. Good design uses the most suitable materials for the program and allows the "look" of the building to emerge from the construction process, exposing all structural elements to the viewer and including no ornamental flourishes applied to the building's skin. If a functional use requires the violation of classical norms such as symmetry, the building's rationalism would nevertheless make it beautiful to both users and viewers.

Although the typical modernist architect did not read Viollet-le-Duc (with the notable exception of Frank Lloyd Wright, a devotee), his principles were repeated and restated so often that they came to seem like common sense.[15] They spread widely and along many axes; for example, they appeared, often in close paraphrase, in Le Corbusier's 1923 *Vers une architecture* (*Toward an architecture*). They also lay behind the best-known dictum of modernist architectural theory, "form follows function," commonly attributed to Wright's mentor Louis Sullivan. Like Pietro Belluschi three-quarters of a century later, Sullivan linked the practice of architecture to nature's ability to produce forms that were beautiful *precisely because* they were functional:

> All things in nature have a shape, that is to say a form . . . that tells us what they are. . . . Unfailingly in nature, these shapes express the inner life, the native quality of the animal. . . . Whether it be the sweeping eagle in his flight or the open apple-blossom, the toiling work horse, the blithe swan, the branching oak, the winding stream at its base, the drifting clouds—over all the coursing sun, *form ever follows function*, and this is the law.[16]

Technological rationalism and naturalist organicism were inextricably melded at the roots of modernist architectural theory as theorists established universal rules of architectural practice through biological analogy.[17]

Functionalism has acquired a reputation for a fatal obsession with technical and financial efficiency, resulting in socially disastrous high-rise housing and uninspired suburban offices. But twentieth-century modernist designers saw the interrelation of form and function as a necessary corollary of architecture's fundamentally biological character. As the Bauhaus émigré László Moholy-Nagy pointed out, Sullivan's catchphrase was not intended to be "a cheap commercial slogan"; rather, it was a commonsense commentary on the similarity between good design and "phenomena occurring in nature," where the form (shape and color) of, say, a leaf articulates its function (its purpose and activities).[18] Despite real philosophical and aesthetic differences, biocentrism united the key figures in American architectural modernism, including Sullivan, Louis Kahn, Eero and Eliel Saarinen, the Bauhaus émigrés, and Frank Lloyd Wright.[19]

Although Wright produced very little work for the Catholic Church, it would be hard to fathom American Catholic modernism without his presence as both theorist and teacher. Musing on Viollet-le-Duc and his mentor Sullivan, Wright emphasized the perceived biological qualities of architecture, calling for an "organic architecture," one that "*develops* from within outward in harmony with the conditions of its being, as distinguished from one that is *applied* from without."[20] Specifically, he argued that "a building should appear to grow easily from the site"; forms, colors, and building materials should harmonize with the specific location and the project's needs.[21] The Beaux-Arts method of design had encouraged architects to see buildings as, essentially, very large and unusually useful pieces of sculpture. Another possibility was to treat buildings largely as technical problems. Wright was both a great artist and an inventive engineer, but the concept of organic architecture treated buildings first and foremost as if they were plants or animals: a building would succeed, or not, because of how well its necessary functions cohered with its form, and because of how well adapted it was to its environment. For Wright, neohistoricism was doomed not merely because it was backward-looking, but because historic styles could never meet the organic criteria for American architecture. By definition, a Gothic, Romanesque, or Renaissance revival building in the United States was removed from its time, place, and landscape. The idea that a church building should be locally adapted led American architects and theorists—though members of an international network and interested observers of European modernism—to focus on generating an "American" architecture.[22]

Wright was not the only influential modernist marrying new engineering techniques and building materials with naturalists' ideas about adaptation, development, change, and growth. A number of architects and artists who admired him, including Germany's Bauhaus group, formally collaborated with natural scientists. During a three-year stint in London, biological and ecological concerns came to dominate the conversation and the design of Bauhaus members including Moholy-Nagy, Walter Gropius, Herbert Bayer, and the future University of Notre Dame professors Aladar and Victor Olgyay.[23] Mingling with English and European biologists, the London Bauhaus exiles reinforced modernist commitments to a "natural" design process that worked from the "inside out," beginning with the metaphorical bones of a project—program, plan, circulation, volumes, structures—and moving to surfaces only later. They soon brought this shared commitment to the United States, where their ideas, along with Wright's, shaped both professional architectural education and the discourse of the press for decades.[24]

"THE LAWS OF SACRED ART": THE *COMMONWEAL* DEBATES, THE LITURGICAL ARTS SOCIETY, AND THE REINVENTION OF "TRADITION"

Although biologically inflected thought came to define much American Catholic building practice and commentary during the twentieth century, even at the height of this influence neohistoricists always contested modernist interpretation of the sources of architectural validity. Their debate unfolded across continents, within Vatican offices, between architects and their clients, between pastors and their congregations, and within the architectural profession. The Welsh priest J. B. O'Connell, in his comprehensive 1955 *Church Building and Furnishing*, inadvertently revealed why the argument remained so impervious to resolution as he explained that the "laws of sacred art" referred to in the 1917 Code of Canon Law were not "a written code of regulations" but rather meant, "apparently, certain qualities of sacred art, certain standards or norms to which artists who work for the Church, and who create sacred art, must conform."[25] Modernists and neohistoricists agreed that church architecture should be judged on those certain qualities, standards, or norms rather than on mechanistic checklists—but they profoundly disagreed about the source of those norms, and therefore about the criteria for judgment.

Several decades before O'Connell's attempt to smooth the waters, emerging modernist and neohistoricist camps tangled in the pages of the Catholic lay journal *Commonweal*. This debate, running from 1925 to 1929, included contributions from priests, architects, "ordinary" Catholics, and interested onlookers, including the well-known non-Catholic architectural theorists Ralph Adams Cram and Lewis Mumford. It caught American Catholics at the origins of a deep divide between modernists and futurists on the one hand, classicists and neohistoricists on the other. For a few years, all the men engaged in these debates worked together to form the Liturgical Arts Society. By the end of the 1930s, however, disagreement over the relevance of modernist architectural theory for Catholic church design had irreparably deepened the fissure between the two camps. Both sought authority through adherence to "tradition" and to the "laws of sacred art," but understood those terms in profoundly different ways. The *Commonweal* debates show how the use of biological metaphors lay beneath this recurrent disagreement.

The architect Barry Byrne (1883–1967), who played perhaps the single most important early role in introducing American Catholics to emerging modernist architectural theory, was the protagonist of the *Commonweal* debates.[26] A talented draftsman, Byrne apprenticed to Frank Lloyd Wright and produced the working drawings for Wright's pioneering Unity Temple (1905–08). He went on to a distinguished independent career, applying Wright's principles to Catholic church design, beginning with Chicago's St. Thomas the Apostle (1922).[27] Two years later, he traveled to Europe with the sculptor Alfonso Iannelli; the pair sketched at Chartres, visited the Bauhaus (where Byrne formed a permanent friendship with Lyonel Feininger and met, among others, Kandinsky, Klee, and Moholy-Nagy), and later, in Berlin, befriended Mies van der Rohe.[28] Byrne returned from Europe—where he had discovered with pleasure that the Dutch, French, and especially German modernists shared his views (and, by extension, those of Wright and Sullivan)—recommitted to modernist practices. He immediately launched the first salvo in an attempt to break the stranglehold of neohistoricism on American Catholic architecture.

The occasion was an ecumenical fundraising campaign for New York's Episcopalian Cathedral of St. John the Divine. Just what, Byrne asked via the *Commonweal*'s letters column, made for good ecclesiastical architecture, worthy of Catholic support? Channeling Wright, he argued that the primary criterion should be whether a given building was "vital and living" rather than a dead "anachronism," a standard that he claimed Ralph Adams Cram's neo-Gothic design did not meet. Church architects should not traffic in vague romanticism, using "a method unnatural and laborious, such as that of numerous and unnecessary pillars, and of cumbrous vaultings of brick or stone for the purpose of producing an effect to a degree that is unnatural and without sense." Rather, good modern churches would be both "natural and economical," their "vitality" achieved through "the constructions of steel and concrete which have had development in our time, and which enable us to build churches free of pillars, in a structural way that is natural and, in our time, unaffected."[29]

Correctly interpreting Byrne's letter as an attack not just on Cram's design but on neohistoricist church architecture generally, the Pittsburgh priest Thomas Coakley and the New York architect Oliver Reagan both replied quickly. Coakley went to the heart of the issue: Byrne's conception of the "natural" in architecture. For Byrne, drawing on modernism's biological and evolutionary analogy, "natural" meant an ongoing development over time in concert with new engineering techniques, liturgical needs, and cultural circumstances. Coakley challenged him on theological grounds, articulating a neoscholastic interpretation according to which the "natural law of function" did not change over time. When Coakley surveyed architectural history, he found that "the instinct for columnar edifices for religious purposes lies so close to the heart of man" that even ancient pagans and heretics understood columns as crucial to religious architecture.[30] The association of columns and religion was a "law of nature" immutably followed by everyone from pagan temple builders to Gothic architects, and still held in America.[31] Although neohistoricists were not all equally dedicated to columns, they, like Oliver Reagan, did agree on the critical point that "our modern requirements" for churches did not "differ greatly in their fundamentals from the needs of the Church in past ages," rejecting the notion that the development of liturgy and national character suggested development in architecture as well.[32] Lacking a principle of change, Reagan also challenged steel-frame construction on the grounds that such buildings made "no serious pretense at being permanent"; masonry, he felt, was better suited to the Catholic Church as a "permanent institution."[33] What was built for an unchanging Church should last indefinitely, not be subject to easy demolition.

This exchange caught, in embryonic form, a still unfinished argument: What criteria should Catholics use to judge sacred art? Both sides appealed to "laws" and "nature," in which classicists, whether priests, theologians, or architects, saw stability. For Ralph Adams Cram and the noted Catholic neohistoricist Charles Maginnis (both of whom soon weighed in), "function and use" of the church had not changed since the Middle Ages; Cram claimed flatly that there were "no new problems to solve" in the twentieth-century United States.[34] A variety of styles—"Romanesque, Norman, Byzantine, Gothic," which had been "left us through our Catholic heritage"—were as suitable for "the unchanging demands of unchangeable Catholic faith and devotion" as the "fad for steel and reinforced concrete construction" were not.[35] Drawing a firm line between sacred and secular, Cram and his allies stressed the need for churches to be "fixed eternal amid a changing world."[36]

Byrne, however, summarizing the ground of modernist theory, argued that the law of nature *was* change; to back this evolutionary point, he consistently used biological vocabulary—natural, unnatural, living, dead, growth—to make the case that "the doctrine [of neomedievalism] requires a denial of the physical facts of the life which surrounds us and in which we participate."[37] Church architecture was not exempt from the rules of life, which required form to evolve from need—in other words, for liturgy and building technology to develop together. Byrne praised the architectural historian and critic Lewis Mumford, a frequent *Commonweal* contributor who had written that "changes of form in building should rise out of a necessity for solving new problems," a maxim Byrne regarded as "a truth so far reaching and so significant in architecture that it may be accepted as fundamental."[38] Invoking the modernist luminaries Walter Gropius, J. J. P. Oud, and Hannes Meyer, Byrne reiterated that "architecture . . . is dependent on current life," since "form . . . is determined by necessity and necessity is created by habits of living," which in their turn are different in different times and places.[39] Gothic architecture, Byrne explained, had developed like other architectures: first came a plan, where "practical arrangement of space for a given purpose" was allied to "an idealistic and imaginative concept of the purpose of the building" and to new developments in structural engineering.[40] "In the Gothic as in all great architectures," Byrne concluded, "the forms were resultant ones," with design determined by "the building plan, the piers and vaults."[41] In the present day also, he argued, "the way for art as for life must be forward, and contemplation of the future and its possibilities profits more than sentimentalizing over the ideality of the past."[42]

Byrne's allies in the *Commonweal* debates and, later, in *Liturgical Arts* circles, did not all share aesthetic preferences. They did, however, join him in using modernist architectural theory to make a biologically inflected case against the key neohistoricist term *style* and in favor of the key modernist term *function*.[43] Mumford, for example, sympathized with neohistoricists, but he agreed with Byrne that architecture and decoration out of their proper time and place were "lifeless"; "living" architecture made "no attempt to catch the spirit, through ornament or constructional imitation, of other 'styles' and periods."[44] Architecture, like the functional structures of animals and plants, evolved to be properly adapted to its own time, place, and circumstances.[45] Crucially, championing a living architecture was not a rejection of the past, but faithfulness to it. Living architecture would "express the continuity of the Church with its own past" without enshrining "dead forms of that past."[46] For the next few decades, Catholic modernists consistently made three points set out in the *Commonweal* debates: first, that the law of nature was change, "life," or evolution; second, that liturgy, and the church buildings in which liturgies were housed, were not immune from this law, but demonstrably had changed across time and space in response to local circumstances; and third, that, as Byrne wrote, "vital historical architecture" had always emerged in tandem with contemporary technologies.[47]

While the Catholic supporters of architectural modernism included priests and theologians, these arguments were drawn from the professional discourse of modern architecture, and mandated respect for creative contemporary architects as the guardians of "life" in the built environment. By the mid-1920s, then, there was already a group of professional Catholics who felt that, as Maurice Lavanoux wrote several years later, while the architects of Catholic churches would always be interested in theology, liturgy, and history, "the solution to our architectural impasse lies in architecture."[48] Barry Byrne, for example, tellingly commented that the problem with neomedievalist Ralph Adams Cram was not his sense of architectural design, but his "writing ability."[49] Cram's rhetorical skill had betrayed him, for he had convinced himself that what was always true of "great, genuine architecture"—that "out of structure and function shall be formed architecture"—was not the case.[50] Although their clerical supporters often cited Jacques Maritain and other philosophers and theologians first and foremost, Byrne and his fellow Catholic modernist architects primarily deployed architecture's professional discourse, though they welcomed theological support for their points. The principles of architecture (defined in biological terms) should guide future church designs, an argument made implicitly and in scattered form in the *Commonweal* debates, then coherently and explicitly in *Liturgical Arts*.

In the summer of 1927, as the *Commonweal* discussion was ongoing, a group of Catholic architects and artists met and considered founding a Benedictine oblates guild, or perhaps even a monastery dedicated to the Christian arts. But they quickly gravitated toward a proposal better suited to their professional identities: raising "standards" in church architecture as a prelude to increasing national respect for Catholic culture and thought. In the late fall of 1930, the Liturgical Arts Society met formally for the first time in the New York office of the Jesuits' *America* magazine, electing Charles Maginnis as president, John LaFarge, SJ, as chaplain, and Maurice Lavanoux as secretary.[51]

While the nascent society's members agreed that the state of American church art and architecture was poor, their solutions varied, in some cases almost directly contradicting one another. Some, like Maginnis and Oliver Reagan, focused on the need for high-quality materials and craftsmanship, but were frankly skeptical about the emergent modernist paradigm. LaFarge's announcement of the society's formation contrasted Albert Einstein's "veneration for [the] strange trinity" of "Time, Space, and Change" with the Church's devotion to the worship of the eternal, infinite, and immutable God.[52] Yet LaFarge, who came from a large family of professional artists and architects, was more open to modernist theory than it initially seemed. Though he felt more positively about "medievalism" than some, he also felt, in keeping with the Maritains, that Catholic art needed to avoid "an over-insistence on the accidental characteristics of medievalism as medievalism"; in other words, a focus on formal elements like Gothic arches over the substance of "the general principle of art coming from a community spirit."[53] Together, LaFarge, Lavanoux, and *Liturgical Arts*' first editor Harry Lorin Binsse slowly channeled the group away from neohistoricism, a development aided by the society's lack of a strong theoretical platform. The early issues of its journal were philosophically inconsistent at best, focusing mainly on elevating the tone of American Catholics' conversations on art and architecture. This frustrated more theoretically inclined members, but it also provided an opening for the biological paradigm to make its way from professional and academic discourse into the journal. Alongside photographs of neomedieval churches, for example, the magazine included a series of essays on early Christian art by the cofounder of Princeton's "humanistic laboratory," Charles Rufus Morey.[54] Morey presented Christian art within a developmentalist paradigm, rather than as the triumphal production of a changeless church—a move that became a hallmark of *Liturgical Arts*' historical and contemporary coverage.

As the prewar years gave way to the postwar building boom, the biological paradigm moved from one among several theoretical options to the central stance of *Liturgical Arts*. Three critical moves, initially made in the *Commonweal* debates, allowed the language and theory of the biological paradigm to eclipse classicist neohistoricism for an ever-growing segment of American Catholics. First, members of the *Liturgical Arts* circle borrowed mainstream secular architectural theory and art history to reinterpret medieval architecture as profoundly "modern." Second, they introduced modernist criteria for judging a building's worth, avoiding "style" in favor of scientific theories of fittingness and adaptation. And third, they argued that to be truly "traditional" was to grow and change—in short, to evolve.

The transition from historic forms like the Gothic arch to modernist notions of adaptation and development was eased by nineteenth-century theorists' reinterpretation of the Middle Ages as a dynamic period whose most notable persons had themselves adhered to a biological and evolutionary paradigm.[55] Men and women in liturgical-movement and *Liturgical Arts* circles propagated these ideas: Lavanoux and the Vermont priest Edward Sutfin cited the art historian Émile Mâle's claim that "the master builders of those days would be as modern today as they were modern in their times. They accepted and controlled the dynamism of their day."[56] Mâle's argument enabled American Catholics to adopt the biological paradigm and develop an interest in moving into the future, without having to sacrifice their attachment to the Middle Ages.

More often than they cited scholars, however, Catholic architects, artists, and writers repeated unattributed ideas, giving the impression that these were common knowledge rather than contestable arguments.[57] In *Commonweal*, Byrne and his allies had advanced "a plea . . . for the medieval spirit," which understood Chartres not as a monument to past faith but as "a new architecture" in which "the 'necessities' of those days had brought about 'changes of form.'"[58] This was a point reinforced by unsourced appeals to Viollet-le-Duc's claim that Gothic forms had emerged from rational responses to contemporary technologies, now generalized into a universal maxim. Jack Wood, a Catholic architect best known for his early work in steel and reinforced concrete housing, commented in 1931 that "good architecture [could] only result from the use of the soundest contemporary methods in building," a sentiment that he regarded as "true today as it was . . . during the middle ages."[59] Catholics who used biological language to discuss Church and church alike opposed this "true" tradition of the Middle Ages to false "traditionalism." The Catholic architect Leopold Arnaud, dean of Columbia's school of architecture, told a 1936 conference that prior to the nineteenth century, "church architecture was the zealous guardian of tradition and at the same time it was experimenting."[60] The Columbia architectural historian and preservationist pioneer Talbot Hamlin—like Arnaud, no radical—described "the essence of the Gothic spirit" as "direct honesty of expression, organic development of magnificent form from the premises of material, structure, and use."[61] Hamlin even praised a new church as "Gothic because it is modern, because it could have been built at no other time and place than its own."[62]

The Liturgical Arts Society increasingly inclined toward this modernist understanding of medieval architecture and art. Lavanoux and others with nonecclesiastical professional backgrounds routinely complained that art courses in

American seminaries and priests' articles about art "were based on the author's trip to Europe and his collection of post cards" and worse, instead of a professionally respectable presentation of the Middle Ages, were "a rehash of Dr. James J. Walsh's *The Thirteenth, Greatest of Centuries*."[63] Lavanoux insisted that an insular, clerical view of art and architecture, embodied in Walsh's bestseller, gave too much weight to a static, classicist understanding of medieval and Byzantine as the only Catholic "styles." He spent the 1940s and 1950s consistently hammering the need for "new life" and "a living tradition" in architecture and the arts alike.[64] In regular articles and in hundreds of slide lectures at Catholic colleges and seminaries under titles like "The Evolution of Church Architecture in Our Day," he presented his argument through a combination of historical examples and, as they became available, European and American modernist churches. His correspondence demonstrates that he helped unsettle American Catholics' attachment to medieval architectural forms. The California priest Anthony Jacobs, for example, saw Lavanoux's writing on "living tradition" as instrumental to his own understanding that neomedieval architecture was "not tradition at all, because it no longer has the spark of life," but rather "just archeology."[65]

By the 1950s, this point of view was standard among critics writing on churches for the secular architectural press, as well as in the liturgical movement. The authors of *Churches & Temples*, a 1953 book of recent designs sponsored by the periodical *Progressive Architecture*, included a "Historical Preface" characterizing medieval Europeans as "dynamic and progressive . . . constantly striving for new means of expressing their new materials, stone and glass." The authors, including the Catholic architect Paul Thiry, repeated a story frequently told by Joseph Hudnut, the radical dean of Harvard's Graduate School of Design, imagining a dialogue between Abbot Suger, patron of the first "Gothic" church, the Basilica of Saint-Denis, and a conservative monk:

> MONK · In the Romanesque the Christian church has achieved its own architectural form. . . . We should take into consideration all of the heritage of the past as a tribute to our forefathers who made this great architecture for us.
> SUGER · You are saying that the Christian church has reached an architectural perfection. This is not admitted as true by all of us who are working on these experiments in the new church. . . . As we develop our new architecture, an architecture which you decry with the word 'modernistic,' we will build new forms, perhaps strange new forms, based on new needs. . . . Architecture, I am trying to prove to you, has always been dynamic, always changing. . . .
> MONK · Your thoughts seem reasonable enough, but are not these new forms foreign to our religion?

SUGER · . . . These new forms of which you speak have been evolving for several centuries. . . . I must admit that these forms are also strange to me. . . . Yet . . . some good is almost sure to grow out of them.[66]

Hudnut's fable associated dynamic, changing, evolving organicism with the unfolding history of church architecture. The true heroes of historical architecture understood that the stream of time moved in only one direction, and looked to the experiments of the future as perhaps "strange" and unsettling, but also "good." The biological paradigm thus enabled Catholic modernists both to claim the great architects of the Middle Ages as their own *and* to justify their explorations into new ways of imagining church buildings.

ADAPTATION: THE RHETORIC OF BIOLOGY IN ARCHITECTURAL DESIGN

The intellectual connective tissue between many of the strategies proposed by the Catholic champions of modernist architecture was the vocabulary of biology and, especially, of evolution. Sometimes this was clearly intentional, but often it seems half conscious at best, as if the biological paradigm had become so accepted that its concepts and turns of phrase simply emerged as adherents offered criteria for judging both finished buildings and the process that produced them. Consensus developed that buildings were not to be judged on faithfulness to medieval stylistic ideals, but should be well adapted to local culture, location (e.g., urban or rural), climate, and specific site and program. Moreover, since modernist theory commended "living"— not sculptural— buildings, an emerging ecological mindset encouraged a holistic approach to design, along with a "natural" approach to construction materials.

The concept of adaptation explains how Catholics besotted by medieval architecture could be so dismissive of the arches and columns around the corner from their American homes. Catholic modernists believed history revealed the evolutionary nature of architecture: good buildings had always been well adapted to their environments. Following Frank Lloyd Wright's lead, they often rejected historic styles for being "European" rather than "American."[67] Fr. John J. Walch of Oklahoma, president of the Catholic Art Association, wrote to Lavanoux in 1949 about his fear that a local priest would call on "a Polish refugee priest who is an architect" to draw up Gothic plans, with the "result [of] a European conceived and carried out Gothic plant, which is about the way a lot of them got here in the first place, I guess."[68] José de Vinck, an émigré author and translator from New

Jersey, complained vociferously about the neohistoricist National Shrine of the Immaculate Conception (1959), remarking that the various historical forms echoed in the shrine had been "pleasing" only when they came as "natural growths" in their own time and place, and castigating the shrine for failing to fit into the American landscape and spirit.[69] Styles could not be transplanted wholesale from one environment to another without doing serious damage to their integrity. Moreover, using "the best she finds in her environment" had *always* been "the tradition of the Church in regard to art," Illinois seminarian John Walsh wrote in 1944.[70] There was plenty of raw material available in the "environment" of the United States. "Why not skyscrapers?" Denver resident G. W. Lancer asked in 1928; this form was, after all, "the American cathedral."[71] If presently skyscraper design was not concerned with the "sublime," that was partly the fault of Catholics who did not "show any inclination of adapting the style to their needs," so that downtown neohistoricist cathedrals were no sooner built than "blotted from sight by the towering cathedrals of business about them."[72]

Critics also praised architects who adapted their work to local environments. Albert Christ-Janer and Mary Mix Foley cited the Catholic architects Antonin Raymond and L. L. Rado for their work in wood, which "reveal[ed] the basic nature of the material and creat[ed] structures that seem as one with nature," while they also, in "the urban scene," worked with "the most advanced designs in slab or shell construction."[73] Christ-Janer and Foley argued that "this is no contradiction"; in both cases the architects were "revealing the basic nature of the material and creating buildings appropriate to their surrounding environment."[74] While some saw the man-made environment as the key factor for adaptation, others, like the St. Louis stained glass artist Emil Frei, approved the idea that "art must be of its time and in its place"—specifically, the local natural environment. Frei found the appearance of steep church roofs in the snowless Southwest disturbing and suggested that architects focus on climate as well as culture.[75] This point (a general theme of modern architectural theory) became a mainstay in *Liturgical Arts*, especially in the 1950s as the journal greatly expanded its coverage of churches in Africa, Asia, and South America and repeatedly evaluated designs on their suitability for the vagaries of local climate.

The rhetoric of adaptation, like the claim of medieval modernism, centered the role of the professional architect. Maurice Lavanoux was often asked to send plans for small churches that could be built cheaply on any site. These prospective clients confirmed the fears of Olindo Grossi, a Catholic and the chair of architecture at Brooklyn's Pratt Institute, that "while the battle for modern architecture, so-called, is won, its general acceptance by the clergy is only very slowly evolving."[76] But Lavanoux rejected them all, telling his correspondents to call in an

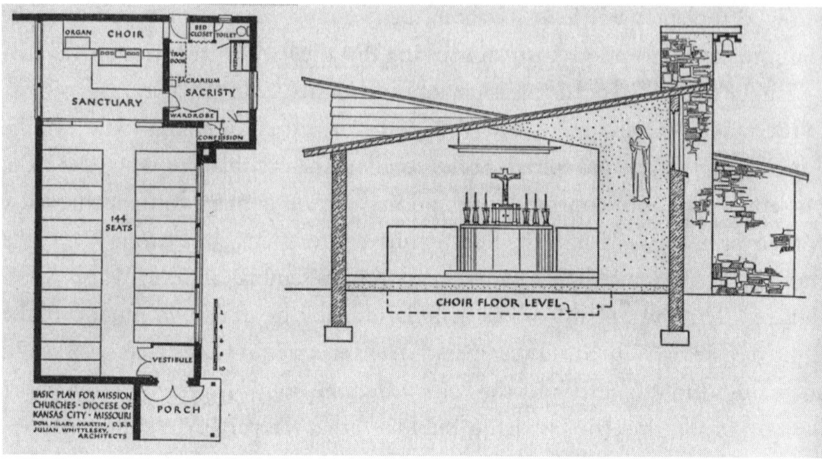

FIGURE 1.4. Adaptable plan for small mission churches in the Diocese of Kansas City (Julian Whittlesey and Hilary Martin, OSB, 1944). Photo: *Liturgical Arts* 12, no. 4 (1944).

architect who could work out a building precisely fitting the situation.[77] In the Diocese of Kansas City, during the building-materials shortages of World War II, Bishop Edwin V. O'Hara took Lavanoux's advice. O'Hara wanted to build ten rural churches as inexpensively as possible. However, instead of choosing stock plans, he hired architects Hilary Martin, OSB, and Julian Whittlesey to produce an adaptable design, "susceptible of change according to location."[78]

O'Hara's mission churches were strongly related to one another, but they were also uniquely adapted to their particular circumstances. Martin and Whittlesey insisted that they "would not undertake the work without seeing the sites," in order that they could "design and locate each building in such a way as to take full advantage of topography, exposures, and surroundings."[79] The architects "held to the thesis that a satisfactory result cannot be achieved by letting a builder *fit* a building design or a stock plan to a piece of property which the designer has not seen."[80] Their simple plan was, therefore, capable of adaptation and elaboration. From the basic plan (fig. 1.4), "schemes were evolved so as to permit variety": four types of wall material were possible, but so was a reverse of the floor plan and a different type of roof framing (also reversible), leading to sixteen potential variations that ultimately would condition the way people encountered and experienced the churches. Like Darwin's finches, O'Hara's mission churches stemmed from the same common ancestor, but also "evolved" to suit their specific locations. When the plans attracted interest elsewhere, Whittlesey refused to simply provide them; he told one South Carolina priest that his firm would have to send a representative to look at the proposed site, and suggested that in any case "some adjustments" would have to be made "on account of South Carolina conditions (local architecture and climate)."[81]

If stock plans offended modernist sensibilities, so too did neohistoricist practices regarding building materials and decoration, which produced what biologically attuned modernists saw as Frankensteinesque horror shows, knit together from without rather than emerging from their own inner logics.[82] The biologically inflected focus on spatial relations, massing, and plan; interest in buildings as enablers of circulation and movement rather than objects of contemplation; and belief that new materials and new construction techniques should be intimately linked to new aesthetics as "form follows function" all proved profoundly important ideas in *Liturgical Arts* circles in the 1930s to the '50s. "A building, if it is to be a vital and living thing," the architect Joseph Salerno argued in 1948, "must take its form from its own inner necessity. . . . Organic law is inherent in all great architecture."[83] For this reason Wright and Sullivan were tremendously important to "the cause of Catholic architecture."[84] They had stated a truth with cosmic implications: in a universe "wherein all is function, all is form," buildings and natural forms alike could be "a glorious revelation of that power which holds us in an invisible, a benign, a relentless—a wondrous hand."[85] Even air-conditioning ducts took on biological significance. In the mid-1950s John Keegan's Yale M.Arch thesis claimed that "building . . . will one day find a natural order not unlike natural growth. . . . The framework [of a building] is familiar to us as the skeleton, the enclosing envelope the skin. With air conditioning, buildings can breathe; pipelines are veins and organs of waste disposal; electricity becomes nerves."[86] If the technical and artistic aspects of the whole were thought of separately, disaster would ensue; but "imagine a living organism of order functioning naturally, unimpeded by the imposition of stylized effects," and church architecture would be vital again.[87]

The majority of Catholic design work in the United States continued to go to local builders with a long history in their dioceses. But for critics influenced by emerging modernist norms, architects' most sought-after skills had little to do with their previous church experience. In *Liturgical Arts*' sixth issue, Harry Lorin Binsse and Maurice Lavanoux remarked that Paul Philippe Cret, professor of architecture at the University of Pennsylvania, was not "a church architect," and had "a fresh point of view and a feeling of detachment which a strictly ecclesiastical practitioner might not have."[88] After this, *Liturgical Arts* consistently looked askance at "church architects," recommending that clients instead seek "creative" men who approached problems individually. The society also encouraged Catholic architectural schools to move away from approaches to training that prioritized students' copying skills. In the late 1930s

Lavanoux wrote to Francis Kervick, head of the department of architecture at Notre Dame, that he felt the Bauhaus had "induce[d] their students to do architecture with intelligence rather than with their pencil and a well stocked library." He suggested that Notre Dame contact Eliel Saarinen at Cranbrook or Moholy-Nagy at the Chicago Bauhaus to find teachers for Notre Dame, for "after all we are going forward and why always stick to outworn forms."[89]

Clients who took *Liturgical Arts*' advice hired architects with distinctly modernist sensibilities, prioritizing a particular style of professionalism. Instead of experts with special skills pertaining to churches or office buildings, modernist architects saw themselves as people who could sensitively discern the individual forms, volumes, and plan best suited to the local environment. Thirty years after Barry Byrne first made this case in an American Catholic forum, Hellmuth, Obata, & Kassabaum described their experience of designing the Priory of St. Mary and St. Louis in terms that had become familiar to readers of *Liturgical Arts*, if not necessarily to cautious building committees. "As we studied the building and the program," they wrote, "the design evolved from our deepening awareness of the needs of this particular church."[90] They added that they had not set out to be "daring"; through a process of discovery, their design "came to seem to us the only way for this church to be."[91] Architects versed in the biological paradigm criticized neohistoricists and classicists for having "the completed building—as a picture—always in the mind of the architect."[92] This prevented the architect from allowing "the environment" of the building to "logically and honestly condition the form."[93]

In addition to their relationship of structure to form, modernist architects' interest in plan and volume—representing an increased interest in how human beings experienced circulating through spaces—led them more and more to think of the built environment as dynamic and holistic, just as biologists were increasingly interested in studying the complex development of entire ecosystems over time. In 1955, the Catholic architect Jean Labatut told a group of Texas architects that contemporary architecture had "a deeper consciousness of the physical and psychological values of that vital architectural 'air space' in which man lives, of that universe . . . called the site, the environment . . . the landscape or the architectural complex of which . . . our mind is a center in motion." He explained that the building itself was only part of the equation; rather, architecture was about "the free space between furniture, walls, buildings, trees, or any other" elements. Considering space, motion, and volume gave architecture "a temporal quality" that in turn suggested "a plastic, organic, dynamic quality." The best building would be aware not only of present needs, but how people would experience the space as their time in it unfolded.[94]

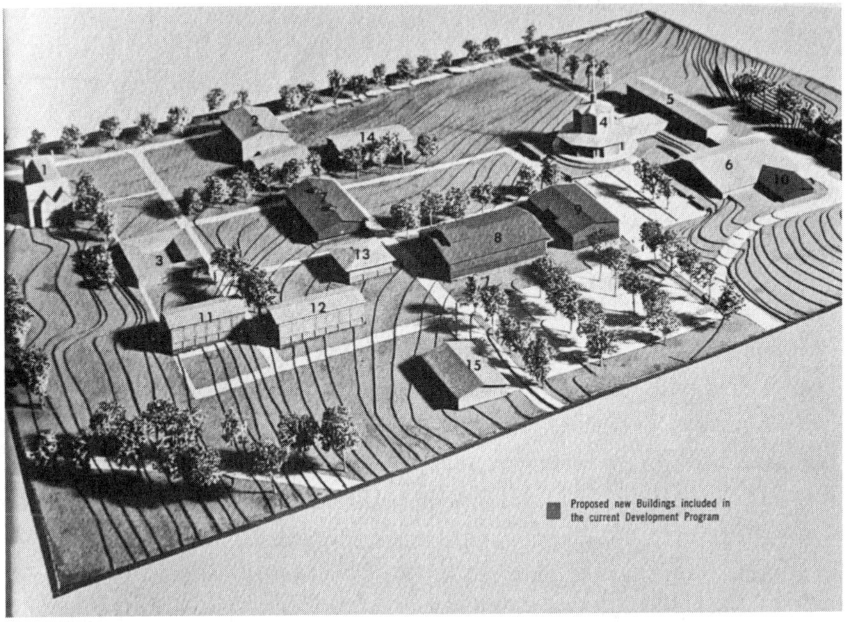

FIGURE 1.5. Model of the master plan for Portsmouth Abbey, from the fundraising brochure "A Time for Advance," 1966 (Pietro Belluschi). Darker buildings (including #7, the school science building) were not yet built; buildings colored white (including #4, the church, and #5, the monastery) were complete. Photo: PAA.

The holistic, environmental, adaptationist approach generated a number of striking trends in midcentury American Catholic architecture. Architects and artists increasingly focused on collaboration, though they often struggled over final control. At a time when most churches were decorated and furnished from catalogues, modernist artists and architects argued for the integration of the arts "naturally" and by design. The Cranbrook-trained stained glass artist Joan Velligan, for example, advertised that her work was for "the contemporary architect who assumes the social responsibility of planning a culturally sound environment in terms of building as an organic art form"; she wanted her own work to be part of "the wall itself creating total integration of interior and exterior."[95] Architects were also increasingly called on to design entire complexes. Parish plants, school and college campuses, and monastic enclosures all seemed to require "master plans" allowing different buildings to work harmoniously with one another, with the natural environment of the site, and with the demands of modern engineering—a gloriously well-adapted state of affairs in contrast to the jumble of transplanted "European" styles in older complexes (see fig. 1.5).

ADDING OUR LINKS TO THE GOLDEN CHAIN: A TRADITION OF CHANGE

For American Catholics who embraced the biological paradigm, stating the case for modernist architectural theory during the preconciliar period meant contending with factions in the Church that saw the maintenance of "traditional" artistic standards as one of the best defenses against the forces of modernism (writ large) and secularism. As the 1930s gave way to the planning fever of the war years and the postwar building boom, philosophical developments within Liturgical Arts Society circles brought members increasingly into conflict with other American Catholics. In the earliest days of the society, a successful future for Catholic worship space had meant, primarily, "better taste," a simplified decorative scheme, the "honest use of materials" in the Arts and Crafts sense, and strict adherence to canonical rubrics. *Liturgical Arts* highlighted such sanctuary renovations, showing only photographs of veiled tabernacles, for example, and assuring readers that the problem to date had been insufficient obedience and submission to Vatican authority. This stance fit seamlessly with the 1917 Code of Canon Law's prescription that "bishops must take care, consulting with experts if necessary, that the forms received by the Christian tradition and the laws of sacred art are observed in the construction or repair of churches."[96]

However, while American liturgists continued to be concerned about rubrical correctness into the 1960s, they were also increasingly convinced that art and architecture—along with the liturgy—should be thought of as living and growing. This stance drew them toward art and architecture that could be "traditional" only if tradition itself was living and growing. Liturgists interested in church design adopted the language of modern architecture, which was oriented toward functional planning and indicated the direction liturgists wished to move the Church as a whole. Functional planning included rubrical adherence, but it had a fundamentally looser understanding of the connection between any individual building and a set of rules. Moreover, this line of thinking increasingly suggested that the rubrics were not eternally valid in the first place.

In June 1954, Maurice Lavanoux was asked to lecture at the Catholic University of America's Workshop in Creative Art on "The Authentic Tradition in Art." Advertising for the workshop noted that "tradition is a living thing, a growing and developing thing," and Lavanoux followed suit, describing "a chain, whose golden links were fashioned in every age and clime, to which chain we can only labor to add the vitality and strength of our link, in our age

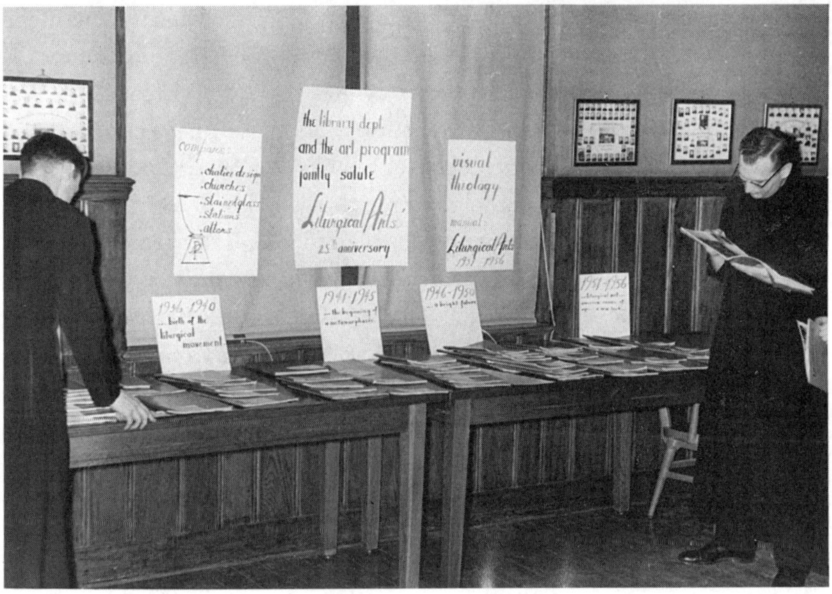

FIGURE 1.6. Display of *Liturgical Arts* at Immaculate Conception Seminary, Darlington, New Jersey, February 1956. Titling the journal a "visual theology manual," the seminarians organized the table into five phases, including "1941–1945 . . . the beginning of a metamorphosis," "1946–1950 . . . a bright future," and "1951–1956 . . . liturgical art . . . america [*sic*] comes of age . . . a new look. . . ." Photo: CLIT, 32-03-01

and clime."[97] The history of Christian art and architecture had emerged in "the evolution of that past tradition," and whatever the difficulties of the present, it was necessary to "work within the framework of the present and the hopes for the future."[98] Within evolutionary logic, the present was no more the final statement on art or architecture than any past age had been.[99] This had been *Liturgical Arts*' basic message for some time; Lavanoux seems to have first used the metaphor of the chain in 1939.[100] While circulation remained small, many copies went to college and seminary libraries where they were read by young Catholics like the Chicago seminarian John Walsh, who confessed to Lavanoux in 1944 that "aesthetically I have been *brought up* these last 4½ years on Lit. Arts" (see fig. 1.6).[101] Walsh had absorbed the quarterly's teaching that "*certainly* tradition grows. What we teach now (the Church) is the tradition of tomorrow and someday the art we now call modern will be part of the tradition that includes all those once modern and revolutionary art-forms—Byzantine, Gothic, etc."[102] As Pietro Belluschi put it to the 1963 National Conference on Church Architecture, in recent decades "tradition, in fact, was found to be change, evolution, search."[103]

This rethinking of "tradition" bridged nearly identical conversations in the professional worlds of architecture and theology—conversations that mutually informed one another and collectively drew on scientific concepts. Was tradition, in any arena, a matter of repetition, or of retaining a clear sense of how modern practices were integrally related to older ones? Catholic theologians, increasingly steeped in historical research, were slowly concluding that it was the latter. The most important preconciliar theological statements in favor of tradition not as "a slavish imitation of the past" but rather a type of "fidelity" to the past that was also "a movement and a progress that goes beyond mere continuity" came from the French Dominican Yves Congar.[104] To argue for theological growth, he cited art, where, he claimed, "tradition conceived as the handing down of set formulas and the enforced and servile imitation of models learned in the classroom would lead to sterility."[105] He further suggested that in the present day, the "mental attitudes" most responsible for "vitality" were to be found in "the world of scientific research," so that theologians and artists alike were justified in turning to science for the language of their own revitalization.[106] Although Congar's work on theological tradition was not widely available until the eve of Vatican II, this type of thinking spread within communities of modernist architects and liturgists far earlier. Around 1960, Columba Cary-Elwes, OSB, provided perhaps the clearest statement of the overlap in theological and architectural approaches when he justified hiring the modernist Gyo Obata to design a radical new abbey church outside St. Louis. "Tradition in theology," Cary-Elwes wrote, does not mean "sticking to the letter of a primitive text." It is "rather an intrinsic growth, a repeated restatement in new terms, intelligible to each age. So too in architecture, tradition is not static but living."[107]

THE LAWS OF SACRED ART: THE BIOLOGICAL PARADIGM AND THE VATICAN, 1917–1960

As their eagerness to reinterpret rather than reject "tradition" suggests, Catholic modernists, while proponents of the biological paradigm, developmentalism, and futurist orientation, were rarely rebels. They appealed wherever possible to papal authority, seeking favorable interpretations of Roman directives related to liturgy, art, and architecture.[108] As with the string of theologians silenced in the preconciliar decades, Catholic modernists tried to balance their devotion to magisterial authority with their conviction that the Church, its liturgy, and its architecture and art needed, fundamentally, to be conceptualized as living and growing, no matter what certain bishops or even curial offices might say. Complicating the situation considerably, Roman documents were often the product of conflicting opinions. Ambiguous phrasing left room for proponents of the biological paradigm to contend that Rome was on their side, while also allowing their opponents to criticize and undermine specific projects. Delays in transatlantic communication and uncertainty about the degree of authority held by various church officials could also sow confusion. Lavanoux, trying to provide authoritative guidance from his office in New York, often found himself chasing down information about rumored denunciations of modern art and countering newspapers' tendency to report every remark by a bishop or curial official as the stance of "the Vatican."[109]

The most important Roman document on the liturgy prior to Vatican II was Pius XII's 1947 encyclical *Mediator Dei*. The American liturgical movement generally received this document as an affirmation of its efforts. However, when it came to art and architecture, the encyclical probably created more confusion than it solved through a failure to define its terms. The key paragraph reads:

> Recent works of art [including architecture] which lend themselves to the materials of modern composition [*recentes imagines ac formae, ad materiam aptiores, ex qua hodie conficiuntur*], should not be universally despised and rejected through prejudice. . . . Thus modern art [*nostrorum temporum artem, "art of our time"*] will be able to join its voice to that wonderful choir of praise to which have contributed, in honor of the Catholic faith, the greatest artists throughout the centuries. Nevertheless, in keeping with the duty of Our office, We cannot help deploring and condemning those works of art, recently introduced by some, which seem to be a distortion and perversion of true art [*quae sanae artis deformationes depravationesque videantur*] and which at times openly shock Christian taste, modesty and devotion, and shamefully offend the true religious sense. These must be entirely excluded and banished from our churches, like "anything else that is not in keeping with the sanctity of the place." (§195)

The American liturgist H. A. Reinhold felt the document itself was generous (or vague) enough to pose no threat to modern art and architecture, but he was all too aware of how useful aesthetic conservatives found it to "hold encyclicals and papal pronouncements with an angry thrust before our faces."[110] Due to an ongoing battle over modern art and architecture between the Dominicans who ran *Liturgical Arts*' French counterpart *L'art sacré* and an alliance of Roman conservatives and French integralists, the Vatican did make a number of interventions clearly hostile to modern art and architecture during the early 1950s.[111] The Holy Office, for example, issued an "Instruction on Sacred Art" in 1952 interpreting *Mediator Dei* as aggressively opposed to the biological paradigm. "Recently the Apostolic See reprobated corrupt and errant forms of sacred art," they wrote. "Of no moment are the objections raised by some that sacred art must be adapted to the necessities and conditions of the present day."[112]

Since much of the French conflict was carried on behind the scenes, American Catholics were largely ignorant about the background of the 1952 instruction. Yet it caused real danger for American proponents of "the art of our day"; in fact, its lack of context probably increased its negative impact by making it seem like a universal pronouncement rather than a focused intervention. It was now quite clear to bishops like Leo Dworschak of Fargo, North Dakota, that "the Liturgical Arts Society is encouraging a form of ecclesiastical art which departs from the traditional form encouraged by Holy Mother Church."[113] The bishop of Galveston, meanwhile, "talked sternly to his priests about using 'good Romanesque architecture' in their churches" in the aftermath of the instruction, causing architect Philip Johnson to predict that "we are sure to have our troubles" over his plans for St. Michael's parish church in Houston.[114] (He was right: the bishop ultimately rejected Johnson's design, despite its formal gestures toward medieval architecture.) At St. Peter's in Kirkwood, Missouri, the 1952 arrival of a crucifix by a local artist, Rudy Torrini, prompted layman Edward Schuster to complain to both Archbishop Ritter and apostolic delegate Amleto Cicognani, arguing with citations from Augustine and Aquinas, as well as "definite provisions of Canon Law recently reemphasized and reinterpreted by the Apostolic See," that the "hideous, blasphemous image" of "a misshapen, ape-like figure" was "a scandal rather than an edification" and ought to be removed.[115] "Is it not the glory of the true Church to stand by objective truth?" he wondered, associating idealized and (as he put it) "orthodox" representations of the body of Jesus with stability and classicist stasis.[116]

Despite this formidable opposition, Maurice Lavanoux insisted that *Mediator Dei* itself was "a most elastic statement and one free from dictatorial overtones" and that it essentially harmonized with his own beliefs, despite its condemnation of some contemporary works.[117] He summarized the biological paradigm's argument neatly in "The Authentic Tradition in Art": "As the Church is a living organism, and its liturgy accommodates herself to temporal needs and circumstances, does it not follow that the external and visual manifestations of that liturgy, on the plane of art, are also living organisms that grow and develop, rather than a dead, lifeless organism, disguised as antiquarianism, also condemned in the papal text?"[118] Increasingly, dividing lines within ecclesiology as well as within architectural theory turned on whether or not a given person subscribed to the biological paradigm.

THE LIVING CHURCH

Why, against substantial opposition from neohistoricists in both the hierarchy and the architectural profession, was the biological paradigm able to gain a substantial foothold within mid-twentieth-century American Catholicism? In part, modernist criteria took root in professionalized American Catholic circles due to the simultaneous movement of biological language and thought into discussions of the nature of the Church itself. Just as proponents of architectural modernism founded their argument on a theory of historical development of forms over time and space, many of the most influential voices in the liturgical movement concluded that the Mass had changed greatly over time. If cautiously at first, they began to assimilate the corollary that it would probably change in the future, a conclusion with serious (though not always explicit) implications for not only liturgy but ecclesiology.[119]

The decades-long reconceptualization of evolution as "proper" to the Church's liturgy and architectural forms built on theologians' retrieval of an ancient ecclesiology. The biologically inflected conversation on architecture both echoed and mirrored the work of theologians like Henri de Lubac and Yves Congar, whose historical scholarship led them to argue not for a return to an earlier and more devout age, but for a theory of doctrinal, ecclesiological, and liturgical development.[120] As this theory spread, the words *organic* and *living* as key descriptors of the Church itself spread with it. While the oldest extant Christian literature—the letters of Paul—memorably described the community as a "body" whose limbs and systems functioned in concert, the implications of organic ecclesial metaphors changed in the aftermath of evolutionary theory. If the twentieth-century liturgical movement adopted an ecclesiology of "organic communion" (as opposed to one of "corporate institution"), this now implied characteristics like adaptation, development, and evolution foreign to premodern Catholics, yet profoundly affecting twentieth-century theology.[121]

The year 1925—when Barry Byrne incited the *Commonweal* debates—also saw the first significant stirrings of the liturgical movement in the United States. In that year, the Missouri-based priest and liturgical pioneer Martin

Hellriegel asserted that the Church itself was "a living organism." This ecclesiological description, once accepted, provided an opening for Catholics to argue that the terminology and ideas of biology were useful in thinking about the Church, just as thinking of buildings as "organic" opened the way for understanding evolutionary theories' relevance to discussions of architecture.[122] Gradually, both Paul's concept of the mystical body of Christ and the related description of the Church as organism worked their way from liturgical and theological enthusiasts into papal documents. In a passage from *Mediator dei* (whose immediate predecessor was 1943's *Mystici corporis*) that Maurice Lavanoux quoted frequently, Pius wrote, "The Church is without question a living organism, and as an organism, in respect of the sacred liturgy also, she grows, matures, develops, adapts and accommodates herself to temporal needs and circumstances, provided only that the integrity of her doctrine be safeguarded."[123] In the United States, preconciliar supporters of organic ecclesiology were similarly cautious. Cajetan Baumann, OFM, warned the readers of *Architectural Record* that while the Roman Catholic Church is "a living organism" that "adapts itself to all places, peoples, periods, and times," it yet has "permanence in its flexibility" and "never changes its doctrines."[124] But by the eve of the Second Vatican Council the notion that liturgy and church buildings should be well adapted to their environment had firmly implanted the idea that they could, would, and indeed should look, feel, and operate differently in the future, along with the idea that the Church itself was best spoken of in biological metaphors.

Within American Catholic architectural circles, these two moves supported each other. The concrete pioneer Jack Wood, for example, argued that the Mass was "not a lifeless survival of the past, but a vital and living spiritual force."[125] A living architecture, Wood felt, would complement a living Mass and a living Church. Leopold Arnaud agreed, opening an argument for "the living tradition in Christian art" with the statement "The Church is a living organism."[126] The architect Paul Thiry's overview of modernist Catholic churches began with a short account of the sacraments, rituals, and liturgical calendar; he foregrounded the first step in a functionalist program, an account of the *use* of Catholic churches, rather than pictures of them. He was careful to note that "development of the sacramental rites has been gradual, organic, and subject to historical change" and "hence is not constant," implying that it would go on changing.[127] The variety of plans that had been used in the past suggested to him that "the ultimate plan [had not] yet evolved."[128] Thiry spoke forcefully to architects: "The design of the church should not concern itself with styles of architecture or forms to follow," for "new forms of structure are ever before the designer and new means of expression constantly possible and necessary."[129]

If the Church was a living body and if the Mass was going to change, liturgists and architects agreed, churches would naturally change, too. The Liturgical Arts Society and its sympathizers began to argue that, as Otto Spaeth put it in 1944, the "vital and creative forces" within the Church "must be allowed to develop free from the shackles of pseudo-tradition or the dead hand of archaeological reminiscences."[130] They tried to calm fears of a "radical break with tradition" by contrasting "revolution" with "normal evolution" that saw forward development as a continuity with "the great art of all periods which *is* tradition."[131] Architects hoped that focusing on plan, volume, space, and circulation rather than on style would be productive. At the 1948 National Catholic Building Convention, Lavanoux defined the "dynamic tradition" of church architecture and the Church itself as a result of a "normal evolution" that avoided an "archaeological and sentimental approach" in order to "plan according to the requirements of our day."[132] He cast aspersions on the idea of approaching a building via "effect," "decoration," and "preconceived ideas," and championed the idea that "whatever style we achieve today" would develop from "the evolution of the plan itself."[133] In 1950, Thomas Locraft, heading the department of architecture at Catholic University, remarked that a good church would provide "spaces . . . for the proper evolution of the liturgical service," suggesting that church architecture and liturgy were co-developing.[134] In the wake of Vatican II, liturgists made this point even more strongly; "the law of life is change and growth," wrote one Kansas City priest in 1966, "and so change [in the liturgy] must come."[135] Frederick McManus, newly installed as secretary to the Bishops' Commission on the Liturgy, agreed: "In principle," the council had clarified, "the liturgy should not be static but should evolve and be adapted to the needs and understanding of each age."[136] By adopting the language of biology, the liturgical movement and its architectural allies had helped prepare the way for the emergence of a full-blown Catholic culture of evolution.

FROM "THINGS IN ORDER" TO "A DRAMA UNFOLDING": THE CULTURE OF EVOLUTION

Increasing commitment to the biological, evolutionary paradigm, in architecture or ecclesiology, was not necessarily a conscious choice. Adherents arrived at their positions between the 1920s and 1960s as a result of education, professional connections, and long-term engagement with conversations like those in *Liturgical Arts*. Sometimes they did not even notice their own shift from a classicist and ahistorical approach to an evolutionary and developmentalist one until it was already complete. John Cogley, *Commonweal*'s editor, summarized a series of 1960s conversations with priests, theologians, and laypeople who had discovered that their "actual cultural values" were conditioning their assessment of the Church—not the other way around.[137] In fact, a number of American Catholics in the conciliar period noted their own surprise at the success of what the young Daniel Berrigan, writing to Lavanoux about the work of the Liturgical Arts Society using yet another biological metaphor, termed an "osmotic process."[138]

The philosopher of science Raymond Nogar, OP, embarked on a lecture tour in 1964 that brought him into close contact with scientists and students, changing his understanding of his own material and spiritual condition profoundly. One night in Chicago, after defending the skeptical view of evolution taken by neoscholastic theologians, he was approached by two geneticists. The scientists suggested to him that while Nogar had conscientiously and carefully presented his case, they were " 'sure that *subconsciously* you think evolution is unquestionable. The conscious reasoning you go through [to leave room for theological doubt] is fascinating, but *it is not you*.' " Nogar was taken aback by the scientists' comment, but had to concede "the large element of realism in the observation. *I did think*, then, that the fact of evolution was incontestable, even by the theologian." Unconsciously, he had concluded that the world was formed by evolution, even as he had continued to defend the legitimacy of Thomistic theology's right to question that judgment. The age of "a picture of things in order" had passed, replaced by an emphasis on "drama unfolding."[139]

Nogar dramatically fleshed out William Birmingham's 1966 conclusion that "Catholics in general . . . backed into evolution."[140] Rather than wholeheartedly embracing the concept, Birmingham argued, American Catholics had kept a cautious distance from the unfolding scientific exploration of evolution, avoiding its potential implications for the Church itself. But the shift in modern thinking had become so widespread, reshaping narratives about all aspects of life, that it had affected many Catholics' thought regardless. The process of absorbing what the Catholic writer George Tavard called "the evolutionist attitude, which thinks of man in terms of his unfolding history rather than of his set nature, and of the universe in terms of its extremely long and slow evolution from an indeterminate past to an indeterminate future," was complex and irreducibly personal, and unfolded over a long period of time.[141] But it happened. By the late 1960s, the theologians Thomas O'Meara and Donald Weisser could confidently cite Walter Ong's analysis that "the principal reason for the thrust into the future which makes our state of mind today different from that of earlier man is our knowledge of cosmic and organic evolution. We are aware that we live in an evolving universe, pitched into the future."[142] They considered that this knowledge, along with increasing technical capabilities, made it possible to consider the immediate future differently, to think of it "as the mutative evolution of what is already active today."[143]

O'Meara and Weisser knew that the theological implications of an evolving universe were not accepted by many American Catholics: "Some see the changing world and the changing Christian mission as disintegration, a personal threat and a betrayal of orthodoxy. . . . Others see changing world and church as a liberation of the true spirit of the gospel . . . so that Christ might emerge dynamically in our world."[144] But even among the second group—those who joined Howard Thorman, the publisher of the new *National Catholic Reporter*, in viewing the late-1960s "situation of crisis" as an opportunity for "beneficial development and change"—there were serious differences of attitude and approach. Some chose projection from statistics, data, and phenomenological analysis of modern society, while others preferred Marshall McLuhan's more fluid, tentative "explorations." (As McLuhan explained to *Playboy* in 1969, "I don't know where [my explorations] are going to take me. . . . My books constitute the *process* rather than the completed product of discovery. . . . I want to map new terrain rather than chart old landmarks."[145]) During the mid-twentieth century, architects and other theorists of new worship spaces attempted practical provision for the immediate future of the worship community, and fantasized about a Church and a church of the far and unknown future.

FIGURE 2.1. Model of St. Ann of Normandy, Normandy, Missouri (Murphy and Mackey, 1951). The model's roof is removable, and the back wall of the sanctuary includes a mockup of the large stained glass mural by the Emil Frei Company. The old church, *at left*, was to be used as a chapel and baptistery connected by a breezeway, which was never built. Photo: GLIT, 28-14-01.

CHAPTER TWO

MODELING THE CHURCH

The Catholic architect Joseph Murphy, the artist Emil Frei Jr., and Bertrand Abell, CP, the pastor of St. Ann's parish in Normandy, Missouri, arrived with some trepidation to visit the newly installed archbishop of St. Louis, Joseph Ritter, in March 1947; "for weeks before," Murphy wrote, "I had wondered and speculated as how my design of the church . . . would be received."[1] During the 1940s, Normandy rapidly transformed from a small country town into a booming suburb; the parish desperately needed a new, much larger church, and its Passionist administrators hired Murphy, an architecture professor at Washington University, to design the new St. Ann's as the first Catholic church in greater St. Louis built using modernist principles.[2] The bulk of the design process, however, had taken place before Ritter's arrival, and his approval was required to break ground.

The archbishop was "cordial" but brisk at first, and Murphy sensed that they should not take up too much of his time. True to modernist priorities, Murphy began by speaking about "our program, the site, and the idea which was the basis for my design." He then displayed his site plan and sketches. Eventually, Abell brought in the architect's model from the car, where they had left it because, Murphy recalled, "we didn't want to appear overanxious to sell our idea." However, by this time Ritter had become deeply interested; the architect now "took possession of the archbishop's office, parking the model in the center of the room" (fig. 2.1). The meeting lasted more than an hour as Ritter investigated the model, made comments, asked questions, and finally concluded (Murphy reported): "*This represents a new era*; the Byzantine, Gothic, and Renaissance served their time; it seems only right that a different architecture would serve our time." Murphy was delighted: "To me [the meeting] appeared to open the door to an era of creative thinking in the Catholic art and architecture of St. Louis."[3]

Ritter was, as it happened, personally inclined to aesthetic reform, becoming one of the Liturgical Arts Society's most reliable hierarchical allies; but his palpably increased enthusiasm after viewing the model was part of a larger story. Mid-twentieth-century American Catholics interested in the evolving future of church architecture created a complex visual culture of projection, aiming to transform the imaginations (and thus the desires) of their coreligionists.[4] Modernist architects engaged in a substantial theological argument about the nature and purpose of the church, one that unfolded in large part through visual means. They sought to convince a wide variety of audiences that church buildings would look different in the future because they would, fundamentally, *be* different: the building would both represent and bring into being a new kind of worshipping community.[5] Using the tools of their trade—the models, drawings, photographs, and other representations sometimes known as paper architecture—they sought to make their hoped-for changes seem at once natural, welcome, and inevitable.[6]

Archbishop Ritter's seduction via model was an event frequently repeated across the United States during the mid-twentieth century. Would-be modernist church designers faced resistance from neohistoricist architects, conservative ecclesiastical clients, and the general public. In response, they mobilized what amounted to a decades-long public relations campaign. A proliferating material culture of visual projection, aimed at a wide variety of Catholic audiences from "ordinary" parishioners to bishops, included prototype plans and models for "ideal" Catholic churches; sketches and study models for specific clients; elaborate M.Arch theses; photographs in promotional and fundraising material; and photographs, plans, and models used in the architectural press and in traveling exhibits to encourage specific future directions. It also included architects' internal deliberations, expressed in sketchpads and classroom projects not intended for public viewing.

The explosion of these materials in American Catholic circles between the 1930s and the mid-1960s was part of a boom in speculative design, what Andrew Shanken terms "a much larger cultural lean towards the future."[7] During the Depression and the war—years of tightly restricted materials and building capacity—Americans could only imagine what might be possible when times were good again. Shanken documents the role played by a "coherent 'unbuilt environment' " in creating a kind of collective unconsciousness of anticipation for modern architecture, due to arrive in the semimythical postwar year "194X."[8] But paper architecture did not decline or disappear when major building programs resumed in the late 1940s. Instead it metastasized, suggesting that it had never merely substituted for a frustrated construction impulse.

Peter Eisenman has noted that architectural ephemera can "have artistic or conceptual existence of [their] own, one . . . relatively independent of the project [they] represent."[9] Models and drawings serve a variety of practical and psychological functions. Some are intended solely for the use of the architect generating ideas; some are technical, like engineering blueprints or models produced for stress tests; and some are essentially propaganda, intended to spark excitement about the future of a particular building or the future of building in general. Since models and drawings liberate architects, at least partially, from "the pressures of reality, the need for practicality or even realism," they offer "an opportunity to experiment with . . . ideas," even if those ideas are, under current circumstances, "impractical or unbuildable."[10]

The unbuilt environment, then, exists primarily as a site of desire. For students and commissionless architects, models and plans can represent an end in themselves but the architect is not the only person whose imagination is in play when considering models, drawings, and plans. To view paper architecture is by definition to imagine; when a client, reader, or museumgoer sees a drawing, photograph or miniaturized version of a building, his or her mind creates a life-sized, situated, three-dimensional image. Models, drawings, and plans of unbuilt buildings are, Robin Evans writes, "projections of a plausible outcome for a set of instructions and proposals already defined elsewhere but not yet accomplished."[11] (See fig. 2.2.) Because of their inherently imaginative quality, in the twentieth century they became a tool for architects to "create a desire on the part of the client."[12] As one architect summed up: after a client views a model building, "he wants it."[13]

Models and other forms of paper architecture, then, serve as a means of shifting aesthetic authority from the existing present to future potential, from the client who already knows what he or she wants to the professional invention of

FIGURE 2.2. "Forward in Faith," fundraising brochure for Portsmouth Abbey, Portsmouth, Rhode Island, 1953. At the top of the hill is a view of Pietro Belluschi's first design for the Abbey Church; several years later, this plan was rejected in favor of the octagonal church in figures 1.1 and 1.5. Photo: PAA.

the architect. The designers of modernist Catholic churches, although always hoping for a client, did not necessarily require money or encouragement to envision new futures for church buildings. Meanwhile, the expanding professional and popular architectural press, along with museum and gallery shows, allowed modernist architects to circumvent skeptical authorities and directly educate the eyes of other architects and, they hoped, potential clients. Sketching and model-making meshed ecclesiology and architectural practice, producing layered visions of church and Church.

THE FUTURAMA OF THE MASS: PROTOTYPING LITURGICAL SPACE

Around the same time Archbishop Ritter viewed the model for St. Ann's, the liturgical-movement leader Gerald Ellard, SJ, was putting the finishing touches on *The Mass of the Future* (1948), which, while carefully presented as the culmination of serious research into the past, deliberately raised the specter of forthcoming change. Ellard's book used science fiction techniques to normalize his ideas about the future of the liturgy. As James Cardinal McGuigan of Toronto pointed out in his introduction, Ellard's section on the future of the Mass was cast in the past tense, "as if at the moment of writing these imagined changes were authorized and announced."[14] Ellard situated himself as the opener of a window on "what we may call the 'futurama' of the Mass, one that is even now partially realized by forces already at work."[15] His reference to Norman Bel Geddes's popular exhibit at the 1939 World's Fair—which simultaneously predicted and prepared an American landscape transformed by expressways and automobiles—clarifies Ellard's multiple intentions: to bring about the particular future he preferred; to describe its arrival as already under way and thus nearly inevitable; to reassure readers that this future would be intimately connected to "deeply-rooted . . . tradition"; and to appropriate American (Catholic) excitement about the technological future prophesied at the World's Fair for the liturgical movement's goals.[16]

Like other liturgists, Ellard borrowed the organicist language of evolution to describe the Mass. While the Eucharist itself, Christ's eternal "work and worship," might be "unchanged and unchangeable," the Mass, as a human practice, was "capable . . . of stagnation or growth," and it needed to grow. Despite Ellard's insistence that his suggestions grew out of the traditions of the earlier Church, he was clear that "we of the twentieth century will . . . strive to work for a richer and better *twentieth* century, and with a view toward a still richer and better twenty-first century," rather than seeking a revival of an earlier period. Like modernist architects, Ellard united the biological language of organicism with an appreciation for technological development, borrowing aviation slang to title chapters "Streamlining for the Age of Air" and "Regrouping the Fuselage Fixtures." Using a radar term meaning "to be headed in the right direction," he also remarked that Catholics interested in reforming the Mass should stay "on the Vatican beam."[17]

Ellard's work demonstrated the close relationship between projected changes in the Mass, changing ecclesiologies, and the (re)design of worship space. He had immediately become a member of the new Liturgical Arts Society; his circle of friends in St. Louis included the modernist stained-glass artist Emil Frei Jr. and the future modernist designer Charles Eames, also a Catholic.[18] As Ellard worked on *The Mass of the Future*, he consulted Maurice Lavanoux on "one of the 'wildest' chapters in the new book," seeking both articles from secular architectural journals that would support his suggestion for new altar locations, and help realizing his "vision of . . . a 'church' in

FIGURE 2.3. Sketch for a modern church (John Kelly, 1955). Photo: CLIT, 32-02-01.

down-town Chicago" that would allow for massive concelebration (help he ultimately received from Barry Byrne).[19] Byrne's projected dome would have accommodated 128 priests and as many as seventeen thousand worshippers. At the time, priests were required to say Mass once a day, as a private celebration if necessary. Liturgists found this practice increasingly disturbing, arguing that it fragmented communities. They therefore advocated concelebration, with all priests present saying Mass simultaneously. Byrne's plans, also later reprinted in *Liturgical Arts*, allowed Ellard's readers to visualize the entire Catholic community unified at prayer.

The effort invested by Ellard and other midcentury liturgists in projecting a new Mass for the future, and by Byrne and other architects in prototype church plans and models, stemmed from the frustrations of the present. Despite what they saw as progress in certain areas, liturgists generally agreed up to the eve of Vatican II that the condition of the liturgy in most places was lamentable, even "squalid."[20] Modernist architects, who believed in uniting liturgical functionalism with structural honesty, had few opportunities to win church commissions as long as the vast majority of clients ignored functionalism in favor of buildings that "looked like churches."[21] Like Byrne's plan for Ellard, or John Kelly's 1955 sketch of a church that he and his partners intended "to build—of balsa wood and for our own edification, between our rounds of the Barclay Street shops," a significant body of paper architecture was intended not to support the building of a particular church, but as an aid for developing visions of a new church that simultaneously commented on and produced a new Church community (see fig. 2.3).[22]

As they worked on drawings and models for their own and others' "edification," architects collaborated with liturgists, either directly or indirectly, by engaging the wealth of new material emerging on the history, theory, and future of the liturgy. Beginning with the earliest prototype church sketches (such as another of Barry Byrne's ideal church plans in the May 1942 *Liturgical Arts*) architects engaged in visual conversation, offering their speculations on the future of liturgical space "in a somewhat suggestive sense and with a view to discussion."[23] Byrne's 1942 plan (fig. 2.4), like the wartime prototypes for schools, factories, and homes printed in the secular architectural press, was intended neither as a specific solution to environmental and cost factors, nor as a detailed model. Rather, Byrne graphically expressed his conviction that "the sanctuary . . . and not the entrances . . . [should be] the dominating element of the building composition," as the overall form of the church should be "expressive of the primacy of [its Eucharistic] function."[24] The dispersed fan shape of the facade with its modest entryways, the seating, and the aisles would distract attention from the walls and doors and direct it toward the large sanctuary.

Prototype models and plans, both before and after Vatican II, redirected discussion from the specific needs of specific sites toward general conversation about the goal and purpose of the future church. While modernist educational practices required architects to research the functional needs of particular

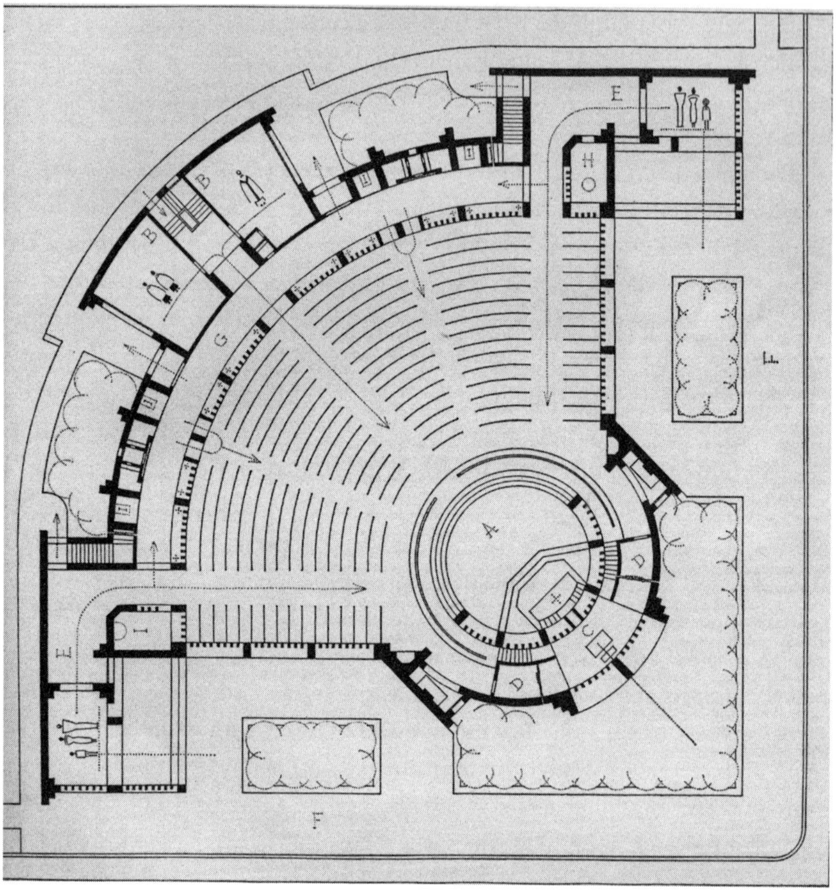

FIGURE 2.4. Prototype church plan (Barry Byrne, 1942). *Arrows* indicate both the proposed circulation of churchgoers and the plan's intention to funnel all focus toward the altar. Photo: *Liturgical Arts* 10, no. 3 (1942).

projects, they also encouraged free experimentation—often in three dimensions, as modeling replaced drawing as the first stage in the design process.[25] Young architects' thesis projects regularly explored liturgical literature, then developed models and plans (see fig. 2.5).[26] Sketching and modeling became a way of thinking through problems that were simultaneously theological, functional, and aesthetic, not only for students but for architects deep into their most productive working years; they recorded, as James Holt wrote, "a flow of ideas which precede the more formal and definitive solution" of final building plans.[27]

Architects like Holt argued that modeling could help avoid "design clichés," such as " 'a structure reaching to the sky or 'pointing to God.' " Explanations like these merely justified preconceived external forms; better designs could be "evolved through internal studies of space, ceremony, light, contrast, mood, and impact" (e.g., fig. 2.6).[28] In theory, a series of "studies" prevented lazy architects and clients alike from falling back on the solutions of the past. The Texas architect and Catholic convert Clovis Heimsath filled two dozen sketchbooks with his notes, musings, and rapid-fire drawings from the 1950s to the 1970s as he experimented with geometric forms and seating patterns that would change the experience of churchgoers.[29] When the New York architect Ray Pavia wanted to meditate on the idea that the Church should move beyond triumphalism, becoming more hospitable and open, he constructed a series of models he called "horizontal cathedrals" (fig. 2.7).[30] Pavia's modeling helped him envision a church that, hugging the landscape instead of dominating it, embraced rather than intimidated.

For architects (and the artists who sometimes collaborated with them), sketching and modeling also bridged the gap between developing their own thought and stimulating "some progressive Church group" to "commission an edifice conceived along similar lines," an aspiration that fueled several highly

FIGURE 2.5. Architecture students working with models at St. John's, Collegeville, Minnesota (ca. 1950s). Photo: GLIT, 06-25-01.

FIGURE 2.6. *Liturgical Arts* layout of studies for a church (James A. Holt Jr., 1968). Maurice Lavanoux's caption notes that "they indicate the flow of ideas which precede the more formal and definitive solution." Photo: *Liturgical Arts* 37, no. 1 (1968).

FIGURE 2.7. Study model for a "horizontal cathedral" (Raymond Pavia, mid-1960s.) Photo: Author.

detailed model prototype churches.[31] To art historians, the best known of these prototypes is the 1950–52 scheme by the Catholics Alfonso Ossorio and Tony Smith for a chapel to be hung with works by their friend Jackson Pollock. The three met with Liturgical Arts Society members, including Maurice Lavanoux, the patron and art-world figure Eloise Spaeth, and former Museum of Modern Art curator James Johnson Sweeney, about to begin his tenure as director of the Guggenheim Museum; however, Smith's model and plans were never printed in *Liturgical Arts*.[32]

Lavanoux did print a far more elaborate and highly developed model made at almost the same time, the 1951 *Church of the Four Evangelists* by Princeton's dean of architecture, Jean Labatut, and the painter André Girard. Like many prototypes, sketches, and actual churches of the 1950s, Labatut and Girard's plan, exhibited at the Carstairs Gallery in New York and then around the United States, projected an overall circular floor plan with semicircular seating, gathering congregants around the altar (see fig. 2.13).[33] What separated the Labatut-Girard scheme was the pair's interest in integrating large-scale narrative art throughout the design. As with classic stained glass, Girard's paintings on a clear glass curtain wall would be strongly affected by changing natural light throughout the day. Unlike stained glass windows, however, the partially painted curtain wall would disrupt the distinction between interior and exterior worship. Labatut and Girard were interested in the relationship between architecture and time, what Labatut called a "twenty-four hour architecture."[34] Using models of multiple sizes, the pair used the architecture laboratory at Princeton to study how lighting conditions, changing through the day and the seasons, might affect worshippers' experience.[35]

Younger architects, in particular, used models and plans both to think through their ideas and to promote their own practices to their elders. The Catholic architect Thomas McNulty and his future wife, Mary Fawcett, both MIT graduates, designed a detailed prototype in 1957 that they hoped would generate a commission from the Archdiocese of Boston (fig. 2.8) Boston was the site of a dense nexus between the Catholic liturgical movement and high-powered modernist design; not only were the Catholics José Luis Sert and Pietro Belluschi deans the schools of architecture (Sert at Harvard, 1953–69; Belluschi at MIT, 1951–65), but György Kepes taught at MIT from 1947 to '74. McNulty, Kepes's former assistant, parlayed a recommendation from his mentor into viewings of his church models by Celia Hubbard, the convert proprietor of Boston's important Catholic modernist gallery the Botolph Group, and liturgical-movement veteran Fr. Edward Sutfin of Vermont.[36] Hubbard and Sutfin in turn passed these "terrific" designs on to Maurice Lavanoux, who promptly published one in *Liturgical Arts*.[37] In addition to a glass curtain wall, McNulty and Fawcett proposed an elliptical floor plan, roofed by a series of individualized concrete shells to be formed separately rather than on a standardized mold.

Architecture students interested in churches, too, regularly sought to publish their thesis projects, which both at Catholic and secular universities straddled the line between dutiful reworkings of current liturgical orthodoxy and ambitious futurist projection. As Harvard MFA graduate Philip Cotton explained to Maurice Lavanoux, his 1959 prototype had "paid little specific attention to the numerous laws and regulations of the church in regard to the liturgy," seemingly a contradiction of the modernist imperative to functional design. Cotton justified his scant attention to rubrical correctness with the comment that he was "looking for . . . a great reform in the liturgy," and had "tried to get some idea of the spirit of the mass and the sacraments" that would be "said and sung in the vernacular in this church." His prototype church, in other words, drew on his understanding of current liturgical-movement projection like Ellard's, seeking a different kind of "function." And both students and recent graduates participated in profile-raising exercises like a 1961 competition, sponsored by the North American Liturgical Conference, whose thirty-three winners were published under the title *Churches for Tomorrow* (e.g., fig. 2.9).[38]

FIGURE 2.8. Proposed Catholic church for the Archdiocese of Boston (Thomas McNulty and Mary S. Fawcett, 1957). Photo: GLIT, 20-38-01.

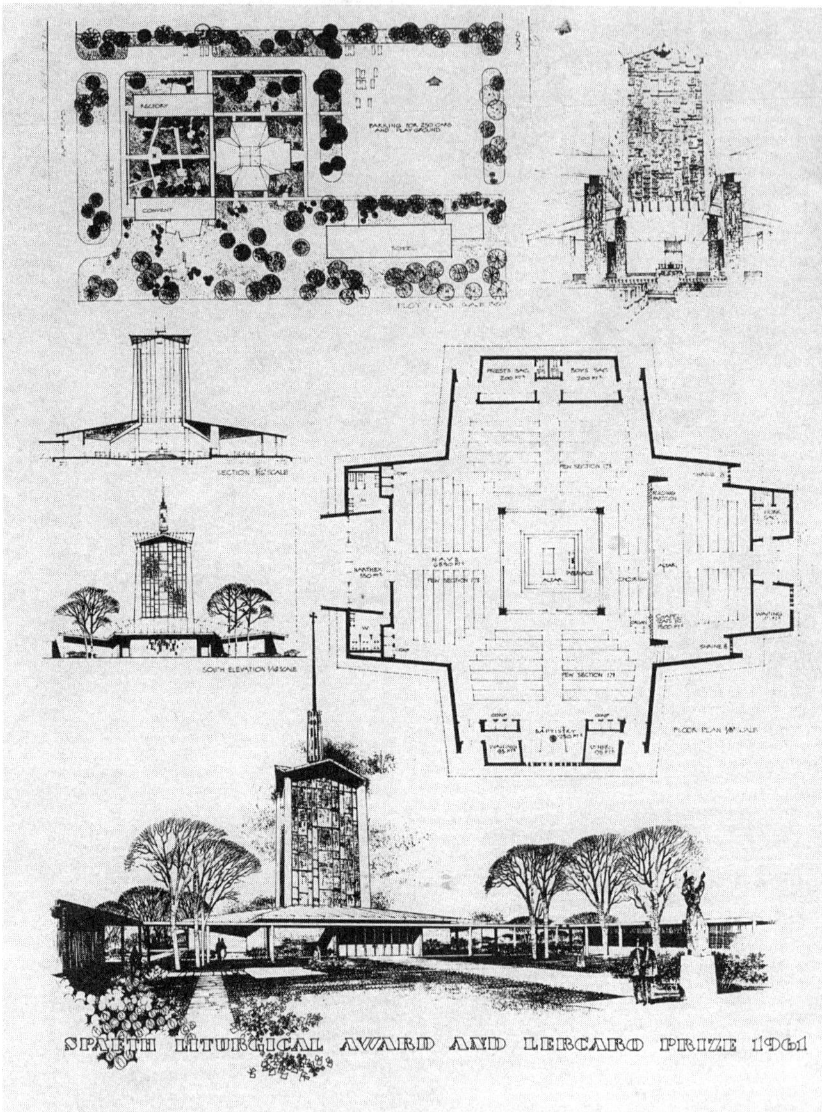

FIGURE 2.9. First-prize entry for the Spaeth-Lercaro Award (Otto Bauer-Nilsen, 1961). Photo: Fr. Patrick O'Donnell, ed., *Churches for Tomorrow: Thirty-Three Designs from the Cardinal Lercaro Prize-Spaeth Competition Sponsored by the North American Liturgical Conference 1961* (Cincinnati: F&W Publishing, 1961). Courtesy Otto Bauer-Nilsen.

In the event, Vatican II disrupted the liturgical future far more than even the most visionary anticipated, and the postconciliar years resulted in another wide swath of prototype church designs and speculations. When Maurice Lavanoux submitted suggestions to the council's preparatory subcommission on sacred art, he begged that "any pronouncement concerning the evolution of sacred art be a *positive* one and a generous one" focused on the use of "the most talented practitioners" in all the arts instead of on rules and condemnations.[39] As it became evident that major liturgical changes would be forthcoming, many Catholic artists and architects resisted the immediate introduction of new rubrics in favor of a prolonged period of spatial exploration. (See chap. 6.) As the lithographer Jeanne Heiberg wrote to Lavanoux in 1966, "We don't have to have [another] set of binding directives that might impede future growth"; she and others preferred "much discussion of trends, possibilities, and experiments."[40] The architect James Holt called on sketching and modeling to provide the meat of that "discussion," noting that while these years were "an exciting period of evolution" and the "revisions in the liturgy allow for the important development of a new liturgical architecture," architects should "resist the superficial development of emotional form credited to . . . the designer's . . . preconceived ideas."[41] Instead, architects would do their best post–Vatican II work if they "evolved [a] final statement through refined internal studies of the space: studies of ceremony, light, contrast, mood, and impacts."[42] Architects ought to collaborate with liturgists and congregations, but they also ought to affirm their professional expertise in space and form and their nonverbal methods of contributing to postconciliar conversation.

THE UNBUILT ENVIRONMENT: THE PUBLIC LIFE OF PAPER ARCHITECTURE

Modeling and drawing, though they might be ways for individuals to work out their ideas, were rarely entirely private practices. Even the least personally ambitious designers of prototype churches, like the teenaged Mary Rose Shaughnessy, participated in a larger conversation at once aesthetic, practical, and ecclesiological. Shaughnessy, an architect's daughter, read books by Gropius, Mies, Wright, Saarinen, and Rudolf Schwarz in the late 1940s and 1950s. Not needing, unlike her father, "to deal with conservative priests and bishops who weren't thinking along those lines," Mary Rose designed her own prototype church, with a Schwarzian parabolic ground plan and a focus on the altar.[43] The consumption and production of even private prototypes and models meant entering a wider conversation about the future of the church; modeling became a way not simply of approaching a specific, isolated building but, as Albert C. Smith writes, "designing a culture's universe."[44] As an increasing volume of modernist material became available to American Catholics through models, drawings, and photographs in brochures, books, magazines, museums, and gallery exhibits, editors and publicists curated the modernist visual imagination.[45]

The timing of Barry Byrne's 1942 prototype plan was not coincidental. In Europe, war activities were destroying churches, while in the United States, everyone awaited a postwar construction boom. With little actual construction to discuss, and knowing that "there will be churches to rebuild" en masse, Maurice Lavanoux settled down during the early 1940s to contest "the old bugbear of 'tradition' versus the 'horrible present,' to say nothing of the future," which he found in more typical Catholic articulations of the postwar possibilities.[46] Roosevelt's "four freedoms," he suggested, should really include a fifth: "freedom from fear of the present and the future!"[47] In the meantime the war years provided an opportunity to take stock and to hope that, as Leopold Arnaud of Columbia put it, "the post-war period" would be "an age of renewed vitality" rather than "an age of disillusionment and despair."[48] This meant printing prototype plans, as well as material on the reconstruction of architectural education along organicist lines.[49] Meanwhile Catholics already convinced by the biological paradigm got a jump on arguing their case to the general Catholic public. One priest felt the "married ladies' sodality" might be "less violent and antagonistic" to modern art if, close to the end of the war, he "talked about the Churches we hope to build and adorn for God in the world of tomorrow."[50]

Despite their hopes for the postwar period, Lavanoux and his allies were somewhat stymied by their sense that very few existing churches could effectively preview the future. As American material did begin to become available after the war, Lavanoux printed it rapidly, composing layouts of photographs, plans, and sketches that, like those in the major secular architectural magazines, were not intended to be copied but rather to be, as Hyungmin Pai writes, "a means for stimulating an idea, a vehicle for conveying the concept of the building portrayed."[51] Unbuilt designs could be particularly useful for conveying the narrative that Church leaders approved of explorations into modernist architecture. In August 1950 Lavanoux printed Joseph Murphy's three designs for St. Louis–area parish churches, claiming they were particularly "fresh ideas" being supported by pastors and bishops."[52] Several years later, he printed the McNulty-Fawcett model side by side with a model for a new church in the

Chicago Loop, asserting that both churches, including Belli & Belli's "daring design" for the Chicago church, had the "hearty approval" of local bishops.[53] As he was increasingly called on to advise architectural students on Catholic church design, he also promoted their work by printing their thesis sketches.[54]

Liturgical Arts' editorial policy was understood by all concerned to be educative, gradually preparing readers to accept the biological paradigm; as Frank Kacmarcik wrote Lavanoux, his printing of modern art and architecture would "no doubt . . . go far in preparing our clergy for a new living liturgical expression."[55] Lavanoux himself commented that his more "extreme and puzzling" items were intended to provoke readers to "perhaps imagine the possibility of other works beyond those they were accustomed to see."[56] His editorial choices ranged from the relatively mundane to the truly unusual. Although earlier phases of *Liturgical Arts* had been less friendly to the nascent ecumenical movement, by 1963 Lavanoux was writing the Anglican Paul Douglas Roller that his MFA thesis "should present this whole idea of an ecumenical center [on Ellis Island] in convincing fashion," adding that Roller's plans would appear during the second session of Vatican II.[57] Lavanoux's printing of these plans, along with other imagined plans for ecumenical centers and churches during the 1960s and 1970s, was meant to help drive the construction of such spaces. He also valued truly unbuildable visions, remarking on Paolo Soleri's "fantastic creations" of the futuristic cities he called "arcologies," and spearheading the creation of drawings and models for chapels on a moon base, a submarine, and a space station (see chap. 4).[58] Lavanoux summed up his editorial philosophy to a friend: "I have long felt that dreams have a way of becoming reality!"[59]

Magazines and books did not, however, always promote modernist work through explicit argument; instead, they often allowed viewers to draw their own conclusions from plans and photos, neglecting to mention what they were rejecting. Like the publishers of the leading secular architectural magazines, by the 1940s Lavanoux declined to print historicist material, writing a prospective contributor in 1944 that "we feel it is more important to devote our efforts to the present and particularly the future, rather than devote our time to any consideration of a style which is definitely of the past."[60] An isolated but telling incident was the Notre Dame architecture professor Frank Montana's selection of plates for the American edition of J. B. O'Connell's 1955 manual *Church Building and Furnishing*.[61] O'Connell—whom Lavanoux noted as "not in tune with recent developments"—had departed for Britain by the time the Notre Dame printed his 1953 lectures, so, as the liturgist Michael Mathis, CSC, carefully noted in the preface, he was "not to be held in any way responsible" for the choice of photographs.[62] Montana, a Beaux-Arts graduate remembered today as "not a radical educator, unlike many of his counterparts," nevertheless selected predominantly modern designs "chosen for the purpose . . . of showing the freedom that is granted by the Church to pastors and architects in meeting the requirements of sound worship."[63] In twenty-six architectural plates, Montana used only one neohistoricist design: St. Patrick's Cathedral. In the other twenty-five, alongside examples from Europe, he printed photographs and plans of churches by the Americans Paul Thiry, Murphy and Mackey, and Mario Ciampi, among the most radical possibilities available in 1955.[64] Americans would have clearly understood the message that modern designs were not only liturgically correct, but (in Mathis and Montana's view) positively encouraged by the Church, which left architects free to "meet the requirements laid down by the Church in any way that local conditions and their own ingenuity make possible."[65] Since the British edition, overseen by O'Connell, conveys a totally different message through its selection of exclusively neohistoricist designs, the American volume stands as an unusually clear example of quiet, yet potent, modernist editorial intervention.[66]

Catholics were not, however, the only people investigating and creating the future of church architecture through their editorial choices. Mainstream architectural magazines took the same tack, printing omnibus articles investigating the question of whether "contemporary architecture [could] meet the spiritual needs and economic limitations of today's church as did the design of the Colonial meeting house, the Gothic cathedral, and the Egyptian temple" and focusing on success stories that showed "the possibility of a new church architecture which could make its own contribution" to the future.[67] Features on new church designs (generally covering both Catholic and Protestant examples, and often synagogues as well) routinely appeared in the December issues of *Architectural Digest*, *Architectural Record*, and *Progressive Architecture*.[68] The editors of these periodicals recognized their kinship with *Liturgical Arts*, and were often in direct touch with Maurice Lavanoux; in 1967, for example, Mildred Schmertz, a Catholic and the senior editor of *Architectural Record*, wrote to mention that she was about to publish "a group of excellent, new, about to be constructed church projects by Pietro Belluschi," adding that "these would excellently demonstrate your thesis that talented and creative responses to the new liturgy, not rubrics, are called for."[69] Lavanoux, meanwhile, often wrote to artists and architects after seeing their work in other magazines.[70] Both formal collaborations and informal shared taste meant that certain churches by certain architects appeared over and over in the architectural press; the "iconicity" of such buildings, as Swati Chattopadhyay points out, is in part "a product of their presentation in the media."[71]

Architectural magazines, along with books like Katharine Morrison McClinton's *The Changing Church* or Thiry, Bennet, and Kamphoefner's *Churches & Temples*, freely mixed photos of finished work with photos of models and plans, the completed churches lending an air of inevitability to projects still in the proposal stage. But models and plans appeared in more explicitly commercial spaces as well. While some prototype church designers, like Labatut and Girard or McNulty and Fawcett, produced highly finished models without a specific client in mind, the majority of polished professional models blurred the line between conceptual study tools and propaganda. *Liturgical Arts* commented (in reference to Paul Thiry's Church of Christ the King, Seattle) that three-dimensional models in particular could "be very helpful for a study of many phases of the building program," meaning that architect and client alike could use models to try out ideas in advance of actual building.[72] Architects like Labatut and Sert used models to experiment with lighting conditions; Pietro Belluschi and his engineer collaborator Pier Luigi Nervi performed stress tests on a large model of their proposed San Francisco Cathedral. But as Joseph Murphy's experience at Archbishop Ritter's office suggests, elaborate and highly finished models and drawings were often used primarily as sales devices, seducing viewers through their miniaturized modernity. Church models partook in the element of showmanship derived from World's Fair exhibits like GM's Futurama and were used in the same ways: as practical study tools, to elicit wonder, to acclimate viewers to a certain look for new churches, and to associate enthusiasm for the future with that look.

Models were exceptionally useful as publicity tools. As early as 1933, Thomas Coakley had two scale models made of his Sacred Heart Church in Pittsburgh. One was a study model for working out interior traffic patterns. The other was a five-and-a-half-foot-long facsimile projecting what the church would look like in exact material detail. "The model had a very surprising effect upon the congregation," Coakley wrote, encouraging other priests to invest in such a tool. "It enlarged their idea of their new Church, made them more proud than ever of their parish, stimulated their enthusiasm, and made the Church 'the talk of the town.'" He loaned the model for exhibition in "a prominent window of the busiest department store in town, where probably 500,000 persons saw it; it was commented on in the newspapers, in store advertisements, and on the radio." Coakley planned to keep the model in the vestibule "as a constant reminder to our generous parishioners of the work still to be done to complete the fabric."[73]

The practice of using models for fundraising increased after the war, as the cost of making and printing images dropped while construction costs and

FIGURE 2.10. Rendering of the proposed Cardinal O'Hara Memorial Chapel, University of Notre Dame (Ellerbe Associates, 1967). Notre Dame commissioned renderings and a large model of a new quadrangle for fundraising purposes. Of five planned high-rise dormitories, only Flanner and Grace Halls (visible in the background of this painting) were built. Photo: University of Notre Dame Archives, GNDL-04-09C-01.

the need for financing climbed.[74] Daring church models made for enticing publicity photographs; a futuristic church slated for the core of a residential tower group lent pizzazz to the University of Notre Dame's 1967 campaign, lending aesthetic weight to the university's quest to "reach out to the future" (fig. 2.10).[75] Photographs of clients with a model church or monastery group demonstrated the collaboration of priests, monks, and nuns with the architect, who had brought his expertise to bear and produced a solution anticipated by all (e.g., fig. 2.11) They were also an important part of the visual portfolio of any project in the fundraising stage, enticing parishioners with the enchanting vision of their new modern building, complete with tiny cars parked in the lot (e.g., fig. 2.12). Suggesting, as Mark Morris notes, that "the project is already a little bit real," models made the planned (but still unpaid for and unbuilt) parish church seem both exciting and inevitable.[76]

Though often models succeeded in converting Catholics to projected churches, occasionally they did backfire badly. In the early 1950s, around the time of the *Instruction on Sacred Art*, the architect Joseph Salerno warned the

FIGURE 2.11. Architects Marcel Breuer and Hamilton Smith showing blueprints and a model of the future bell banner to sisters of Annunciation Monastery, Bismarck, North Dakota, including Mother Edane Volk (in profile, holding pen) (ca. late 1950s). Photo: Benedictine Sisters of Annunciation Monastery.

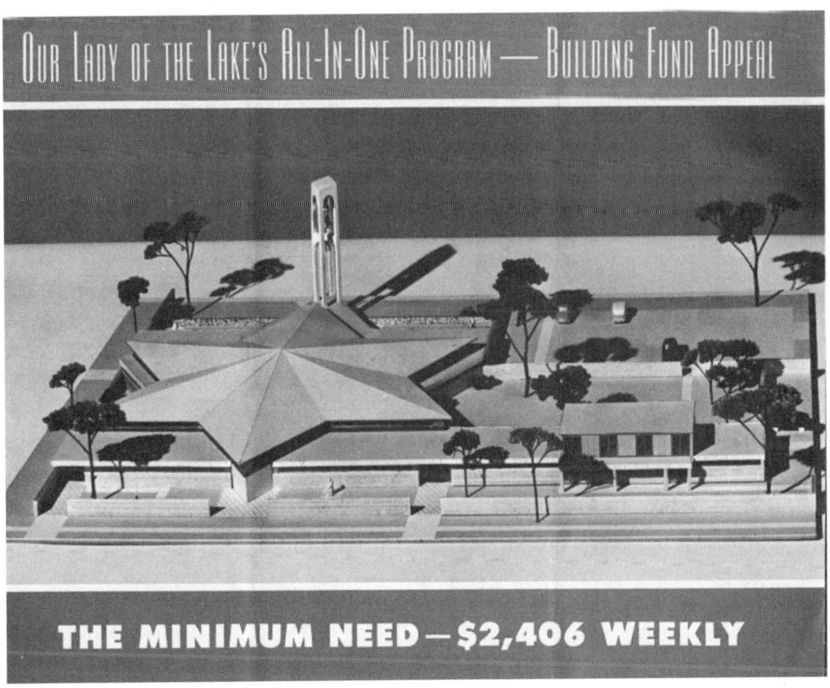

FIGURE 2.12. Brochure for Our Lady of the Lake, Mound, Minnesota (Voight & Fourre, 1965), ca. early 1960s. Photo: Courtesy of the Archives of the Catholic Archdiocese of Seattle.

parish building committee at St. Francis of Assisi in Weston, Connecticut, that choosing him would mean "fireworks," a prophecy fulfilled when the town dentist "made a captive audience of his patients to protest the building of a 'modernistic' church within sight of his house. All this before even I knew what the church would look like."[77] Nevertheless, the committee accepted Salerno's drawings and agreed to have a model made, which was eventually shown to the parish with, Salerno reported, "enthusiastic approval."[78] He prepared working drawings and the project was put out for bidding. But after an extended silence, the diocesan building commission rejected the design, apparently offended, in part, by the appearance of the model in *Architectural Record* prior to its final acceptance.[79] This last-minute disruption after years of work shows why Catholic clients were so often deeply concerned about the presentation of the model and/or drawings to religious authorities, typically the bishop or, in the case of monastic communities, the motherhouse.[80] Bishops could and did scotch even fairly well-developed plans, as Wendelin Nold of Galveston-Houston did with one Philip Johnson–designed parish church. Johnson wrote Lavanoux in April of 1953 that "I am going down on the 7th with the new model full of hope," but ultimately, the Houston Catholic architect Donald Barthelme reported, the model was not convincing and the bishop "put his foot down."[81]

EXPANDING THE AUDIENCE FOR THE CHURCH OF TOMORROW: LECTURES AND EXHIBITIONS

While magazines and books reached many architectural professionals and liturgists, most potential church clients—both lay and clerical—could not be educated through these means. Yet for modernists it was extremely important to win over rank-and-file clergy and the "man in the pew." This was true for reasons both practical (those who despised modernist architecture might refuse to donate to the building of such a church, or derail a project with complaints to diocesan authorities) and spiritual (as aesthetic education functioned as a kind of evangelism).[82] Modernists could be quite explicit about this parallel. "I hope you are completely converted to modern architecture by now," Clare Boothe Luce wrote to Fr. John Tierney in 1950. "Incidentally," she added, "I read a rather clever article by a great critic who suggested that a conversion to modern art is almost as startling as a conversion to Catholicism: i.e., one day ya hates it, and the next, nothing else will do."[83] Even as architects guarded their professional prerogatives and attempted to retain control over their designs, they therefore welcomed opportunities to put their paper architecture before the public.

Even in the late 1950s, only a minority of American religious buildings were built in the "modern style" (and fewer still according to modernist principles.) With a general lack of local examples, slide lectures and exhibitions became important tools in the modernists' educational arsenal, circulating images to communities that might never have laid eyes on a modern church. Maurice Lavanoux crisscrossed the country in the 1940s and 1950s, giving hundreds of lectures at seminaries and colleges using worldwide examples of modernist churches, under titles like "The Evolution of Church Architecture in Our Day." He primarily spoke to Catholics, but also at secular architecture departments; and he occasionally appeared on radio and TV.[84] These lectures began as an opportunity to ease the Liturgical Arts Society's financial troubles, but also served to promote modernism to diverse Catholic audiences. To take three examples from 1948, in February Lavanoux joined the St. Ignatius Loyola parish discussion club in New York, whose chair said the group had "realized that, within the limits of the law, there is room for growth and the creative change that are the principle of life."[85] In June, he appeared at the National Catholic Building Convention in Chicago, where he took the opportunity to use slides of Barry Byrne's " 'multaealterae' " and "gave a plug for" Ellard's *Mass of the Future*.[86] In November, he lectured at the Catholic University of America.[87] While others lacked his reach, they often wanted to follow his lead, and he fielded frequent requests for the loan of slides and photos from teachers, Newman Clubs, and other would-be lecturers.[88]

Everyone interested in Catholic modernist architecture agreed that the annual Liturgical Weeks, which drew potential clients from all over the country, should be an excellent opportunity for education. Their demonstration liturgies projected "the mass of the future," and, like the World's Fair's Futurama, "created a total environment, which immersed spectators in the dramatic action" and inspired attendees to recreate the experience in their own parishes.[89] But liturgical-week art displays frequently drew modernists' wrath for being too heavily commercialized, dominated by catalogue vendors. The 1957 show, at St. John's Abbey under the direction of the liturgist and architect Cloud Meinberg, OSB, did win approval for its selection of liturgical objects and photos and models of churches; Lavanoux longed for such an exhibit to circulate nationally for the enlightenment of "the general public."[90] Prioritizing professional expertise over commercial viability, Lavanoux hoped to transfer the art show to museums, who could ensure that "the result would be kept at a high artistic level." Such exhibitions promised "the opportunity for church officials and the general public to see and appraise a movement which promises a great future."[91]

The midcentury Catholic galleries and bookstores where proponents of the liturgical movement gathered were frequently owned and staffed by women, and exhibitions—which often relied on volunteer labor—were also often the domain of genteel laywomen.[92] Eloise Spaeth, wife of the industrialist Otto Spaeth and former convent school student, became the most energetic link between the museum world and the Liturgical Arts Society. In the spring of 1944, she organized "Religious Art of Today" at the Dayton Art Institute, rejecting any submissions that were "merely a copy of the traditional," and accepting only those which were "of this day and time."[93] Spaeth wanted to demonstrate that "the artist of today is freeing himself from traditions which, no matter how great, still belong to the past."[94] She borrowed paintings, sculpture, and liturgical objects from museums in New York and Chicago as well as from private collectors; Francis Taylor, director of the Metropolitan Museum of Art, came to Ohio to open the exhibit in person.[95] The architectural section of the exhibit contained photos, drawings, and models of Protestant, Catholic, and Jewish buildings, but it was a painfully small selection, since so few American religious buildings had even gestured at modernism prior to the war.[96] (By 1963, an American Institute of Architects–sponsored exhibit of modernist churches drew 150 entries, of which 25 were chosen for display in the lobby of the Pepsi-Cola Building in New York.)[97] The Dayton exhibit did have, as its "high point," a walk-in, life-sized model of a modernist church: a Chapel of Christ the Worker, designed by Barry Byrne with windows by Emil Frei.[98] This, as a newspaper pointed out, was a "new theme; it belongs to the 20th century."[99] Visitors walked through a narrow passageway into the model chapel, which invited them to inquire whether their own parish church buildings were, or could be, able to stimulate "20th-century" thought.

Spaeth's first exhibit had great propaganda value, with "urgent appeals" from both the Offices of War Information and of the Coordinator of Inter-American Affairs for copies of the catalog to send to Brazil, as proof (against "a German build-up" focusing on the destruction of monasteries in Europe) that the people of the United States cared about "art and religion."[100] After the war, Spaeth developed further as a patron, exhibition chair, and key supporter and organizer of the Archives of American Art.[101] Circulating publicity overseas about contemporary religious art continued to be a government concern during the Cold War; for example, the State Department requested photos for a 1953 exhibition on "The Church in America" intended "to combat the impression of many Europeans that ours is a purely materialistic society."[102] While Spaeth worked tirelessly to promote American modern art overseas, she also campaigned to have it accepted by American Catholics. In August 1954, she opened a show in East Hampton, featuring Joseph Murphy's model of Resurrection Church and Marcel Breuer's model for St. John's Abbey Church.[103] Simultaneously, she solicited assistance from wealthy Catholics for the American Federation of Arts touring exhibition *Today's Religious Art* (1957–1960) and the Museum of Contemporary Craft's *The Patron Church* (1958).[104]

Eloise Spaeth was unique in her combination of personal wealth, leisure to focus on promoting contemporary church art, and connections in both the Catholic and the museum world, but other Catholics also organized exhibits with a modernist bent.[105] The Madonna Guild, a Catholic women's group in Memphis, Tennessee, began a novena when, two weeks short of the submissions deadline for a 1958 show on contemporary art, they had received only ten photographs; by the time their nine days of prayer were up, over a hundred more had come in.[106] University and seminary students organized smaller-scale exhibitions, generally relying heavily on photographs and on their own work. The Newman Club of Washington University in St. Louis, however, obtained Joseph Murphy's model of Resurrection church for its 1951 sacred art show.[107] On a more professional level, Celia Hubbard's Botolph Group, assisted by exhibit designer György Kepes, showed contemporary art and architecture at the Margaret Brown Gallery in Boston for three weeks in December 1955, including Breuer's model of St. John's Abbey and models, photos, and plans of churches in Venezuela and El Salvador by modernist luminaries Paul Lester Wiener, José Luis Sert, and Oscar Nitzchke.[108] Hubbard's catalogue introduction noted that "the exclusive copying of styles of the past implies that Christian art is dead in our time"; she wanted to demonstrate that, rather, "the same spirit that has always inspired true religious art is still alive."[109] Everywhere exhibits like this appeared, they advanced the same point. As the reporter Jack Harwell noted of a show at the Contemporary Arts Museum in Houston featuring the Labatut-Girard model, "a major metamorphosis of church architecture is taking place in the United States. The pattern of the old church building is changing and in its place is arising another which may, in our time, create a distinctive style of its own" (fig. 2.13).[110] Harwell encouraged readers to see the exhibit, which also featured plans of Houston's St. Rose of Lima and the model of St. Ann's parish that had so enthused Archbishop Ritter in 1947, in order to see "the direction that may be taken."[111] Architects no doubt joined Sert in the wish that these shows would "give the courage to at least one pastor" to commission a modernist church.[112]

FIGURE 2.13. Exhibition-goers viewing one of several models for prototype Church of the Four Evangelists (Jean Labatut and André Girard, 1951). *At right*, the curved rear wall of the sanctuary features paintings from the four evangelists; *at center*, a model worshipper kneels at the communion rail while a priest stands facing the congregation across the altar and tabernacle. Other models included a painted glass wall encircling the nave. Photo: GLIT, 16-70-01.

ARCHITECTURAL ECCLESIOLOGY: MODELING THE CHURCH

In 1974, the Jesuit theologian Avery Dulles surveyed the state of contemporary ecclesiology in *Models of the Church*. Dulles noted that recent theology had reemphasized the ancient Christian conviction that "at the heart of the Church one finds mystery."[113] Therefore no single idea or image or characteristic, no matter how resonant and grounded in tradition, could adequately express the "complex reality" of the Church. Even to approach adequacy required Christians to perform "a kind of mental juggling act," keeping multiple aspects in the air.[114] Dulles called these images or aspects "models," emphasizing the partial but real self-sufficiency that prevented them from fully synthesizing and presenting a false coherence.[115]

Dulles distinguished his ecclesiological models from architectural models, dismissing the latter as merely "scale reproductions of the reality under consideration," which they certainly were not.[116] Rare was the model of an American church that copied, rather than projected, a built reality. The extensive network of architectural images made and used by Catholics from the

1930s onward—in trade journals like *Church Property Management*, in *Liturgical Arts* with its distinctive visual language, in the secular architectural press, in exhibits, and in privately circulated plans and drawings—was both produced by and stimulated thought about "new directions," "creative thinking," and "the future." Catholic modernists saw themselves moving, as the title of a 1962 collection of essays by the New Churches Research Group in England put it, *Towards a Church Architecture*.[117]

But if Dulles misunderstood the nature of architectural models, he nevertheless showed why they mattered so much. Models—and photos, plans, drawings, and slides—showed midcentury American Catholics that it was possible for the church of tomorrow to look very different from the existing churches in which they worshipped. Paper architecture did far more, however, than normalize modernist aesthetics or entice building fund contributions. Like Dulles's "heuristic models," models and drawings of future churches raised the possibility that the Church, too, might change, as the universal and local community responded to the imperatives of its new buildings. Ray Pavia's horizontal cathedrals suggested a profoundly different conception of authority; John Cates's underground church projected humility and service. Many models silently argued the possibilities of new construction materials and techniques, helping Catholics believe that these new technologies could be "baptized," allowing the Church to be part of the modern world rather than rejecting it. The modernist unbuilt environment imagined a future church with less separation between clergy and people, adequate space for the entire community to gather around the altar, and a focus on the creation of a universal community through the Mass.[118]

Architects and their allies, in short, invested substantial time and resources during the 1940s and 1950s to create a collective vision for a type of church that American Catholics rarely encountered in their daily lives. They drew on their general knowledge of architectural principles and on this emerging collective vision to generate proposals in the same architectural family—a contemporary church architecture that would, per the principles of the biological paradigm, be clearly functional for its time and place. That they largely succeeded in linking this formal vision to the cause of liturgical change became evident in the later 1960s, when American Catholics often interpreted the mandate of the Second Vatican Council through this lens, despite the council's lack of outright endorsement of "modernist" aesthetics. When the Servite priest Gabriel Weber studied the conciliar document *Sacrosanctum concilium* with a Denver junior high class in 1967, he required his thirty-five students to submit a model of "a modern church, illustrating the recent changes in the liturgy"; the class

FIGURE 2.14. Models of modern churches by a junior high school class in Denver, Colorado, 1967. Photo: GLIT, 47-02-01.

read books on modernist church architecture and spent several days discussing "the purposes of a church and the function of various areas and furnishings."[119] The students' models indicated that most of them understood the connection between liturgical change and a distinctly 'modern' look of concrete, glass, and wide-spanned roofs (fig. 2.14).

In generating this large body of architectural ephemera, American Catholics interested in church architecture were engaging in a common midcentury cultural practice: the creation of verbal and visual "images of the future." These images became so widespread by the 1960s that an academic subdiscipline emerged to articulate their psychological rationale and effects. "Futurists" not only projected futures, but also tried to understand why futuristic speculation seemed increasingly appealing and what effect it had on the people who engaged in it. In Robert Bundy's words: "Images of the future . . . speak to what will be or can be or should be." They are not divorced from the present or the past, but are "born and refined in the light of specific interpretations of the past." But they also "tell of a counterreality radically different from the present, of another and better world in another time," and in doing so they "pull a civilization forward in search of the destiny the images foretell." If a particular vision is compelling enough, to enough people, it may even shape what comes to be: "The actual future of a civilization . . . is prefigured in the shared images of the future possessed by its people in the present."[120] In short, futurists concluded, people use images both to speculate based on current developments, and to affirm particular futures they desire. Preexisting churches, uncooperative clients, and lack of funds constrained Catholic modernists' building; in their paper architecture, they created an unbuilt environment that opened up real future possibilities.

FIGURE 3.1. Chapel of the Holy Cross, Sedona, Arizona (Anshen + Allen, 1957). Photo: Author.

CHAPTER THREE

THEOLOGY IN CONCRETE

> Was the last stone in sublime church architecture laid seven hundred years ago? Have we no greatness to contribute? Has all steam and oil and electricity, all this building and expansion and industry, all this vision and invention and labor, all this creation and munificence, brought not one small thing to the House of God?
>
> MYLES CONNOLLY, *Mr. Blue*, 1928

The sun shone brightly over the Atlantic Ocean on the morning of May 8, 1936, as Paul Schulte, OMI, a missionary en route to the United States, raised his chalice above his head. It was completely steady, and Schulte was relieved, since he had obtained permission to say the world's first Mass aboard a dirigible only after promising several Vatican offices that the *Hindenburg* would not sway midair, spilling the newly consecrated wine, now the Blood of Christ. Triumphantly, Schulte turned to his small congregation of crew and reporters and proclaimed:

> Let the Amen be pronounced by the skies with the wonderful clouds surrounding us, the ocean over which we are hovering, the sun, the breeze, the stars. Let the Amen be spoken by the motors, the wonderful airship, the crew, the passengers. *Gloria Tibi*, Glory be to Thee today, tomorrow, and in all eternity, Amen.[1]

Schulte and the Jesuit editors of *America* who devoted two full pages to his Eucharistic adventure were not the only twentieth-century Catholics intrigued by the relationship between the liturgy and the new technologies of modernity. *America* had earlier noted the first Mass on an airplane and on the deck of a submarine; in later decades, Catholics would wonder about the sacramental possibilities of travel into outer space and into the depths of the seas.[2] In this context, the new construction technologies Catholic modernists employed in more conventional worship spaces represented more than cheap but fungible alternatives to the techniques of the past.

Modernist architects deployed new materials and techniques in a century defined by cascading revolutions in technologies of transportation, construction, and communication that ultimately transformed almost every aspect of life. These changes were particularly visible and acutely felt in the mid-twentieth century, when wartime R&D budgets produced new compounds of plastic, rubber, glass, and metal, while government policy and consumer demand drove innovation in audiovisual and climate-control technologies. American Catholics' views on the relevance of these developments for the design of their churches ranged from distaste for—and even revulsion against—the materials of modernity, to a practical acceptance of their benefits in the service of missionary ends and material comforts, all the way to Schulte's ascription to the *Hindenburg*'s motors of the capacity for mystical communion with the divine. Whether they responded positively or negatively to exposed concrete, innovative floor plans, or plexiglass sanctuary furniture, American Catholics understood church designs incorporating concrete, plywood, plastic sealants, and video projection as part of a wider conversation about the relationship of technology and the sacred. The engineering developments that made modernist churches feasible raised questions that were, for many Catholics, fundamentally theological. Catholic modernists made three interlocking claims in favor of new technologies as fundamental to valid worship space. First, in line with their evolutionary understanding of technological and design development, they believed that new technologies were necessary because they were well adapted to the twentieth century American environment. Second, they argued that the specific properties of new building materials would enable priest and people to unite in the celebration of the Mass. And third, the use of new technologies in postwar church buildings and, further, their potential to transport the Mass to previously impossible corners of the cosmos also caused Catholic modernists to reflect on God's sacramental presence in the world, and on their own role in enabling divine indwelling.

TECHNOLOGICAL CIVILIZATION AND CATHOLIC MODERNITY IN THE AMERICAN CENTURY

While wide-ranging conversations about the aesthetic and economic properties of new materials occupied Catholic builders, the defense of the use of new materials and technologies was ultimately rooted neither in their cost-effectiveness nor their beauty, but in the claim that, as the Catholic architect Leopold Arnaud put it in 1939, "the age of eclecticism is irrevocably past, and technological civilization has been recognized and accepted."[3] The open use of modern materials for Catholic churches was founded on the conviction, as Pietro Belluschi informed critics, that "the industrial revolution cannot be undone."[4] Because evolution moved only in one direction, wrote the Catholic architect Robert Lawton Jones in his 1960 concept statement for the parish church of SS. Peter and Paul (Tulsa), Catholics and architects alike could "no longer speak the language of Chaucer nor wear the powdered wig of Washington, for our age demands different expressions to be meaningful."[5] Jones, a student of Mies van der Rohe, claimed that "architecture should naturally evolve from certain functional requirements and also be a statement of its time. We must use the 'esthetic vernacular' of our technological age if art is to be representative of its time."[6] Architects like Belluschi and Jones, steeped in modernist design philosophy, believed the use of technology *was* natural; it was only cowardly discomfort with the perceived ugliness of the industrial revolution that led society to resist "learn[ing] with humility what nature has to teach us, namely the inherent quality of structural logic and appropriateness, never monotonous but dazzling in its variety of forms."[7]

The belief that contemporary civilization was, by its nature, "technological," put engineers and inventors at the center of modernists' evolutionary narrative. Accused by their detractors of rejecting history, they in fact had discovered an alternative origin story for themselves by reaching outside the architectural establishment. The architectural historian Walter Behrendt, whose book *Modern Building* Maurice Lavanoux often recommended to young Catholic architects, looked back in the late 1930s to the dark neohistoricist days of the nineteenth century and retrieved "a line of creative building" not among architects, who had been too concerned with the "roving fancy" of beaux arts and neo-Gothic eclecticism, but among "the new iron bridges and derricks, the furnaces and cooling towers, the silos and wide-spanned worksheds, in short, the works of the engineers which wholly changed the face of the cultivated land."[8] Heroically practical engineers had saved architecture from itself during a period of dishonest eclecticism that ignored structural function in favor of pure form. If the logic of the biological paradigm required evolutionary development from identifiable ancestors, the modernist narrative retrieved the utilitarian structures of everyday life—grain elevators, dams, and factories—as the true representatives of the nineteenth-century building arts.[9] Now that architecture as a whole was (as modernists saw it) coming to its senses, it discovered a lineage that had avoided the errors of neohistoricists' evolutionary detour and, without fuss and with admirable ingenuity, used contemporary techniques to fill contemporary needs.

Catholic modernists therefore appealed to the American industrial vernacular as they sought to reform the Church's architecture, arguing that "native art only is genuine."[10] As early as 1936 the convert artist E. Charlton Fortune was arguing that the contrast between the aesthetics of everyday life and the historicist church favored the former: "While the future priest is studying in the seminary," she wrote, "his future parishioner is busily concerned with mundane things such as ice-boxes, stream-lined cars and well made furniture, buying excellent things on the installment plan, and learning a considerable amount about beauty in the process."[11] This perceived dichotomy continued to disturb Catholics in *Liturgical Arts* circles during the following decades.[12] The midwestern industrialist Otto Spaeth, Eloise Spaeth's husband and then president of the Liturgical Arts Society, noted in the mid-1950s that while the average parishioner "drives a streamlined car to work in an office or factory where everything has been designed for maximum efficiency and comfort," nevertheless "every Sunday he is asked to hurl himself back centuries to say his prayers in the pious gloom of a Gothic or Romanesque past."[13] At Spaeth's own 1952 Meta-Mold Aluminum factory, featuring a mobile by his friend Alexander Calder, he had adhered to the highest standards of contemporary design; he did not see why he or anyone else should be asked to do otherwise in his religious life.[14] The problem, however, was not only that Catholics would (modernists believed) begin to ignore or marginalize the Church because of its backward aesthetics, but also that the "best" architecture of the day was serving secular ends.

Those undergoing clerical education sometimes agreed with modernist critiques. In 1945, seminarian John Paul Harding wrote Lavanoux to praise the spacious designs of the Museum of Modern Art and Radio City Music Hall, not to mention "the finest building in New York City," an asphalt plant on the East River. "But what of our churches[?]" he lamented, noting that these were not taking modernist lessons to heart.[15] Harding joined a group of Catholics embarrassed that, as architectural historian Nikolaus Pevsner had recently written, "no church designed anywhere after 1760 is among the leading examples of architecture."[16] He, the Spaeths, and Fortune—none of them architects—spoke for American Catholics who wanted to see church architecture make far more explicit use of the technologies of modernity, both to reclaim the Church's dominant role in contemporary life and to help Catholics reconcile their faith lives with the modern world. Some of the most striking churches of the period set out to perform one or both of these tasks.

THE CHAPEL OF THE HOLY CROSS, SEDONA, AZ

The pharmaceutical heiress Marguerite Brunswig was studying art in New York in the early 1930s when she received the vision whose realization consumed much of the rest of her life. As she wandered Midtown Manhattan, she became fascinated by the contrast between its ambitious skyscrapers and St. Patrick's Cathedral, which had "exhausted itself in copying the Gothic instead of bravely pioneering, giving an expression of the day in contemporary language as did its laity [*sic*] neighbor, the Rockefeller Center."[17] One day, either while the Empire State Building was under construction in 1931 or after its completion in 1932 (her accounts varied), she suddenly realized that its structural elements formed a cross. Deeply disturbed by "how small even the most magnificent cathedrals appear compared with the striking eminence of this gem of modern architecture," she immediately had a "vision of the church in the form of a cross, overtowering an entire city in majestic simplicity, which would express and guide the spirit of modern architecture just as the majestic cathedrals of the medieval ages dominated the architecture of their times."[18]

After returning to Los Angeles, Brunswig contacted Lloyd Wright, Frank Lloyd Wright's eldest son, who "evolved the structure" of a cruciform skyscraper (fig. 3.2).[19] Wright's towering concrete-and-steel design, at a height of roughly five hundred feet, articulated the cross form over and over, not only in the screen walls but in the plan and elevation.[20] The design, "conceived for America in American streamline language," resembled Wright's 1925 City of the Future sketches, and envisioned the church as both complementary and competitive with the powerful futurist forms of Le Corbusier's Radiant

FIGURE 3.2. Sketch for a Chapel of the Holy Cross (Frank Lloyd Wright Jr. [Lloyd Wright], ca. 1931). Photo: GLIT, 31-54-01.

City.[21] Although the Depression, and disinterest from potential diocesan patrons, prevented the realization of Wright's plan, Brunswig (now married to Tony Staude) continued to develop the idea of a church whose main symbolic form, the cross, was also its main structural form. In the early 1950s, having inherited her parents' considerable fortune, she began to plan seriously for its implementation.

By this time Staude's ambitions had shifted from the massive futuristic skyscraper of the 1930s to a more modest plan. She had now seen the small church of Notre-Dame-de-Toute-Grâce du Plateau d'Assy, built between 1937 and

1946 under the direction of Marie-Alain Couturier, OP. Couturier's journal, *L'art sacré*, offered an even more dramatic modernist aesthetic than *Liturgical Arts*, with striking images of American concrete dams alongside churches.[22] Staude still wanted to use modern construction techniques to "express the cross in . . . the elevation" of her church, but she now envisioned a church on the scale of Assy, not the Empire State Building. In 1950 she turned to another Frank Lloyd Wright disciple, Theodore van Fossen, who designed an eighty-five-seat chapel for a site near the Staudes' Sedona, Arizona, ranch.[23] But this plan, too, came to nothing. Finally, in 1953, Staude discovered *House Beautiful*'s influential article on Anshen + Allen's Herschel and Sonya Silverstone House (1949). The San Francisco firm had built a low-key house true to key tenets of the biological paradigm in architecture: "fitness to purpose and site," the "effortless combination" of "the beauty of sculpture and utility of structure," and "a theme of simplicity in design . . . in construction, in maintenance, and in decoration."[24] After an initial meeting, the Staudes and the architects surveyed territory near Sedona by airplane and Jeep. They found a dramatic double spur of red rock on Forest Service land just outside the town—use of which required approval from the secretary of the interior as well as Bishop Bernard Espelage.[25]

Bob Anshen's design, which one of his employees remembered as "a couple of lines," was magnificently simple but an extraordinary technical challenge.[26] His ninety-foot-tall Chapel of the Holy Cross both dramatically awes with its scale relative to human visitors and modestly accepts its role as a small focal point in a dramatic landscape, at the foot of a 1,500-foot cliff and built with simple planes of sandblasted concrete (fig. 3.1). A long ramp spirals up from the parking lot so that visitors approaching on foot must engage with the red rocks and open sky. The site was so isolated that when the construction supervisor arrived, he discovered there was no road, no electricity, and no water. But ground was finally broken in April 1955—more than thirty years after Staude's initial vision—and the chapel was dedicated in the spring of 1957. A thirteen-foot iron corpus by the sculptor Keith Monroe, sometimes known as the "Atomic Christ," hung directly on the structural concrete cross. As Staude pointed out, Wright's complex multilayered crosses had become a single "monolith with the Christian connotation of the one cross—organic to the structure. From without the building hangs *upon* it, and from within, the body of Christ is hanging *from* it" (fig. 3.3).[27]

Troubled by the association of the era's most spectacular and compelling buildings with commercial rather than ecclesiastical interests, Staude coopted contemporary engineering to serve God. Though scale and complexity

FIGURE 3.3. *Christus* ("Atomic Christ"), Chapel of the Holy Cross, Sedona, Arizona (Keith Monroe, ca. 1957.) Photo: GLIT, 31-56-01.

changed dramatically over her thirty-year odyssey, at any given time, Staude wanted to build a church that would, as the *New York Times* put it, "anticipate the future instead of reflecting the past."[28] In contrast to the recently opened neohistoricist National Shrine of the Immaculate Conception, she asked, "should not we in America . . . have a national shrine where God can be worshipped as a contemporary?"[29] And despite the dramatically different aesthetic impact of the design's two major iterations, both Wright and Anshen relied on the latest construction technology to serve this goal.

Both during its construction and after its 1962 dedication, another major modernist Catholic church lured engineers, contractors, architects, and TV crews to the far suburbs of St. Louis. The curvaceous building inspired rapturous comparisons to waves, wings, and flowers, and attracted admiration for its daring construction technique (fig. 3.4). Yet less than a decade earlier, the new Priory of St. Mary and St. Louis had been slated for a neohistoricist design—an artifact of its funders' attachment to old-world Catholicism. The 1954 foundation was the brainchild of a group of Catholic businessmen who wanted serious academics alongside religious formation for their sons.[30] Formally organizing themselves as "Catholic Preparatory School for Boys, Incorporated," they quickly came to be known as simply "Inc," and sought out the Benedictines at Ampleforth Abbey in Yorkshire to begin a school and monastery.

By the time Columba Cary-Elwes, OSB, and two other English monks arrived in St. Louis in October 1955, some architectural intrigue had already taken place. Knowing that an entire monastery would involve a substantial commission, Patrick Holloran, SJ, of St. Louis University tried to get Leo A. Daly's firm hired on the grounds that it was "a good Catholic company."[31] Inc, meanwhile, was eager to employ a local architect, Ray Maritz, who had built the colonial-style house already on the property.[32] Their 1955 fundraising brochure featured sketches of a vaguely Gothic cloister, low buildings with steeply pitched roofs, and a church with a longitudinal plan and a heavy square crossing tower. Shortly after the monks arrived, Maritz produced a more formal proposal to join all the preexisting buildings—house, barn (to become the chapel), and sheds—into one continuous plan.[33] The monks and Inc discussed a temporary monastery in "the Georgian style," to be eventually replaced by permanent buildings that would "use contemporary methods and style, and yet keep in mind the traditional character of a monastic foundation"—revealing the ambivalence that the monks were already feeling about the aesthetics of their enterprise.[34] But the idea of temporary building was quickly discarded as prohibitively expensive.[35] Despite serious doubts that the monks were now raising about building in "the Georgian style" at all, Maritz's more permanent plan was put out for bids in January 1956.[36] When the lowest estimate came in at nearly three times Maritz's guess, the monks seized the opportunity to rethink their entire approach. They would live and open the school in the preexisting house and barn, and take more time to investigate architectural options.[37]

None of the founding monks had architectural training, and their English motherhouse was an imposing neo-Gothic pile. However, as they journeyed

FIGURE 3.4. Church of St. Mary and St. Louis, St. Louis Priory, Creve Coeur, Missouri (Hellmuth, Obata, & Kassabaum, 1962). Photo: Author.

around the United States researching American school standards, they also took in the latest American architecture. They found that their fellow Benedictines were on the cutting edge of both the liturgical movement and modernist church architecture.[38] At St. John's Abbey in Collegeville, Minnesota, the monks were collaborating with Marcel Breuer on a hundred-year building plan.[39] They regarded themselves as a "forward-looking order," and were committed to the idea that their new church "should be of a form valid for the future, and expressive of contemporary technology."[40] During 1955, the St. Louis group also saw Barry Byrne's St. Benedict's Abbey Church in Atchison, Kansas, and made an extended visit to Portsmouth Priory, in the midst of developing a long-range plan with Pietro Belluschi. Timothy Horner, OSB, made a solo visit to MIT, where he admired Eero Saarinen's new thin-shell concrete Kresge Auditorium (1955).[41] Even before the failure of the Maritz plan, these experiences had led the immigrant monks to feel that they needed buildings that would "project the image of the monastery and school that we wanted"—and this meant building not in a style that was "English" but rather "American" and contemporary.[42] In early 1956, the monks reopened their search for an architect, this time focusing on modernists. Saarinen's work at MIT dominated their thought, and locally, they particularly admired the new airport terminal designed by Minoru Yamasaki of Hellmuth, Yamasaki, & Leinweber. On March 22, 1956, George Hellmuth agreed that his new firm, Hellmuth, Obata, & Kassabaum (HOK), would prepare a proposal for the school and monastery and would consult with Pietro Belluschi.[43] Thirty-nine-year-old Buddhist Gyo Obata, a student of Eliel Saarinen's at Cranbrook, would be the primary designer.[44]

HOK's collaboration with the monks was an exemplary modernist process.[45] The first meetings saw no discussion of design or style at all; HOK told the monks that they would first make a complete program, then study individual buildings. Obata saw the entire site as a work of architecture, sensitive to "the existing natural land contours" and a "whole complex of relationships between groups of building as well as between one building and another"—a complex in which the negative spaces between buildings, "increasing in carefully planned steps from intimate courtyard to great plaza," would serve to integrate the entire suite into one great flowing environment.[46] The first master plan, dated October 22, 1956, showed simple rectangular placeholders for both church and monastery. As at contemporary complexes like Portsmouth and St. John's, the monks wanted both a flexible plan leaving room for expansion, and buildings that, as Horner wrote, would not be "discard[ed] . . . after a mere 100 years."[47] Working with an architect who not only had never designed a monastery but was not himself a Catholic proved determinative; the monks recalled for decades how, in articulating the purpose of each space for their architect, they also clarified it for themselves.

By the summer of 1957, ongoing discussions had developed the rectangular cipher of October 1956. It first transitioned, at HOK's suggestion, to a Greek cross; a monk raised the possibility of an octagon; initial thoughts of stone moved toward cheaper and more elastic concrete.[48] In January 1957, HOK brought two models to the monks; a pyramid, with a series of triangular arches ringing the bottom layer, served as the basis for the final design.[49] At this stage Hellmuth and Horner teamed up to "sell" their funders on the "uncompromisingly modern" design.[50] Yet both Inc—which deferred to the monks but remained uneasy—and the abbot of Ampleforth, whose approval was required, were profoundly unconvinced that this was appropriate monastic architecture. Finally, a meeting between Obata and the Italian engineer Pier Luigi Nervi softened triangles and straight lines into parabolas and curves, a design paradoxically not only more appealing to the conservative eye, but also more technologically radical.[51]

What HOK ultimately built was consistent, Obata felt, with the "the spiritual program from the Monks," which "was to design a Chapel in a strong and living architecture using structure and materiel of today."[52] Obata and the monks had studied, together and separately, "a variety of plan shapes," but "as the plan evolved," Obata settled on a circle, bringing both a monastic choir and a large lay assembly near a central altar, along with a graceful periphery of daily Mass chapels.[53] The church's most distinctive forms—parabolic arches of varying sizes in three layers—"reflect[ed] on the exterior what was happening inside": the first layer of arches held the chapels and four entranceways, the second defined the circular nave and choir, and the third "reflect[ed] the central altar and also [became] the bell tower."[54] If this was a fairly straightforward statement of form following function, its realization required cutting-edge technique and materials.

Between August 1960 and the dedication in September 1962, the contractors, McCarthy Brothers, used a then-experimental technique, spraying concrete on a single wooden form rather than poured into a double form—very similar to Frank Lloyd Wright's recent landmark Solomon R. Guggenheim Museum (1959) (see fig. 3.5).[55] The flowing concrete shell "creat[ed] various volumes of spaces," articulating different segments of the building while also keeping them united into "one total continuous space"; with few internal walls, Obata employed "light to give form to a space."[56] He commissioned the Kal-Wall company to develop a new color of their experimental fiberglass compound: a dark smoky gray that allowed the whitewashed concrete to read in sharp contrast to the fenestration.[57] On the inside, however, a layer of white Kal-Wall diffused a soft glow into the building, continuously forming and re-forming the sense of interior space as the quality of light changed through the day and the seasons.[58] Through these and other new techniques and materials, the whole project acquired an aura of experimental flair. Along with the Chapel of the Holy Cross, it was routinely featured in the secular architectural press as an example of thrilling new technology.[59]

FIGURE 3.5. Church of St. Mary and St. Louis under construction, 1961. Wooden forms support the arches under construction, as well as five workers; steel reinforcing bars are stacked in the foreground. Photo: ASLA.

BRINGING THE ASSEMBLY CLOSER TO GOD: NEW CONSTRUCTION TECHNIQUES AND THE LITURGY

By the time the Second Vatican Council opened, American liturgists had largely acceded to modernist architects' proposed relationship between modern materials, modern engineering techniques, and contemporary America. "We shall have liturgical churches," H. A. Reinhold exclaimed in 1961, "not so much by improvement of taste alone, but by functional construction and trueness to new materials!"[60] But what constituted a "good" liturgical space, and how did new building technologies help produce common answers to this question? The American liturgical movement argued that building technology could facilitate the uniting of priest and people in common worship of the divine at Mass. Practical liturgists had long employed technology to bring Eucharistic assemblies together; during the interwar years, rural missionaries used specially fitted trailers and train cars as chapels (see fig. 3.6), Alaskan Jesuits traveled to far-flung villages by bush plane, and the Catholic press kept a close eye on the use of airplanes, submarines, and zeppelins as temporary chapels.[61] For more conventional worship spaces—churches—however, the core question for liturgically minded modernist architects was how best to "gather" the congregation around the altar. The creation of visible unity between priest and people focused on the incarnation of Christ in the Eucharist was meant to simultaneously reflect the liturgical movement's claim that the congregation had an active role in the Mass, and to produce a better understanding and performance of that role in both clergy and laity alike. It brought liturgists into further alliance with secular modernist architects interested in buildings' social function and led both groups to closely examine the new possibilities offered by, among other materials, reinforced concrete.[62]

TRUENESS TO NEW MATERIALS: THE PROPERTIES OF REINFORCED CONCRETE

As a young man, Maurice Lavanoux had worked for several years in the offices of the neohistoricist architects Maginnis & Walsh, where he became increasingly disturbed by his growing realization that his employers were not, in the moralistic terminology derived from the Arts and Crafts movement and universally employed by modernists, "honest" in their use of construction technology. "I found the system one of steel beam and trusses where the thrust was not outward but downward," he wrote years later, comparing neohistoricist practices to the genuine Gothic engineering he had seen at Reims; after a church's modern skeletal structure was erected, "fake buttresses and plaster vaults would make the whole building a bastard of architecture."[63] Lavanoux's concern was not with the formal elements of buttress and vault themselves, but with their lack of structural significance. They were only what the critics Albert Christ-Janer and Mary Mix Foley later called "a frosting of past styles."[64] If Catholic architects were to be "honest," they would have to choose: either

FIGURE 3.6. *Liturgical Arts* layout with three views of the Paulists' Saint Lucy Catholic Motor Chapel. The bottom two pictures show the back of the trailer opened for mass, with loudspeakers mounted to the roof, as well as a view through to the living space and circulating library in the body of the trailer. Photo: *Liturgical Arts* 6, no. 2 (1937).

build neomedievalist churches using medieval materials (stone) and techniques (flying buttress and groin vault), or not only exploit but simultaneously reveal recent developments in construction methods.

During the 1930s, the Liturgical Arts Society was still divided between an Arts and Crafts contingent who felt that "honest" church-building required the sole use of natural materials like stone and wood, and an emerging group who argued that man-made materials, used appropriately, could be ecclesiastically acceptable: "Stone," Frank Brannach noted exasperatedly in 1932, "is not more religious . . . than brick, concrete, steel, or glass."[65] By the 1950s, this debate had been settled almost entirely in favor of the modernists, the holdouts having either retired or left the society in favor of the Catholic Art Association, which, inspired by William Morris's disciple Eric Gill, continued to advocate for a purist interpretation of medieval craft practices. But during the society's formative years, as *Liturgical Arts* noted in its sixth issue—devoted entirely to concrete—"there [was] perhaps no building material concerning which there has been greater controversy."[66] The loudest arguments swirled largely around whether concrete's aesthetic properties were acceptable. Everyone knew that this material was "economical," but many could "see no beauty in what they call[ed] the 'lifelessness' of concrete surfaces" and believed, therefore, that its use was ecclesiastically inappropriate. Catholic architects like Jack Wood, Barry Byrne, and Leopold Arnaud, however, argued passionately that "properly handled," the material could indeed be beautiful.[67]

Whether or not concrete was intrinsically beautiful, the idea of "honest" building appealed to a wide variety of Catholic patrons. The Benedictines of St. John's Abbey, Collegeville, wrote in their famous 1953 letter to prospective architects that "the Benedictine tradition at its best challenges us to think boldly and to cast our ideals in forms which will be valid for centuries to come, shaping them with all the genius of present-day materials and techniques. We feel that the modern architect with his orientation towards functionalism and honest use of materials is uniquely qualified to produce a Catholic work."[68] But these views had first been advanced by architects, not priests; and it was largely architects who drove the conversation about the liturgical possibilities of building technologies.[69] Their sophisticated professional interpretation of "trueness to new materials" led them to consider not just the aesthetics and economics of concrete surfaces, but the "honest" use of its specific properties. For modernist architects, the excitement of reinforced concrete (and, eventually, new types of glass, steel, plywood, plastic, and other materials) was embedded in the promise of entirely new methods of solving, with ever greater "efficiency, economy, and elegance," the fundamental problem of architectural engineering: counteracting the downward and outward forces exerted by the weight of a building's roof and therefore enabling a structure to withstand both the ordinary pressures of gravity over time and the extraordinary pressures of rare events such as earthquakes.[70]

Modernist theory understood changes in architectural aesthetics as responses to the evolutionary development of new engineering systems, and the *Liturgical Arts* circle increasingly shared this analysis, expressed in secular work ranging from Walter Behrendt's 1937 *Modern Building* to James Marston Fitch's 1966 edition of *American Building*.[71] Lavanoux and Binsse informed readers in 1933 that historical forms of architecture had not been invented at random but instead had "grown": "The traditional styles of church building," they claimed, "all grew out of systems of engineering imposed by the older masonry of stone-upon-stone or brick-upon-brick."[72] In December 1949 the editors of *Architectural Record* updated this narrative, claiming that "primarily, historic religious architecture has always been a series of wholly rational solutions of very real problems, paramount being the necessity of sheltering a large number of people, the congregation."[73] Romanesque builders had relied on thick lower walls and attached buttresses to support the roof and upper walls, leading to a massive effect and dim interiors. The classic Gothic aesthetic was the natural evolutionary result of thirteenth-century masons' discovery that the stresses exerted by the roof could be channeled away from the wall structure via "flying" buttresses. The walls themselves, no longer needing to carry the burden of the roof, could be light, thin, and pierced with massive expanses of glass.

For modernists, the necessary corollary was that the use of new techniques and materials would always require, as *Liturgical Arts* put it, "novelties of design."[74] Christ-Janer and Foley, presenting Catholic and Protestant designs in their 1962 *Modern Church Architecture*, organized the book in part as an explanation of the "nature" of reinforced concrete, structural steel, plate glass, stone, and wood. Using the now-familiar argument that the flow of evolution had been interrupted by an abortive attempt to use new materials in the recreation of historic "styles," Christ-Janer and Foley focused on new designs that had "evolved" directly from the properties native to these materials.[75] The languages of nature and technology relied on each other. Paul Thiry, for example, borrowed Frank Lloyd Wright's concept of "organic" building, commenting that just as the Romanesque had given way to the Gothic through successive advances in engineering, so in the twentieth century "new materials . . . made new structural concepts possible and through their structural influence alone" would change "the direction of an architecture."[76] That these architects' buildings sometimes had serious structural or materials problems (leaking roofs,

FIGURE 3.7. Concrete folds in a longitudinal section of St. John's Abbey Church, Collegeville, Minnesota (Marcel Breuer & Associates, 1953–61). The "bell-banner" stands at left; at center right, the baldachino hangs above the altar. Photo: GLIT, 25-56-01.

disintegrating plexiglass or plywood, cracked concrete) lends credence to the notion that modernist church builders, like their Gothic forebears whose towers occasionally collapsed, were working on the cutting edge of these new technologies, developing new practices through trial and error.[77]

Reinforced concrete—for Catholics the most controversial of modernist materials—had become the preferred building material of the twentieth century after a series of revolutionary advances in engineering.[78] Beginning in the 1860s, builders discovered that they could encase cast iron and, later, steel rods, in concrete to provide a skeletal structure that combined the advantages of the two materials, enabling their handiwork to effectively resist both compressive and tensile forces simultaneously. Because its strength came from form rather than mass, reinforced concrete made possible structures that combined the virtues of wood, such as a feeling of lightness and openness, with those of heavy masonry, such as size and durability.[79] Buttresses, thick lower walls, and interior columns became unnecessary even for very large buildings. Load-bearing walls became curtain walls, which, since they were no longer required to support the roof, could now be constructed primarily of glass or any other weatherproof material.

Alternatively, engineers could produce strong walls from folded concrete slabs, avoiding post-and-lintel construction or interior columns. Antonin Raymond and L. L. Rado designed several folded-concrete churches during the 1930s and 1940s, taking decorative inspiration from Auguste Perret's pioneering Église Notre-Dame du Raincy (1922–23); more famously, concrete folds played the key structural and aesthetic role in Marcel Breuer's St. John's Abbey Church (see fig. 3.7).[80] Concrete had a special place for biologically inclined modernists because, in Jack Wood's words, it could "truly be said to form the basic anatomy of an architecture, for it not only can form the bones and muscles of a structure, but also its enveloping surfaces."[81] But even when Catholic modernists employed supposedly "natural" brick, wood, and stone, the technical contributions of "industrialized materials of the machine age: steel, reinforced concrete, plate glass, and glass brick" still encouraged a new aesthetic.[82] Thiry's 1941 design for Our Lady of the Lake, Seattle, for example, was in brick, but a concrete structural frame (dutifully exposed in the nave) made it possible for the walls to be far thinner and visually light than if they had been the primary roof support.

The American pioneers of concrete Catholic churches, including Byrne, Raymond and Rado, and Thiry, were succeeded in the 1950s by a group of young architects who, steeped in the modernist theory developed by the previous generation, took advantage of another series of technological advances. Increasingly finely ground cement greatly increased compressive strength, while improvements in the design of steel reinforcing bars also reduced the weight necessary to achieve the same amount of strength.[83] However, postwar designers did not only rely on better versions of old materials; they also grew to understand the possibilities inherent in reinforced concrete as a medium that was not simply a stronger, lighter, cheaper substitute for wood or stone, but had its own distinctive fundamental quality: plasticity.

Concrete is produced by pouring wet cement, sand, and gravel between prebuilt wooden forms, which are removed when the mixture is hardened, revealing concrete imprinted with their shape. This can then be covered with another material like brick or stone; surfaced with some kind of tool and perhaps painted; or left in its unvarnished state for an effect known as *brutalism*, after the French *béton brut*, "raw concrete." Plasticity—the ability of concrete to take on the shape of its forms—enabled twentieth-century engineers to generate the nonrectilinear shapes that give the swooping designs of the 1950s and 1960s their distinctive character. It was plasticity, according to Wright, that gave this industrial material "organic" capacity.[84] German and French engineers began experimenting with very thin concrete poured between curved forms in the 1920s, but these techniques were first popularized by a pair of European engineers: the Spanish Félix Candela and the Italian Pier Luigi Nervi, both Catholics by birth who made their careers building commercial and public structures but maintained strong interests in church design.[85] Exiled in the aftermath of the Spanish Civil War, Candela convinced the architect of Mexico City's planned Cosmic Rays Laboratory (1951) to change his design from a barrel shell to a pair of hyperbolic paraboloids. Because it can be developed entirely out of straight lines, this shape, with the double curves of a saddle, was both inexpensive and relatively easy to plan mathematically.[86]

FIGURE 3.8. Main chapel, Annunciation Monastery, Bismarck, North Dakota (Marcel Breuer & Associates, 1954–63). The concrete roof's hyperbolic paraboloids are echoed in the baldachino above the main altar. Photo: Author.

Candela's career was made when, after the success of his first paraboloids, he developed an "umbrella," a hypar form with straight edges combining the strength and thinness of the hyperbolic paraboloid with rectilinear formal characteristics.[87]

Curved thin-shell concrete was the apotheosis of developments structural engineers had worked toward for a century; lightweight and chary of materials, it could simultaneously provide structural support and enclosure while distributing stress with tremendous efficiency (figs. 3.8, 3.9).[88] It also elegantly represented how technology both drew upon and supplanted forms evolved in nature. In using the term *shell* to describe thin, curved concrete walls, architects reinforced the intimate connection they saw between biological and technological development. Frank Lloyd Wright often spoke about seashells as "housing produced by God," and in this vein Candela and Nervi suggested yet another new direction for technologically driven architecture: instead of decoupling "support and enclosure" as earlier concrete wizards had done, they conceived of the shell wall as both at once.[89] Candela in particular was intrigued by nature's building lessons:

> It has always been desirable to observe natural examples in search for inspiration to solve a vaulting problem. . . . Reinforced concrete is not only very akin to the stuff of natural shells, but it can also withstand considerable tensile stress. The properties of continuity and tensile strength of reinforced concrete offer us a unique opportunity to emulate the economy of material in natural methods of enclosing space.[90]

In Candela's Mexican church La Virgen Milagrosa (1953–55), as Albert Christ-Janer and Mary Mix Foley wrote, the walls, roof, and structural supports are "amalgamated . . . into a multiwarped slab, having a thickness of only 1½ inches or less. No rivets, welds, bolts, or nails are used in the entire construction, since it is in truth a continuous shell."[91]

Thin-shell concrete dominated the unbuilt "churches for tomorrow" of young Catholic architects in the 1950s and early 1960s.[92] It also characterized a number of built American Catholic churches from that period, as congregations sought to demonstrate that a church as "modern as a Cosmic Capsule, spiraling towards the stars" might nevertheless "carry genetic seeds born from

FIGURE 3.9. St. Rita's, West Allis, Wisconsin (Mark F. Pflaller Associates, 1963). The roof consists of four hyperbolic paraboloids, three inches thick, weighing in total six hundred tons and entirely supported by the corner buttresses. Photo: Author.

the primeval seas . . . the aura of tradition"—that is, how a futuristic church might nevertheless be understood within the legitimate evolutionary development of the Christian tradition.[93] Gyo Obata's St. Louis Priory Church, the liturgical consultant William Schickel noted, was also a "shell concrete building" that had "in the traditional sense, no walls"; the very quality that made it difficult to design, requiring an "entirely new approach" to elements like candle brackets, also placed it in the stream of time in which "the norms for church building must be constantly revised."[94] The drama of the hyperbolic paraboloid and other new concrete techniques shored up modernists' claims that their churches developed recognizably out of the Gothic tradition of technological daring.

TECHNOLOGY AND THE "LITURGICAL" CHURCH

Whether folded or thin-shell, reinforced concrete liberated architects from the visual obstructions inherent in earlier building techniques. Concrete's ability to span large interiors made it possible for architects to conceive visually unified spaces for the participatory Mass.[95] Barry Byrne's *Commonweal* argument against interior columns was tied to his contention that "vital" church architecture brought the assembly and celebrant into close contact and focused attention on the altar; a good modern church, therefore, would use "the constructions of steel and concrete which have had development in our time, and which enable us to build churches free of pillars, in a structural way that is natural and, in our time, unaffected."[96] He argued that "vital historic architecture" had always responded to currents in technological development, particularly with regards to spanning roofs.[97] Since modern construction could easily span the "broad shallow church" that gathered the congregation close to the altar, "to then fill this space with columns that are of no use" in an attempt to be "artistic and churchly" would not be "honest."[98] Byrne's preferred "broad shallow" columnless floor plan, made possible by contemporary engineering, quickly became standard in American modernist church design. Whether rectangular or semicircular, naves stretched short and wide; article after article applauded a design's ability to bring the entire congregation within a few rows of the altar. The unity of walls and roof eventually made possible by thin-shell concrete promised to further accentuate the unifying action of the Mass.

New technical abilities could support the liturgical movement's preferred ends in other ways, as well. The theologian Harvey Cox invoked a frequent 1960s theme when he lectured on "The Church's Mission to Technopolis" at

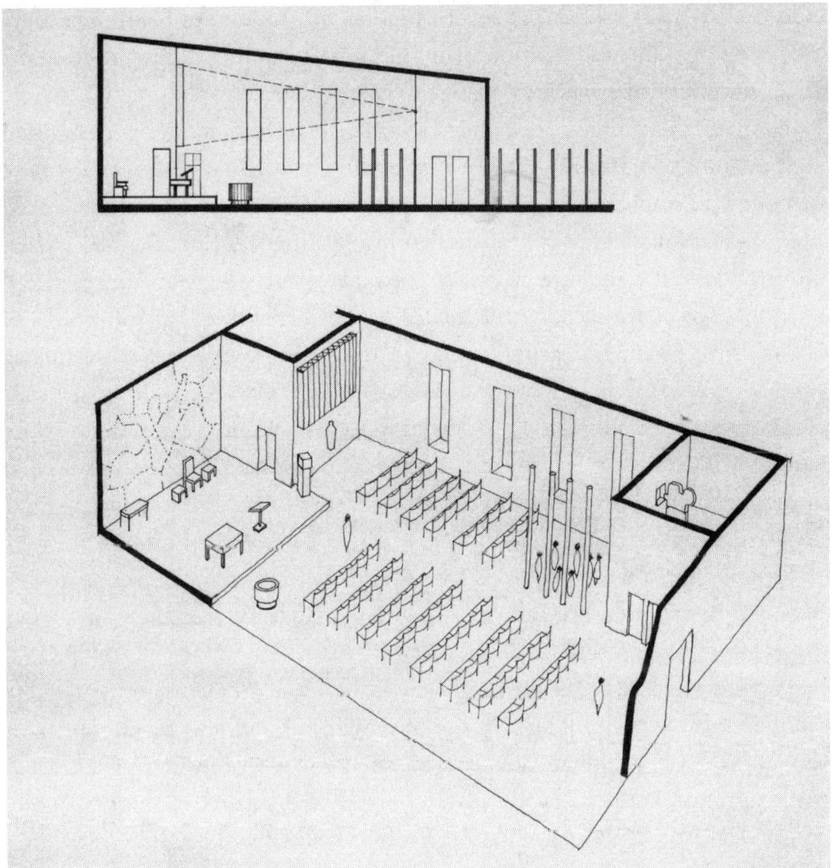

FIGURE 3.10. Prototype church with video projection capabilities (drawings by Viggo Mathieson from a concept by Patrick J. Quinn and Maurice Lavanoux, 1970). Photo: *Liturgical Arts* 38, no. 2 (1970).

Oakland's Holy Names College in 1967, describing the "forming [of] a world civilization through technology."[99] Churches could participate in this eschatological development through their use of the latest audiovisual techniques. Collaborating with the architect Patrick Quinn, Maurice Lavanoux suggested a small church, seating no more than about 350, that would make it easier to include elements that would not be possible in "the old, static interiors," such as a small projection room and screen for "visual explanation of the Word" as well as "vital events of the day which bear increasingly on our lives as Christians" (fig. 3.10).[100] Through both the 1950s and 1960s even small parish churches routinely bragged about their use of technology to support liturgical unity: St. Mary's in Storm Lake, Iowa (1954), for example, announced in its dedication program that it had Waylite cement block, plastic floor covering, and loudspeakers with a system of special support for the hard of hearing in fourteen pews, for "the elimination of undue and distracting noises" that might draw attention from the Mass.[101]

Architects, meanwhile, responded to criticisms that they were too obsessed with their own engineering prowess by arguing that they were leveraging new structural possibilities to draw attention toward the altar. The asymmetries of Thomas McNulty and Mary Fawcett's prototype (fig. 2.8) disturbed critics like the priest John Reinhold, who complained that it might be "more 'interesting' aesthetically to have the altar off the main axis . . . but does this solution bear in mind that the altar has a dignity and a purpose that takes it out of the line of charming new angles?" The architects responded, "The altar is the generating point of the roof shells which further stress its focal point in the church." Further, they insisted that "liturgical and aesthetic purposes cannot be separated in the design," and claimed that the off-center altar allowed them to avoid "rigid seating patterns," which they thought made "many people cluster in the rear of the church."[102] They intended the swirl of both roof and seating patterns to be not merely odd but functional, with "circular movement" converging toward the altar.[103]

McNulty and Fawcett's defense rested, therefore, not on their plan's aesthetic interest as such, but on its use of new forms and new technologies to solve a liturgical problem: how to generate a focus on the altar. Traditional basilican church plans, modernists contended, habitually muddied congregational focus. While the altar was usually raised and brightly lit in such churches, it was also distant from the vast majority of massgoers, who were therefore practically compelled to direct their attention to side altars, statues, and paintings. In contrast, designs like Joseph Salerno's proposed St. Francis of Assisi supported the roof on a small number of columns, causing it to visually "float" and directing attention away from the walls (fig. 3.11). A glass-and-steel enclosure directly over the crossing focused light more intensely in the altar area.[104] Pietro Belluschi was called in to rework the new San Francisco cathedral after an architectural outcry over a "safe" local church architect's neohistoricist basilican design; he collaborated with Nervi on a hyperboloid structure funneling light toward the altar. At St. Procopius Abbey in Lisle, Illinois, not just the church but the entire monastic complex spiraled toward the altar (fig. 3.12). In his dedication sermon, Abbot Daniel W. Kucera, OSB, defended the monks' decision to build as "a pledge for the future," and described architect Ed Dart's concept of a "volute, meaning that the building spins out like a spring, unwinding, from the church . . . to the various common and public rooms and finally to the monastic cells winding back to the starting point, to this House

FIGURE 3.11. Model for St. Francis of Assisi, Weston, Connecticut (Joseph Salerno, ca. 1955). Photo: Copyright 2017 Pedro E. Guerrero Archives.

FIGURE 3.12. Architectural model of St. Procopius Abbey, Lisle, Illinois (Edward Dart for Loebl Schlossman Bennett and Dart, ca. 1965–67). Photo: GLIT, 30-21-01.

of God . . . to this table from which Our Lord's Body and Blood will animate, sustain, and unify the brethren."[105]

Particularly during the 1960s, when theologians, laypeople, and architects alike spoke more often about modesty than grandeur, disputes among Catholic modernists over thin-shell concrete often turned on concrete's contested liturgical functionality. Competition judges and critics looking at student work sometimes charged young architects with merely expressing technical skill. Yet even on projects involving experienced practitioners, fault lines could emerge between the use of advanced building technology as an end in itself, and as an aid to liturgical goals. The difficult design process for the parish church of St. Patrick's, Oklahoma City (1959–62), pitting the architect Robert Lawton Jones against the engineer Félix Candela, reveals the stakes modernists saw in these disputes. How, Jones wanted to know, could the engineer's vision of the secular, technological future be used to enhance the liturgical movement's vision of the sacred, eschatological future—or, in his own words, how was the design to "express both [the church's] supernatural purpose and nature of construction"?[106]

Jones (1925–) was born in Oklahoma, to a Catholic mother and a Presbyterian father. Like Barry Byrne before him, Jones first thought seriously about architecture as a career when reading about Frank Lloyd Wright.[107] Following a wartime stint in the navy, Jones enrolled at the University of Notre Dame in 1946, where he studied with Victor and Aladar Olgyay, the Hungarian refugee brothers, alumni of Le Corbusier's office, and ecological design pioneers. For his graduate work in city planning, he enrolled (at the Olgyays' suggestion) at Mies van der Rohe's Illinois Institute of Technology. Jones's last stop as a student was the technical university in Karlsruhe, Germany, where he held a Fulbright in 1953/54; there, he worked in the office of Egon Eiermann, one of the best-known architects in postwar Germany and a sometime friend and associate of Mies. Now fully inducted into the transatlantic community of modernist architecture, Jones moved back to Oklahoma in 1954 and formed an architectural practice with the brothers David and Lee Murray; Murray Jones Murray, with Jones as lead designer, built a diverse collection of Oklahoma modernist landmarks, including the Tulsa International Airport.

Jones had learned from Mies that "express[ing] the spirit of our period in history" meant paying the most attention to "technology as a seminal force." Yet his interest in technology was not distinct from an acceptance of the biological paradigm; modernist architects saw technological developments as part of the specific "environment" in which they worked. Form was not "an end in itself," because "an organic concept of order provide[d] the means of achieving the proper relationship of parts to each other and the whole. The built environment and the natural one should respond to, and interact with, each other." Therefore, "the tradition of architecture" had been "one of change," as "each civilization has decided for itself what best provides for its needs," and a good church, therefore, like any other building, was a "living thing," responsive to the demands of its inhabitants.[108]

An active Catholic, a member of the Christian Family Movement, and a veteran of one of Michael Mathis's liturgical design workshops at Notre Dame, Jones received commissions for two parish churches in Oklahoma in the late 1950s: SS. Peter and Paul (1957–61) in Tulsa and, shortly thereafter, St. Patrick's. The latter's energetic pastor, Fr. Donald Kanaly, also enlisted as consultants both Frank Kacmarcik of St. John's–Collegeville, and Felix Candela, whose work he had seen while on vacation in Mexico. He was unaware, however, that Jones despised Candela's signature religious design, La Virgen Milagrosa, for its application of a twentieth-century technology (thin-shell concrete) to a long, narrow thirteenth-century plan. Candela—fundamentally an engineer—was primarily concerned with structural daring, while Jones contended that daring alone did not serve the liturgy; the ensuing polite battle illustrated the distinction between sculptural and functionalist design technique and nearly foundered the project. The first design period began with a disastrous meeting during which Jones sketched a foot, telling Candela that they needed to understand the foot before they put a shoe around it. Candela disagreed, preferring to start with the "shoe." He floated a shamrock-shaped plan, a symbolic move anathema to Jones because it expressed a designer's "idea" instead of attending to the needs of the congregation.[109]

An overly rigid separation of priest and congregation, undercutting the ideal of unity around the altar, caused the quartet of Jones, Candela, Kacmarcik, and Kanaly to scrap their initial site plan. The four, who had been communicating largely by letter, decided to meet in Oklahoma City to start from scratch. While there, Jones spoke to parishioners, one of whom praised the special occasions when the whole parish met for Mass in a nearby field. This chance encounter spurred consideration of methods to facilitate unity not just among the roughly five hundred people at a typical Sunday Mass, but also the entire 1,700-person parish. Jones's final design nested two spaces: a fully weatherproofed and heated inner church enclosed in plate glass, and a roofed and semienclosed ambulatory. For larger crowds, the glass doors slide open to allow direct visual and aural access to the inner church. Inner church and ambulatory are united within a thick concrete exterior wall. The ceiling design melds the two spaces further with ten 4-inch-thick concrete "umbrellas," each using four of Candela's famous thin-shell hyperbolic paraboloids.[110] A single umbrella covers half of the inner nave and an entire ambulatory aisle, ensuring visual unity across the glass walls (figs. 3.13, 3.14).[111]

Jones's and Kacmarcik's decorative scheme played subtly on the bipartite design's suggestion that congregational unity in Christ was not yet accomplished, but was in process toward a fulfilled eschatological harmony. For their theme, they borrowed a phrase from the preconciliar church dedication ceremony: "This is a fearsome place; it is the house of God, the gate of heaven." St. Patrick's aggressively plain exterior and its low-ceilinged, dark narthex/baptistery gave way to a dramatically lit and decoratively rich, if simple, Eucharistic space representing the heavenly Jerusalem. Kacmarcik enlisted Josef Albers to design a subtle apse screen in concrete block with gold leaf. He also directed the parish in fabricating the procession of angels that forms an integral part of the cast-concrete panels of the exterior wall. The church thus obtained a sense of "early Christian simplicity . . . consistent with a truly Christian spirit of poverty" while avoiding a "slipcover approach to houses for worship" that

FIGURE 3.13. St. Patrick's, Oklahoma City, Oklahoma (Robert Lawton Jones for Murray Jones Murray, 1962). Angels and sanctuary furniture by Frank Kacmarcik. Photo: GLIT, 22-65-03.

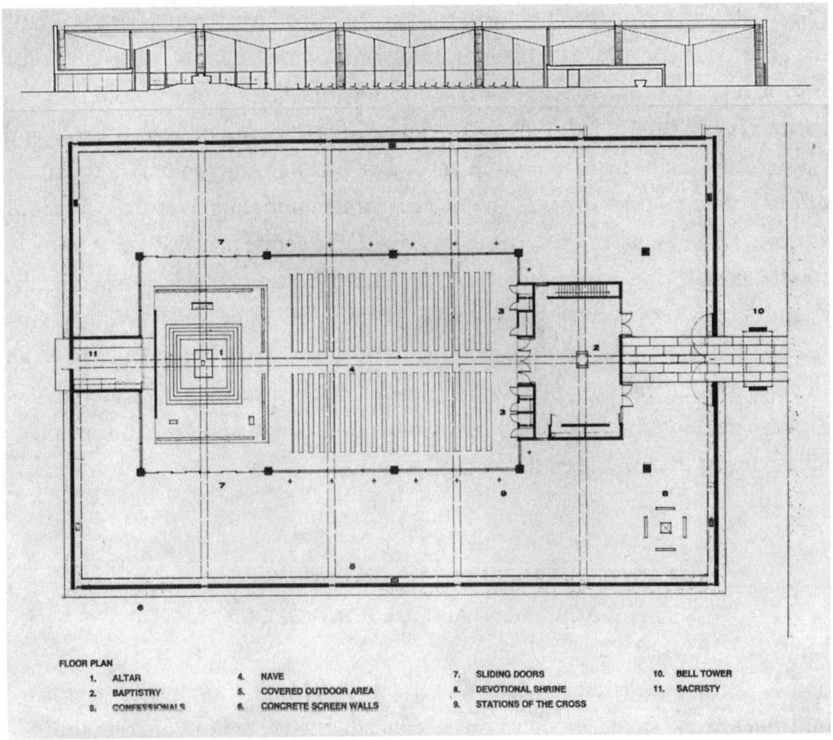

FIGURE 3.14. Plan and longitudinal section of St. Patrick's, Oklahoma City, Oklahoma (Robert Lawton Jones for Murray Jones Murray, 1962). The plan shows an exterior wall (*the thick black line*) and an interior glass enclosure (*the thinner black line*) united by a wide ambulatory and roofed by ten concrete "umbrellas." The black squares indicate the centers of the umbrellas. Photo: Courtesy of Robert Lawton Jones.

"simply [applied] modern clichés to the floor plans or building arrangements of the past."[112]

The contrast between "early Christian simplicity" and the refusal to remake "building arrangements of the past" is telling. For Jones, it was one thing to reference and evoke traditional sensibilities or theological and liturgical emphases, and quite another to do so through historicist architecture; further, it was essential not to build in concrete, steel, and glass while ignoring the necessity of a new plan that would encourage the congregation to develop properly in the future. He deployed Candela's concrete umbrellas, along with plate glass, to encourage the congregation to work toward unity; but he also assiduously organized interior space so that "the facilities for private devotion" were not "scrambled with those of public worship." In other words, while "every part of the church should be related to the whole"—a maxim that inevitably (for Jones) followed from "the organic principle upon which beauty depends"—the whole should still be composed of separate units for separate functions, a principle for organizing space (drawn from ideas about the organization of the body) dear to modernists of this period.[113] At St. Patrick's, this meant moving the Stations and a devotional shrine into the ambulatory aisles, highlighting the symmetrical axis of the baptismal font and Eucharistic altar, and eliminating a separate space for a choir.[114] The use of transparent sliders and the concrete umbrellas that visually and structurally joined the ambulatory and the nave/sanctuary unit suggested the distinct characters of earth (the congregation inside) and heaven (the angels outside), while simultaneously proclaiming their essential unity, particularly when the sliders were thrown open. At St. Patrick's, Jones used modern materials in a modern plan that evoked the Christian journey through history but fundamentally pointed toward the eschatological future.

A WORLD DEDICATED TO GOD: TECHNOLOGY, SACRAMENTALITY, ESCHATOLOGY

Shortly before the end of World War II, Charles Maginnis complained to *Architectural Record* that, while he could "concede the value" of concrete for "realistic building," he was "still puzzled why it should be thought capable of the dignity of a cosmic revolution"—fearing, correctly, that it was "certain to intrude presently in ecclesiastical design."[115] The spate of new materials (plywood, plexiglass, and plastics along with concrete) were certainly modern; did they have the capacity for sanctity? A succession of skeptical bishops, pastors, architects, and laypeople argued the contrary through the mid-twentieth century, preferring stone to concrete and seeing interest in the "ecclesiastical" possibilities of engineering developments as a betrayal of the Church's heritage. Yet Catholic modernists' interests in the interplay of technology and liturgy went beyond sheer practicality or the thirst for novelty sometimes attributed to them. They saw the question not as one of Church discipline, but of ecclesiological mission and identity.

Catholic modernists argued that the Church had a responsibility to embrace new technology. They often acknowledged the new order as strange, unsettling, and potentially destructive, but claimed that it was nevertheless capable of sacramental salvation; just as human beings existed outside of God's grace until formally enfolded into the Church, so too did new technologies. In Sedona, builders scattered a sack of holy medals into the foundations of the Chapel of the Holy Cross, seeding the concrete with sanctity. Twenty years

FIGURE 3.15. Sanctuary renovation of St. Francis de Sales, Philadelphia, Pennsylvania (Venturi and Rauch, 1970). Photo: Architectural Archives, University of Pennsylvania, by the gift of Robert Venturi and Denise Scott Brown.

later, when the pastor of St. Francis de Sales in Philadelphia was forced to gut a controversial renovation by removing the cathode light Robert Venturi had run around the sanctuary, Maurice Lavanoux was outraged (see fig. 3.15).[116] The parishioners did not see in Venturi's design, as Lavanoux did, a combination of "reverence for the history of the building" with "hope that man can bring the presence of grace to this frightening and at times uncomfortable new world of technology."[117] He called the dissidents "parish pussyfooters" who were refusing Venturi's offered "great hope" that plexiglass, vinyl, and cathode light could be "baptized" before human beings destroyed themselves through their own technological prowess.[118] Glenmary Fr. Patrick O'Donnell, introducing the "Churches for Tomorrow" competition in 1961, shared Lavanoux's concern about "imminent cataclysm," writing that Catholicism "demand[ed] structural incarnation . . . flesh and bones of wood and steel and brick using every modern device and material" to help "shout the praises of God together, publicly, while there is still time."[119]

Mid-twentieth-century Catholic futurists often used the term *humanization* to express the role they felt the Church should play in transforming a threatened civilization into one filled with God's grace. Catholic university chapels, especially Newman chapels at secular universities, bore significant weight in this program.[120] Newman chaplains and their supporters argued in favor of modern architecture on campus as an effort to transform, rather than reject, students' interest in technology. "Concrete, glass, steel," Shields Remine wrote of New York University's new modernist Catholic student center; "these are the tools needed by growing minds. But unless religion is a part of that growth the student cannot really mature."[121] If the technological world was to be saved, it was essential to blur the boundary between secular technologies and sacred spaces; this was the job that the liturgy could perform, whether in a concrete church or in technologically aided forays to parts of creation never before accessible to God's presence in the Eucharist. In February 1963, *Jubilee* readers encountered Daniélou's claim that "this world that technology has developed may itself be sacralized; there is no reason why it cannot be capped with a temple in which God will have his dwelling and the whole consecrated to him."[122] Daniélou's "temple" was no metaphor; for him, contemporary religious architecture was "like the expression of the modern soul" and "one of the first beginnings of what may be a consecrated world of technology."[123] Sanctuary furniture and Eucharistic vessels also received attention. In 1968 seminarian William Wilson, supported by the sacristan of Our Lady of the Assumption Abbey in Missouri, explained his desire for an unusual chalice to the liturgist Frederick McManus.[124] "As a member of the 'steel nation' in the 'steel age,'" he wrote,

> I would like to bring a pure steel chalice to the Altar. Steel symbolizes "homo faber" of today. Man uses steel for everything from cookery to building Space Craft, from life-saving medical equipment to (horrible to say) life-destroying armaments. I want to use a piece of uncovered, i.e., unplated steel, now for the sacred purpose of the Liturgy. In this way I hope to bring grace to man, the steel user, so that his use of steel may be directed more effectively to the welfare and benefit of the entire human race.[125]

Thus, decades after Schulte's *Hindenburg* liturgy, Wilson asked the materials of modernity to pronounce with him the "amen" of the Mass.

While Catholic modernists baptized new technology and used it to transmit Eucharistic presence in the unlikeliest of places, their sacramental actions looked beyond the present into the deep future. Both liturgists and architects countered Maginnis's dismissal of concrete's potential for "cosmic revolution." The Catholic lay intellectual Justus George Lawler wrote in the 1950s that one of the key contributions of the liturgical movement to theology was its revival of the classic Christian doctrine of the "sacramental nature of being."[126] The liturgy, according to the liturgical movement, derived its meaning from its function: it was a conduit that revealed and made possible God's presence in the world. Ultimately, liturgical performance allowed Catholics to participate in God's great work of redeeming all creation. This interpretation of the liturgy had significant implications for the Catholic assessment of the material world. Because Catholics expected the eschatological glorification of the whole creation, "matter, even as now existing, can be known by the man of faith to possess certain filaments of perfection which require that it be treated reverently."[127]

This understanding of matter's potential required theologians to respect the nature of materials as they were, aligning the interests of liturgists and modernist architects. Concrete and steel, too, were part of God's creation and would one day be redeemed. At St. John's Abbey, for example, commenters related Marcel Breuer's modernist idiom to eschatological openness. The distinguished British liturgist Illtud Evans, OP, noted that St. John's might "enshrine the unchanging mysteries." Nevertheless, it had done so "with the newness of [the] apocalyptic vision of the New Jerusalem," giving "concrete, too, a word to say" in proclaiming God's glory.[128] Aelred Tegels, OSB, a monk of St. John's, concurred. Functionality, he wrote, included the practical necessities for celebrating the Eucharist. But a church also needed to function as "a sign, or sacramental" that would help the assembled worshippers "situate themselves in salvation history and relate themselves to the entire New Covenant people, on earth and in heaven, in time and in eternity."[129] The anticipation of redemption needed to find expression in the best of modern architecture, which alone could convey that apparently "profane" materials shared in "the vocation of all things to recapitulation in Christ."[130] If "the true grandeur of creation" really " 'await[ed] the revelation of the sons of God,' " then creation's "potentialities are constantly being revealed in the development of new materials." The concrete church was not merely "an authentic contemporary expression" but one looking forward to the cosmic redemption of all things in Christ.[131]

"A WORLD WITH THE BARRIERS DOWN"

In September 1962, *Life* magazine surveyed a group of "Bold Steps to a Glowing Future."[132] "All over America," the editors wrote, "young people, bold people are casting off the old solutions and the tried and true ways and building new and unorthodox challenges to their world." Alongside new alloys for intercontinental missiles, medical treatments, radiation research equipment, and a gigantic radio transmitter/receiver that was "helping man fling his first, hesitant challenges into space," *Life* ran photos of the newly dedicated St. Louis Priory Church. The inclusion of Obata's technological marvel in this parade of scientific triumphs is an indication of American liberals' tremendous Cold War–era interest in uniting the interests of science and of the nation with those of faith.[133] But even as many Catholic modernists would have applauded *Life*'s approval of "Christ served in concrete," by 1962 others were beginning to build on one premise, the fundamental sameness of these enterprises, in order to question another: the wisdom of a Christian focus on building technologically forward-looking churches.

Throughout the 1960s and early 1970s, American architects continued to design Catholic churches with an eye to the technical and liturgical future. But simultaneously, new sets of concerns appeared that raised doubts about relying on literally parochial Catholic churches—no matter how futuristic—to resolve the vast contradictions of modern civilization. By 1967, Maryknoll priest Eugene Kennedy spoke for many when he magisterially dismissed "celibacy, the liturgy, catechetics, the institutional church, [and] the creation of community within religious orders" as "non-problems" and "intramural" issues that were causing Catholics to miss their chance to respond to "the real challenge to Christianity today."[134] Citing Alvin Toffler and other secular futurologists, Kennedy announced, "The future has burst above the world like an errant rocket and its fiery motes fill the air around us. An age to come has inched in under our skin and infected us with a new and unnamed anxiety."[135] Kennedy, like many postconciliar Catholics, turned to a revived eschatology to help him make sense of the Christian role in the new order, what *Life* described as "a world with the barriers down."[136] He asked Catholics to recognize that "the awesome gut problem of the present is to face the future in faith, to inform it with hope, and to give it the love that is man's sole source of life to the full."[137] It was this sacralization that had connected the mastering of new technologies of building to the eschatological renewal of creation, what Kennedy called "the real business of salvation history."[138] But what if the upheaval of the present, opening the way toward the future, was so vast that it would sweep away both Catholic churches and the Catholic Church? And what if the sacramental task of Catholics, whose Eucharistic liturgies infused matter with God's spirit and opened the world toward God's future, was itself a temporary and passing responsibility necessary only in an unredeemed world? To resolve this ecclesiological paradox, futurist Catholics turned to the biological paradigm, and to its greatest twentieth-century theological exponent: the controversial Jesuit Pierre Teilhard de Chardin.

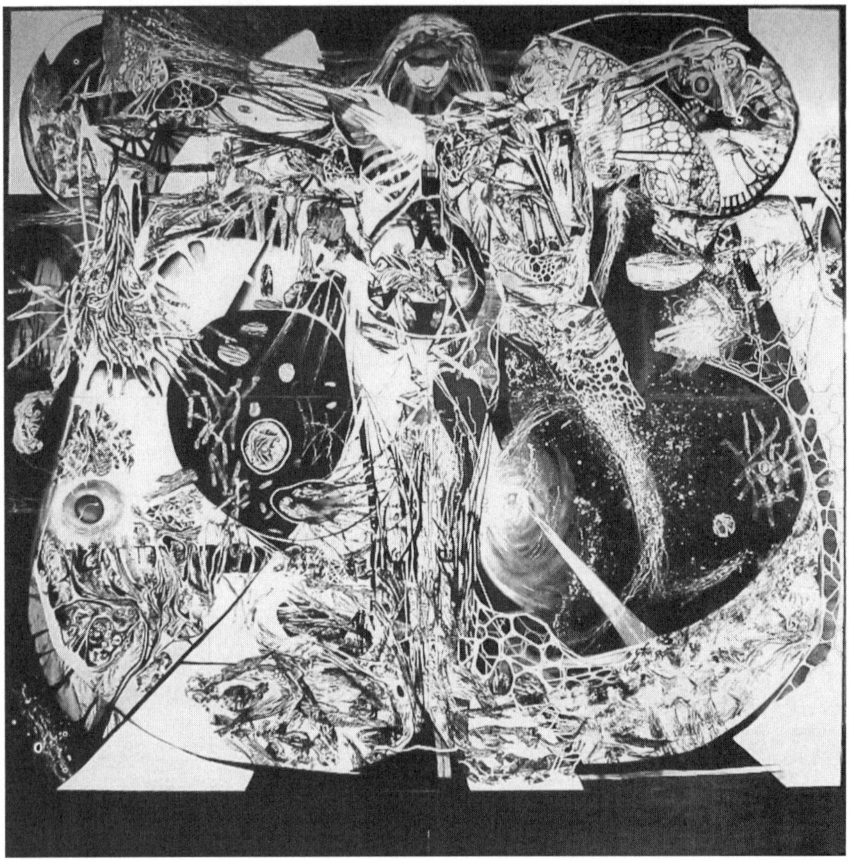

FIGURE 4.1. *Christ Invests Himself Organically with the Very Majesty of the Universe*, paint and mixed media on canvas (Michael Dvortcsak, 1967). Photo: Author.

CHAPTER FOUR

PILGRIMS OF THE FUTURE

As an MFA student in painting at the University of California–Santa Barbara beginning in 1966, Michael Dvortcsak spent as much time in the library as he did in the studio. His reading program, encompassing works by R. Buckminster Fuller, György Kepes, Albert Einstein, Alan Watts, and Pierre Teilhard de Chardin, was shared during the 1960s by many Americans who saw eclectic work in science, art, and religion flowing into a single unified field. All these thinkers, Dvortcsak wrote in his thesis, shared an interest in discerning "the relatedness of the microcosm to the macrocosm," with similarities and convergences among seemingly disparate aspects of reality.[1] Their research seemed to be producing growing evidence of cosmic interrelatedness that, their admirers felt, incentivized the pursuit of a future with artificial political and intellectual barriers lowered.

Holism—the belief that "reality can only be understood as a whole . . . [and by] focusing on relationships between the parts and the whole," in the process "emphasiz[ing] unity, interdependencies, and integration," as Linda Sargent Wood puts it—was a defining vision in American life during the long 1960s, shaping everything from civil rights activism to incipient environmentalism to countercultural experimentation.[2] The perception of fragmentation and the need for healing dominated much of modern thought, ranging across socialist theories of alienation, psychological concerns about the divided self, and theological fears about the division of the Christian churches and the perceived gulf between Christians' "religious" and "secular" lives. Holist hermeneutics, in response, "worked to . . . bring together what others treated separately: mind, body and spirit; individuals and community; human beings and nature; nature and technology; science and religion; the material world and the sacred."[3] The 1960s holists were delighted that, as Dvortcsak wrote, "after centuries of describing how things differ to the senses, Western man has begun to ask how things resemble other things."[4]

Despite his Catholic baptism, Dvortcsak had no plans to work for the Church. Nevertheless, when another student introduced him to Newman chaplain Bob Donahue, who wanted an altarpiece for the brand-new St. Mark's chapel, Dvortcsak found the idea compelling. He presented Donahue with sketches for a triptych: one with "images from the microcosm . . . tiny little parts of the body, tissue samples, small images," a second with "images from the macrocosm, spiral galaxies and so forth," and a third with "an image of Christ in two attitudes, one crucified and another with hands in prayer." Explaining why his vision was appropriate for a Catholic liturgical space, he shared a favorite quotation from Teilhard de Chardin:

> *Christ invests himself organically with the very majesty of his creation*. And it is in no way metaphorical to say that man finds himself capable of experiencing and discovering his God in the whole length, breadth and depth of the world in movement. To be able to say literally to God that one loves him, not only with all one's body, all one's heart and all one's soul, but with every fibre of the unifying universe—that is a prayer that can only be made in space-time.[5]

Dvortcsak installed his massive painting, *Christ Invests Himself Organically with the Very Majesty of the Universe*, in 1967 (fig. 4.1). The Newman Center explained to visitors that it was "a statement about the universe, about God, about Christ," a statement made in "science . . . the language of the university"; staff and students alike "wanted to show that our world, seemingly divided in so many ways—spiritually, intellectually, socially, and economically—really is not. It is one."[6] An outline of the human brain was the first thing Dvortcsak laid down on his enormous canvas, and this formal shape dominated the work, encircling galaxies and cells, webs of lines that might be seen as coastlines or blood vessels, but were, understood properly, both.[7] Viewers were not meant to identify particular forms as soap bubbles or nebulae; their task, rather, was to understand that these things were fundamentally similar, unified within the embrace of the cosmic Christ. The mural was an instant draw on a campus, where the names of Aldous Huxley and Alan Watts were on everyone's lips; Donahue reported an increase in attendance of up to 30 percent, with students not merely attending Mass, but remaining to meditate (and trip out) in front of the painting for hours on end.[8]

The theological defense of new materials and technologies outlined in chapter 3 rested on matter's potential for sanctification. The doctrine of creation and a reemerging interest in cosmic redemption ultimately helped Catholic modernists see these man-made materials as "natural" in their own way, to be appreciated as God's works. The 1960s saw Catholics extend these arguments as many of the same people and their younger contemporaries self-consciously took up what Holy Cross Father Bernard Murchland called, in 1966, "the prophetic principle." Prophets, he claimed, were "attentive to the variables of human evolution," and "interested in . . . possible developments." The prophetic principle, as opposed to the "institutional principle," could be defined as "the discernment of present predicaments in the light of future possibilities." Putting this in more biblical (and more biological) language, Murchland reminded his readers that the Kingdom of God, "like a seed . . . takes root and matures slowly; it grows and deploys itself in the evolution of history."[9] The Catholics interested in these ideas sought to illuminate developments of the present with the clarifying light of the divine future.

The making and installation of Dvortcsak's mural brought together a number of key threads in Catholics' 1960s quest to discern, build, and experience the future of the Church—threads that, united within the larger frame of the biological paradigm, mutually strengthened and reinforced one another. The first is cosmic holism, especially as shaped in the long 1960s by the short-lived but intense American obsession with Pierre Teilhard de Chardin, whose devotees saw both past and present as oriented toward a future of fulfillment in the divine. The second is the great interest many American Catholics shared in seeing scientific research (exploration into outer space, the visible natural world, and the secrets of microscopic cells) as a type of revelation, a window into the nature of God that could both illuminate and be illuminated by the sacramental practice of the Eucharist. Finally, the new presence of psychedelic drugs gave many people—whether they thought of themselves as part of the "counterculture" or not—a "brilliant glimpse of a living cosmos . . . pour[ing] through," and granted them "an unprecedented vision of a different world."[10] As much as the developments of the late 1960s horrified many American Catholics, some of their coreligionists saw the new drugs as tools, provided by scientific research, that could help human beings achieve insight into their own full potential as part of a great ingathering of creation toward its redemption.

THE PHENOMENON OF TEILHARD

Word spread quickly after the 1955 publication in French of a thick book containing a heady mixture of theological speculation and scientific data. Parts of the work that became *Le phénomène humain* had circulated in manuscript to a small group for years; now a wider audience became aware of its author, Pierre Teilhard de Chardin, SJ, as something other than a geologist and paleontologist. He had been working out a grand theory of the universe, a scientific theology inflected by his study of philosopher Henri Bergson's concept of evolutionary dynamism.[11] Hierarchical discomfort with his ideas had suppressed his theological work until his death simultaneously unleashed nearly forty years of writing on the past, present, and future of creation.

The English translation of his masterpiece, *The Phenomenon of Man*, with an admiring foreword by the English biologist, Bauhaus collaborator, and avowed atheist Julian Huxley (brother of Aldous), appeared in mid-1959.[12] American audiences had been primed by the writings of early admirers, especially his fellow Jesuit, the St. Louis–based historian and cultural commentator Walter Ong.[13] *The Phenomenon* sold fifty thousand copies in the United States alone in its first two years, and was followed by eleven more English-language books between 1960 and 1975, in addition to several volumes of letters. Its author, obscure and controversial in his lifetime, became in death the household name "Teilhard," with followers deeming him as significant as Aquinas and Darwin.[14] He was read far beyond Catholic circles, quoted by everyone from Episcopalian priests to the *Whole Earth Catalog*, a trend enhanced by the slightly later popularity of his admirer Marshall McLuhan.[15] But his status as a Catholic priest—even one who had fallen under official suspicion—meant that his reception was especially rapturous among the largely college-educated American Catholics already convinced by the biological paradigm and hungry for a theological framework to fill it out. The artist Patricia Malarcher was working at Harper Brothers, Teilhard's American publisher, several months before *The Phenomenon* appeared, and still recalls her delight at hearing people in the hallways discussing a Catholic scientist's work on evolution.[16]

Teilhard's books were shared between Catholic friends, colleagues, and spouses, purchased in bulk for Catholic college libraries, and discussed endlessly in Catholic magazine articles, study circles, symposia, and classrooms.[17] By December 1960, Sr. M. Madeleva Wolff, president of Saint Mary's College in Indiana, was certain that her friends Henry and Clare Boothe Luce had already "received more than one copy of Pierre Chardin's *Divine Milieu*," though it had been published only in late summer.[18] Many American Catholics reported that they did not find Teilhard's work simply interesting on a theoretical level; rather, reading it was like discovering something they had always known, but had been unable to recognize or articulate. When a student passed a copy of *The Phenomenon* to the architect Patrick Quinn, he recalled, "I was deeply moved . . . it made theological sense to me in the context of both creation and evolution."[19] Sr. Madeleva expressed the intimate relationship readers often reported with Teilhard when she wrote that *The Divine Milieu* was "one of the most completely luminous books that I have ever read. . . . To me it is, in parts at least, another self."[20]

The initial flood of Teilhard's own work was followed in short order by so many book-length studies and articles that as early as 1964, an author was begging readers not to "allow [themselves] to be checked by an initial feeling of surfeit at the prospect of 'another book on Teilhard.'"[21] Teilhard and his explicators earned a perennial place in regular periodical features for Catholic Book Week and Christmas shopping.[22] Publishers advertised heavily, gambling that even books they had to admit were Teilhard's "most technical pages" would contain enough of his "boundless faith in the greatness of man's ultimate destiny" to prompt another ascent to the top of the bestseller list as Harper & Row did when announcing the publication of "the scientific findings of the 'pilgrim of the future.'"[23] Enthusiasm spread well beyond academic commentary: nuns wrote Teilhardian poetry, and the musician Sebastian Temple (best known for his composition "The Lion Sleeps Tonight") not only released an album of Teilhardian folk songs, but embarked on an American lecture tour to promote Teilhardian ideas.[24]

The deeply emotional reaction to Teilhard helps explain why many Catholic readers evidently discounted official concern about his views. Intra-Catholic battles in the early years of Teilhard's popularity previewed the high-profile conflicts that tore some communities apart in the aftermath of Vatican II. When the young priest Hugh McElwain returned from Rome to teach theology in the fall of 1959, he saw Teilhard's name mentioned in conjunction with the centennial of *On the Origin of Species*. He acquired a copy of *The Phenomenon of Man*, then put it on reserve for his seminary class on the theology of creation, only to discover later in the semester that the rector had removed it due to a 1957 Holy Office *monitum* banning Teilhard's books from libraries and Catholic bookshops. Rather than quietly acquiescing, McElwain "became intensely curious, and immersed myself passionately into Teilhard's writings. . . . His vision of the evolving universe literally 'blew my mind.' "[25] Seminarians like Greg McAllister, increasingly uncomfortable with the neoscholastic theology of their teachers, could acquire Teilhard's work from local bookstores outside the Church's official reach; McAllister and his friends took their reading literally underground, holding a Teilhardian study circle in the subbasement of the San Francisco archdiocesan seminary to avoid their rector's disapproving eye.[26] Laypeople interested in Teilhard paid the Vatican even less mind. *Jubilee*'s editors glided over Teilhard's controversial reputation, noting evasively that "a series of events conspired to prevent [*The Phenomenon of Man*'s] publication" in the early 1940s.[27] After a second *monitum* emerged in 1962, they noted crisply that it was "a warning and not a prohibition, nor does it consign the works mentioned to the Index of Forbidden Books."[28] Faithful Catholics could read and discuss Teilhard to their hearts' content.

"LORD, LET ME SEE": TEILHARD'S THEOLOGY OF VISION

The eagerness with which many college-educated American Catholics devoured Teilhard's dense, voluminous work testifies to their tremendous desire for a theology accounting for the evolutionary theory in which they had already come to believe.[29] Despite his unusual analytic vocabulary, Teilhard's basic ideas were relatively easily grasped. He used his immersion in the study of the deep past (as a geologist and paleontologist) as a hermeneutic for his investigation of Christian theology, and vice versa. He argued that scientific study of the past demonstrated that the universe is slowly evolving in the direction of greater and greater life, greater and greater consciousness. Deep geological time had given way to the "biosphere," where life emerged; now the biosphere was giving way to the "noosphere," an evolutionary leap forward in consciousness where thinking human beings would develop a unified network of thought and spirit, a single consciousness, driving the "complexifying" universe ultimately in the direction of a moment of total convergence, the "Omega Point." In keeping with the theological tension between human free will and the gift of God's grace, Teilhard described the universe both as moving toward the Omega Point, and as being drawn in irresistibly. God's act of creation must not, he insisted, be understood as having occurred at a single moment. Rather, creation is an ongoing activity beneath the surface of evolution, and the fullness of God is only to be found in the future of the ever-evolving universe. In short, as Linda Sargent Wood puts it, Teilhard made a "religion of evolution."[30]

I. F. Clarke, in a sweeping survey of futuristic visions from 1644 to 1979, quotes from Teilhard's description of "the men of the future" who, "forced together by the growth of a common power and the sense of a common travail," would "form a single consciousness," collectively choosing a "yes" to God "individually affirmed by beings in each of whom will be fully developed the sense of human liberty and responsibility."[31] This prediction, Clarke says, is simply "the most ambitious in the history of futuristic literature."[32] Teilhard's "ambition" attracted substantial critiques from scientists who pointed out that he ignored the evidence of evolution's randomness, waste, and tragedy, and from theologians who criticized his sometimes mystical treatment of war and its weapons.[33] Nevertheless, even when it required them to elide aspects of his writing, American Catholics during the 1960s typically read Teilhard as a visionary of evolution toward cosmic peace.

Catholic artists and architects had a special affinity for Teilhard's work, which affirmed the importance of creative energy in the cosmic renewal of the universe. *The Phenomenon of Man* opens with a brief essay on "Seeing."[34] Scriptural themes configure the healing of blindness and the conferral of new sight as critical parts of human transformation; in response, Teilhard framed his entire work as "an attempt to *see*," arguing that "the whole of life lies in that verb." According to this salvific theory of sight, his projected unity of creation could arise only out of a vision of "increased consciousness," and it would be the "elaboration of ever more perfect eyes" within an evolutionary cosmos that would enable human beings to "see more and better."[35] The particular qualities of vision he enumerated include "a sense of spatial immensity . . . a sense of depth . . . a sense of number . . . a sense of proportion . . . a sense of quality, or novelty . . . a sense of movement . . . a sense, lastly, of the organic."[36] Newly evolved eyes, conditioned by a deeply felt understanding of organic growth in time and space, would launch humanity toward the Omega Point.

Teilhard affirmed artists' personal and professional experience of seeing the world more deeply and with more attention than others seemed to, and of "ever more perfect eyes" that could discern the true reality at the heart of things, rather than their immediate external surfaces. Catholic artists and architects particularly appreciated his stress on the dialectic between matter and sanctification. The painter Rose Sulymoss, commenting that "our century aims toward unknown directions; the space age tears down all previous rules, accepted forms, and laws," took an equivocal stance toward the material world: it should not be "the objective, the idol." Teilhard had rightly honored and praised matter but understood that it was "only the means toward the goal." Her own art tried to "manifest a searching spirit toward God" and to "sanctify art." She could only portray matter using matter, but at the same time avoided a strict realism that would, paradoxically, not be able to show the fullness of reality. Explicitly Teilhardian paintings, sculpture, and stained glass are typically characterized by a strong sense of movement. A number of artists hit on the formal strategy of semiabstraction (depicting recognizable shapes and subjects in a non-photorealistic manner) as a way of seeing the inner truth of matter without rejecting firsthand observation.[37]

Architects and urban planners, meanwhile, seized upon Teilhard's call for human beings to participate in "building" the new world.[38] His theories on the biological basis of social organization and its potential for evolution under the right physical circumstances easily cohered with the views of modernist designers. Having promoted Teilhard through his introduction to *The Phenomenon*, Julian Huxley—who had become friendly with many of the Bauhaus émigrés during their time in London—highlights the fluid international network of scientists, artists, architects, theologians, and men and women of letters who shared these interests.[39] So, for example, a *Liturgical Arts* review of Richard Neutra's *Survival through Design* opined that Neutra was close to Teilhard's view that people are "arriving at '. . . the conception of a common task; namely to promote the spiritual future of the world."[40] Le Corbusier, too, found a kindred spirit and inspiration in Teilhard. As Flora Samuel writes, the architect and the theologian "linked the 'physical sphere of organised "Nature"' and the 'moral or artificial sphere of human institution,' blurring the boundaries between nature and culture."[41]

While Teilhardian architects focused on how their building skills could contribute to emergent human development, or "hominization," their technical expertise existed, they felt, to serve this overall vision of cosmic evolution. Their task was not to unimaginatively give a client "what he asked for"; it was to use their talents and expertise to promote what Teilhard called "planetisation." William Schickel commented that "the idea that all human works have a final obligation to mankind itself to be a positive force in human evolution" had "deeply influenced the approach to [his post–Vatican II] renovation" of Kentucky's Abbey of Gethsemani.[42] The Catholic architect Ray Pavia, lecturing to Brooklyn college students in 1963, set out his prescriptions for the future of church building following a brief tour of modern thought, which "perceived and predicted space in every direction and dimension"—past, present, future; outer space and "inner psyche."[43] Teilhard was part of the Church's engagement with and sacralization of modernity; he had discerned "the essential principle" that "to divinize does not mean to destroy, but to sur-create."[44] Salvation would come not through the destruction of evil (or of modernity, whether philosophical or technical), but rather, through the creation of new dimensions for materiality.

Pavia's Teilhardian vision for the church building of the future was not a prescription for materials, elements, or forms, but for a particular type of community and set of behaviors from which any given formal solution would emerge organically. "The client must be capable of shedding his conventional attitude of what a church should look like," Pavia argued, "and must be able to grow with the architect in the experience of creating a church." A church building that met these requirements would engage in a "functionalism of a higher order," divinizing the community through "a spiritual dialogue . . . established between God and man."[45] As with Pavia, it was the social function of architecture that most engaged Catholics thinking about cities and buildings within a Teilhardian framework; Teilhardian designs derived their aesthetic not from their visual representation of theological ideas, but from Frank Lloyd Wright's and Le Corbusier's modernism and the vernacular aesthetic of science fiction illustration, among others. Their Teilhardian inspiration lay in their promotion of enhanced human consciousness, progress, and the unity and redemption of creation.

JOY AND HOPE, GRIEF AND ANXIETY: TEILHARDIAN DREAM CHURCHES IN A NUCLEAR AGE

Teilhard's almost incredible popularity among Catholic and other intellectuals during a period of roughly fifteen years raises the question of why, exactly, it seemed so urgent to build a world urging human beings into greater and greater unity. In short, American Teilhardianism is best understood as a Cold War phenomenon.[46] The powerful dialectic of hope and dread generated by midcentury scientific, military, and geopolitical developments provided fertile ground for the growth of Teilhardian enthusiasm.[47] This dialectic emerged as American intellectuals felt their way forward from the atomic conclusion of the Second World War. The Jesuit Daniel Berrigan, for example, wondered if nuclear warfare was powerful enough to signal an end to evolution. "The laws of man's spiritual life, as his destiny goes forward, seem to be analogous to the laws of his biology," he wrote in 1962. "These latter laws, especially in light of the writings of Blondel, Bergson, and Teilhard de Chardin, are seen more and more today as symbols of the spiritual progress of man."[48] But Berrigan argued that the present situation, while in one sense a normal development, also represented a true crisis. "No revolution, no scientific breakthrough prior to our own generation—nor all of them taken in their sum—could have brought us to the brink where we stand today," he thought. "There was never before a time, that is, when men could announce the simple power to end time, to end man, to end history, to bring down the world."[49] Ten years later, the German theologian Jürgen Moltmann addressed St. Louis Catholics with the reminder that "world peace has become the absolutely necessary condition for the survival of the human race. . . . The one alternative to world peace is world annihilation, whether by atomic suicide, the escalation of social injustice, or the creeping ecological death of industrial societies."[50] In this context, it was radically hopeful to embrace Teilhard's faith that "mankind as an organic and organized whole possesses a future."[51]

Although Berrigan and a few others argued that technological progress had been so co-opted by the Cold War that rejecting it altogether had become necessary for human survival, Catholics writing for periodicals like *Commonweal*, *Jubilee*, and *Liturgical Arts* mostly resisted that conclusion. In a special May 1962 *Commonweal* issue on "The Arms Race and the Christian Obligation," Justus George Lawler recounted that Teilhard had looked forward to Russian cooperation in the International Geophysical Year of 1957/58 in the hope that it might signal "year one of the Noosphere," the first step on the road to the "spiritual unification of man." Lawler observed sadly that the hope had proved false. "For it is not clear at the present time," he wrote, "whether we are moving towards the dawn of the Noosphere, or whether we have instead taken the first step towards Armageddon." But Lawler thought that it was possible that these two options were not, perhaps, mutually exclusive after all, for "the growing realization that we are faced with an unimaginable and utterly incomprehensible fate may drive man toward the unifying of all peoples on this bruised planet. Compelled by the fear of extinction, we may be facing the most dramatic evolutionary leap in the story of man."[52] Paradoxically, the threat of total annihilation might represent a step forward. The human race might be so frightened by the "alternative to the United Nations" that it would overcome its insularity and take the steps toward interconnection and mutual communion that were the absolute prerequisite of further evolution toward the Omega Point (fig. 4.2).

Meanwhile, in an essay claiming that the modern world had been entirely reoriented around "the fact of evolution—cosmic, organic, and intellectual,"

FIGURE 4.2. "This Is One Alternative to the United Nations," advertisement. Photo: *Commonweal*, December 20, 1963.

Walter Ong, SJ, argued for a Teilhardian revolution in political organization. In "this thermonuclear, quasi-unified world," the sovereign state, whether American or Soviet, was ultimately doomed. So too was the supposed separation between the Church and the modern world, rendered irrelevant by "the slow, and sometimes exceedingly painful, elaboration of a more profound understanding of [the Church's self] and of her role in God's designs forced by the changing world view." After a long evolutionary period of divergence and differentiation, creation was now "converging" again; "greater and greater contact" through communications and technology were binding people together inextricably, "and the space age has in some sense begun."[53]

Immersion in Teilhard offered a distinctive eschatological answer to nuclear terror: the option not only for "a peace generated by mutual fear," but for the "practical reality" of the "Peace of God."[54] In 1960 and again in 1965, *Jubilee* printed excerpts from Teilhard's writings in its Christmas issue, the second time with the editorial note that "hope for the future has become virtually an act of faith" and that Teilhard's essay was intended by the magazine as a "gift, with hope that the world will soon be ransomed from the horrors of war."[55] In *Commonweal*, James Schall disputed Margaret Mead's recent argument that "the threat of the bomb, of material destruction, is more serious than we suppose on our psychic structures. Work and confidence in the future depends upon . . . the assurance of a tomorrow. . . . Yet we cannot be guaranteed tomorrow."[56] Mead's analysis was valid but incomplete; the malaise caused by the bomb,

Schall suggested, was merely a special case of a general inability to believe that human actions might matter for the future of the world. The solution was the Incarnation, the guarantee "that all things return through man, through Christ to the Father, that therefore what man does has cosmic significance."[57]

Schall's answer held a special appeal when set against the ever-present nuclear threat. Teilhardian "optimism" offered a way for Catholics to see, in Teilhard's words, "the atomic age" as "not the age of destruction but of union in research."[58] Whether or not there really was "a total synthesis happening in our times" in which "a great ingathering of people and movements and ideas, many of which . . . appeared to rival each other" were now "coalescing into one renewal" (as the liturgist Godfrey Diekmann described the scene of 1965), Teilhard's devotees could forecast a pattern of convergence from within the most frightening conflicts of the postwar era.[59] Diekmann related the "coalescence" of the Church to "the great upheaval throughout the world in the name of human rights, the achievements in social and economic reform right here in the U.S. . . . Even the technological revolution and man's new adventures in space," all of which were "related to the moment in Salvation History in which we now find ourselves."[60]

Within this context, Maurice Lavanoux both delighted and infuriated readers of *Liturgical Arts* with a series of projects that seemed to some to push over the line from practical planning into pure speculation: a "Chapel on the Moon" (November 1967), an ecumenical submarine chapel (November 1971), and a space station "Spiritual Research Center in the Sky," unpublished due to *Liturgical Arts*' 1972 demise. With these three interventions, Lavanoux and his architectural and theological collaborators became part of a small group of American Catholic science fiction creators—or perhaps purveyors of what Jacques Maritain dismissed as Teilhard's "theology-fiction."[61] But against the grim vision of Walter Miller's *A Canticle for Leibowitz,* in which the Catholic role after nuclear disaster is to protect the last surviving fragments of civilization, in Lavanoux's more optimistic forecast the Church was to broker an antinuclear peace within the logic of Teilhard's cosmic vision, "show[ing] the wholeness of *creation*, etc."[62]

In the spring of 1963, Lavanoux went to Princeton University, at the invitation of Jean Labatut, to comment on that year's architecture theses. The projects included a lavish set of plans for a permanent lunar colony by the military engineer William Sims, future co-designer of Disney's Epcot Center.[63] Lavanoux, always enthusiastic about the possibilities of new technology, was entranced by the idea of a moon colony, and especially intrigued by the inclusion of a chapel in the plans. He wanted to publish them immediately, but Sims never provided the full set of drawings. To his extensive reading on ecumenism in the Vatican II years, Lavanoux now added Arthur C. Clarke and Isaac Asimov, R. Buckminster Fuller, futurist literature like the essay collection *Toward the Year 2000*, and, of course, Teilhard.[64] *Liturgical Arts*' editorials began to sound like copy for *Astounding Worlds*. "Out of man's dreams of the possible emerge the realities of to-morrow," Lavanoux wrote in 1967. "The fantastic speed with which man has reached outer space may leave us bewildered and fearful of all the implications inherent in the exploration of the unknown. Yet the known of today was the unknown of the recent past. Those of us 'over thirty' can think back to the discovery of electric light, the telephone, the radio (the crystal set), the airplane, radar, television, and now photographs *from* the moon, via a man-made machine."[65]

In May 1967, the California artist Louisa Jenkins introduced Lavanoux to her son-in-law Mark Mills when the editor was on one of his periodic information-gathering trips. A fiercely independent, quietly stubborn introvert, Mills had grown up in the mining town of Jerome, Arizona, watching residents fight the slope of the mountain to keep their homes level.[66] In high school he read Frank Lloyd Wright's *Autobiography*, and in 1944, after completing a degree in architectural engineering, he struck a deal: Mills would provide labor, and in return he would receive room and board at Wright's compound Taliesin West. In 1949 he left Taliesin along with Paolo Soleri, with whom he had been working on a radical architecture suitable for extreme environments. After a few years at loose ends, during which he (with Soleri) constructed a dome house in the brutally hot Arizona desert and did a short stint in the offices of Anshen + Allen (the designers of the Chapel of the Holy Cross), Mills moved to Monterey, California. At a dinner party, he was introduced to Louisa Jenkins's daughter Barbara, a Catholic convert like her mother. When the two agreed to marry in 1954, Mills, who had grown up Catholic, decided to return to the Church.[67]

Mills's projects demonstrate his great respect for the natural qualities of their environments; he built to accommodate features rather than level a site—a preference developed during his childhood in Jerome and his time with Wright.[68] His sinuous organic forms seem to grow out of their surroundings, and he blended exterior and interior both by incorporating skylights and large windows, and by using found material to build interior elements like fireplaces, a technique shared with Wright. Mills's houses gracefully alternate smaller, enclosed spaces and open, light-filled areas; they generate both a great sense of calm and a desire to move further into or out of the structure.[69] Wright's ideas about seashells affected Mills as deeply as they did the concrete wizards working at the same time. His favorite of Wright's sayings fit beautifully into a holistic and biologically inflected eschatology: "There must have been a sense of God in these little (seashell) forms to produce this infinite beauty of form. Just as there must be slumbering in all of us. There is in us, too, that interior sense of becoming which we call God, working in us all, and which, you will see, has infinite capacity which no human mind can ever encompass and imprison."[70] Mills admired architecture, and architects, who could convey both a deep respect for the natural world and a sense of forward motion.[71]

Mills—quirky, immensely talented, interested in integrating architecture into extreme natural environments, used to designing for the pleasure of it rather than for financial reward, and open to futuristic collaborations—was just the man Maurice Lavanoux had been looking for. In Jenkins's kitchen, Mills and Lavanoux chewed over ideas for a "dream church."[72] With the moon landing now on the horizon, Lavanoux was impatient to proceed. By the end of June 1967, Lavanoux had sent Mills articles and pictures about possible moon installations from the *New York Times*, and Mills had sent back architectural notes.[73] Lavanoux wrote excitedly to Mills: "I can visualize the 50th anniversary issue of *Liturgical Arts* having a report from our MOON correspondent!!" He signed off, "Enthusiastically yours."[74]

In November, Lavanoux published a special issue of *Liturgical Arts*, "A Chapel on the Moon, 2000 AD." Mills's plans were accompanied by a series of real and imaginary images: Ranger 9 lifting off from Cape Kennedy; a NASA artist's conception of Apollo and a lunar module; illustrations of Jules Verne stories—tying together "The Past, the Present, the Future: 1865—1967—2000." Lavanoux also borrowed an illustration of a lunar colony by the science fiction artist Roy Scarfo from a *New York Times* article by Isaac Asimov.[75] Scarfo and Asimov envisioned a self-contained bubble of living, food-growing, and lab space buried under the moon's crust, protecting the colony from the harsh environment of the surface. Moving sidewalks and personal mechanical wings would convey residents between farming areas, dorm-like housing, and two university/lab buildings. On the surface, a nuclear power plant would make peaceful use of this technology, while antennas for space research and an observatory would provide the colony's raison d'être. Lavanoux made only one modification to this detailed projection: inserting Mills's chapel (fig. 4.3). The entire structure was to be buried underground along with the rest of the colony; but at the very top, an oculus would give onto the surface, on axis with the altar so that the celebrant raising the host would look up into the stars (fig. 4.4).

FIGURE 4.3. Maurice Lavanoux's edited version of *Advanced Lunar City* (Roy Scarfo, 1967). At the center of the painting (8A), Lavanoux inserted Mills's chapel in place of a university building. Photo: *Liturgical Arts* (original, copyright 1967 by Roy Scarfo).

In keeping with the spatial restrictions of a moon colony—and with Mills's gift for economy—the chapel design neatly packaged everything necessary for a complete lunar mission. The material of the "walls" would not have to withstand the harsh exterior atmosphere, so Mills suggested a translucent plastic film covering a web of cable suspended from a concrete collar. While the worship space itself extended from the floor of the chapel (sunk six feet below the rest of the colony) to the oculus, a mezzanine level ringed the exterior diameter. Six small cells, a kitchen, bathrooms, conference rooms, and library/study spaces all gave onto an open walkway overlooking the worship space. Mills named the chapel after Emeric Doman, CO, his friend and the provost of the Monterey Oratory, and solicited Terence Mangan, CO, to write a

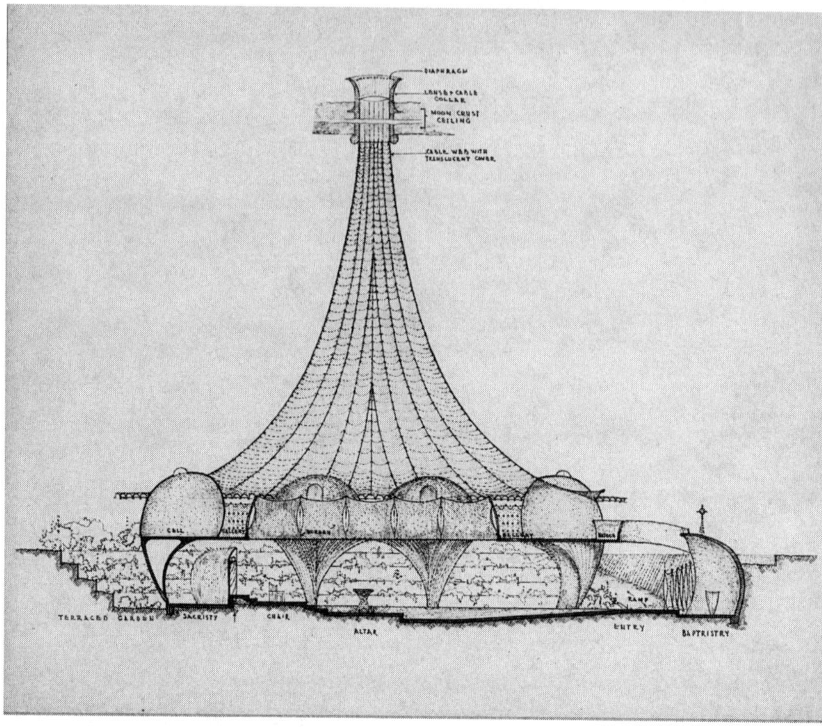

FIGURE 4.4. Mark Mills, section, *Doman Moon Chapel* (1967). Photo: Courtesy Mark Mills Papers, Special Collections and Archives, California Polytechnic State University.

commentary on its appropriateness for the order's priests; Mangan saw it as a "futuristic symbol of [the] effort" to integrate scientific and religious beliefs, and to integrate priests and their communities, joining "the Christian vision of the 'new creation' . . . to the rapidly changing technological universe that is their home."[76] Despite the compactness of their individual cells, the Oratorians would have felt they were in a larger unified design, for each small space opened into the larger space of the chapel. At the end of the gallery, a bridge and ramp flowed downwards into a baptistery and toward the main entrance.

The chapel itself was to be ringed by a terraced garden, which entering worshippers would pass as they walked down the ramp. Because of the translucent wall materials, the garden would be visible from within the worship space. The layout of the nave, sanctuary, and sacristy were the least unusual aspects of the space; Mills envisioned a modern but (by the late 1960s) fairly standard arrangement, with the priest and people brought together by an intimate semicircular nave around an altar on a moderate thrust. Apparently, he did not expect the liturgy to develop in ways that would preclude a seated congregation or a separate space for the celebrants.[77] What defined Mills's moon chapel as futuristic was its determined use of the most advanced "secular" materials available. Plastic films, cables, and (for the statuary) cast aluminum and welded steel predominated. Only a decade earlier, a leading figure in the Bay Area Catholic art scene had barred a stainless-steel sculpture from a religious art exhibit because it was "made from inferior material"; choosing to avoid traditional "precious" materials entirely, Mills declined to notice any difference between the type of material used for "sacred" art and architecture and that used for "secular."[78] Mangan framed this choice in a Teilhardian key, concluding, "Time and progress change man's world-image; hopefully, they strengthen and enlighten his world-view. Pierre Teilhard de Chardin summed up this incarnational worldview of Christianity when he wrote: 'Nothing is profane for those who know how to see.' "[79]

Four years later, Lavanoux and Mills produced a second in this series of "dream" churches for *Liturgical Arts*' fortieth-anniversary issue. This new "chapel" was to be a submarine, christened the *Cardinal Bea* in honor of the great ecumenist and head of the Vatican's Secretariat for Promoting Christian Unity (fig. 4.5). Crewed by representatives from all the Christian churches and all the world religions, the *Bea* would travel around the world, spreading

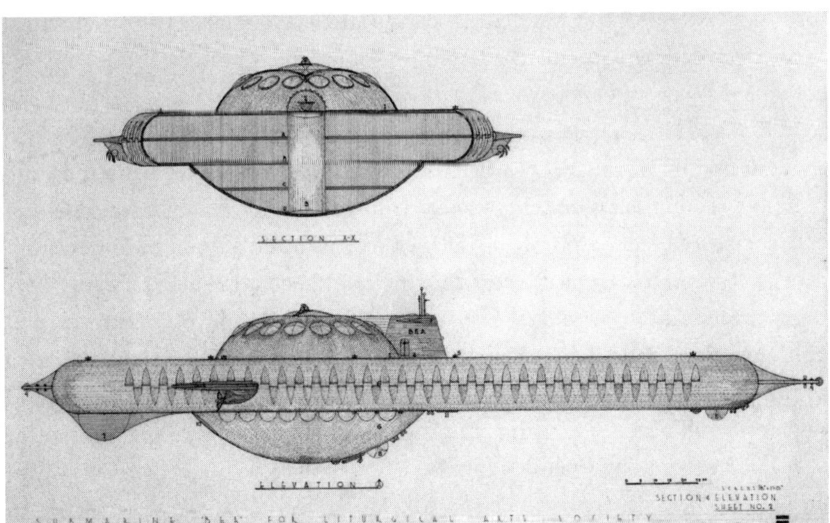

FIGURE 4.5. *Cardinal Bea* submarine chapel, with the elevation and latitudinal section showing four decks (*A–D*) of living quarters, the nuclear power core (5), and the chapel (*upper portion*; note the altar, portholes, and, at the very top, the dove) (Mark Mills, 1971). Photo: Courtesy Mark Mills Papers, Special Collections and Archives, California Polytechnic State University.

peace and understanding at each port of call until it arrived in Philadelphia in 1976, just in time for the World's Fair and bicentennial celebrations. Again, Lavanoux printed Mills's detailed plans alongside commissioned articles, this time mostly by Jesuits: Clement McNaspy, SJ, on "Man, the Sea, and Peace"; Neil Hurley, SJ, on "Liturgy and Play in Our Expanding Tele-civilization," and Francis P. Sullivan, SJ, on "Saline Theology: For a Church at Sea."

Mills and Lavanoux conceived the *Bea* as a solution to conflict among nations, designed, in Hurley's words, "to stress the evolutionary unity of the species as a worshipping community, beginning with the origins publicized by Charles Darwin and pointing toward the supernatural unity of the race in God as foreshadowed in the writing of Father Pierre Teilhard de Chardin, S.J."[80] Peace in this view was not merely the absence of war; it was the attainment of Teilhard's Omega Point. Just as Mills and Lavanoux had earlier turned to one extreme environment, the moon, in an attempt to get theological perspective on the actions of nations on earth, they now traveled to the depths of the ocean seeking to "humanize ('hominize' is the more accurate and Teilhardian term) . . . the sea."[81] Mills decided that the traditional shape of a submarine, long and shark-like, was inappropriate for a peace-building ship.[82] Instead, he based his design for the hull on the manta ray, an equally hydrodynamic but far less aggressive creature. He saw a peace sign in the overall shape as the stern forked to port and starboard, and echoed it in the steel frame of the chapel. As if to emphasize the twin characteristics of both secular science fiction and Teilhardian projection—speculative playfulness alongside quantitative, scientific accuracy—Mills gave precise measurements for his plan, indicating that the sub would be 246 feet long. But his original drawing demonstrates that he obtained those figures by working backward from a natural constraint. He drafted a sub precisely as long as his drawing paper, minus a quarter-inch margin on either end, then used a standard scale of 1/8 inch to the foot to obtain the dimensions.

The *Bea* was to carry a crew of 220, including scientists and chaplains. Living quarters and labs would take up most of the space in the massive horizontal volumes of the A and B decks. The chapel itself rested atop the four decks, with the altar poised directly over the central core of the nuclear reactor that would power the submarine—putting potentially destructive technology to peaceful use. Fourteen small portholes formed a clerestory; through them worshippers would be able to see water and fish, lit by deck lights on the outer hull. Mills designed retractable cages so that the portholes could become temporary aquariums, and he intended for sound to be transmitted from the ocean during services. Serving and both stained glass windows and Stations of the Cross, the portholes, like the moon garden, creatively integrated the natural world into a human-designed space for extreme and hostile environments. In a final touch, Mills set a glass dove (symbolizing peace) into the hull directly over the altar, refracting light downward into the chapel. The inhabitants would live in harmony both with the natural environment in which they were submerged and with the rest of humankind.

Lavanoux asked the Catholic painter Brenda Bettinson to send something appropriate for the chapel's main artwork. He initially suggested *Our Lady of the Seas*, but later wrote to Bettinson: "I wonder if it might not be better to think of something abstract. . . . After all, this chapel will be for *all mankind*."[83] He sent her a copy of *Profiles of the Future* by Arthur C. Clarke and suggested that "perhaps the subject of your painting could encompass all creation."[84] Bettinson settled on a warmly colored painting she called *Oculus*. An editorial note indicated that the yellow sun on the green field stood for "the light power of the sun" that illuminated "the oceanic depths"; further, the eternal circle combined with the square, symbolic of the earth, to "add up to perfection."[85] Its heavy impasto suggested the motion of the waves and the volume of the ocean and graphically expressed the cosmic natural harmonies of holistic philosophy.

Lavanoux partnered with the sculptor-architect Pierre Székely on a third entry in this series, a space station in permanent orbit, which Lavanoux called a "Spiritual Research Center in the Sky."[86] He was tremendously excited by the prospect of adding the final element to his "trilogy" on "intangibles, the possible, the fantastic . . . within the orbit of God's grace!"[87] Once again the editor acted as broker, planning to incorporate Székely's designs with the ideas of the French physicist Pierre Baruch and join them with solicited theological articles and essays culled from other sources like the AIA *Journal*'s "Science Fiction Becomes Fact."[88] He did extensive research, including on possible technical challenges to the liturgy in orbit. Reading about Skylab 2, he recalled Teilhard's "Mass on the World," conducted in the desert with none of the usual liturgical objects available. If Teilhard were in space, Lavanoux realized, "the problem of weightlessness" would mean "he could not use bread, wine, NOR an altar." (A letter to NASA brought back the response that "any technical difficulties caused by weightlessness could be overcome in the instance you cite." "So that's settled for the time being!," he commented.)[89]

The Spiritual Research Center in the Sky would have been the culmination of Lavanoux's science fiction career. After closing down *Liturgical Arts* in 1972, he continued writing his "editor's diary," constantly hoping to find enough funding to revive the magazine. He kept working, too, making a trip to NASA headquarters in May 1973 to look for photos; he thought that perhaps his third dream church could be published simultaneously with the Apollo-Soyuz

American-Soviet joint mission in 1975. "Would it not be a wonder," he wrote, "if *our* Space spiritual research center, devoted to PEACE, should also join this American-Soviet rendezvous . . . ? One member of *our* crew could join the American Apollo, another join the Soviet Soyuz, & perhaps bring to both thoughts just a bit *higher* than technological achievements." His research stimulated thoughts on the connection between space science and liturgical art, and he remarked that the results of the space program should, at the parish level, "feed an awareness of the wonders of Creation and their practical application in the liturgy of the Church and its physical aspects in the form of art and architecture. *It is all of a piece!*"[90]

Lavanoux's ambitions did not stop with solving American-Soviet relations. In July 1973, he tried his hand at a little science fiction of his own, in a diary entry dated "June 23, 2025":

> This morning edition of the *Martian Daily Blast* brings disturbing news. Militant elements on Mars have challenged the governments of Saturn and Jupiter to a final confrontation to determine the mastery of outer space. The Martian prime minister, Amas Dubious, has contacted his counterparts on Saturn and Jupiter in an effort to *cool it* but the danger is ever present. The *Spiritual Research Center*, launched in 1975 under the aegis of the Liturgical Arts Society . . . has again rendezvoused with American and Soviet space ships & will bring to Earth a representative from Mars, Saturn, and Jupiter for a *peace* conference in an environment that should make these ambassadors feel at home—*The Painted Desert in the Petrified Forest National Park* in Arizona. . . . Because of Vatican Council III the late secretary of the Liturgical Arts Society . . . now heads a Vatican division of the Congregation for Celestial Affairs and it is expected that all the representatives from Mars, Saturn, Jupiter, and Earth will choose him as a totally disinterested chairman, entirely devoted to PEACE. The next decade will tell the story and we hope that the year 2025 will go down in history as a final acceptance of the fullness of the Holy Spirit![91]

Lavanoux and his "dream trilogy" collaborators proposed a creation- and Creator-centered spirituality and practice as an antidote to national and ecclesiastical deadlocks and a prophylactic against the threat of nuclear war. All three fantasy chapels would have drawn worshippers into communion with the natural world and the universe through their use of transparent and translucent materials connecting the interiors of the chapels to fauna and flora, water and space. Lavanoux—who had clearly been asked one too many times "what all this has to do with liturgical art"—responded testily in October 1971: "A great deal.

It deals with all the interacting activities of the universe—quite simply, with creation, with God!"[92] His collaborators agreed that technological achievement would lead to greater things; Neil Hurley proposed that the ecumenical liturgies that would take place in the chapels would emphasize, in a Teilhardian fashion, "the cosmic nature of human worship, especially in the 'jet-atomic-space' age." Hurley concluded that the projects gave "a fantastic but not fanciful glimpse of what is now possible as mankind marches dramatically through the space-time arc which unites Alpha and Omega—man the tool-maker, the dreamer, and the worshipper—a restless pilgrim fulfilling a sacred mission."[93]

In creating these "dream chapels," Lavanoux and his collaborators appropriated the classic science fiction strategy of using imaginative creations to get a grip on the unknown future. Fr. Clifford Stevens, in his commentary on the moon chapel, pressed the point, writing that "man stands on the threshold of a vast unknown, and the theologian, with the rest of the human race, gazes into the darkness," and went on to claim that the chapel, in the face of frightening darkness, could be "a torch to guide [man] into the future."[94] Terence Mangan likewise commented that the chapel "is the reassurance to the Christian pilgrim of tomorrow, who has exchanged staff for space-helmet."[95] Both men invoked an anxiety which betrayed the other side of midcentury technocratic optimism: fear of what the future *might* look like if contemporary problems were not dealt with productively. As Isaac Asimov commented, Hiroshima had "made science fiction respectable."[96] It seemed obvious to many Americans that the Federation of American Scientists was correct that there would be "one world *or none*."[97] Out of this belief came a variety of Cold War jeremiads from both the right and the left—the former positing that the "one world" should be *American,* the latter that peace on earth required cooperation among all nations.[98]

Where normative science fiction antinuclear visions were, like *Star Trek*, decidedly secular, Lavanoux and his associates staked out a role for Catholic belief and practice, claiming Teilhard's work as both an accurate scientific guide, and as a theological exposition of why and how all things were related. To the proposed cooperation of the American and Soviet governments, Lavanoux added proposals for the cooperation of representatives of all religious groups. He wrote in a 1969 letter that the submarine's mission would be "all keyed to peace, but without any international or even religious entanglements; in other words, supernational and superecclesiastical—with God, the creator, as skipper."[99] The sub's round-the-world trip was to include "*atonement* stops at Bikini, Hiroshima, and Nagasaki."[100] The *Bea* was to proactively promote ecumenical peace as the opposite of ever-more-dangerous war; the sub's fantasy voyage was to include regular telecasts "showing scenes of cooperation and international understanding, and ventures of a multiracial and transconfessional nature" to counter scenes of "hatred, tension . . . and conflict" on the daily news.[101] In developing these proposals, then, Lavanoux and his collaborators sought a realistic response to the promise of technology, on the one hand, and on the other, the nuclear threat. The moon, sub, and space station chapels were not "mere" fantasies, but serious attempts to grapple with a stark choice between the Omega Point, where cosmic unity would be crowned in God's glory, or a disastrous alternate path toward annihilation in both physical and theological senses. For Lavanoux, architectural backwardness—the continued building of neo-Gothic "archeological horrors in church buildings"—was the direct opposite of better "relations with our separated brethren and with non-Christian communities" and with nature.[102] To slow down, to move backward, to self-isolate, was to die, and to change and unite with others was to live—in architecture, in the Church, and in all other domains. Imagining futuristic "dream chapels," thus encouraging Teilhardian understandings that the world was all of a piece, might help creation survive.

INNER SPACE AND THE TOTAL ENVIRONMENT

Michael Dvortcsak's immersion in holistic thought was typical of artists involved in what James Nisbet describes as a "widespread reconceptualization of the material world as bound to the shapes of ecological change" during the 1960s.[103] *Ecology* in this period was a fluid word, encompassing "a technical concept, a condition of the earth, and a way of imagining the material world," available to poets, philosophers, artists, and scientists alike.[104] Holistic thinkers like Rachel Carson and Jane Jacobs pointed out the interdependence of many kinds of systems, stressing their strength when functioning harmoniously and their fragility when disrupted by human arrogance.[105] But Teilhardian enthusiasts were often less cautious in the lessons they drew from Teilhard's narrative framing of scientific evidence; they posited human creativity as the main driver of the next phase of evolution, enlisting art, science, and religion in their quest. If the next physical frontier was outer space, then, the Jesuit William Lynch mused in the early 1960s, "how much further can we not go in imagining the creation of the new by the inner life of man," the "creative liberty" granted to humanity by God.[106]

During the first years of Teilhard's popularity, a new genre emerged, called, following the artist Allen Kaprow, "environments." These works, as Nisbet notes of Kaprow's 1961 *Yard*, "paradoxically . . . aspired to generate [their] own complete environments, while at the same time working in conjunction with the existing environmental conditions of [their sites]."[107] Like modernist architects, these artists sought to organize an entire space and condition the response of viewers, while acknowledging that changing natural conditions like weather, as well as the irreducibly chaotic actions of people within the space, would defeat aspirations to complete control. The cosmic vision of holism—which insisted that outer space, the inner space of the psyche, and the physical spaces human beings inhabited were all related—shaped a number of Catholic "environments" of the long 1960s, both imagined and real, as architects and artists sought to overcome a lengthy history of dividing the sacred space of the Mass from the supposedly profane spaces of the world. (See chap. 5 and 6.)

This development was already well under way in the 1950s. The Chapel of the Holy Cross mutated from a skyscraping marvel in Lloyd Wright's decontextualized 1930s design to a structure that, while in its own way a technological triumph, was deeply concerned with its intimate relationship to its surroundings and with visitors' immersion in the dramatic landscape visible beyond the altar. Postwar interest in master site plans, too, prioritized the relationship of buildings to one another within a complex landscape. The desire to symbolically align "religion" and "science," particularly, surfaced in educational design.[108] Pietro Belluschi and the monks at Portsmouth Abbey, for example, reframed their master plan to bring the school science building into direct sight of the new church, while monumental artworks like Louisa Jenkins's mosaic at the College of the Holy Names, Oakland (1957) and Roman Verostko, OSB's ceramic tile mural at St. Vincent College in Latrobe, Pennsylvania (1958–60), graphically associated the colleges' joint interest in science, the arts, and religion. Monasteries themselves attracted architects as a kind of total environment: Marcel Breuer, Gyo Obata, Louis Kahn, and others jumped at the chance to design entire communities—spaces eschatologically framed as "signs and foretastes of the New Jerusalem" as well as protective enclaves where, in the heart of aerospace country, a new generation of desert monks planned to "keep alive the values necessary for the survival of the world."[109]

Monastic environments had for centuries invited inhabitants and visitors into a constructed physical space focusing concentration on the ecology of a small area and on the depths of the soul, Lynch's "inner life of man." As countercultural spaces avant la lettre, it is unsurprising to find monastic design strategies recreated by, among others, the Catholic-raised Timothy Leary, whose Big House at Millbrook, New York (along with the "Time Chamber" he created at his home in Massachusetts) testified to his belief that controlled environments were necessary for truly "fostering cognitive transformation" with the aid of psychedelic drugs.[110] Although the counterculture's interest in

"Eastern religions" is better known, in its quest for holistic spirituality it also maintained intimate engagements with Catholic theology and practice, both because Catholic thinkers like Teilhard attracted early counterculture theorists, and because Catholics sought out countercultural experiences for their own spiritual development.

In *The Joyous Cosmology*, the sometime Episcopalian priest and counterculture guru Alan Watts suggested that psychedelics were truly Eucharistic, incarnating and revealing divine presence in the world. According to Watts, overcivilization had sundered primordial humanity from nature and people from their own integrated humanity; but he hoped that from the "sacramental" drug-induced insight of the basic interconnectedness of all life, Western culture was "beginning to evolve a new image of man, not as a spirit imprisoned in incompatible flesh, but as an organism inseparable from his social and natural environment." Because of the Catholic theological recognition of " 'extraordinary' graces, often of mystical insight, which descend spontaneously outside the ordinary or regular means that the Church provides through the sacraments and the disciplines of prayer," he felt that "only special pleading can maintain that the graces mediated through mushrooms . . . and scientists are artificial and spurious in contrast with those which come through religious discipline."[111]

Watts was far from the only person to associate the Eucharist with the opening of the doors of perception. Henri Bergson's theory of evolutionary dynamism, so crucial to Teilhard's thought, was also important to early assessments of LSD.[112] Al Hubbard, a Canadian Catholic businessman who saw (per Aldous Huxley) "LSD-25 as an instrument for validating Catholic doctrines and giving new life to Catholic symbols," introduced hundreds in North America to what he identified as the beatific vision, newly and reliably accessible through psychedelics.[113] In 1960s Berkeley, Timothy Leary and the Berrigan brothers mixed in the same social circles, all interested in investigating human evolution, while the theologian John Courtney Murray, SJ, not only experimented with LSD but suggested its use to assist in the spiritual exercises of Ignatius Loyola, which for hundreds of years had called on practitioners to use their imaginative inner sight as a route to divine encounter.[114]

The biography of the artist Louisa Jenkins illustrates how Catholic thought and practice, Teilhardian evolutionary theology, radical architecture, and psychedelics could mesh easily in the search for holistic unity. Jenkins, a resident of the artists' colony at Big Sur, had studied yoga, Eastern religions, kabbalah, alchemy, and Jungian archetypes during the 1950s. Her reading of Teilhard and her experience of taking LSD jointly developed a holistic vision that permeated her life and work from the late 1950s until her death in 1989. She originally undertook both pursuits in the company of her friend Clare Boothe Luce, who, like Jenkins, had converted to Catholicism in the aftermath of a beloved child's death. Initial contact as Jenkins worked on mosaics for Luce's memorial Chapel of St. Ann in Palo Alto deepened into a long-lasting spiritual companionship, beginning when Luce translated *Le phénomène humain*, a gift from the Jungian ethnologist Maud Oakes, during an extended visit to Jenkins's Carmel home. Jenkins was initially more skeptical about LSD, writing to Luce in February 1959 that she should

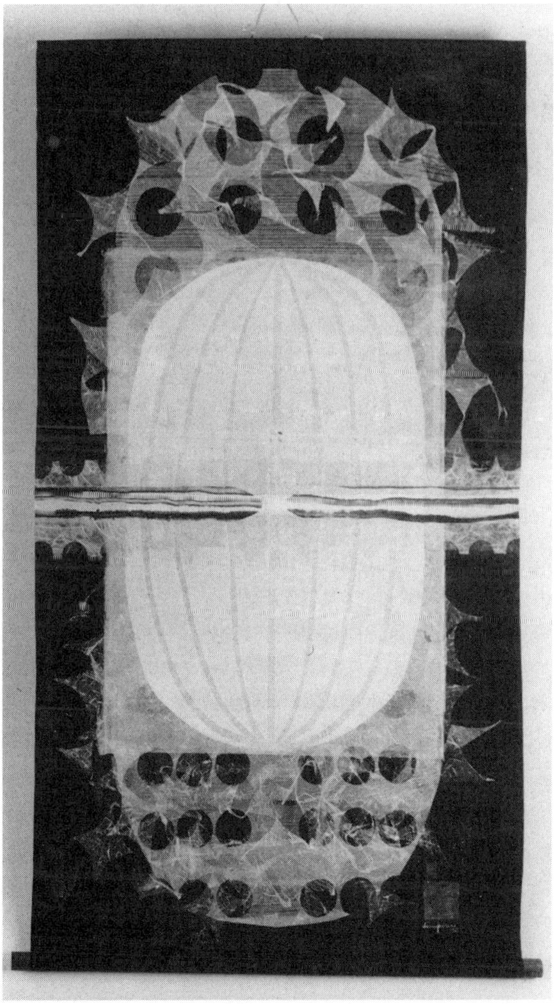

FIGURE 4.6. *Threshold of Reflection*, ink and paint on Japanese paper (Louisa Jenkins, mid-1960s). Jenkins described this, the eleventh in a series of fourteen scrolls on Teilhardian themes called the *Stations of Life*, as "that place where the expanding frontiers of our world change to converging ones." Photo: GLIT, 15-19-01.

"think twice about taking it (the drug)."[115] But by December, she was thanking Luce for giving her "Bucky [Fuller], Gerald [Heard], LSD . . . my very works in the studio."[116] Jenkins's introduction to psychedelics occurred in a sacramental context. Following a monastic "day of recollection" and an early-morning Mass said by John Courtney Murray at Luce's Arizona ranch, Gerald Heard "gave [her] the tiny pill with his blessing."[117] Her experience suggested that access to cosmic vision through the mind's expansion was a vital moment in cosmogenesis: "[Scientists are] trying to uncover the mystery of the mind and how it works. This is the great frontier of our age, and how exciting it is to be living now. We are poised for that new leap into the unknown area of the noosphere foreseen by Teilhard de Chardin."[118] LSD would help change the mental structures blocking evolution toward the Omega Point.

Jenkins's wide-ranging pursuit of new vision, like that of many countercultural denizens, was both articulated in spatial terms and sought through immersive experiences in physical spaces blending the constructed with the natural.[119] She was particularly interested in R. Buckminster Fuller's geodesic domes, planning several times to build one for a studio or living space.[120] She also sustained long and fruitful collaborations with several American monasteries, many of which were rethinking the meaning of the cloister in the wake of Vatican II. In June 1969, for example, the normally enclosed Benedictine sisters of Regina Laudis in Connecticut spent a day sitting on hay bales in the cow barn along with their lay guests, including Jenkins and Maurice Lavanoux, while Fuller held forth on "spaceship earth."[121] Jenkins not only visited St. Andrew's Abbey in California frequently but taught a number of artistic workshops for monks and lay guests alike. Although her plan to build a geodesic dome there never came to fruition, her mosaics and a rare stained glass design remain the complex's dominant decorative elements.

Despite burgeoning moral panic over psychedelics during the later 1960s, some Catholics continued to be intrigued by the spiritual possibilities of countercultural total environments. Priest-sociologist Andrew Greeley, predicting in 1969 the contours of *Religion in the Year 2000*, suggested that "one of the best places to look for hints as to the liturgy of the future is the world of psychedelia, where much of the authentic, yet bizarre 'liturgical' innovation is going on."[122] The UC–Santa Barbara students tripping out in communion with Michael Dvortcsak's Teilhardian painting evidently intuited this same connection. Catholics, often in collaboration with other Christians, were also interested in creating total environments for worship, as at Montreal's Expo 67, where the Christian pavilion drew on McLuhanite and Teilhardian ideas, immersing visitors in a mixed-media overdose.[123] Many of the eight hundred participants at the 1967 International Congress on Religion, Architecture, and the Visual Arts attended a "be-in" worship session, which drew mixed reviews; Maurice Lavanoux thought it bordered on the sacrilegious, while some younger Catholics, like the artist Robert Rambusch, felt it was a positive experience.[124]

Architects and congregations building less far-out Catholic worship spaces, however, were also interested in the abrogation of boundaries and the creation of revelatory total environments. The integration of art, architecture, and the natural world, of interest to modernists for decades, took on new urgency within a holistic frame of reference. The stained glass artist Robert Frei wrote that "in a period of environmental aesthetics . . . unrelated gems have no place," meaning that his own work could not be done independently of either architects or the natural world.[125] A glass artist working in the "total environment" of a church needed to think about "working with sunlight . . . directing transmitted light over other forms, of the movement of the sunlight, of surface texture."[126] This type of integrated environment might produce new spiritual progress; the Benedictine artist Roman Verostko argued that abstract art could create shared worship experiences in this new age where "barriers of self [were] being broken for inter-subjective communication."[127] He wondered "what marvelous things [could] happen" now, when the challenge of art was not to delineate separate forms but rather to "reach beyond with creative imagination to unveil the living face of Christ."[128] What would it mean to build a sanctuary "where sacred space is created with cosmic implications that enlarge the action of liturgy, the truth of the Eucharist, and challenge the soul-searching of modern man?"[129]

In seeking to answer this question, artists, architects, and their clients renewed their attention to organic forms and natural found materials, seeing in them an openness to growth.[130] Jean Labatut's mid-1960s Stuart Country Day School of the Sacred Heart took "pains to pay nature the compliment of fruitful alliance," with construction "merely provid[ing] the needed voids for buildings, but [leaving] trees and boulders, even to the extent of incorporating a number of these boulders in the various sections of the buildings and cloister garden."[131] He used a two-ton stone from the grounds as the convent chapel's altar. William Granger Ryan, the president of Seton Hill College, asked the artist Gary Jurysta to create a chalice that would be "alive" and "unfinished" and thus "express . . . the quality of both human life and the liturgy." The two men finally settled, for the chalice's stem, on a piece of grapevine that Ryan had found while walking. They sought to leave open the possibilities of growth and change that they felt were impossible with typical "cold" and "machine-like" chalices, "well-polished" and "precisely made."[132]

FIGURE 4.7. Temporary student chapel at the University of St. Thomas, Houston, Texas (Glenn Heim, 1966). Photo: GLIT, 30-40-01.

Liturgists and architects of the later 1960s also thought differently about what it meant to create a "distraction" from the altar and the Eucharist. Only a few years earlier, modernist churches had minimized not only side altars and statues but visual contact with the world beyond the church, sometimes to the point of having no windows at all, as at St. Richard's in Jackson, Mississippi. New thought about the integration of the Eucharist and creation, however, now suggested that visual contact with the outside world might enhance, rather than detract from, the liturgy at the altar. Liturgists suggested using filmstrips or slides showing the stars, or the Earth as seen from space, as part of special services or even during Sunday Mass.[133] Liturgical dancers practiced in "natural" public parks before bringing their prayer back to the rest of the congregation.[134] Architects of new buildings, meanwhile, provided expanses of clear glass through which worshippers could be fully aware of the natural world.[135] A temporary chapel at the University of St. Thomas in Houston, designed by seminarian Glenn Heim in 1966, featured backless benches and a wall of glass opening out to the college's famous Philip Johnson–designed mall (fig. 4.7).[136] Ralph Rapson, the architect of St. Thomas Aquinas parish church in St. Paul Park, Minnesota, took a special interest in uniting inside and outside.[137] His 1969 design incorporated heavy redwood beams, the remains of which were also used to build sanctuary furniture and benches for the narthex, and a clerestory inviting congregants to relate the trees they could see through the windows with the Eucharist. Rapson used more clear glass in the narthex as well, and further elided the inside/outside distinction by using the same pebble flooring for both vestibule and plaza. At St. Peter's in Pacifica, California, Mario Ciampi surrounded his 1965 church with a sunken garden, visible through, as the manufacturer put it, "a continuous, encircling wall of ASG's Starlux plate glass," chosen because it would "bring in all the natural beauty of the wooded basin in which the church is set" (fig. 4.8).[138]

Finally, the search for a meaningful total environment often meant the use of flexible architecture, understood as more permeable than monumental and enclosed buildings. At the Chapel + Cultural Center at Rensselaer Polytechnic Institute in Troy, New York, the congregation insisted on an exterior plaza, visible from the baptistery, as another kind of unifying worship space (see chap. 6). Clovis Heimsath's flexible design for Texas Southern's Newman Center also expressed this idea; in its dedication booklet, the congregation proclaimed that the building "is not to be a refuge or an escape" but to "encompass the real world inside and outside." As Maurice Lavanoux commented, the

FIGURE 4.8. Advertisement for Starlux plate glass, showing St. Peter's, Pacifica, California (Mario Ciampi, 1965). Photo: *Architectural Record*.

"elastic operation" of Heimsath's design served a purpose, with the entrance "not present[ing] a barrier, a wall," and "outside flow[ing] inside to make one world. Inside there is still openness of space, the light of the sky, the beauty of nature."[139] Heimsath's carefully constructed environment sought to create a space where students could understand the coherent integration of all facets of creation.

THE OMEGA SEED: PAOLO SOLERI'S ARCOLOGICAL SALVATION

Teilhardian evolutionary theory presented both a solution to ecological and political crisis and the promise of a salvific expansion of consciousness as individuals melded with the emerging world soul. To participate in noogenesis was a matter of mysticism, an exploration into the "inner space" of the collective unconscious, but it also called for performance of the practical and scientific tasks that might lead humanity into the eschatological future. Remaking the inner self through the practices of immersive integration was not only, for Teilhardians, a matter of personal salvation, but a step toward collective evolution and the erasure of interpersonal and political boundaries. The political work involved in this evolution tended to be conceived of in the postatomic spatial terms of "one-worldism," as Fr. Jim Nielsen put it in a sermon at New Mexico State University in early 1967: "I'm sure you have heard people say, 'I don't like this one-worldism implicit in the United Nations and the ecumenical movement of the churches.' But . . . does not our American hope for all mankind plus our Christian vision of God's kingdom move us towards a new internationalism?"[140] Catholic astronaut James McDivitt invoked the same language to describe his experience of space travel, commenting that the documents of Vatican II "talked about a one-world community and . . . when you look down from space you don't see the boundaries of nations; all you see is the boundaries between land and water. It's really and truly just one world. . . . You know that there's a lot to be done down there, and it should be done together" (fig. 4.9).[141]

Nielsen and McDivitt, invoking the language of ecumenism, implied both the promise and the risk of Teilhard for Catholic theology: with interpersonal and political boundaries collapsing as humanity's new sight pushed it toward the noosphere, did the Church have a role? While many Teilhardians retained both an interest in his theology and an attachment to Catholicism itself, others found themselves drifting farther and farther from the institutional Church. Perhaps the most idiosyncratic and simultaneously the most brilliant of these figures was the Italian architect Paolo Soleri (1919–2013), who rejected formal

FIGURE 4.9. "Theology makes man as ancient as the universe itself, with a wisdom ever ancient and ever new, stretching from end to end mightily / whether lost in the cosmos or securely rooted to the earth." Banner, St. Alfred the Great Newman Center, Las Cruces, New Mexico, n.d. (ca. 1960s). Photo: GLIT, 17-43-01.

association with the Catholic Church but drew heavily on Teilhard for his own philosophy of design for salvific evolution.[142]

Soleri came to the United States in 1946 to live and work with Frank Lloyd Wright at Taliesin West, where he befriended Mark Mills. After several years back in Italy, Soleri returned to Arizona in 1956 and began making ceramic bells to support his family. He also read Teilhard intensively, and, in the desert near Scottsdale, continued to work out the principles that would make him one of the most important pioneers of ecological design. Soleri's handwritten comments on a December 1964 sketch show him in the final throes of establishing his core idea. "It follows," he wrote, that "under the pressure of the population explosion, complexification of life, reverence for nature, [and?] maturing consciousness about the aesthetic-compassionate nature of matter, and armed with the skill and power of self [adjusting???] technology: man will transfigure the earth and construct human ecologies. Architecture become [*sic*] archology. . . . Archology is architecture blossoming into the ecological. Archology is compassionate ecology." Soon spelled *arcology*, Soleri's solution to the ecological crisis of a finite planet and a growing human population called on architects to exploit technology in the service of, not just building, but transfiguration.[143]

Soleri's 1972 essay "Religion as Simulation" navigated between his devout Teilhardianism and his suspicion of Teilhard's ecclesiastical commitments. Religion, he wrote, was "instrumental, not in discovering our origins, but in creating the future." God, "a hypothesis life cannot do without," was "a hypothesis in the process of implementing fragments of itself." Religions, as the creations of unevolved humankind, were at best simulacra of the "possible reality which would occur if the process of sensitization going on now on the earth and elsewhere would . . . develop exponentially, calling into cause the whole of the physical universe, transforming its bleak emptiness and the isolation of its sensitized species, man included, into the radiance of the Omega God." Like other Teilhardians, Soleri held out hope that technology could be harnessed by "sensitizing" humanity to develop the seed of a new creation. Omega, the end, would be a new genesis.[144]

Soleri elaborated dozens of arcologies—designs for compact vertical cities that would enable human beings to make sustainable use of the Earth's resources while simultaneously engineering an evolutionary society. His twenty-sixth speculative arcology, titled "Theology," invited humans to a "restoration, on necessarily new levels" of monasticism (fig. 4.10). In this "learning center," with space for thirteen thousand people on eighty-three acres of surface and cave shafts for research, study, and industrial production, Soleri hoped, "physical or territorial interdependence" would be "the first step into a practicable ecumenism." As members of varying religious and ethnic groups were forced to rely on each other in tightly packed arcological spaces, humanity might take evolutionary steps toward the Omega Seed, even if only in the small beginnings of "a little more hope, a little more grace, a little less bigotry."

The Corcoran Gallery and the Whitney Museum showed Soleri's work in 1970, the year after MIT Press released his collection *Arcology: The City in the Image of Man*. Maurice Lavanoux visited the Whitney in July, spending "several

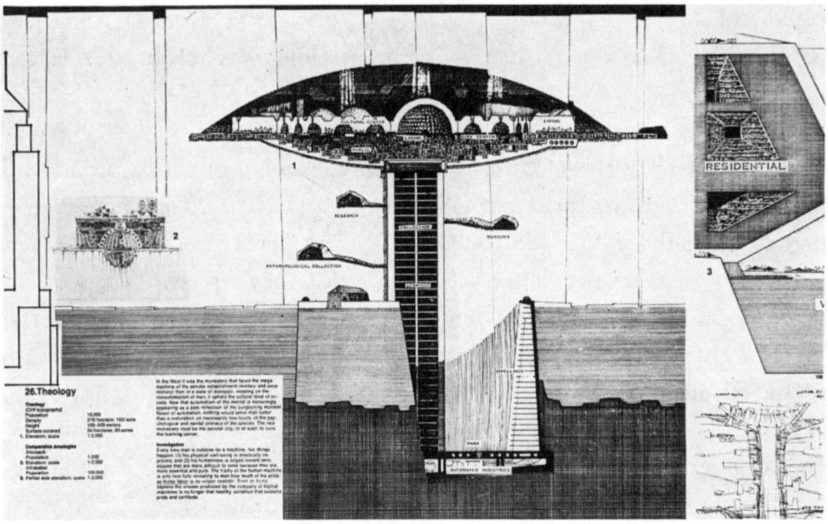

FIGURE 4.10. Paolo Soleri, "Theology." Arcology designed for a population of thirteen thousand. From *Arcology: The City in the Image of Man* (MIT Press, 1969). Photo: Cosanti Foundation.

hours" in the "fantastic" exhibit. "What an extraordinary person [Soleri] must be," he wrote to Mark Mills; "at least his work, as exhibited, is overwhelming."[145] Catholic or no, Soleri's theological commitment seemed plain. In 1970, he began building his first livable arcology, at Arcosanti, Arizona, a project that consumed the rest of his life. In an early progress report soliciting students, labor, and financial support, Soleri made it clear that "the arcological commitment" was not just a matter of developing technocratic solutions for population explosion and environmental trauma; it was "indispensable" because its physical elements would make "the state of grace (esthetogenesis) possible for a socially and individually healthy man on an ecologically healthy earth."[146] His work drew pilgrims ranging from the hippies of experimental communes to older and more experienced architects and builders—the Catholics Mark and Barbara Mills and Clovis and Maryann Heimsath among them.[147] Still under construction today, Arcosanti stands as a physical link to the Teilhardian moment in American religion and architecture.[148]

The *New York Times* architecture critic Ada Louise Huxtable might have had her doubts about Soleri's quixotic project, but she knew what to call a man who intended to revolutionize city design with "six shovels, some rakes, a cement mixer, some stouthearted graduate students and a firm intellectual conviction." If Arcosanti was "a dream," Huxtable concluded, "it is the very best kind." Her review of Soleri's Corcoran exhibit was headlined "Prophet in the Desert."[149]

"Prophecy" was an apt description, applied frequently to Teilhard's thought, as well as to the work of his followers who sought to, as Bernard Murchland put it, "go forth to conquer the future" and who set themselves in opposition to those Pope John XXIII called "prophets of doom."[150] Rather, like their secular science fiction contemporaries, they discerned the seeds of a new beginning in the apocalyptic threat technology posed to their world. Variously turning their attention to space travel, to intricate vertical cities, to art and architecture revealing the organic world, and to mind-expanding drugs as the basis for cosmogenesis, they participated in the twentieth-century revival of Christianity's eschatological vision even as they wondered if the present form of the Church prevented evolution rather than assisted it. But other Catholics—who also sometimes thought of themselves as prophets—kept that far horizon in mind while directing their gaze closer to home, to the crumbling American cities where, they insisted, God was present, too.

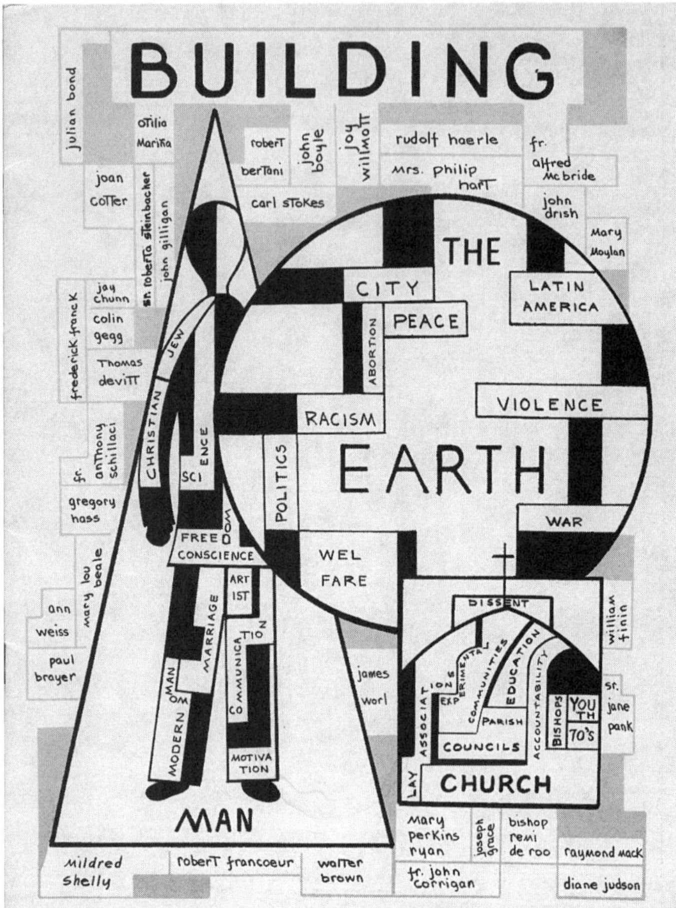

FIGURE 5.1. Program cover for the National Association of Laymen's 1969 convention. With a design invoking the famous Trylon and Perisphere of the 1939 World's Fair, the NAL's convention cover invited attendees to consider the overlapping interrelationship of "Man," "Church," and "Earth." The names listed around the edge for attendees' consideration include Catholic intellectuals like the Teilhard expert Robert Francoeur and the education theorist Mary Perkins Ryan, as well as other notable figures like the civil rights activist Julian Bond. Photo: JAL series 4, "Building the Earth" program cover, 1969, Marquette University Archives.

CHAPTER FIVE

THE SECULAR CITY

To this people you said,
I did not make the earth to lie idle,
I made it to be your home.
And so they drew from it bread and wine,
and opened rivers in the rock.
They raised up cities from the ground,
and sang new songs in the air.

ERNEST C. FERLITA, SJ, "The Canon of the Pilgrim Church," 1967

On December 11, 1966, just a few days after the first anniversary of the closing of the Second Vatican Council, Richard Cardinal Cushing released a pastoral letter to his archdiocese of Boston titled "The Servant Church: A Beginning and a Blueprint." It was also the third Sunday of Advent—known as Gaudete Sunday, after the first word of the introit of that day's Mass, "rejoice"—itself the one-year anniversary of the release of the council's final document

Gaudium et spes, the Pastoral Constitution on the Church in the Modern World. The council, Cushing wrote, had "drawn up a pattern of action for the years ahead, a clear blueprint for the future." Now it remained to build from the blueprint, to "make alive locally the renewal of faith which had been the special work of the council."[1]

Cushing's letter answered the council's "two basic questions": namely, "what is the Church and what is her mission in the world today?" The Church, he wrote, following the council's conclusion in *Lumen gentium* (1964), "is fundamentally a mystery, which is to say that it is the sacramental presence of Christ in the world." Its mission, then, was "to spend herself in realizing the Kingdom of God among men." After a discussion of war, poverty, racism, and the "division of churches" as major problems preventing this realization, Cushing devoted the balance of his letter to explaining how he intended to reform archdiocesan administration in Boston to address them, establishing new commissions and apostolates and revamping clerical formation. He concluded with a brief meditation linking the political, the sacramental, and the eschatological:

> Christ comes to us in every problem to be solved, in every situation to be reconciled, in every human being to be healed. Theologians often speak of "future eschatology" (the fact that Christ will come again at the end of time), it is imperative that we also speak of "realized eschatology" (the fact that Christ comes to us in the here and now). . . . One of the happy results of the current aggiornamento in the Church is that of deeper insights into the meaning and significance of the Eucharistic Celebration. This is our principal preparation for Christ's Second Coming. . . . Here we are given 'food for the journey' so that we can pursue the difficult work of healing and reconciliation which is the ministry of this Pilgrim Church. . . . Let us . . . go forward together to build the Kingdom of God among men.[2]

Sacramental action united the new Jerusalem of the future eschaton, the city of Boston in which Christ could be met here and now, and the churches where massgoing Catholics could receive the Eucharist and so be fed for a journey through the spaces of the earthly city on its way to the future. Faithful Catholics, the Cardinal wrote, were called upon to "leave behind that narrow . . . notion that religion is purely 'otherworldly,' that it has nothing to do with 'the secular city.'"[3]

Cushing's pastoral—like many other mid-twentieth-century Catholic efforts to encourage "this-worldly" religious observance—invoked two influential theological statements on the relationship of Church and world, both released in late 1965: *Gaudium et spes*, promulgated by the Catholic bishops of the world in solemn council; and a slim polemic by the young Baptist theologian Harvey Cox, *The Secular City*, written rapidly as "a study resource . . . for the National Student Christian Federation" then published by Macmillan.[4] Despite their dramatically different institutional contexts, these two documents were taken collectively to heart by thousands of American Catholics. Both contended that the fates of Church and city were intertwined, and both inspired Catholic architects and liturgists—not to mention diocesan bureaucrats—to think through their implications for worship space during a decade of rapid urban transformation. At a time when American cities were being remade by federal intervention and by the simultaneous migration of whites (often Catholics) to the suburbs and Southern blacks to Northern cities, many American Catholics read these documents as calls to ask how church buildings could both reflect the Church's salvific urban mission and better promote the future success of that mission. As ways of building out Vatican II's "blueprint," they proposed renovation techniques, the rethinking of interior spatial organization, close attention to the relationship between church buildings and neighborhoods, innovative sites for urban worship, and ecumenical partnerships unthinkable only a few years earlier.

Unlike Paolo Soleri's arcologies and other fantastical future-city projections, many of these proposals were immediately practical, based on up to the minute sociological studies, sometimes immersing architects and liturgists in the minutiae of federal housing policy. In making them, architects and liturgists drew on a long Catholic tradition of transgressing the boundaries between interior and exterior worship spaces. Yet they also signaled a new approach to the relationship between the sanctuary and the city, one driven by the imaginative co-location of worship space, political activity, and eschatological salvation suggested in Cushing's pastoral. Residents and nonresidents, Catholics and non-Catholics, priests and urban planners—all saw the city as a matter of apartments and potholes, but also as a spiritually powerful place, potentially both destructive and salvific. In Robert Orsi's words, "Spaces on the urban landscape [became] both geographical sites where real people live and constructions of terror and desire."[5]

This understanding of the city was not entirely new to the postconciliar period. Catholic ambiguity toward the city existed prior to the 1960s, but *Gaudium et spes* and *The Secular City* spurred development of a true Catholic "secular theology." Drawing on and transforming preconciliar urban ministries, American Catholic futurists of the 1960s looked to new kinds of church buildings to encourage the mutual eschatological salvation of Church and city.

Taking up the architect Patrick Quinn's call not to "*forget that the future city is already with us, we are living in it*,"[6] they challenged the meticulously maintained dichotomies between future and realized eschatology, between "sacred" and "profane" space, projecting an incarnational mysticism into the entire urban complex. In many ways, this vision extended the reach of the Church into new corners of the city, and so it was often supported and even funded by dioceses and religious orders. But while the Church's institutional power centers typically focused on the responsibility of the Church to save the city, other Catholics saw the relationship as reciprocal: the city was to be understood as a salvific gift to the Church. As the Church's role in the Vietnam War and American racial politics came under increasing activist scrutiny in the late 1960s, this aspect of secular theology called into question long-standing spatial norms that had previously carved out worship space as politically inviolate. The eruption of political demonstrations within church buildings during the late 1960s represented both the logical extension of secular theology, and its institutional limit.

"A PEOPLE WHOSE CITY IS TO COME"

The history of Catholic engagement with the twentieth-century American city is marked by profound ambiguities of thought and action. On the one hand, chanceries and lay societies alike claimed responsibility for and control over the city as a whole, well beyond the boundaries of the Catholic community. Catherine de Hueck Doherty, Dorothy Day, and members of their Friendship House and Catholic Worker communities wrote movingly of finding Christ in the tired faces of the urban poor.[7] Meanwhile, Catholic presence in the form of churches, convents, schools, land speculation, urban processions, and festivals had shaped and ordered the land planning and visible street activity of all major American cities, and powerful lay and clerical Catholics were intimately involved in pre-1960s urban regulatory regimes of both land use and social morality.[8] These campaigns ranged from the eradication of "indecent" entertainment to the improvement of housing policy and (not coincidentally) race relations. The layman Dennis Clark, for example, worked with both the Philadelphia Housing Council and the Catholic Interracial Council in the 1950s; his book *Cities in Crisis* (1960) called for greater attention to housing and racial issues by the institutional Church.[9] A "Workshop on Housing and Planning" at the National Catholic Social Action Conference (NCSAC) of August 1960 revealed the depth of lay expertise in this area: five of seven participants were lay professionals.[10] Priest-sociologists like Andrew Greeley and Gerard Murphy, SJ, took an interest, as did the National Catholic Welfare Council's Social Action Department, which, through the extensive correspondence of its director Msgr. George G. Higgins, served as a hub for those interested in urban issues, just as the Liturgical Arts Society did for those interested in the arts.[11]

The massive urban planning projects of the mid-twentieth century also seemed to demand some kind of Catholic response. The Washington office of the National Conference of Catholic Charities (NCCC), for example, attempted to "humanize" an urban renewal project displacing thousands of residents from Southwest Washington, DC, during the 1950s.[12] The NCCC hired Fr. Robert Howes of Worcester, Massachusetts, then on a summer break from a master's program in city planning at MIT, to study government policy related to the project, particularly its effects on lower-income residents.[13] As part of NCCC's effort to make sure that urban renewal had "an interest in the human aspects of renewal"—specifically, community cohesion and low-income housing—Howes testified before the Committee on the District of Columbia in the House of Representatives.[14] The Archdiocesan Council of Catholic Men devoted an entire day of its annual convention to discussion of the project, keynoted by Francis X. Servaites, director of the National Capital Housing Authority. Servaites, in a classic Catholic Action moment, used the platform provided by his government position to excoriate that government for its inadequate attention to the problems of low-income families.[15] Later Catholic interventions in urban planning were built on these and other 1950s efforts to secure better housing for low- and lower-middle-income families, to consider the effects of urban renewal on the population, and to work with and within government agencies to pursue a better urban environment for all.[16]

Despite claims of concern for and control over the entire urban complex, however, until the mid-1960s, institutional Catholic participation in informal and formal urban planning more typically took the form of enclosure: parish complexes of church, rectory, convent, and school frequently occupied entire city blocks, with a ring of Catholic homeowners surrounding the lot.[17] Seminaries and novitiates were generally located away from cities and imposed news blackouts on their students, preventing them from having much contact with or even knowledge of urban life. This defensive building pattern had developed in the context of Catholic immigration into often hostile nineteenth- and early twentieth-century American urban territory, but also from deep theological roots dating to the earliest centuries of the Church.

The monastics of the Egyptian desert had abandoned the luxuries of Alexandria in pursuit of the spiritual life as early as the third century. As he watched the Roman world collapse after the city's sack, St. Augustine, the West's most influential theologian, played brilliantly on biblical images of the eschatological city, the "new Jerusalem" that would replace the sinful world, to contrast the temporal, and temporary, earthly city (or city of man) with the eternal, triumphant city of God, to be inhabited by those who were focused on the divine rather than on present cares. Augustine's dichotomy was repeated endlessly by many who distrusted and feared the supposedly corrosive effects of urban life on Catholic faith. As late as the 1960s, a priest wrote skeptically that "New York is what we might call the city of man, as opposed to the city of God. . . . Can the Christian soul grow in this environment?"[18] Concerns like these drove a series of episcopally backed efforts during the first half of the twentieth century to move immigrant Catholics away from the coastal cities.[19]

Despite the technological optimism and skyscraper-building energy in some twentieth-century American Catholic periodicals, editorials and articles in the pre–Vatican II period much more often revealed distaste for the city. This phenomenon was not confined to the Church's more politically and theologically conservative precincts. *Commonweal*'s 1925 editorial "The Terrible Super-City," for example, contrasted "fatuous pride" in the prospect of growth with "the misery and essential loneliness of the wretched millions" forced to live in massive futuristic cities.[20] The liturgical movement and the Catholic counterculture of the 1930s through the 1950s, too, persistently attempted to alter the basically urban character of American Catholic life, arguing that the rural life and liturgical movements were "two halves of a circle."[21] A belief in the ennobling nature of rural life impelled the Catholic Worker and other liturgically invested groups to found a variety of communal farms as an alternative to the city, despite the swift collapse of most of these projects beneath the romantic inexperience of the would-be farmers.[22]

Before the late 1960s, American monastic theory joined this generally negative assessment of city life's effect on the soul. Thomas Merton documented his flight from the temptations and distractions of New York to rural Kentucky's Gethsemani Abbey in *The Seven Storey Mountain*, a postwar bestseller that left an enduring mark on the liturgical movement.[23] Twenty years after Merton's entrance into Gethsemani, Aelred Wall, OSB, and several companions left Mount Saviour Monastery in Elmira, New York, for a site in New Mexico so remote that even today reaching it requires favorable conditions for navigating a thirteen-mile dirt road. In December 1964, Wall wrote to supporters that the name of the new foundation, the Monastery of Christ in the Desert, reflected not only their "physical surroundings" but their desire to be "a people of the desert—not a 'settled' people but a people 'whose city is to come.' "[24] For

Wall's countercultural community—as for their contemporaries at Arcosanti, Esalen, Tassajara, and Drop City—the real city, "final and permanent," was located in the eschatological future; reaching it required turning one's eyes away from distractions of metropolis.[25]

THEOLOGIES OF HOPE: *GAUDIUM ET SPES* AND *THE SECULAR CITY*

At the same moment, however, other American Catholics were beginning to draw on different theological resources and to turn toward understanding the city not as a place of temptation or, at best, of rest on pilgrimage, but as a site of God's self-revelation and collaborative action with human beings.[26] Although this phenomenon built on American Catholics' consistent attention to and sacralization of urban space, developments in the 1960s and 1970s ironically turned many Catholic futurists toward a mysticism of the city even as suburbanization had finally drawn an enormous number of white Catholics away from their traditional urban strongholds. This movement, as Robert Orsi notes, sent monks and nuns to build ministries in the new "deserts of Syria and Egypt," now represented by the South Bronx.[27] Thousands of largely white, middle-class Catholics—including the Jesuits of Woodstock College, who left their "setting of grazing land and rolling hills" in rural Maryland for the "contact with urban problems and with secular disciplines" offered by the Upper West Side of Manhattan—committed themselves to temporary or permanent residence in the physically decaying, and increasingly African American and non-Catholic, inner cities.[28]

On one level, questions about building patterns, government services, and economics associated with suburbanization and "urban renewal" were sociological and technocratic. But as Donald Campion, SJ, pointed out in 1966, this population shift coincided with a major ecclesiological development. It was no longer possible or sufficient, Campion argued, for the Church to " 'get out the vote' by simple fiat"; rather, the Church's new consciousness of itself as "the People of God, as the Pilgrim Church, as a missionary community" implied major changes in mission.[29] A year earlier, Campion's fellow Jesuit, the cultural commentator William Lynch, used a four-part series on NBC's *Catholic Hour*, "Images of Hope," to make a similar point. "The City of Man," Lynch narrated, was itself an "image of hope . . . built on our hope and our trust in each other." This City of Man was not a danger to the Christian soul but rather a place where "cousins and co-citizens . . . all of us totally human" found that "kinship in this city is the salvation of" all.[30]

In rethinking the Church's relationship to the city, Catholic futurists married sociological and theological analysis. As the Second Vatican Council came to a close in the last months of 1965, theologically literate American Catholics closely followed its final debates and the release of its culminating document, formally the Pastoral Constitution on the Church in the Modern World, but known to most by its opening words, *Gaudium et spes*. Explaining their new outlook, the council fathers wrote: "The joys and hopes, the griefs and anxieties of the men of this age . . . these are the joys and hopes, the griefs and anxieties of the followers of Christ. . . . The news of salvation . . . is meant for every man. That is why this community realizes that it is truly linked with mankind and its history by the deepest of bonds" (§1). While *Gaudium* mentioned the old dichotomy of the transient city of man and the permanent city of God, it focused on the "fact accessible to faith alone" that "the earthly and the heavenly city penetrate each other." This interpenetration had consequences, the council claimed, for the relationship of Church and city. If "the Church has a saving and eschatological purpose which can be fully attained only in the future world," nevertheless "she is already present in this world, and is composed of men, that is, of members of the earthly city who have a call to form the family of God's children during the present history of the human race" (§40).

Although *Gaudium*'s words on cities challenged American Catholics, it was the document's theological anthropology, its assessment of human nature in light of Christian doctrine, that urged Catholics to rethink their attitude toward crowded urban areas. Human beings can be understood, according to the council, only in the light of Christ; "for by His incarnation the Son of God has united Himself in some fashion with every man" (§22). This was true "not only for Christians, but for all men of good will in whose hearts grace works in an unseen way." Chapter II, "The Community of Mankind," assessed the contemporary world as one of "interdependence," which called Christians to work with one another and with other "men of good will" for both "the progress of the human person" and "the advance of society itself" (§23–25ff). Catholics who saw *Gaudium* as the council's key document took its themes of hope, pilgrimage, eschatological transformation, and "humanization" as their banner in the later 1960s. It was Christians' task not to flee one city for the other, but to live in both at once, drawing the earthly city closer to eschatological transformation while understanding that Christ's incarnation had, in *Commonweal* editor Daniel Callahan's words, "redeemed man and matter," and that "if this is so, then the sacred and the secular have entered into a relationship of unity."[31]

Gaudium did not stand alone in encouraging American Catholics to rethink their engagement with the contemporary city. The revival of eschatology in academic and popular thought focused readers of Protestant and Catholic theology in the later 1960s and 1970s on the doctrine of Christian hope for the redemption of the world, not its abandonment. Very shortly before the promulgation of *Gaudium*, meanwhile, Harvey Cox's *The Secular City* created a popular sensation. The book purported to be about contemporary action but, as the religious historian and Lutheran minister Martin Marty noted, had "a consistent if sometimes hidden obsession with the future."[32] Cox's "affirmative vision of the urban world as man's responsibility" and as the arena for God's action toward a renewed future struck a nerve among Americans of many denominational commitments. Catholics formed a noticeably disproportionate share of Cox's audience, and his work shared with Teilhard's the distinction of being, as Callahan noted, "eagerly passed from hand to hand and quickly adopted by a variety of study groups."[33] Within a year the book, whose first printing had been an already substantial ten thousand copies, had a revised edition, and within a decade it had sold a million copies—astonishing figures for a work of academic theology. Even Catholics who had not read it soon became familiar with Cox's basic ideas through venues such as Cardinal Cushing's pastoral letter, or events like the 1966 Liturgical Week, dedicated to the theme "Worship in the City of Man."[34]

Cox made several arguments eagerly adopted by American Catholic futurists. First, and fundamental to the whole work, he asserted the theological importance of the city and the compatibility of urban life with belief in the biblical God. *The Secular City* projected a future of continued urbanization, technologization, and secularization (in the form of "the collapse of traditional religion").[35] Since the book is littered with statements like "secularization is the liberation of man from religious and metaphysical tutelage," it was easy for careless critics to conclude that Cox belonged among the death-of-God theologians, who saw Christianity as a dead letter in the modern world.[36] But those who read the book more closely saw Cox's real point: one young Catholic woman came away convinced that she "must be committed, *involved*, in the secular world, in my family, with everyone I am associated with, in a Christian way. *Nothing is secular.*"[37] Cox's polemic was directed not against theism, but against the (as he saw it) artificial divide between the "sacred" and the "secular" perpetuated by the external elements of religion: church buildings, vestments, denominational administrative structures.

Arguing that these elements were vestigial, Cox emphasized instead incarnation, emergence, and evolution. New ways of understanding and proclaiming God, new ways of living together in the city, new ways of being the church would come in God's good time, for secularity was not "a static fact but . . . an emergent reality . . . a process."[38] This did not mean that the process would be peaceful and pain-free; Cox thought that the "transition today from the age of Christendom to the new era of urban secularity" would be no less traumatic than the Israelites' passage from slavery to freedom. But while *The Secular City* chastened aspirants to a new Christendom, it exhilarated those with ambitions to heroic sanctity and who, in Teilhard's words (as quoted by Cox) had "in the name of our faith . . . become passionate about the things of this earth."[39] If Christians must reject an ambition to be the keystone of an imperial establishment, they could nevertheless be "God's avant-garde," called to practice a "diakonic function" of "healing the urban fractures" and a "koinoniac function" of making hope visible through fellowship.[40] They could look forward to a future of constant change, since "the church is . . . a people whose task it is to discern the action of God in the world and to join in his work"; the Church's compulsion must not be to maintain itself, but rather to constantly shift locations to wherever the action might be. Therefore, the Church "must allow itself to be broken and reshaped continuously by God's continuous action." It would have the honor of "struggling alongside people of many persuasions" to do God's will.[41]

On the strength of these ideas, Cox became one of the most influential public theologians of the 1960s. *Commonweal* hired him as a columnist in the fall of 1966. In the opening installment of "The Secular City," he commented wryly that the editors, "in a moment of unprecedented insight," had commissioned him "to deal with the whole gamut of modern urban secular life, with all possibilities and pitfalls, illuminated of course by a lucid theological perspective." He undertook, therefore, to provide readers with a sampling of urban forecasting theories, but also with a clear argument that cities would not "develop" of themselves. Rather, human beings, decision-makers, would bear responsibility "in full consciousness" for "what kind of city (and thus what kind of world) we want to build."[42] The comprehensiveness of this brief appealed to the many Catholics who sought an integrated, synthetic approach to religious practice and ethical action.[43] And like *Gaudium et spes*, *The Secular City* obligated Christians to learn about and from the modern world, envisioning a future of mutual enrichment. Catholics who took up this charge were invited to proclaim, with the influential African American liturgist Clarence Rivers, that

> There's a city in the making
> Call it any name you will—
> Utopia, Jerusalem
> Or better, better still
> It is everywhere, no special place;

And yet is never seen
Except by men of vision,
by men who dare to dream. . . .

There's a city in the making
Call it by a million names
New York, New Delhi, Amsterdam
Kinshasa, Moscow, or Berlin
It's where you are and work for it;
Your blood and sweat and tears,
Your care, my friends, will build its walls;
Your love will make it real.[44]

Catholic ministries of incarnational, eschatological presence built on *Gaudium et spes* and *The Secular City* would not require withdrawal to the desert; they would instead transform the cities of the present into the city of God's future.

"THE MAXIMUM USE OF OUR FACILITIES": TRANSFORMING PARISH PLANTS FOR THE URBAN FUTURE

By the mid-1960s, many former Catholic urban strongholds had been hollowed out by suburbanization and huge new investments had been made in suburban parish plants.[45] One realistic response would have been to close city churches and schools with sharply decreasing revenue and, due to their age, sharply increasing maintenance costs. This was the approach taken by many Protestant and Jewish congregations during this period. Yet the Catholic administrative structure of the territorial parish significantly raised the logistical difficulty of such a move.[46] In addition, American Catholics attuned to new secular theologies concluded that the Church had an obligation to "continue to inhabit the inner city" in order to fulfill its "incarnational role in the contemporary community."[47] For many, this meant continuing or developing a presence of, in the sociologist Sr. Marie Augusta Neal's words, "trained Christians" who could "express compassion for existing conditions and understanding of ways to remedy them" and who were committed to living as coworkers with others in the city as they undertook "the long and arduous task of reshaping the city into a community of the people of God."[48]

If Catholics were dazzled by the possibilities inherent in rethinking the role of the church in the city, they were also aware of the constraints imposed by preexisting structures. It might have been true that "there [was] nothing in Revelation that would oppose the decision of a pope to destroy every existing church building in the world and to order that, henceforth, priests should minister to the people exclusively in their homes or places of work"; but even Daniel Callahan did not go quite as far as advocating that outcome.[49] Catholics who regarded their massive parish plants as expensive and forbidding white elephants might fantasize about destroying them, but they seldom if ever actually did so. In practice, preexisting buildings affected how Catholics conceptualized the future of their worship space. The priests serving one Chicago parish consulted an architect and repainted their "ungainly three-story parish house" in "reds, blues, whites, oranges, and other hues not usually associated with rectories." They hung prints by Gauguin, Matisse, and Corita Kent, with a new sign out front reading, "Presentation Parish House—Welcome." Their seven-hundred-seat school and separate community center began to serve many non-Catholic children and other neighborhood residents. But despite success in turning their plant to new uses, the priests conceded that if they hadn't had it, they "might have selected a different kind of apostolate, one perhaps headquartered in a storefront or in one of [their] overpopulated apartment buildings." The legacy of the parish's past constrained its future. Instead of moving into unconventional new spaces, the priests had to do their best to "exploit [our] buildings and turn them into assets rather than liabilities in the work of Christ."[50]

As at Presentation, Catholics seeking new ways to incarnate the church in the city were generally renovating rather than building from scratch, rethinking rather than inventing. St. Michael's and St. Edward's, a Brooklyn parish, opted for a new altar made of repurposed rails from the nearby Myrtle Avenue El, a striking choice that brought the everyday technology of the city to the heart of the liturgy.[51] Visual interpretations of Cox's theme envisioned the church in service to the world and vice versa. After he designed banners for the Vatican Pavilion at the 1964 World's Fair, Norman Laliberté was commissioned by the Church of St. James the Less in Jamesburg, New Jersey, to create a vast banner entitled "Man in the Religious and Secular City" for its 1967 renovation (fig. 5.2). Laliberté's visual interpretation of Cox's theology melded panels on classic biblical and ecclesial themes with symbols signifying the arts, technology, and human love, culminating in panels on peace, "death now seen as a new beginning," and the judgment of Church and world alike.[52]

The theme of judgment and responsibility sounded beneath secular theology's surface optimism. For Marymount (Manhattan) College administrators, a postconciliar chapel renovation was not just a response to changing liturgical norms but "an opportunity to cooperate with secular society for a 'good' city,"

FIGURE 5.2. Renovation of St. James the Less, Jamesburg, New Jersey (1967). Willy Malarcher for Rambusch Company, liturgical consultant. Banner ("Man in the Religious and Secular City") by Norman Laliberté. Note the brighter lighting over the nave, the altar moved forward, and the tabernacle moved off-axis (*right side of photo*). Photo: GLIT, 17-24-01.

to "assist in defining and realizing the city's aspirations." The chapel would be "a service . . . an 'investment' in reviving the core of the city. . . . An experiment, an opportunity."[53] More soberly, the liturgist Robert Hovda wondered, "Isn't it time to stop and think about church property and community responsibility, about the uses to which we put the buildings and other property of the churches and synagogues?"[54] The "maximum use of our facilities" for poor (and often African American) city residents would be a way of repenting for the Church's part in creating the conditions of racism and poverty; Catholics should be open to what neighborhoods needed space for, rather than dictating what use could be made of their churches, schools, and parish halls.[55] In fact, Hovda and others suggested that there was no contradiction in using a space for liturgy and for other purposes. Such spaces might help people understand better how liturgy and daily life were related to each other. Hovda's championing of the multipurpose church saw the future of the ecclesia, the assembly, and the future of the polis, the city, as profoundly intertwined.

The concept of the multipurpose church space—perhaps not even administered by Catholics—signals that American Catholics intrigued by secular mysticism responded through political and social action, but also by attempting to transform centuries-old attitudes about sacred space. They argued that rather than setting certain places apart for the worship of God, the Church needed an aesthetic of openness and transparency, and locations in places of need. While economics and migration patterns ensured that most church projects in American cities of the 1960s were renovations rather than new buildings, architects and liturgists did put significant thought into what kinds of churches might be appropriate for the secular city of the future. These proposals interrelated church and city, focusing on architectural and spatial blending rather than on drawing Catholics out of the city into a timeless celestial world. As José Luis Sert commented, "Today, instead of bringing people into church, we must bring the church to the people."[56]

Architects and Catholic patrons alike seized on the idea of downtown churches amid the daily buzz of office work. Urban chapels—which could operate simultaneously as traditional mission efforts and as new engagements of the sacred and secular—generated enthusiasm from both conservative and progressive diocesan officials, priests and religious, and laity. The Chapel of St. Christopher, which opened in 1965 in an office building on East 43rd Street in Manhattan, invited urban workers to daily Mass and gave them a quiet space in which to focus on the presence of the reserved Eucharist, while constantly reminding them of their "responsibility to sanctify the business world in God's name."[57] The chapel attracted more than five hundred massgoers a day; it was a simple space with a central altar, revolutionary neither in conception nor purpose, but nevertheless clearly understood as part of an overall archdiocesan effort to update the relationship between the Church and the city.[58] The Capuchin priests who as late as 1945 had celebrated their move from the Bronx to Staunton, Virginia, on the grounds that "the City was not an ideal place for a Religious House of Studies," announced plans in 1972 to build a new friary a block from Penn Station, complete with sidewalk-facing windows and a large, street-facing stained glass and metal sculpture, "Christ in the City" (fig. 5.3).[59]

More elaborately planned than the Chapel of St. Christopher was the Chapel of St. Botolph, intended for the Government Center development in downtown Boston.[60] The Archdiocese of Boston, in collaboration with several religious orders, developed what amounted to an entire program of urban

FIGURE 5.3. Detail of *Christ in the City*, stained glass, stone, metal, and bronze, Capuchin Monastery Church of St. John, New York, New York (Benoit Gilsoul, 1975). Roughly thirteen feet in diameter, this installation on West 31st Street shows an overhead view of Manhattan with the East River and Brooklyn docks (*top*) and the Hudson and New Jersey docks (*bottom*). Photo: Author.

chapels in the 1950s and 1960s: St. Francis Chapel in the Prudential Center, the Shrine of St. Anthony on Arch Street, a Paulist center on Park Street, a Jesuit chapel on Newbury Street, a chapel in South Station, and the church of St. James the Greater on Harrison Street. These spaces were only part of a midcentury urban strategy that included deep involvement in civic land-use planning. Msgr. Francis Lally, Cardinal Cushing's close aide and editor of the archdiocesan newspaper, was an original member of Boston's urban renewal agency, the Boston Redevelopment Authority (BRA).[61] Perhaps inspired by the recent success of the shrine on nearby Arch Street, Lally expressed Cushing's desire to build "a free-standing chapel" somewhere in the Government Center project.[62] At least two BRA planners expressed reservations about a possible conflict of interest, given Lally's position as chairman of the board, and wondered whether an interfaith rather than a Catholic chapel would be more suitable.[63] This suggestion, however, was disregarded, and the archdiocese moved swiftly to hire José Luis Sert, a Spanish-born Catholic, well-known urban theorist, and dean of the Harvard Graduate School of Design.

The land intended for St. Botolph's was a narrow slice at the corner of New Chardon and Cambridge, dominated by office and government buildings. Sert thought in terms of the rhythm of the entire city of the future, whose skyline could be judiciously managed rather than grow randomly.[64] His eventual solution was a three-hundred-seat concrete-and-brick structure without windows along its side walls, which, hemmed in on all sides, would have let in relatively little light (see fig. 5.4). Instead, the building's illumination would come from skylights, allowing it not only to be successfully lit but also to relate intelligently to the "massive" Government Center of the future, when "thousands of office workers and West End residents" would "see the building from above."[65] Four "light towers" at the building's corners would create visual interest for those looking down on the chapel from their offices and apartments, as well as provide the main interior decoration. Glass in primary colors would filter light onto the concrete interior walls during the day, in patterns changing with the movement of the sun, while at night interior lighting would cast color

FIGURE 5.4. José Luis Sert shows his model for the Chapel of St. Botolph to Richard Cardinal Cushing, late 1960s. Photo: Josep Lluis Sert Collection, courtesy of the Frances Loeb Library, Harvard Graduate School of Design.

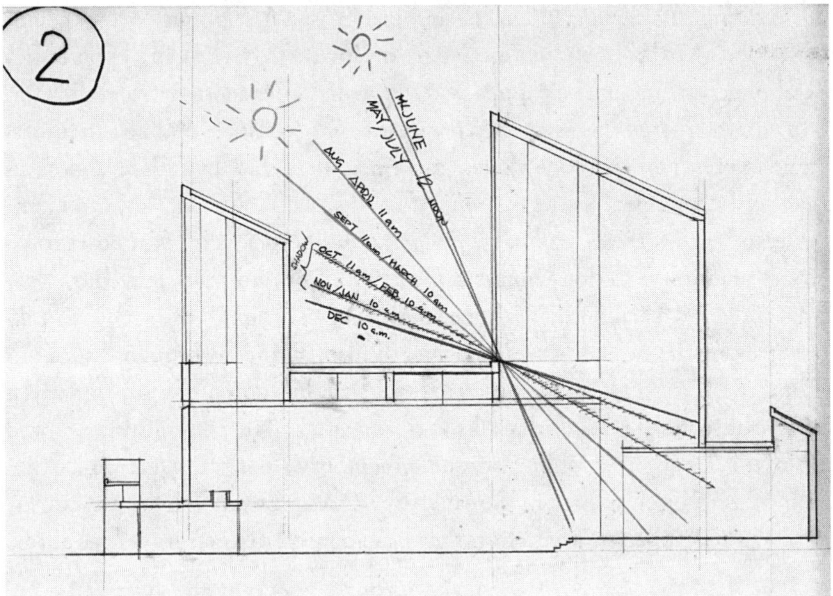

FIGURE 5.5. Drawing of the proposed Chapel of St. Botolph, Boston, Massachusetts (José Luis Sert, 1960s), showing how light would enter the chapel at different times of the year and day. Photo: Josep Lluis Sert Collection, courtesy of the Frances Loeb Library, Harvard Graduate School of Design.

onto nearby buildings and "halo the chapel in variegated light" (see fig. 5.5).[66] One commenter missed the point, noting that "the Rudolph building will not provide the chapel with the quietest of backgrounds."[67] But others did not; Maurice Lavanoux of *Liturgical Arts* was especially interested in publishing "a plan showing the location of the chapel in the general complex of buildings around it."[68] The chapel was intended precisely to provide a grace note of stillness within the busy city. Sert saw visual change both inside and outside the chapel as taking place naturally and cyclically, as sunlight shifted through the day and the year. The chapel would have been a small part of an urban ecology planned to include spiritual succor on a human scale, "intimacy" and a "sense of involvement that suits liturgical change" in the midst of a towering city.[69]

In addition to strategizing small urban chapels, architects rethought cathedral design for the age of secular theology. Was a cathedral, as had historically been the case, an expression of raw Catholic power within a downtown neighborhood? Or was it, too, ideally a tool to enhance collaboration between Church and city? In San Francisco, plans for the new St. Mary's cathedral evolved from a Romanesque structure in early 1963 to a strikingly modern design by January 1964 (fig. 1.2).[70] Between 1964 and 1970, however, the design underwent one more significant change. What the archbishop had first proposed as expanses of stained glass between the massive pylons of Pietro Belluschi's hyperbolic-paraboloid roof became clear glass, so that worshippers look beyond the altar onto unobstructed views of the city (fig. 5.6).[71] As usual, though, architects could express new theological ideas more readily in their hypothetical designs than in those subject to the consent of cautious archbishops. Richard Gemperle, in his 1965 thesis for Rice University, designed a church for downtown Houston that had "a dominant characteristic of openness," achieved by clear glass walls and a ceiling that is "one tremendous skylight" (fig. 5.7).[72] Utterly transparent, the cathedral would be "seen into, and seen through;" without proper walls to speak of, "the internal space of the church [would extend] in all four directions across sidewalks and streets. . . . The church space [would extend] itself to include the city, and a member of the congregation [would feel] himself to be at once in the sanctuary and in the city." This was consonant with Gemperle's prediction that "the church of the future" would be

FIGURE 5.6. View of the city from the Cathedral of St. Mary of the Assumption, San Francisco, California (Pietro Belluschi with Angus McSweeney and John A. Ryan, with consulting engineer Pier Luigi Nervi, 1964–1970). Photo: Author.

FIGURE 5.7. Model cathedral for downtown Houston, Texas (M.Arch thesis by Richard Gemperle, 1967). GLIT, 14-43-01.

"less 'religious,' more open, less authoritarian, and more human."[73] His design would "bring the Church to the people," since "the Church's ineffectiveness in modern life is related to its isolation in space and time."[74]

Gemperle's cathedral remained unbuilt, as did Ray Pavia's design (with Cajetan Baumann, OFM) for the Rockford, Illinois, cathedral.[75] But the shared idea for a "horizontal cathedral" that did not try to compete with towering office buildings but instead concentrated on hospitality and openness, on moving beyond "monumentality" as a dominant theme, was a popular idea through the 1960s. (See fig. 2.7) As the Catholic architect John Cates noted—sounding like Marguerite Brunswig Staude decades earlier—in the contemporary city steeples did not serve their intended purpose; they were being "reduced to obvious impotence by the mighty commercial concrete peaks around [them]."[76] Cates proposed, instead, sinking churches underground, with a public park on the roof and skylights to illuminate the worship space.[77]

THE PARISH OF THE FUTURE

In the fall of 1965 at UC–Berkeley's College of Environmental Design, Patrick Quinn's class "Religion and Architecture in the Future City" began with a discussion of "the concept of architecture as the establishment of 'places' within a dynamic ecological order."[78] Robert E. Park had introduced the concept of the city as an "urban ecology" in 1915, but the idea that religion was a part of a "dynamic ecological order" still came as a surprise to some of Quinn's architecture students, let alone the Catholic and Protestant seminarians also taking the course.[79] Quinn passionately criticized city planners who, though they would "seldom . . . mention or even acknowledge religion as a vital part of man's life," did "recognize the existence of the organized churches and . . . make some unassigned lots with little black crosses on the map. What kind of church, or what kind of group doing what, is not indicated."[80] Not understanding what a church was for, they unthinkingly repeated the patterns of the past, separating church buildings from other lots. But Quinn understood secular theology as Harvey Cox intended it: "a trend which no longer separates the sacred from the secular, but sees the potentially sacred in all creation."[81]

His students soon did, too. The Catholic seminarian Greg McAllister, in his final essay for the course, explored recent developments in the theology of God. Many theologians now saw "God" not as a transcendent being, but the "ground of being"; accessible not by separation from the world, by embarking on a journey to Elsewhere, but rather "attainable through total involvement with the human." In support of this position, McAllister cited, among others, both Teilhard and Cox. With his seminar teammate, Unitarian architectural student Sigrid Lorenzen Rupp, he argued that this theological shift demanded a spatial shift: liturgical spaces that immersed people in the city rather than detaching them from it. New Catholic buildings ought not to be "separate and exclusive structure[s] existing over and against the structures of human society" but should "become one with them and give up [their] separate identity." They should be "functional human complexes" that provided spaces for "lectures and dinners" (including Eucharistic celebrations), meetings including group prayer and bible study, and individual "reading and meditating."[82]

Proposals like McAllister and Rupp's were part of a widespread attempt by those interested in secular theology to envision different ways of organizing church life. This was a worldwide conversation in the post–Vatican II period, and Americans sought information on parochial experiments in Paris and Rome as well as at home. Maurice Lavanoux, fresh from reading *The Secular City* in the summer of 1966, suggested a planning competition on "how to integrate church needs (I don't necessarily mean large church buildings) in new developments and also in any re-development of existing conditions, etc."[83] The prominent German Catholic architect Justus Dahinden, who had recently published *Bauen für die Kirche in der Welt* (Building for the church in the world), told the American Protestant magazine *Your Church* in 1970 that he thought the future held "less of a tendency to isolate the church building—it will be brought more into the middle of a housing development, more into the midst of the community activities."[84] Many other Catholics, both architects and not, predicted that the territorial parish (hitherto the foundation of American Catholic life) would dissolve or radically transform under the joint pressures of population shifts and secular theology.[85] By 1968 it seemed "obvious" to Lavanoux that "the problem is to find a way to take care of a fragmented worshipping community"; to him, this meant "smaller churches, or chapels in apartment houses, even office buildings," as "the set, territorial parish of old can no longer be adapted to changing living patterns."[86] The objection to the built environment of traditional parishes included both their forbidding appearance (Sr. Marie Augusta Neal claimed, with Cox, that true Christian communities were "communities without walls"[87]) and their inflexibility, their inability to respond to the swift reconfiguration of the urban landscape. Neal, like the priests of Presentation Parish, argued that if Catholic buildings like churches, parish halls, schools, and even convents and rectories could be transformed from fortresses to open environments, then new residents of inner-city neighborhoods could become "creative and responsive initiators of action" alongside Catholics who chose to live there.[88]

That those populations were frequently non-Catholic partially explains why the dissolution of architectural boundaries was so often seen also as the dissolution of invisible boundaries between Catholics, Protestants, and Jews. Urban chapels, in addition to serving the needs of Catholic office workers, were expected to serve as a locus for ecumenical life, an area in which the "secular city" was already excelling and that many Catholics expected to become increasingly important for the Church as a whole. By 1968 many shared Fr. Joseph Nolan's belief that "the forward thrust of ecumenism . . . is manifestly the work of the Spirit. Christian unity is not a matter of *if* but *when*, because it is God's will."[89] Architectural and liturgical practice during the late 1960s responded directly to this belief. In 1969, Cardinal Cushing anointed Boston's Prudential Center chapel as a place where "people of all faiths" could "come . . . and speak to God through their own prayers," positioning the chapel as a gift to the city, paid for by Catholics but available to all.[90] Other models for the "church of the future" claimed that buildings actively designed for interfaith activity might encourage and hasten union; Maurice Lavanoux made a point of printing elaborate proposals for ecumenical and interfaith churches in classic urban crossing grounds like New York City and Philadelphia.[91]

The desire to have church space used to the maximum by all members of the community—a hallmark of *Secular City*–inspired spatial thought—also suggested ecumenical leanings. By August 1970, Lavanoux, who had been cautiously encouraging interfaith encounter since a tentative endorsement of the

Air Force Academy chapel in the late 1950s, thought that as a matter of course new churches should "provide ample space for worship and allow that space to be used for community needs—that is, the needs of the *total* community, not necessarily the needs of one denomination." Should anyone suggest that this meant "a dilution of beliefs," he noted that he rejected syncretism; rather, support for ecumenical space signaled "a willing acceptance of the fact that certain community needs can be shared by all in a *common* space."[92] While Catholics routinely participated in shared worship space in military and academic settings, two experiments in ecumenical building, in Kansas City, Missouri, and Columbia, Maryland, generated particular excitement and appeared to point the way toward future building norms for city parishes. Though these two projects had very different contexts, both were seen by Catholics, Protestants, and the secular press as viable models for urban religious space.

St. Mark's, Kansas City, was a multidenominational church uniting many of the core desires expressed by 1960s Catholic futurists: ecumenicity, flexibility, multipurpose space, inexpensive and unpretentious construction, suitability for avant-garde liturgical art, and a church building conceptualized as a service to the surrounding city. The project, which made *Time* as "the first joint Protestant-Roman Catholic congregation in the U.S.," originated with a joint Presbyterian-UCC parish that invited Catholic and Episcopalian participation.[93] Unlike the Chapel of St. Botolph (where a lengthy development process apparently diminished chancery enthusiasm and derailed construction), the St. Mark's project, with the support of Bishop Charles Helmsing, raised funds quickly. Formal development began in July 1966, and by July 1967 ground had been broken.

This swift action resulted from years of shared work by the initial participating clergy. The neighborhood was in the end stages of racial transition; by the mid-1960s, towering new housing projects packed nearly fifteen thousand residents, mostly black, into a six-block radius. While these buildings were being planned in 1957, the Presbyterian minister Kenneth Waterman took over a congregation of twenty elderly whites, only to have his church burn down within two weeks. Rather than reassigning Waterman, the United Presbyterian Board of National Missions decided to rebuild on the spot, and Waterman threw himself into community work, befriending the local director of Catholic Charities, Fr. Lawrence McNamara, and working jointly with Kansas City's Catholic Interracial Council and Bishop Helmsing.[94] From 1963 to '65, Waterman, Helmsing, McNamara, and Fr. Allen Hingston collaborated with Episcopalians and Disciples of Christ to bring the community organizer Saul Alinsky to Kansas City, an intensely controversial project that nevertheless laid the groundwork for St. Mark's.

Both Waterman's church and a nearby UCC congregation increasingly saw their membership coming from the Wayne Miner housing project. The two churches federated in the fall of 1964 and jointly bought land closer to the towers. Soon the Catholic and Episcopalian dioceses became involved in St. Mark's as well. McNamara explained that he saw "standing at the side of the racially dispossessed and politically exploited as only the first step in a long process that will give a few inner city dwellers a chance to find God now and may, hopefully, build a foundation for other generations." He was highly aware that "the decision to join the program has long-range implications for the Catholic diocese in years to come; it ties the whole diocese more closely to the inner city."[95]

The St. Mark's participants knew that all eyes were on them; they promoted their project as "a unique new church that represents a real ecumenical breakthrough at the grass-roots level."[96] The building committee prioritized community availability: "worship space which will be used many times every week and which can accommodate a larger congregation"; "flexible activity space" for larger social activities that could also be "rearranged and sub-divided for small groups and classes"; and office space.[97] Despite the somewhat forbidding appearance of architects Mantel and Steele's windowless concrete building, it was intended to relate clearly to its neighborhood, with a transitional plaza sweeping the congregation into the building and sending the resources of the church out into the city[98] (see figs. 5.8 and 5.9). Staff were "determined not to be captive to the building in terms of ministry to the inner city," as the UCC minister William Hayes wrote; though the church building itself was "an essential ingredient," it was primarily to be "a launching pad which makes involvement possible."[99]

Ecumenical expectations positioned St. Mark's as a guide to the future.[100] But its building also exposed the tension between those Catholics who wished to push toward full unity, and those who more cautiously noted that doctrinal, liturgical, and administrative barriers still existed between the churches, feeling that physical structures should reflect this fact. On the one hand, Catholics like layman Donald Thorman noted that *Nostra aetate*, Vatican II's 1965 document on ecumenism, was not "the final word on the subject, for it really only opens the door to future thought and experience."[101] On the other hand, the complex legal and financial structure behind St. Mark's made it clear that the eschaton had not yet arrived. Officially, St. Mark's was a "chapel of ease" for Roman Catholics, attached to the regular parish of St. Aloysius, which created administrative distance from full Catholic participation.[102] News coverage also carefully stressed that the four "faiths" would "respect the distinctiveness and integrity of each parent church body."[103]

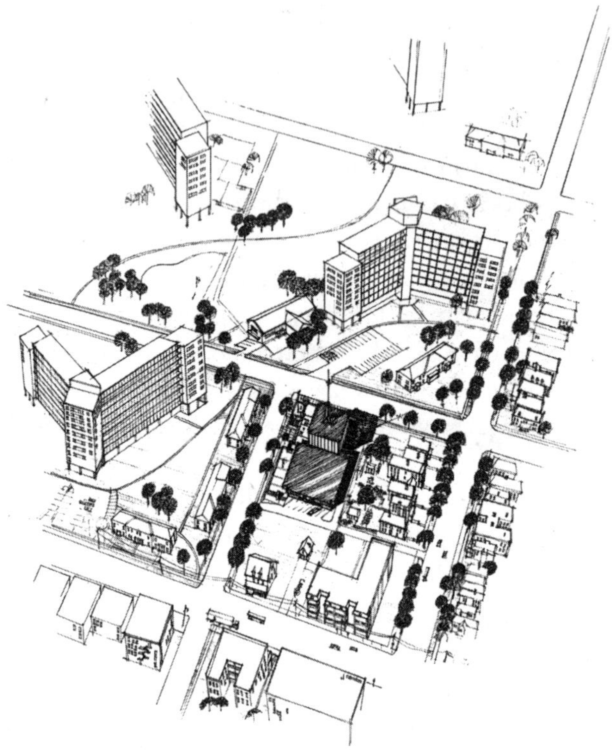

FIGURE 5.8. Architect's study drawing for St. Mark's Church, Kansas City, Missouri, overhead view of plan within the neighborhood (Mantel and Steele, 1967–68). Photo: GLIT, 29-25-01.

Despite denominational wariness, however, the building itself was meant to encourage more future unity than the groups had at the outset. The Presbyterian pastor David O. Shipley claimed that the "flexible media of concrete and steel permit the expression of unifying liturgical principles while they provide for the variety of needs common to the city."[104] Robert Ready, OSB, a veteran street preacher from nearby liturgical-movement stronghold Conception Abbey, was assigned to lead St. Mark's Catholic contingent in March 1968. Ready was cheerfully frank about the challenges of ecumenical life: "Since November 1968 Protestants and Catholics have been living and working together under the same roof in St. Mark's . . . and the roof is still on!"[105] But he felt that the fragile emerging practices were a beginning, and that avoiding syncretism now might signal the emergence of a new reality. "We on the staff at St. Mark's," he wrote, "are daily reminded in our work that 'what is not possible with man, is possible with God.'

In our common prayers, daily conversations, discussions and planning sessions we perceive that a community is beginning to form, and we are impelled to 'stir up the Grace of God that is in us.' We expect to grow in our understanding. . . . We believe that our work together at St. Mark's is a step forward in ecumenism and 'a journey of a thousand miles begins with the first step.' "[106] Ready's comment revealed the eschatological and mystical spirituality underlying his community's practical engagement with the realities of the secular city.

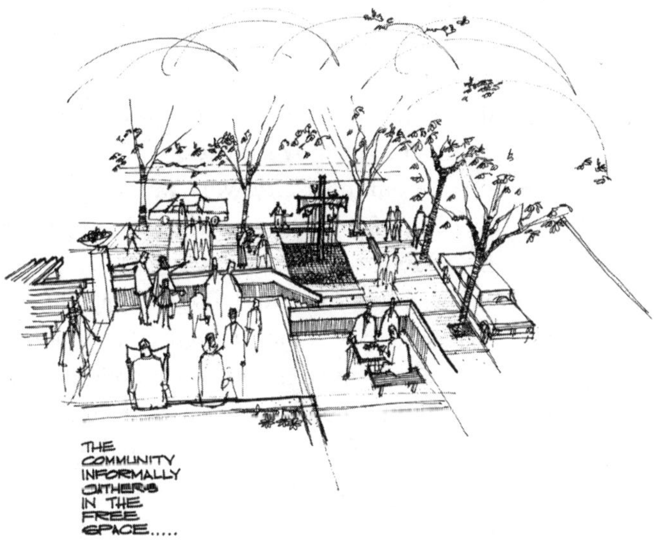

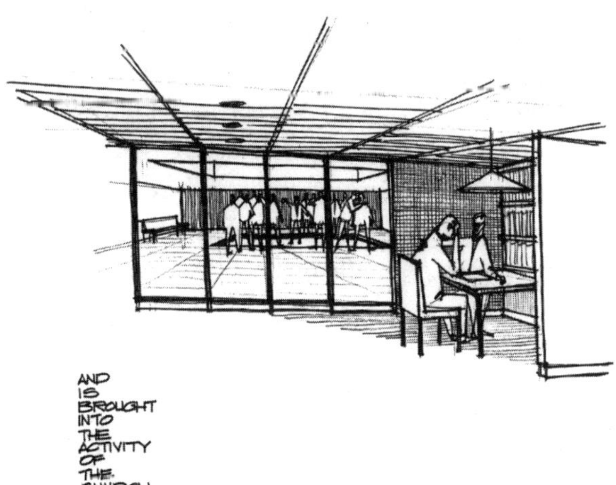

FIGURE 5.9. Architect's study drawings for St. Mark's Church, Kansas City, Missouri (Mantel and Steele, 1967–68). *Top*: "The community informally gathers in the free space . . ."; *bottom*: "And is brought into the activity of the church . . ." Photos: GLIT, 26-26-01 and GLIT, 29-27-01.

As St. Mark's was opening, the Catholic Archdiocese of Baltimore was also investigating the possibilities of ecumenical worship space in the "new town" of Columbia, Maryland. As in Kansas City, ecumenical liturgical collaboration in Maryland began with joint work in social services. Columbia's developer, James Rouse, wanted from the beginning to have all worship space be ecumenical. Archbishop Lawrence Shehan preferred to build typical suburban parish plants on dedicated land. However, both Shehan's leadership in Vatican II's ecumenical-relations efforts, and the development of relationships with Protestant and Jewish groups through the Interfaith Housing Corporation, a group chaired by Fr. John Walsh of the archdiocese, shifted Catholics toward a decision to participate fully in ecumenical worship space there.

Rouse's idealism and commitment to solving the problems of cities in a deliberately integrated community attracted attention from priests who were deeply engaged in interracial and inner-city work in Baltimore, including Austin Healy, head of Shehan's inner-city commission. Healy's interest in the archdiocese's footprint in Columbia, he wrote, was "born of interest in the Inner City, because planning a city for the future should have built-in cautions and positive measures to avoid the causes and oversights that create todays [*sic*] problems in city living."[107] John Walsh agreed that Catholic participation in building Columbia was not (unlike suburban efforts to create isolated "parish plants") about a flight of the Church from the city. "Building new towns is justified only if it helps to rebuild our older cities," he said in 1969. "This is why the churches are getting into the low-rent housing business. If that is not our reason, we are temporizing and should get out."[108]

The postconciliar loosening of restrictions on Catholic ecumenism facilitated a final agreement, hammered out over 1966/1967, to participate in building an interfaith center in Columbia's Village of Wilde Lake, and to establish a full Catholic parish (as opposed to a "chapel of ease"). The plans for this arrangement mutated from a "Village Religious Center," a plaza on which Catholics would have their own building, to a building comprising two large multipurpose rooms—one primarily dedicated to Catholic and one to Protestant worship—joined by a shared baptistery and social space.[109] The Wilde Lake Interfaith Center, designed by Boston architects Huygens and Tappé with assistance from local Catholic architect William Gaudreau, opened in September 1970.

Like St. Mark's, the Wilde Lake IFC generated national excitement. Reports praising it as the church of the future linked ecumenical enthusiasm, distaste for excessive spending, and technocratic optimism. A Rouse Company press release highlighted a Catholic priest's claim that churches would have to "lose their 'fixations on monuments and real estate' or become 'museum pieces' in the city of the future." Old patterns of development represented sheer inertia, while a "divorce" from "the present 'laissez-faire' type of operations" would leave the churches "better equipped to handle the common problems" of the city.[110] Addressing the future with creativity practically demanded interfaith centers. Protestant minister Clarence Sinclair drove the point home by comparing Columbia's interfaith center to a " 'launching pad' for mission work of the faiths," borrowing the futuristic excitement of the Apollo missions for the more prosaic establishment of a neighborhood church.[111]

The tendency of the Rouse Company, the archdiocese, and the ecumenical Protestant group at Columbia to ignore or minimize conflict publicly gave outsiders the impression that relations were smoothly and unprecedentedly harmonious, although behind-the-scenes matters were more complex.[112] Before ground was even broken on the IFC, the New York–based Interfaith Research Center on Religious Architecture (of which Robert Rambusch was treasurer and Maurice Lavanoux a director) wrote Rouse to inform him that the directors believed there were "rich possibilities [in Columbia] which could point the way of the future."[113] The Jesuit art historian Thomas Mathews optimistically recorded that Columbia had "begun at last to show signs of scoring a radical breakthrough" both in interfaith relations and in "the relations of church planning to city planning."[114] Meanwhile, the Columbia planners were keeping track of other "experiments"; the Interfaith Center's files contained material on St. Mark's in Kansas City, as well as the syllabus for Patrick Quinn's Berkeley course on "Religion and Architecture in the Future City."[115]

What, exactly, did the project look toward? Both participants and observers sometimes struggled to grasp its full meaning. However, several themes emerged from contemporary discussion. Thomas Mathews highlighted the "open-ended" aspect of the plan for its "great flexibility suited to the flux and mobility of the modern city."[116] The architects deliberately avoided interior load-bearing walls, on the theory that "Catholic" and "Protestant" spaces could be combined later with minimal fuss as the groups grew closer together.[117] Flexibility in architecture was not a construction end in itself; Anthony Tappé hoped that the building's "flexible framework," its movable partitions and ample flow space, its lack of fixed furniture, would allow the "interfaith principle" to "flourish."[118] It was a "non-traditional building" for a "non-traditional concept," and its "non-static quality" would, in a classic expression of environmental determinism, "encourage experimentation with new liturgies and their physical expressions."[119] At their most soaringly optimistic, Columbia's Catholics hoped that the center was actually leading in the direction of the ultimate future, the fulfillment of God's kingdom. John Walsh's prayer at the dedication of the Village of Wilde Lake asked God to "help us to see that today is not an isolated event but is linked to all that has gone before—to all that is now—and to all that is to come," putting Columbia in cosmic perspective as a place that was not secular, since "nothing is secular," but "on the contrary . . . made sacred by its origin in You and its destination in You."[120]

"PLEASE WAIT UNTIL THE SERVICE IS ENDED": PROTEST, LITURGY, AND THE INSTITUTIONAL LIMITS OF SECULAR THEOLOGY

Attempts to structure new partnerships between Church and city, between church buildings and city needs, attracted tremendous energy in the late 1960s and early 1970s: chanceries created new commissions dedicated to partnership with city residents; rectories and convents opened their doors to their neighborhoods; storefront and urban chapels attracted a cross section of workers, residents, and energetic volunteers; Catholic schools welcomed increasing numbers of non-Catholic, frequently African American students; representatives of Catholic, Protestant, Jewish, and civic offices worked together to create new social services, housing, and worship opportunities; and young architects envisioned new ways of relating church buildings to the city. Yet despite real desire to reshape relations between Church, church, and city, the spatial convictions of secular theology were ultimately incompatible with an equally strong desire to protect sacred spaces from secular intrusion.

This conflict appeared between post–Vatican II "conservatives" and "liberals," but also divided Catholics who wanted church buildings better suited to the future from those who saw no future for dedicated churches at all. In 1966, for example, Michael Barnes of Milwaukee wrote to *Commonweal* to complain that the architect Clovis Heimsath's recent sketch of a church as "a place apart" was insufficient: a church "must also say and be other things if it is to be true to the full meaning of the Eucharistic celebrations." It might be true that a church was "a good place to escape for a while the weight of the world," but for Christians, "religion is not merely a consolation in a troublesome world, but also a challenge to transform that world." Barnes concluded: "To be both in the world yet looking beyond each here-and-now, to be God-centered by being man-centered—in this lies the paradox of the meaning of the Eucharist."[121] But if Heimsath wanted a church in which to pray to God apart from the world, and Barnes wanted churches in storefronts in order to remind Catholics that (as Cushing had pointed out) the Eucharist was food for an earthly and not only a heavenly journey, a third option for relating earthly and heavenly city existed: take secular theology's spatial implications to their logical conclusions by bringing "secular" concerns into dedicated liturgical space.

During the 10 a.m. Mass in St. Patrick's Cathedral on January 22, 1967, twenty-three men and women "rose to their feet and held placards [containing antiwar slogans and pictures] aloft," according to a report filed with the Archdiocese of New York. "Amid the confusion occasioned by this act," the celebrant "announced to the congregation that they should remain seated and the Police would handle the situation." The demonstrators were promptly arrested and charged with a variety of wrongdoing, ranging from creating a public nuisance to disturbing a religious meeting.[122] Meanwhile, more protestors picketed outside, loudly objecting to Cardinal Spellman's recent statement, during a Christmas visit to American troops in Vietnam, that "less than victory is inconceivable" in "a war for civilization."[123] A week later, Gary Youree wrote Spellman to explain the demonstrators' position: "When the Church indulges herself in affairs of a 'secular' nature, she transforms the aisles of her buildings into two-way streets." Further, Youree noted pointedly, "Our Lord conducted a much less peaceful demonstration in the Temple at Jerusalem," and therefore the police response was inappropriate to the nature of the action.[124] But lay opinion on the demonstration was anything but singular; the incident also prompted a one-line letter that read simply, "Forgive us our trespasses."[125] Were "secular" demonstration techniques inside church buildings a way to heal the Church of its sins? Or were they traumatic events exacerbating postconciliar wounds on the Catholic body?

After the St. Patrick's protest, archdiocesan spokesman Msgr. Thomas McGovern, taking the latter position, noted ominously, "It would be tragic if religious-minded Americans worshiping in their churches and synagogues had to have a constant concern about such desecration of God's house."[126] McGovern's fears were realized over the next several years, as urban Catholic churches became a favored target of demonstrators against the Vietnam War and in favor of civil rights and reparations.[127] In the summer of 1969, for example, weeks of protests by ACTION (Action Committee to Improve Opportunities for Negroes), a "local militant organization," rocked the cathedral of St. Louis.[128] On June 29, "12 teen-age black militants" walked past one thousand worshippers waiting for the noon Mass and "lay down in front of the communion railing." When they refused to leave, the cathedral's rector canceled Mass.[129] The next Sunday, during the fifth straight week of protests inside the cathedral, three demonstrators were arrested and charged with "disturbing a religious assembly"; this time "a scuffle broke out when a member of the congregation leaped from a pew and knocked a mock bishop's mitre off [protestor William Calvin Mitchell's] head as he and the others were marching out of church chanting 'Racists, racists, white Christian racists.'"[130]

In the wake of several similar incidents connected to the issuing of the "Black Manifesto"—a demand for financial reparations from white churches and synagogues—John Cardinal Dearden of Detroit, one of the nation's most progressive bishops and the president of the National Conference of Catholic Bishops, issued instructions to his priests.[131] "Do not call the police, or attempt to physically force anyone out of church," Dearden ordered, although he clearly preferred that Mass proceed in an orderly manner. If activists came into the church during Mass, they were to be "treated with utmost courtesy," but were to be asked to "please wait until the service is ended." If they would not agree to this, however, the priest was to "stop the service and allow them to make their presentation," but inform parishioners that "they may leave if they so desire, and . . . are excused from the obligation of hearing mass for this Sunday."[132]

As Cardinal Dearden predicted, it was a summer of liturgical protests. In Washington DC, James Gibbons and his Center for Christian Renewal attempted, ten Sundays in a row, to hold a teach-in on race at St. Matthew's Cathedral. Finally, they "staged a walk-out from a mass," protesting the use of archdiocesan funds for "church and school construction rather than . . . improving conditions for people living in Washington's black ghettoes [*sic*]." Denied the opportunity to speak inside the cathedral, the group stood outside and "sang songs such as 'We Shall Overcome' as parishioners filed out after mass."[133] Catholic reactions to these events showed deep divides over the propriety of activists' presence within church buildings. While some pastors called police or canceled Mass, the pastor of St. Gabriel the Archangel in St. Louis, Msgr. Harry Stiltz, invited ACTION members to tell his congregation they "should set up committees to fight hunger and poverty in the inner city"—at which point half of Stiltz's parishioners left, but half stayed, a percentage Maryknoll Sister Cecilia Goldman found "very good."[134] Others tried to walk Dearden's suggested line; on the eighth consecutive Sunday of ACTION protests in St. Louis, a group of protestors agreed to Msgr. Clarence White's invitation to speak after mass, rather than during it.[135] White shared Dearden's preference for keeping political activism out of the church building itself: following the liturgy, seventy-five of White's parishioners convened to hear Luther Mitchell in the church's basement meeting room, while Dearden's guidelines directed that similar post-Mass meetings be conducted in the parish hall. Msgr. Francis Kennedy, the administrator of Cincinnati's St. Peter in Chains Cathedral, tried a riskier compromise. When fifteen demonstrators from the Black Economic Development Committee appeared in the first rows during a Sunday Mass on May 11, 1969, they agreed to remain "in a respectful manner" throughout the service, including the formal dismissal, at which point Kennedy invited Marvin Gentry to the pulpit to read the manifesto before the recessional hymn.[136]

Cox- and *Gaudium*-inspired Catholics and chancery officials had formed many partnerships to increase the Church's "presence" in the wider community. Low-income housing, service organizations, and unconventionally located downtown chapels could be seen both as "forward-looking" uses of the Church's resources in ministries of incarnational presence, and traditional expressions of Catholic charity and mission activity, in which "the Church" went outside of its strongholds to save "the world." But these partnerships were strained beyond their limits when the "secular" world came into the "sacred" precincts of the church, a development Catholics deeply informed by secular theology saw as a natural, necessary step toward a more just future, but many other Catholics saw as an invasive violation of holy space. At best, many massgoers simply refused to engage with protestors' attempts to insert discussions of race, economics, and social conditions into the physical space of the church, walking out themselves; at worst, they violently objected to what they saw as the city's intrusion on the sanctuary, the "desecration of God's house." In either case they insisted on maintaining what the architect Patrick Quinn dismissively called an "inner security" derived from "retreating from the world to meet [God] once a week in some sacred enclave." But Quinn and his fellow partisans of secular theology saw another option available. After all, "the future city is in the making around us and we are its makers," Quinn wrote; Catholics could choose, instead of retreat, "a freer, more mobile, more committed community whose inner security stems from discovering God in the world of its daily life."[137] Creating this community would require completely restructuring the Catholic understanding of sacred space. Quinn, along with many other architects and liturgists, understood this task as vital for building the world—and the Church—that Catholic futurists sought.

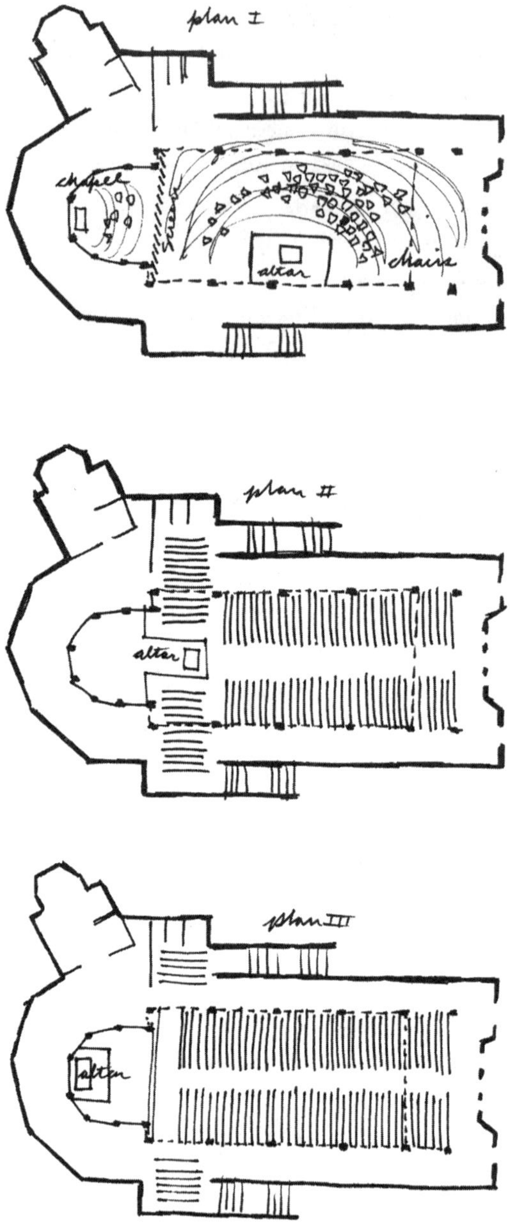

FIGURE 6.1. Three possibilities for renovating a pre–Vatican II basilica for the new liturgy (William Schickel, 1970). Photo: *Liturgical Arts* 38, no. 2 (1970).

CHAPTER SIX

"WHAT IS A CHURCH?"

On the evening of June 21, 1968, Americans tuning their televisions to NBC saw what was to some a welcome, and to others a shocking sight: a jubilant interracial procession of adults and children carrying balloons and banners, circulating through a cramped and nondescript school cafeteria, and finally arriving at the front of the room, where a small guitar choir was assembled. The next shot found the group settled down around tables to listen to a speaker, identified as Fr. William Nerin, who told them: "We are leaving an environment in the Church which we have had for many years. We are leaving an environment of monarchy and we are leaving the king-subject relationship." The remainder of *The New American Catholic* presented a full hour of interviews ranging from the "anonymous . . . 'man in the street'" to Auxiliary Bishop James P. Shannon of St. Paul, Minnesota.[1] Despite its inclusion of a few conservative viewpoints, the program clearly sympathized with the balloon-carrying massgoers: the Community of John XXIII, a "floating parish" that owned no property, claimed no territorial boundaries, and met, most Sundays, in rented and borrowed spaces in and around Oklahoma City.

Dozens of American Catholics wrote NBC and Shannon to express their feelings, both positive and negative. They commented on liturgical and administrative change within the Church, social activism by priests and nuns, and clerical celibacy. But those who disliked the program saved a special vitriol for NBC's footage of the "sacreligious mass(???)," wondering if it was actually "a Mardi Gras? A Hippie Party?"[2] Several letters concentrated on what their writers perceived as a disconnect between the dignity due to the sacrament and its surroundings: "*My Lord and my God* what's happening to our lovely Church? . . . I was so upset when I saw the darling children marching through the church [sic] with banners and balloons, like a circus, and the priest standing laughing like a fool."[3] Sr. M. Paulissa, SSND, expressed her exasperation with the "Modern Catholic" in a withering question: "Why build beautiful churches if some few people prefer tavern-like atmosphere for the Holy Sacrifice?"[4]

Why indeed? The Vatican II era was experienced by many American Catholics as a spatial crisis.[5] Church renovations, innovative new buildings, and unconventional Eucharistic spaces like the Community of John XXIII's cafeteria simultaneously exhilarated and unsettled postconciliar Catholics feeling their way toward a new understanding of the Church.

By 1969, as Minnesota pastor Leo Howley pointed out, conciliar developments had "force[d]" Catholics "to answer a question we have taken for granted all our lives. . . . What is a church?"[6] In the wake of the council, always intimate ecclesiological and architectural questions intertwined with reflections arising from the highly mobile nature of the American population during the 1950s and 1960s. As in the years prior to Vatican II, Catholics across the political and liturgical spectrum shared the conviction that the future of the Church's magisterial and spiritual "environment," in Nerin's term, was bound up with its liturgical environment. But if the Community of John XXIII's cafeteria Mass was a harbinger of the future, was its spatial innovation a sign of hope for the Christian community or a betrayal of the Church's core mission?

Many American Catholics regarded the development of new kinds of worship space as integral to the Church's postconciliar future, but "New American Catholics" of the late 1960s and early 1970s who tried to discern a functional church of the future had a distinct set of ecclesiological and architectural problems. Unlike their preconciliar counterparts, they could no longer assume that the Church's rituals and its corresponding architectural demands were basically stable; "the liturgy of the future," as Frederick McManus wrote in 1966, now meant "different things to different people."[7] The early liturgical movement had complained bitterly that the main problem lay with priests and designers who ignored rather than engaged the strict rules, called rubrics, governing ritual activity.[8] Architects were encouraged to consult canon law and study ritual scripts, along with theological appreciations of the liturgy; architects promoted by the preconciliar liturgical movement sought functional plans that allowed for correct ritual performance and emphasized the meaning of sacramental action. Summarizing three decades of recommendations on the cusp of Vatican II, the liturgist H. A. Reinhold advised that devotional shrines and other possible distractions be located away from the main altar, perhaps in side chapels or a basement.[9] The baptismal font should be located to stress that "we have all entered the Church through baptism."[10] Confessionals were to be aligned with the baptistery, indicating the relationship between the two sacraments. "A useful floor plan" would avoid nonfunctional although pious and "symbolic" uses of space, like the cruciform plan that looked good from the air but divided the congregation; instead, the various parts of the church should be both "organically distinct" and "hierarchically organized," just as a body or any other biological entity would be.[11] Above all, everything about the design would "direct attention to the altar," which should be "the focal point of the church."[12]

As a practical matter, many American liturgists hoped that if the council did opine on church architecture, it would affirm the necessity of, as Gerald Ellard had predicted in the 1940s, first "putting the altar farther down into the body of the building, and secondly, turning the altar towards the people."[13] As the first conciliar documents emerged from Rome, however, and as debate over what they meant for church design gathered steam, liturgists increasingly framed the problems of worship space as much more complex than they had appeared only a few years earlier. The preconciliar consensus on functional liturgical architecture frayed as Catholics of the 1960s and 1970s faced the twin tasks of remaking older churches and developing new ones; their conversations, simultaneously practical and existential, unfolded in an atmosphere of deep uncertainty about when, or whether, liturgical requirements would ever stabilize. As two liturgists from St. John's Abbey wrote in 1963, just prior to the promulgation of *Sacrosanctum concilium*, "It is quite clear that Vatican Council II will have a profound effect on the design of the church," and it would not be "practical to do nothing when the times demand action." However, they conceded, "many people seem[ed] to be confused as to just what this effect [would] be."[14]

Sacrosanctum's release did not clear much up. "It was repeatedly stated" at a January 1964 meeting of liturgists in Boston that the Church was "in a period of transition and that there were different valid sources possible to the same problem" of liturgical space. The only thing the liturgists could agree on was that "many possibilities exist and it is the architect's challenge to shape his churches to fit the needs and conditions of the people and the place."[15] The wide variety of liturgical spaces proposed and produced in this period show the immediate consequence of Vatican II for liturgical architecture was not a sudden shift in beliefs about the relationship of Church and church. Rather, the council's perceived diffusion of responsibility and authority into the Church as a whole created an efflorescence of ideas about what both the liturgy and the church of the future should be. There were many variations on three types of postconciliar worship space: renovations of older churches; new church buildings; and "non-church" spaces like the Community of John XXIII's cafeteria.

Fr. William Nerin's broadcast homily, like much postconciliar theology, cast his Catholic community as pilgrim voyagers: leaving a place of safety and stability for the uncharted waters of God's eschatological kingdom. While some postconciliar futurists developed and refined theories about floor plans, modern building materials, and sanctuary arrangements, others drew on secular theology and sought to erase physical barriers between the Mass and the everyday life of the people of God. "Experiments" by both groups tied the post–Vatican II liturgy to the spaces where it was created, performed, and received, as architects and liturgists alike insisted that an authentic future must, in the architect Robert Lawton Jones's words, involve a return to "fundamental questions"—not the question of what a church should look like, but rather, "what should a church be?"[16]

FUNCTIONALISM AND FLEXIBILITY IN THE VATICAN II ERA

Early in 1967, Msgr. John E. Kelly invited the Rambusch Decorating Company artist Willy Malarcher to his new parish of St. James the Less in Jamesburg, New Jersey.[17] Kelly, a media relations expert for the American bishops in Rome, had recently been reassigned to the semirural Jamesburg in his home diocese of Trenton, arriving to a ten-year-old brick Romanesque basilica, long, narrow, dark, and decorated with an assortment of plaster statues. He immediately organized the area's first parish council, although at its opening meeting in September 1966, he had to explain what the purpose of this unfamiliar body was. Despite a recent "noticeable drop" in Mass attendance, the parish began planning to renovate the church and to build a permanently open daily Mass chapel.[18] Malarcher, a Louisiana-born painter with an MFA from Catholic University, had been at Rambusch when, at the outset of Vatican II, the liturgist Frederick McManus had come to tell its artists and designers he hoped the Church would turn to people like them to help guide it toward a future free of the strict rubrics that had previously governed most aesthetic choices within the sanctuary. Now Kelly told Malarcher, "We have to change this [church]," and handed him a slim booklet hot off the presses: the Sacred Congregation of Rites' *Instruction on Eucharistic Worship.*[19] This document, Rome's instructions on the implementation of *Sacrosanctum concilium*, focused on Eucharistic theology rather than on instructions about step heights and tabernacle placement. As Catholic modernists hoped, instead of prescribing new rules, it invited artists, designers, architects, and others to envision different ways of embodying the great mystery of God's presence in the design of churches.

What made a "functional" church in the postconciliar era? In the 1940s, Barry Byrne summarized his work as "an analytical study of liturgical and practical needs, as these exist in modern life," leading to the production of church plans "gather[ing] the congregation intimately around the altar, or close to it."[20] While this task included studying the meaning of the Eucharist, for Byrne's generation of architects it also included close study of the practicalities demanded by fixed ritual scripts. A functional church needed to consider a slate of processions over the liturgical year; the placement of the choir; circulation needs for distributing communion; and numerous other details. As the postconciliar era unfolded, however, architects like Patrick Quinn noted a "state of flux" in the liturgy that made this kind of functional design impossible. In 1969, the liturgist Joseph Champlin expressed the the new situation's challenge for those who believed that form should follow function: "What liturgy is, should be, will be, determines the kind of building we must design for sacred worship. But to define the liturgy is difficult, and to describe its future extremely hazardous. . . . The liturgy of tomorrow cannot be precisely determined at this moment."[21] On the one hand, good churches would both express and make possible the liturgy; on the other, the preference of documents like the *Instruction on Eucharistic Worship* for a theological (rather than formal) approach to architectural guidelines meant a highly fluid situation for church architects and renovators.

The first wave of liturgical changes—including the dramatic moment on the first Sunday of Advent 1964, when many priests across the United States faced their congregations for the first time across the altar at Mass—sparked a series of makeshift sanctuary makeovers.[22] Veterans of the era recall, with pleasure or horror, "renovations" that consisted of wrenching the high altar away from the back wall. Many churches did no renovations at all, properly speaking, simply abandoning the old high altar and introducing a table closer to the congregation; still others ignored the changing liturgical situation as long as possible. Eventually, however, even the most reluctant pastors conceded the need to think seriously about redesigning their churches. Under orders to "modify the interiors [of older churches] as quickly as possible within space and budget limitations," as the *New York Times* put it in a 1972 article on "slowly evolving changes in Roman Catholic church architecture," parishes across the United States scrambled, with varying degrees of enthusiasm and aesthetic competence, to renovate.[23]

In letters, phone calls, magazine articles, and in-person visits, architects, artists, and pastors struggled to predict what changes might be coming, and how limited money might most intelligently be spent during a period of upheaval. Roger Jacobs of Milwaukee's Conrad Schmitt Studios wrote to a Kentucky pastor in 1967 to suggest a low-key renovation: moving the tabernacle to a side altar and moving the main altar forward to the edge of the existing predella, without changing any levels in the floor. "It is not necessary to do so now," Jacobs added, "but we feel that eventually we will be exhorted to remove the communion rail completely in order to eliminate all actual and visible barrier between the minister and the participating congregation."[24] The pastor had to decide: do only what was required, or potentially save money in the long run by removing the rail now and obviating a possible later renovation. This type of practical decision presented itself in both old churches and new. As the architects of San Francisco's new cathedral noted in 1964, "a real problem in trying to build the church of the future" had to do with the height of fixed elements such as the sanctuary steps. If "the time should come when people would receive Communion standing," at what height should the priest be for distribution?[25] How could an architect both design for the rubrics currently in force, and for those expected but not actually legislated?

By the early 1980s, most liturgists agreed that the main physical requirements of the postconciliar liturgy were a freestanding altar, a separate lectern for reading the scriptures, and a tabernacle away from the main altar.[26] However, during the postconciliar decade, it was far from clear either that these items *were* required, or that they were *all* that would be required. While frustrated priests and laity demanded to know when the postconciliar liturgy would stop changing, many liturgists—building on the evolutionary insights of the biological paradigm—had come to believe not merely in the necessity of corresponding liturgical and architectural reform but in their ongoing development. As Godfrey Diekmann told *U.S. Catholic* in 1965, "If the Council is successful, the principle of adaptation will be accepted," and this would "naturally lead to diversity and flexibility in the liturgy," not to a new norm.[27] Frederick McManus put it even more starkly in a memo to Oklahoma Bishop Victor Reed before the Vatican Council closed: "*In principle*, the liturgy should not be static but should evolve and be adapted to the needs and understanding of each age."[28]

In this situation of uncertainty (both in practice and in principle), many renovators did not plunge ahead alone, but sought out artists and architects who had guided the handful of preconciliar churches that seemed to be "clearly in anticipation of the changes in worship that were expected."[29] These men and women (including the pioneering independent liturgical consultants Frank Kacmarcik, Adé Bethune, and William Schickel, as well as studio-associated professionals like Malarcher and Jacobs) were overwhelmed with work, given how many extant churches seemed unsuited for the changes that had already occurred, let alone those anticipated.[30] Even while commending one of Schickel's low-cost renovations, Maurice Lavanoux worried about the consequences of the sudden national transformation: "The problem solved in [St. Therese, Detroit, Michigan] is one that needs to be met on a rather massive scale throughout the country. In order not to fall into a new and rather tiresome stereotype the work will have to be entrusted to a competent and creative designer and the local authorities will have to be aware of the liberty and variety allowed by the new directives."[31]

The liturgical consultants by and large agreed with Lavanoux that "liberty" was key, in part due to the stressful experience of retrofitting so many older churches without major—and very expensive—architectural surgery. Struggling with the results of the past led Adé Bethune, after a whirlwind tour of a dozen rural churches in need of renovation, to request no more rubrical "straitjackets."[32] Beyond the practical frustrations of renovation, however, Catholic futurists welcomed the collapse of rubricism because it coincided with their overall rethinking of the nature of the world as dynamic, evolutionary, rather than static. William Schickel, commenting on the application of *Sacrosanctum concilium* to churches, claimed that his main "fear" was not the technical problems of ongoing renovation but rather "the fixed point of view."[33] While liturgists and architects should not "expect . . . drastic revision to take place every year," Schickel felt that "the basic instinct of the Council was to move from a static position to a fluid one, and if one realizes that the idea would be to move toward a variety and fullness of life rather than rushing pell mell to tie down by directive a new set position, a new static point."[34] By the late 1960s, the liturgist Joseph Champlin could comment that a certain set of "familiar directives" was arising out of magisterial documents on the liturgy, but he did not mean a new set of rubrics. Instead, postconciliar consensus demanded "full, active, conscious participation in rites which possess noble simplicity, which are short, clear, and within people's powers of comprehension; taking part by means of songs, actions, gestures, and bodily attitudes, as by reverent silence; assembling for mass in such a way that a sense of community develops."[35] Functionalist design for the future would foster participation and community; the amorphous nature of these goals, and the awareness that rites seemed likely to go on changing, meant that it would also prize physical flexibility.

BUILDING COMMUNITY: "PARTICIPATION" AND WORSHIP SPACE IN THE POSTCONCILIAR DECADE

Experiments with the design and use of liturgical space during the Vatican II era, whether mild or radical, sought to encourage lay participation in the Mass. For the preconciliar liturgical movement, the architectural encouragement of participation meant minimizing visual distractions and shrinking the distance between the average pew and the altar, thus enabling massgoers to see and hear the priest, to focus on the liturgy rather than private prayer, and to make predetermined responses in set dialogues. In keeping with this goal, the last chapter of *Sacrosanctum concilium*, "Sacred Art and Sacred Furnishing," included a terse paragraph of great significance: "When churches are to be built," the council fathers wrote, "let great care be taken that they be suitable for the celebration of liturgical services and for the active participation of the faithful" (§124). They added, moreover, that the Church did not subscribe to any particular historical style and that the rubrics governing furniture and arrangement should be revised and even abolished if they were not "suited to the reformed liturgy" (§123–29).

Preconciliar churches built in the United States along the lines suggested by the liturgical movement were relatively well prepared to respond to the mandate for participation. But many Catholics in the 1960s and 1970s faced the necessity of retrofitting churches like St. James the Less for a very different future from the one envisioned by their original builders, often only a few years earlier.[36] If "the Council has handed us a brief for a new approach to church design," Patrick Quinn wondered, "what shall we do with the old ones, especially those neo-classic romantic hybrids whose plaster is hardly dry?"[37] Successive growth waves during the century prior to Vatican II had left American Catholics with a stock of buildings featuring long, narrow floor plans, high roofs, and altars placed against the back wall of the sanctuary and raised high above the nave floor. And this arrangement was not only a practical problem because of the strong "preference" now advanced by the Vatican that the main altar should allow for circumambulation and for Mass facing the people.[38] More pressingly because more difficult to correct, the typical floor plan, which divided the sanctuary strictly from the congregation and forced people into orderly rows facing the backs of one another's heads, seemed, in *Liturgical Arts*' terms, a "straitjacket" that "made *participation* impossible."[39] Liturgists now concluded that seeing and hearing the priest was necessary but not sufficient for full and active participation.

The simplest, cheapest, and most popular solution for renovators of basilica-plan churches was the one Malarcher and Kelly implemented at Jamesburg: moving the altar as far forward as possible, cleaning up the walls, and redoing the lighting to unite sanctuary and nave. (The Rambusch Decorating Company's preconciliar handbook had mandated strong light on the sanctuary and low light in the nave to stress the separation already imposed by communion rails and steps.) This kind of renovation was efficient, but, from the point of view of increasing participation, not optimal. Long naves, in Joseph Champlin's view, were too restrictive of the congregation's mobility during the service. If future congregations needed to be "listening, speaking, singing, watching, standing, sitting, moving about the church," in order to be deeply involved in the main action of the Mass rather than distracted by the statues, stained glass, and so forth that had served to "fill the [inspirational] gap" left open by the distance between congregation and Eucharist, then a renovator's job was "to make this as effective, as convenient as possible." *Liturgical Arts* suggested instead a more "desirable," though also more "costly" reconstruction of interior space in basilica churches (fig. 6.1). This reorganization of space screened off the former sanctuary as a chapel. In the former nave, new seating would be arranged around an altar set close to one of the side walls. The ninety-degree rotation would transform a longitudinal space focused on a distant sanctuary into a horizontal arrangement with a shallow semicircle gathered around the altar. Minor altars and devotional accoutrements previously located along the side walls of the nave would be removed or relocated out of the congregation's immediate sight. "The advantages," Maurice Lavanoux commented, were clear: "distances from the altar cut in half; greater visibility and better sound contact [with the presider]; less distractions to one's communication with Christ."[40]

Churches renovated in this way, as at St. Joseph's Chapel at Boston College and St. Sebastian's parish church in Greenbrae, California, pushed much more dramatically against the concept of the nave-sanctuary divide than renovations that merely brought the altar toward the congregation but maintained intervening steps and/or communion rails.[41] At St. Joseph's, the only gesture toward a spatial divide was a low one-step predella on which the renovators mounted the altar; since this movable platform was covered by the same wall-to-wall carpeting as the rest of the renovated interior space, the renovators minimized any visual distinction between "sanctuary" and congregation. Yet even this solution did not go quite far enough for many postconciliar Catholics. Was it not more consistent with the call for full and active participation to do away with the nave-sanctuary divide altogether? Could worshippers gather around the altar directly, rather than be separated from it by steps, let alone communion rails (see fig. 6.2)? This was an especially controversial question for groups that had long been barred or discouraged from entering the sanctuary during Mass: African Americans and women. One issue in a multifaceted controversy over Afrocentric Catholic liturgies in Chicago was the right to determine access to and design of black parishes' sanctuaries.[42] In 1966, the newly released sacramentary still barred women from proximity to the altar, establishing that if no "qualified man" was available as a lector, a woman reader would be permitted as long as she was "standing outside the sanctuary."[43] Postconciliar communities sometimes did not wait for official episcopal permission to invite laity, including laywomen, into the sanctuary—a practice that could invite censure, as when a priest wrote Frederick McManus to demand whether it was licit for nuns to gather around the altar during the communion ritual.[44]

As communities meditated on the meaning of active participation in the Mass, some concluded that people should also "participate" in making the church itself, and not merely by donating money to hire a construction company. Proponents pointed to everything from medieval cathedrals to Arts and Crafts modernism as precedent for communal building.[45] But many Catholics in the late 1960s strengthened the association of craft with full and active participation, and questioned architectural overdetermination. Maurice Lavanoux, after an evening Mass at a Jesuit artists' workshop in 1967, recorded in his diary that he had seldom been "so conscious of the need for simple and relatively unencumbered *space*." Most churches, he thought, were so hemmed in by encrusted decoration and furniture that they now found themselves unprepared for "the great evolution of the mass."[46] Some congregations, like the student groups at Boston College and New Mexico State–Las Cruces, took pride in designing and building church spaces themselves. Others encouraged massgoers to remake the liturgical space each week by rearranging seating and creating rotating or disposable visuals, in theory both engaging them in offering the Mass and preventing spiritual stagnation. The artist Corita Kent, IHM, commented that "the people who worship in each church" should "do the decoration," which "should always be temporary, I think."[47] New multipurpose worship spaces like St. Mark's, Kansas City; St. Leo, Pipestone, Minnesota; or the Chapel + Cultural Center, Troy, New York, came not with permanent art,

FIGURE 6.2. Daily mass at the Chapel+Cultural Center (C+CC), Troy, New York, early 1970s. The lay massgoers sit in the "sanctuary" area (see figs. 6.7 and 6.8) as they listen to a female lector read. The edge of the altar is visible to the right. Rotating photos of the poor around the world hang on the rear wall in place of biblical narrative art, a crucifix, or statues of saints. Photo: GLIT, 26-43-01.

but with hooks, clips, and tracks for the easy hanging of rotating or disposable art, "objects which are created not to last centuries, but weeks (or hours)."[48] In Jamesburg, Willy Malarcher advised the use of "disposable," congregation-made art "to assist the spirit of rededication" (see fig. 6.3).[49] Constantly enlisting parishioners' creativity to rearrange and replace elements of their worship space enabled them to actively participate not just during the hour of the liturgy, but during its preparation.

The end goal of all this activity was the discovery of ways to build a stronger community both within the immediate worship group and on a larger scale. It was not only the Church's radicals who promoted the community-building function of unconventional liturgical spaces in the Vatican II period. Chanceries were deeply concerned about keeping a mobile population connected to the institutional Church, and the late 1960s saw a spate of creative spatial efforts aimed at strengthening ties with Catholic suburbanites.[50] While bishops regularly created new parishes to serve that growing population, many worried

FIGURE 6.3. Paper fans, an example of "disposable" congregation-made art, carried into the church of St. James the Less, Jamesburg, New Jersey, during its rededication ceremony. Photo: Courtesy Rambusch Decorating Company, established 1898.

that offering Mass regularly in parish churches was not sufficient. Alarm over the future of the traditional parish was widespread, and the decline in mass-goers over the 1960s bore out some of these fears. While some attributed this to post–Vatican II changes having gone too far, and others to them not having gone far enough, a third group suggested that the problem was that the American parish plant as traditionally constituted was, as Bishop John Mussio of Steubenville, Ohio, claimed in 1964, "totally incapable of doing the job demanded of it."[51] Mussio meant, in part, that chanceries could not expect the new residents of the suburbs to treat parish churches as had their parents and grandparents in dense urban settings. Hartford, Connecticut's diocesan liturgical commission suggested that it was time to face the "disconcerting facts" that "the celebration of the Sunday liturgy in the large parish church (however well the changes have been implemented) gives the people little taste of genuine Christian community-spirit."[52] This staggering indictment, followed up by the blunt statement that "few people are coming to weekday liturgy in our churches," suggested that radical measures had to be taken. If the parish itself was not to be abandoned as a building block of Church life, it would have to be reconstituted as a composition of small, intimate groups tied to a central administrative and physical structure.

Home masses had been a part of Catholic life for decades, but they struck a new chord in the 1960s. They appealed to those who exulted in the promiscuous mixture of sacred and secular; the *Sign* highlighted one priest's use of a flat TV-set top as an altar as a symbol of "Christ coming to His people in a new, intimate way" (fig. 6.4).[53] As Mary Henold points out, in home masses, "women could stand within feet of the altar," a development not yet possible in many parish churches.[54] Yet Mass in community living rooms had impeccable credentials: it dated to the practice of the Apostles, who met "in their houses for the breaking of the Bread."[55] Bishops encouraged home masses on the grounds that they "contribute significantly to growth in awareness of the

FIGURE 6.4. Fr. Lawrence Dannemiller reads the gospel during Mass in Mr. and Mrs. Ivan Hubbell's living room, Elk Rapids, Michigan. Dannemiller brought vestments, an altar cloth, a chalice, and paten, and used the Hubbells' television as his altar. Photo: *Sign*, August 1966, courtesy Passionist Historical Archives, Helen Gallagher McHugh Special Collections, University of Scranton.

parish as community, especially when the faithful [also] participate in the parish Mass on the Lord's Day."[56] Priests beginning home Mass programs were to view them as an opportunity for evangelization; the intimate environment would make it possible to instruct "many who have assisted at Mass for years from the last few pews in Church," as well as an "opportune moment for the priest to probe his little audience for their reasons for always preferring the rear pews."[57] But this did not mean priests were to view the exercise cynically. Rather, an earnest concern for the spiritual care of the community appeared in one Kansas liturgist's plea to use home masses to help congregations understand that the Eucharist was not an individualistic experience; its purpose was "to mold a community through the bond of charity."[58] The properly celebrated, episcopally authorized home Mass would tie participants more closely to the parish as normative unit, inspiring families to attend Mass in the church on Sunday with a more committed spirit because they would understand their home life as part of parochial life, not as distinct from and possibly in opposition to it.

Concern for suburbanites also manifested in the movement of the liturgy into shopping malls. In Portage, Indiana, priests set up a fifty-foot long trailer with a glass-enclosed altar in a mall parking lot, offering the occupants of 150 cars Mass via loudspeaker.[59] Most such ministries, however, rented a storefront within the mall. The Franciscan proprietors of a chapel in Colonie, New York, which opened in 1970 and racked up half a million worshippers by 1975, justified their enterprise in terms familiar to the radicals simultaneously calling for storefront chapels in decaying urban areas: they wanted to "go where the action is and be with the people," in this case not the urban poor but bored teenagers and housewives with shopping bags (fig. 6.5).[60] Local blue laws required the mall—and thus the chapel—to close on Sunday, but a priest stayed on duty six days a week from 10 a.m. to 9 p.m. The church flowed into the mall space via worshippers who could not get a seat inside and via an information counter in the mall corridor, a space that Fr. Fabian Joyce, OFM, considered "one of the most important parts of the chapel" since it was the first point of contact with the many people arriving at the mall who had not intended to pray.[61]

Shopping-mall ministries were aimed squarely at the concerns, ease, and comfort of the suburban middle class. If it was no longer simple for a woman driving rather than walking to her errands to stop by the parish church for a quick prayer or to light a candle, she could now do so between visits to mall shops. "Busy mothers and many retired people," a reporter noted, "find the chapel schedule more convenient than ordinary, early-morning parish Masses." One woman brought visiting relatives to the chapel's Saturday vigil

FIGURE 6.5. St. Francis Chapel, Northway Mall, Colonie, New York (ca. 1974). "Motherhood Maternity Shops" was immediately to the chapel's left. Photo: *Sign*, April 1974, courtesy Passionist Historical Archives, Helen Gallagher McHugh Special Collections, University of Scranton.

Mass "because 'it's so difficult to get two families out of the house on Sunday morning.' "[62] Not everyone appreciated the semidifferentiated flow of space between mall and chapel; one woman complained that if she arrived late and had to stand outside the chapel, she couldn't hear anything but records blasting from a nearby shop.[63] Yet as even this concern demonstrates, despite their easy blend of consumerism and worship, the mall chapels were as spatially radical as American Catholic churches ever became, insisting by their presence that the sacred was not excluded from—and did not exclude—the secular.

The sense that the future would be very different from the present, requiring great flexibility in spatial arrangement and surface decoration, did not preclude postconciliar architects and liturgists from considering themselves as part of an ongoing evolutionary tradition, or from looking to "basics" of the Christian tradition to provide new answers for the future. Using the same biologically inflected language of the "living Church" that theologians and liturgists had elaborated during the first half of the twentieth century, *Living Worship* reminded its readers in 1966 that "experimentation and adaptation must begin in earnest and in public, but to be rich and full of power, they must be organically related to our past."[64] The architect Patrick Quinn dismissed ongoing arguments about modern "style" with the comment that "the future historians" could delineate all that; meanwhile, "our task is to continue a great living tradition."[65]

Quinn and other architects interested in "basic" questions about the function of a church were particularly attuned to early Christian spatial practices, just as liturgists inventing the "Mass of the Future" were often students of early Christian liturgy.[66] As the Middle Ages had been claimed for the cause of evolutionary modernism, so now was the early Church: "the whole history of early Christianity," *U.S. Catholic* asserted in 1965, "reflects [an] attitude of change and adaptation according to local circumstances."[67] Both in Europe—where Dom Frédéric Debuyst, the Belgian editor of the quarterly *Art d'église*, elaborated this idea—and in the United States, the supposedly early Christian concept of the "house church" recurred frequently as a joint ecclesiological and architectural response to contemporary problems.[68] If, as Vatican II had declared, the Church was "the people of God," then, as Adé Bethune summarized in 1968, "the church building is the house of the people."[69] Like any modern house, it ought to be "roomy, bright, pleasant, restful, open, hospitable" so that the "family" would be "able to see each other, hear each other rejoice in each other's presence."[70]

The "house church" appealed to many postconciliar Catholics because it prioritized community creation. The Lutheran architect Ed Sövik commented that understanding the church as basically a house meant thinking of architecture as an expression of the "ethic of love"; the building must not overwhelm or overpower its visitors, but meet them in "the open, dynamic, self-denying, and possibly dangerous form of the dialog."[71] Architects experimented with various ways of achieving the correct feeling. In the mid-1960s, Joseph Diviney, a student at Washington University in St. Louis who later joined Walter

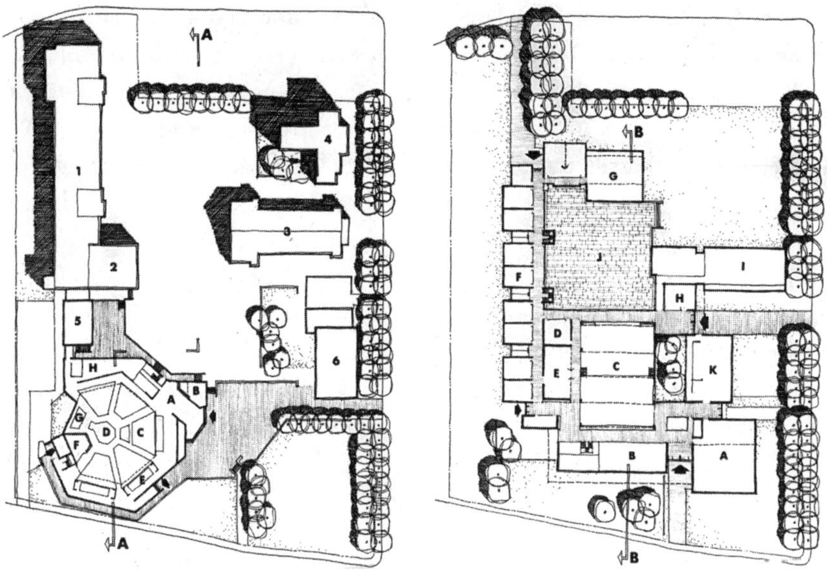

FIGURE 6.6. Two plans for a parish plant on Long Island (Joseph Diviney, ca. 1967). *On the left*, a typical layout with a "modern" church; *on the right*, a rethinking of the entire layout so that all elements are integrated into a single house-like unit. Photos: GLIT, 09-25-01 and GLIT, 09-26-01.

Gropius's Architects' Collaborative, undertook the design of a new church, seating approximately 1,000 to 1,200 people, for a parish on Long Island (fig. 6.6). He began with a plan that would have looked familiar to liturgically sensitive preconciliar architects, a heptagon with five blocks of seating arranged around a projecting sanctuary; but after several months of work, he concluded that this was "at best a compromise of the concept demanded by Vatican II." The move from a long, narrow nave to a gathered congregation still left the church building "segregated . . . from the other buildings of the parish . . . [and] from the daily lives of the parishioners."[72] Diviney reblocked the entire site, grouping a variety of buildings—including a large multiuse space that would be the primary site of worship as well as community activities—around a central courtyard. The new plan resembled a courtyard-oriented house, whereas his "compromise" solution had strung a series of unrelated buildings along the edges of the plot. He also suggested breaking the large parish community into two units of 1,200 families (still far larger than many liturgists of this period suggested) so that they might be able to realistically have "meaningful involvement" with one another during liturgical celebrations.

While Diviney's thesis project went unimplemented, several parishes did explicitly set out to build a "house church," including St. John the Evangelist in Hopkins, Minnesota, guided by liturgical consultant Frank Kacmarcik. Located in the liturgical-movement hotbed just a short distance from St. John's Abbey in Collegeville, the parish had been meeting in a converted movie theater and then the school gymnasium since its founding in 1950.[73] Pastor W. Leo Howley, however, had studied architecture, and had become interested in modern churches while serving as a military chaplain in Germany in the 1940s.[74] Howley and his parish building committee worked closely for several years with Kacmarcik and architect George Rafferty of Progressive Design Associates. As the design emerged in the mid-1960s, the building committee developed a lengthy document based on its conviction that the current congregation had "a serious responsibility to God for the spiritual formation of countless souls for generations."[75] They wished to "produce a living edifice," which acknowledged that while altar, pulpit, and other elements were important, "the most important items in the church are people, i.e., Christ and his people," and "everything" was to be "oriented around them and their functions."[76]

In his dedication sermon, Howley tied the building's house-like quality to a theological recognition of God's incarnational presence in the community. His parish had come to realize, like "the early Christians," that "God does not dwell in buildings but within men. . . . Wherever God's People gather for worship the place is called the house of God's people."[77] Around 1970, in the midst of serious financial troubles, parishioner Patricia Witte wrote that the people of St. John's had decided to build a "church of tomorrow," and they were aware that "its potential for celebration [would] perhaps not be fully realized in this generation, steeped as it [was] in the traditional idea of the church as the house of God" more than the "Paschal living room" represented by St. John's.[78] Rafferty made a conscious effort to design a church that would blend into the neighborhood of "well-maintained single-family houses," rather than dominate the block.[79] A Mediterranean courtyard house sheltered from the Minnesota elements, the plan organized a "paschal living room," chapel, library, community room, office, and school around a substantial atrium where, per the community's building philosophy, "the people of God should get to know each other" so that they might "love one another."[80]

Despite the community's and the architect's many references to early Christian practice and architecture, both looked to the far future. A *Progressive Architecture* jury saw the house-church as "a very mature solution . . . a growing, evolving kind of plan" allowing for multiple community functions. Witte, too, believed the building was pointing toward a reality not yet achieved.

Rafferty, she wrote, had been faced with "creating a church for the future in a parish where the congregation, to a large extent, might have preferred a traditional church." The church therefore did not represent a finished reality, but was "a symbol of hope . . . conceived, designed and built in a time of turmoil and chance." The parish's struggles through a post–Vatican II adjustment "all contributed to resistance and suffering that at some future date [would] be understood to have been necessary in the transformation to a mature, twenty-first-century community in Hopkins." As a church of the "*Risen Christ*," the community was "in the process of transformation towards the fulness of redemption," and would be helped in its journey by its church building.[81]

"USES WHICH WE CAN'T FORETELL": MULTIPURPOSE CHURCHES AND THE UNKNOWN FUTURE

Progressive Architecture, keeping tabs on development in Protestant, Catholic, and Jewish buildings, commented in 1968 that secular theology's abrogation of the distinction between sacred and the profane meant a shift in the definition of a church. A church was no longer "a very special place, with its own etiquette," or even "an embassy from the beyond with extraterritorial powers"; the term now conjured "the Judaic idea of what might be called a sacred quorum."[82] The word *church*, in other words, now frequently referred not to a building, but to "the assembly of Christians gathered for worship."[83] Nevertheless, the shifting "assembly of Christians" had to come together somewhere—at least until, as some projected, technology would enable the liturgy to unfold over telephone lines.[84] Understanding the church as a "tent" or other temporary space to house the people of God, rather than as a permanent edifice, resulted in the development of multipurpose spaces that could be converted or abandoned as the future unfolded.

Temporary church spaces, intended to eventually become a school gym or social hall, had been a staple of preconciliar parishes in the growing suburbs; sometimes they previewed postconciliar strategies of folding doors and moveable sanctuary furniture. Folding doors and even a folding communion rail helped St. Matthew in Norwalk, Connecticut, opened in 1960, do double duty as church and social hall.[85] But most preconciliar parishes regarded this as a fiscally prudent stopover while funds were raised for a permanent church. By the late 1960s, however, some Catholic groups felt that convertible worship rooms signaled the kind of church they *intended* to be. Four of the six buildings profiled in *Progressive Architecture* in 1968 under the heading "The New Church Architecture: The Passing of Sacred Space?" contained multipurpose spaces meant to house both worship and other activities.[86] This included the Catholic-sponsored Chapel + Cultural Center (C+CC) in Troy, New York, which *Progressive Architecture* described as "the secular nave," referring both to Harvey Cox and J. G. Davies's *The Secular Use of Church Buildings* (1968). The C+CC, which houses the Newman Center at Rensselaer Polytechnic Institute (RPI), was a thoughtful architectural response to the challenges laid down by Cox. Typically staffed by priests sympathetic to their young, energetic congregations, 1960s Newman Centers were often loci of lively liturgical and architectural experimentation. College chaplains were among the most eager to renovate their buildings, cheerfully ripping out pews so that students could sit cross-legged on carpet around the altar; meanwhile, programs that needed new buildings responded to up-to-the-minute liturgical and theological imperatives to situate themselves in their environments and provide multipurpose space. At the University of Maine–Orono, the 1972 Newman Center used local materials to "relate . . . to the Maine environment"; chaplain Blase Schauer and his students at New Mexico State–Las Cruces went so far as to build their chapel by hand, using local stone and wood.[87] Both, like the C+CC and others, provided multipurpose space.[88]

RPI's Catholics had celebrated Mass for several years in a convent chapel just off campus. When this building was sold to the university, the group decided to build its own church, despite the postconciliar liturgical upheaval, expressing the "strong" feeling that "the renewed Church needs to find expression in a new building."[89] The Newman group's postconciliar ecclesiology translated into an ambitious desire to create a space suitable for the entire college and city community to use for ecumenical and interfaith worship, and for as many secular purposes as future imaginations could devise. The architect Peter Levatich, an RPI alumnus, expressed both excitement and frustration at the challenges of designing "for uses which we can't even possibly foretell."[90] But the building's program charged it to "be a statement of the Church's openness to all individuals and institutions and its changing role in a society which is radically secular," be available for "maximum use" (rather than only a few hours a week), and provide for "maximum flexibility" due both to its projected secular and religious uses and to "the present state of transition in the worship forms of the Church."[91] As *Jubilee*'s article "Revolution on the Secular Campus" described, the Newman group had transitioned from an inward-centered "club" to an "apostolate" evangelizing and serving the campus to, finally, a self-conception as a "community" sharing many things with the larger community.[92] Their new building would "embody in brick and stone the new dialogue that has been opened between churches and between church and community" and "step beyond the once-narrow confines of serving one religious belief and into the broader concept of involvement and exchange."[93]

Rev. Thomas Phelan, RPI's Newman chaplain, had been involved for some years with the national Catholic Art Association. Prior to the council, this group had maintained a mutual cordial dislike with the Liturgical Arts Society; CAA had continued the more philosophical and intra-ecclesial discussions associated with the early discussions at Portsmouth Priory, while the society developed in a more practical, ecumenical, professionalized direction.[94] In the mid-1960s, however, the visions of the two groups converged. Phelan's long-standing interest in the arts and in "good work" ensured that despite a low budget everything would be entrusted to accomplished artists. Adé Bethune served as liturgical consultant and George Nakashima did the woodwork and furniture. In consultation with the Newman group, the team emphasized interior flexibility. Levatich arranged a series of rectangles in a shallow curve, with three main public spaces: a lounge/meeting room and a large multipurpose room linked with an open foyer and baptistery (fig. 6.7). The lounge has a folding wall capable of dividing a parish living space from a conference room. The main multipurpose space, meanwhile, includes a mechanized folding wall and a series of configurable floor platforms (fig. 6.8). At one end of the room, a shallow rectangle with a fixed bench on three sides serves as either the sanctuary, when the main space is filled with a congregation, or, with the mechanized wall in place, as a chapel (see fig. 6.2). To one side of this sanctuary/chapel is a small area functioning as a chapel of Eucharistic adoration, with a curtain that can be pulled around the tabernacle to hide it from view when the space is in use by other faiths or for secular purposes. The sanctuary/chapel, when the altar and lectern are removed, also serves as a stage for readings and performances; alternately, if a stage is built in the center of the entire space using the platforms, it can be used for extra seating. When the mechanized wall is closed, a projection screen can drop from the ceiling, and events can take place on either side of the wall. Artwork (except for Bethune's multicolored rose window) consists of easily changed banners and paintings.

Phelan later recalled, "We did not want to build another church and rectory. We wanted to build a building that would be used 'all the time.'" In collaboration with RPI's Protestant chaplain Herb Hodgson, Phelan was particularly interested in using the arts to "get at religious and moral themes" and awaken

FIGURE 6.7. Chapel + Cultural Center (C+CC), Troy, New York (Levatich and Miller, 1967). Note that the altar and sanctuary furniture have been removed for a secular performance, while a white curtain has been pulled around the tabernacle with the reserved Eucharist (*right side of the photo*). Banners, including one with a quotation from Teilhard de Chardin, hang along the hall and to either side of the sanctuary/stage. Photo: GLIT, 26-43-02.

FIGURE 6.8. Chapel + Cultural Center (C+CC), Troy, New York (Levatich and Miller, 1967). Section of main multipurpose space showing sliding wall and movie screen. Photo: C+CC.

the 'human' side of his technologically oriented students.[95] In service of this goal, Phelan's own vision of multipurpose space changed during the design process. In 1966, he told the Catholic Art Association that while in the Middle Ages churches had been used for secular purposes and could be again, a church building still ought to have a permanent fixed altar, lectern, and presider's chair. By the time his building opened a year later, he had accepted that movable sanctuary furniture was more suitable for a multipurpose building.[96] He also originally intended for the building to be a meeting place of the sacred and the profane.[97] But by April 1968 he was echoing Cox, saying that the building committee wanted "to demonstrate that everything is sacred in its own way and that there is nothing totally secular."[98] While Phelan continued to believe that the need for dedicated worship space would not disappear, he had decided that it was more important to be flexible and open than to insist on permanent churches. He began to claim that the Newman group was "building a building to be given away."[99] If the Catholic community came to feel that the C+CC "was a millstone around our necks," the flexibility of the space would make it possible for the university to take it over.[100]

Such multipurpose spaces seemed both to provide the flexibility Catholic futurists craved, and to resolve the long-standing dilemma of the separation of liturgical and civic life that had troubled countercultural Catholics for many years. In one of many proposals for more compact community worship space, Maurice Lavanoux suggested that a space for 250 to 300 people could "allow for great elasticity of seating arrangement so that the space could be used throughout the week. . . . Parish activities of all kinds would become a beehive of community involvement."[101] He felt that new multipurpose spaces could "welcome the evolution of liturgical awareness and the living liturgies of the faithful *in action*."[102] Catholic parishes that requested multipurpose spaces, such as St. Leo's in Pipestone, Minnesota, prioritized movable sanctuary furniture so that the space could be available for "non-cultic community events." St. Leo's architect, Ed Sövik, commented that the priests and their parish council "were eager to look onto the future as far as they could, and had the courage to venture beyond what has already been accepted as change."[103] In other words, they were not content to stop with providing for Mass *versus populorum* or even creating a more community-oriented feeling. They tried to provide for a future where community events and worship interpenetrated freely, and tried to make their space responsive to future liturgical possibilities as well as present celebrations. At Our Divine Savior in Chico, California, Patrick Quinn argued that his plan, which used heavy sliding curtains to divide the space, acknowledged that the liturgy was "only one of the 'encounter' situations" that might occur in the building—so that the new church space "should be *people-centered* rather than *liturgy-centered*" (fig. 6.9).[104] At a Texas Newman Center, Clovis Heimsath solved a similar problem geometrically, "carving" a cube into related parts with sliding doors, with smaller living and study spaces constellated around a multistory "center bay" that was conceived as a "flexible space for liturgical functions, art exhibits, dances, student meetings, and recreations."[105]

A number of new churches, like Our Divine Savior, relied on moving parts and flexible furniture to achieve multiple ends. Our Lady Queen of Heaven in Lake Charles, Louisiana, had what the architect Robert Biery described as a "main paschal room," which could be "converted quickly to an auditorium for lay meetings."[106] Liturgical designer William Schickel built configurable furniture of blocks held together by pegs and used them in projects like a temporary chapel for St. Charles Borromeo in Kettering, Ohio (fig. 6.10). Others, like St. Leo with its deliberate allusions to warehouse architecture, bridged the sacred and the secular through architectural forms. St. Thomas Aquinas in Indianapolis (Evans Woollen and Associates, 1969) drew on theater architecture, with a sloping nave arranged around a three-quarter-thrust stage for the sanctuary and exposed lighting trusses in lieu of a baldachino. On the sanctuary wall, a massive red cross cutout "inspire[d] a kaleidoscopic array of changing meanings"; the stainless steel sanctuary furniture could "be removed so that the great high space becomes a multi-purpose auditorium or theater." The architects added that while "romantic richness" had been "lovely and valid in its

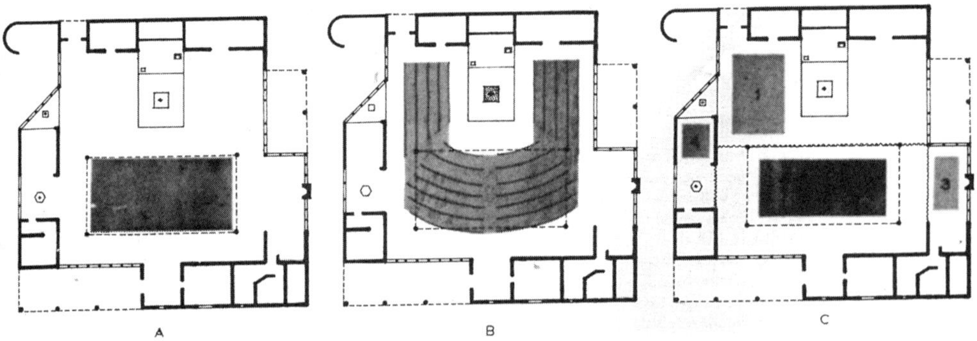

FIGURE 6.9. Three plans for configuring Our Divine Savior, Chico, California (Patrick Quinn and Francis Oda, 1969–70). *On the left*, a congregation sits in the gray block while Mass is celebrated at an altar directly beneath the main skylight. *In the middle*, for a larger group, congregational seating is extended to all three sides. *On the right*, the space has been subdivided using heavy curtains, screens, and sliding doors. A congregation of seventy gathers in the sanctuary for worship (*1*); up to 150 people can meet near the entrance (*in the dark rectangular block*); fifteen can meet for a conference or seminar (*3*), and about ten can do private prayer in a Blessed Sacrament chapel (*4*). Photo: Courtesy Patrick Quinn.

FIGURE 6.10. William Schickel's flexible furniture for St. Charles Borromeo, Kettering, Ohio, mid-1960s. Photo: GLIT, 25-28-01.

own day," it "properly belong[ed] to eras now irrevocably dead," associating the flexible, multipurpose, metallic space with the green shoots of the living church.[107]

LITURGICAL EXPERIMENTATION AND THE WORSHIP SPACE OF THE FUTURE

Postconciliar Catholic communities who built or renovated dedicated or multipurpose churches during the late 1960s often suggested that they hoped to serve the entire local community. But some also justified the time and expense involved with the hope that local investment could serve the universal Church.

When the rector of the Cranwell School in Lenox, Massachusetts, hired Peter McLaughlin to design a new chapel as "a laboratory where full participation in the liturgy could be experienced by the students," he invoked one of the key words of the postconciliar decade: *experimentation*.[108] The ubiquity of this term indicated the extent to which professionalized American Catholics had internalized the scientific model of approach to reality. While opponents of liturgical and related architectural experimentation accused proponents of a desire for excessive individualism and anarchy, proponents wondered how Catholics could responsibly determine the best forms for liturgy, parish life, bureaucratic organization, or anything else, without trying out various options and seeing what worked. The American priest George Casey had seen this type of thinking coming as far back as 1963, arguing that the Vatican Council's work on the liturgy was important because "this is the day of exploration: of space . . . of the insides of the atom; it is the day of research and of an unending effort to solve problems and mysteries; of the insatiable quest to know. The Catholic people are not apart from all this; they too want to know what is going on."[109]

Evolution and *experimentation* worked together in postconciliar discourse, despite their different connotations: if *evolution* reassured the anxious that change was natural and the future could retain an organic connection to the past, *experimentation* offered a greater level of human control over the process of discovering and building the future. The liturgists Robert Hovda and Gabe Huck argued that although "historically, certainly, liturgy evolved by means of a less formal kind of experimenting and adapting," nevertheless "contemporary tools of research and measurement" were making it possible to participate in "a public and scientifically measureable effort to draw from the experience of a concrete assembly rites and modes and styles of worship that are particularly meaningful in and congenial to its culture."[110] Maurice Lavanoux, meanwhile, scolded postconciliar Catholics who sought to fall back on "ingrained habit" since the liturgy was "now evolving in the chrysalis of experimentation."[111]

The desire for some form of postconciliar liturgical experimentation was hardly universal, but it was widespread, ranging from laypeople to bishops like Paul Hallinan of Atlanta and Victor Reed of Oklahoma City. The Notre Dame sociologist Donald Barrett summed up a wide-ranging 1966 discussion by pointing out, "We're all struck with the need for experimentation—experimentation which is observed, so that we can learn from it."[112] For Thomas Ambrogi, SJ, "experimentation" was the only way to make a "truly significant liturgy," which would have to "emerge out of an authentic development from below."[113] However, Ambrogi's further explanation pointed to the tensions inherent in the term. "Genuine scientific experimentation," Ambrogi told his audience at the 1967 Liturgical Week, was not "just the trying of something different every day to see if it might be relevant for 'me' or for 'us.'" It was to be "fully authorized . . . by legitimate episcopal authority." Three characteristics would make liturgical experiments properly scientific: "carefully and professionally prepared," they would be repeated for a substantial period of time, and finally "they would be so structured as to allow for thorough critical evaluation." Ambrogi envisioned an experimental liturgy as popular only in a very limited sense; "tentative new rites" would have to be composed by teams of scholars including psychologists, theologians, anthropologists, historians, and "liturgiologists," approved by the hierarchy for temporary use, and then "evaluated scientifically with an eye toward acceptance into the ordinary worship of the church."[114]

The question of whether experimentation could grow out of local communities, or was to be undertaken and supervised ("controlled") by professionals, was one of the most contentious in postconciliar Catholicism.[115] At the local level, priests and laypeople alike often read the Vatican II documents *Lumen gentium* and *Sacrosanctum concilium*, with their emphasis on the local Church, as tacit permission to experiment. Collections of potential liturgies including dozens of variations on the text of the Mass began circulating, first in mimeographed and then published form, with suggestions ranging from those based on extensive historical research into early liturgy to those referencing twentieth-century literature and events.[116] Yet shortly it became clear that official permission for this kind of experiment would not be forthcoming. The years 1967 and 1968 both brought pronouncements from the Vatican against local and "private" experiment, and proposed centers for liturgical experimentation at universities like Notre Dame and Fordham never materialized.[117] Both Rome and the American hierarchy took an increasingly dim view of the idea that Vatican II had signaled "a permanent effort of experimenting in order to adapt" continually to new circumstances.[118]

In practice, however, the paucity of official channels for liturgical experimentation did not destroy the desire to experiment, but instead created sometimes intense conflict over control of liturgical space. If some Catholics saw experimental liturgies as the best ways to "discover how best to meet the human and Christian needs of the People of God," others saw them as a blow to the Church's unity and authority structures.[119] In Chicago, Archbishop John Cody engaged in a multiyear battle with African American activists over control of the city's black parishes and the use of Afrocentric symbolism during Mass.[120] At St. Cecilia's Parish in Englewood, New Jersey, an overflow Mass for families in the school cafeteria became more popular than Mass in the main church; lay leaders including the liturgical artists Willy and Patricia Malarcher and Richard Anuszkiewcz, a student of Josef Albers, hung their own artwork from the cafeteria ceiling and arranged the space differently each Sunday. But the arrival of a new priest in the late 1960s put an end to this Mass on the grounds that it was distracting from parish unity.[121] The fragility of lay-led activity in spaces controlled by priests and bishops was a frequent theme of postconciliar experimentation. In St. Louis, the pastor of St. Francis Xavier expelled a 2,500-person experimental community, "so formless that even members refer to themselves as 'the group from the lower church,'" from its weekly liturgy.[122] He explained that the group, which had its own bank account and paid rent to the church, was diverting money from the regular parish collection; he also had "theological" and "liturgical" concerns about parochial unity. When, after a month, a new pastor agreed to restore the basement masses, Cardinal Carberry emphasized that he "should seek to preserve the parish's life as 'a single totality.'"[123]

Tension over physical and liturgical control of churches was far from the only factor leading experimental groups to go underground, in a common spatial metaphor. But the relative ease of conducting experimental liturgies outside of church buildings certainly helped build unconventional liturgical spaces' popularity. Authorities often condemned this strategy; the editor of the Sacramento *Catholic Herald*, for example, accused the 1966 Liturgical Week of condoning a "liturgical orgy" by "sponsoring a series of Eucharistic celebrations offered in various hotel rooms and on home dinner tables where priests made up their own ceremonies."[124] Three years later, Archbishop John Whealon resorted to University of Hartford security personnel to prevent attendees of the New England Congress of Religious Education from celebrating unauthorized masses on campus.[125] Heavy-handed tactics could exclude experimental liturgies from churches. But this was a dangerous road, as proponents of a more openly experimental climate warned. Donald Thorman of *National Catholic Reporter* told the hierarchy, "Face it: the Underground Church proves there will be experimentation, with or without permission."[126] The Illinois priest James O'Brien made the dire prediction that Rome's disinclination to allow experiments in the liturgy would create "what might be called the *Humanae Vitae* effect," the exposure of magisterial authority as a sham.[127] The watchful eye could not be everywhere. At the same time a guard and a Hartford diocesan priest were interrupting a midnight dorm liturgy during the Congress of Religious Education on Whealon's orders, experimenters at St. Thomas seminary were celebrating "an unsanctioned mass . . . without the intrusion of the church establishment" in a lounge only a few feet away from the sleeping archbishop.[128] In dormitories, basements, private homes, parks, and cafeterias, experimenting Catholics slipped beyond hierarchical supervision to seek the future of the liturgy.

While frustrating restrictions on buildings owned by the Church led some Catholic experimental groups away from them, others deliberately sought to decouple parishes or communities from stable locations or buildings. "Floating" parishes—those that rented or borrowed a variety of nonpermanent liturgical spaces—shared some spatial values with the ad hoc protest groups of the Catholic left, who were arrested variously while celebrating a Mass for peace on the Pentagon concourse in 1969, burning draft files while reciting the Our Father at Catonsville, Maryland, in 1968, and performing a quasiliturgical ritual involving throwing shredded draft files in the Rockefeller Center plaza, also in 1969.[129] If, as Teilhard's holistic universalism and Cox's secular theology had suggested, God was everywhere, Catholic liturgical performance outside of permanent church buildings was a powerful tool for both affirming and manifesting that presence.[130] These theological and historical convictions joined the widespread concern that traditional territorial parish organization would not prove effective in the future Church, and that "experimental parishes" and "experimental non-parochial forms" were necessary.[131] Seventy-eight percent of respondents to a 1970 *U.S. Catholic* poll agreed that "some parishes without [territorial] boundaries should be tried." One respondent, Wisconsin priest George Hinger, knew that detaching parish communities from parish churches would have "dangers," but these were "of the kind that must be faced by any growing and developing community." Hinger felt that "the greatest danger [was] that by not experimenting along new lines of parish structure, our present churches may well be paid for, but stand as the most costly mausoleums in history."[132]

Hinger captured both the financial and the more existential concerns that generated floating and other experimental postconciliar parishes. Catholics who had spent decades paying for huge parish plants were now highly aware that building and maintenance expenses constrained their attempts to reconceptualize the postconciliar future. As a result, both futurist prognosticators and groups beginning new Catholic communities in the late 1960s often chose to envision a future without permanent and dedicated churches.[133] Experimental parishes like the Community of Christ Our Brother in Atlanta did not have territorial boundaries, relying on communities of interest instead and drawing participants from a relatively large geographical area. These communities conceptualized themselves as alternatives to traditional parish structures, and both because they regarded the future as inherently open and uncertain and because, in the words of Christ Our Brother administrator Fr. Conald Foust, they preferred "to use what small amount of money we have to respond to human needs, rather than build a church or hall," they were mobile by design.[134] They often met in non-Catholic churches: Christ Our Brother was meeting at a Methodist community center in August 1967, while a community sponsored by the relocated Woodstock Jesuits rented the Columbia University chapel for several hours a week.[135] Although members of experimental communities sometimes put the choice sharply between spending money on buildings or antipoverty measures—a member of the radical Emmaus House in Harlem remarked, "We're more concerned with stopping all church-building and trying to feed the hungry"—they were also capable of articulating a sense that this mobility, as much as poverty, was a necessary quality of the church they envisioned.[136]

Hundreds of experimental, underground, and floating groups were meeting across the country by the late 1960s, and many sought not just personal spiritual achievement and social action, but a significant "potential effect on the structure and function of the parish of the future."[137] If shopping mall ministries were directed at the suburban middle class, floating parishes were closely aligned with the self-image and experiences of mobile, highly educated professionals. Moving frequently in pursuit of career goals and living apart from their extended families and ethnic communities, these men and women tended to self-segregate into social groups of similarly situated professionals. They saw themselves as problem-solvers, and in their religious life, they rejected the idea that they should be either mere recipients of sacramental services, or foot soldiers in hierarchical campaigns. Instead, they hoped to actively shape the church of the future.

A detailed study of two Oklahoma-based experimental nonterritorial parishes by the Center for Applied Research in the Apostolate (CARA) provides a rare window into the mechanics of these communities. The Community of John XXIII, Oklahoma City, and the Community of the Living Christ, Tulsa, had been given official permission to embark on a period of experimentation by Bishop Victor Reed, whose episcopal motto, according to CARA, could have been "Let a thousand flowers bloom."[138] In August 1966, Oklahoma City priest William Nerin and roughly thirty laypeople petitioned Reed for formal recognition of their nascent community. In November, the members signed a declaration of their intent:

> To provide the Church with an experiment in living parish life in a way more suited to the demands of our time, the Gospels, and the needs of the

> members, themselves; to be a true servant of man in secular society; to leave a record of our successes and failures for the benefit of the Church, God's people here on earth. . . . We, the undersigned, realizing the seriousness of our endeavor will demand a suitable length of time to test fully this experiment, herein pledge ourselves for a minimum of two years to this effort.[139]

They promised that their liturgy would be "in keeping with the dictates of Vatican II and the rules and regulations of the American Bishops," but they felt "that some experimentation needs to be made for the sake of the Church."[140] Reed gave permission for two years' experimentation, followed by an evaluation; the first lay chair of the community kept a detailed diary during this period, intending to make the experimental "data" available to the diocese. The news generated widespread publicity and more than two hundred letters of inquiry to Reed from outside the diocese.[141]

Within a year, the community had grown to approximately one hundred members—far short of the thousands in a typical city parish. This, too, was intentional. John XXIII's members hoped that in a small group they could develop a better community life and a "relevant, meaningful" liturgical experience in combination with social action. "Impatient to get on with the renewal promised by Vatican II," they firmly rejected "building programs, a huge debt, two thousand unknown faces, and numerous organizations," illustrating that many Catholics had come to view the financial sacrifice associated with ambitious parish plants not as a point of pride and an investment in the parish's future, but as a stifling burden.[142] Instead, as a brochure clarified, the community "own[ed] no real property and [did] not contemplate such a move in the future."[143] This was essential to members' spiritual growth: the lack of property "causes us to be less secure in our 'parish life' and encourages us to see and understand more about our city and our neighbors. It enables us to go where we're needed—where the problems are."[144] John XXIII thus envisioned permanent mobility. During its first years, liturgies moved frequently, including full weekends spent at "regional parks and church camps."[145] This reconceptualization of liturgical space was powerful enough that one of the community's masses led NBC's 1968 *The New American Catholic.*

Tulsa's Community of the Living Christ, including founding member Robert Lawton Jones, was less vocally committed to mobility, but also resisted property ownership. Their 1972 self-evaluation established their intention to have an "outward thrust" aimed at the larger community—a choice that underlay their disinterest in church-building.[146] Eventually, their special focus came to be not mobility but ecumenism, and by the early 1970s they shared a downtown storefront with a small Presbyterian group. The two communities ran the building as a drop-in center for teenagers during the week, and the Presbyterians celebrated their liturgy on Saturday nights. Living Christ's Sunday liturgies reorganized the storefront into a banquet hall, gathering four or five massgoers at small tables around a central table serving as the altar. In lieu of a reredos, a bulletin board illustrated a weekly theme; the group also had decorative banners that they occasionally shared with similarly minded parishes.[147] However, Living Christ expressed the feeling that their other activities, in other places, "often" saw "involvement and participation" to a greater degree than "at the actual Sunday liturgy"; they cited weekday evening meetings that might feature a "home mass" but might also be formatted as a "song fest" or "simply dialog with personal problem-sharing," along with informal and formal liturgies to dedicate a playground they had built, at a picnic on a farm, to celebrate Easter outdoors, and jointly with various neighborhood churches, highlighting their ecumenical activity.[148]

Catholic communities that opted to float often attracted people both deeply rooted in Catholic life (Living Christ's initial membership was drawn almost entirely from the Christian Family Movement) and with increasingly fragile ties to the institutional Church. John XXIII's note-keeping on experiments was not matched by outreach from within the chancery during its crucial first years; as time went on, the record-keeping ceased and membership turned increasingly inward, a situation facilitated by the community's spatial instability. This helped it stay restless and searching, and prevented ruinous debt, but it presented difficulties for recruiting new members. Floating communities also reflected the transience of their largely professional-class base; members often found themselves not moving "where the action was" but away from the city altogether, as one former member of Living Christ did when his family relocated to St. Louis in what he described as a "typical corporate transfer move."[149] Due to increasingly mutual disinterest between chanceries and floating communities, the results of these experiments in the 1970s and beyond did not match the widespread predictions in the late 1960s that they would be a guide to the church's future.

BEYOND THE CHURCH OF TOMORROW

"Why build beautiful churches?"

Sister Paulissa's question echoed across the American Catholic community during the postconciliar decade, as many of her coreligionists disputed the definition of "church," seeking new kinds of worship spaces to express a new ecclesiology and decorating them with flexible, fragile, even disposable furniture and art. Adé Bethune spoke for postconciliar Catholic futurists when she lamented that "too many of our older church buildings are granite and marble palaces, unsuited as homes for the new liturgy. Too many of our newer churches are still pretentious architectural constructions." What was to be done? Bethune's solution was exactly what Sister Paulissa disdained:

> We should not only feel free to re-arrange existing buildings more radically than has generally been done so far, but also we must have the courage to give up buildings that are a financial liability. We must feel free to sell, or to tear down our marble palaces and build along more modest and suitable lines for the family of the Christian people to do their work. We should also feel free to use a plurality of places convenient for small group assemblies—homes, schools, shopping centers, apartments in housing complexes.[150]

If some postconciliar parishes found renovating their churches a "growth experience," and others built new structures combining multipurpose use with intimate, flexible, but recognizable worship space, a few pushed the limit beyond what their community would accept. In Cottage Grove, Minnesota, a building committee including the liturgical artist Gerald Bonnette agreed to implement a spatial solution by Frank Kacmarcik—one so unusual that the dedication program began with the statement "Yes, this is our church."[151] It being "difficult to build an old church," the committee remarked, they had chosen to "build a new one." The committee had not "set out to build a building that looks like a church"; it wanted, instead, "a religious building designed with careful attention to function and built in flexibility," one that "would encourage total involvement" of the parish in worship and service. The full plan, in addition to a multipurpose room, called for an auditorium with movie theater–style seating, a stage, a screen, and projection equipment where the Liturgy of the Word would be carried out (fig. 6.11). A separate "Hall of Celebration," not yet built, would be used to celebrate the Eucharist; the time of transition from one room to another would be used to "build up friendly encounter." But the parish never became reconciled to the building, and never added the Hall of Celebration; many even departed for nearby St. Thomas Aquinas (itself a notably "modern" building) on the grounds that St. Rita's would "never be a church."[152] In the 1980s a new church, with a layout combining nave and sanctuary in a single large space, was attached to one end of the building.

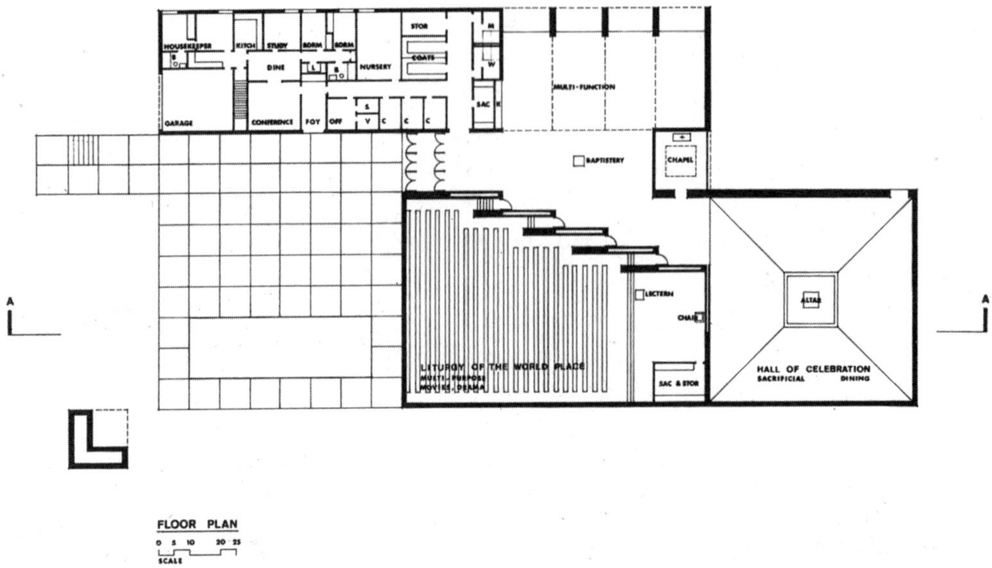

FIGURE 6.11. Plan for St. Rita, Cottage Grove, Minnesota (Ted Butler for Hammel, Green, Strahanson, 1971). The plan shows the auditorium (*bottom middle*), "Hall of Celebration" (*bottom right*, never built), and multipurpose room (*top middle*). Photo: GLIT, 21-39-01.

St. Rita's proved a pastoral failure, but it represented the kind of "basic" postconciliar experiment called for by architects and designers like Kacmarcik, Bethune, and Patrick Quinn. In a lecture to the Catholic Art Association in August 1966, Quinn argued that "any real work of architecture manifests much more than the technology and fashion of its time . . . because it bears witness to the activity it shelters, and even fosters its development." Therefore, "if that activity, its inner life, changes so radically that the building can no longer cope with it or facilitate it, then the building must be altered or entirely replaced." He wanted to know how "the churches of the future" would "manifest Christian life in their making." Where a more conventional statement might have looked to Vatican II's documents on the Church and the liturgy for clues, Quinn instead turned to John XXIII's 1963 encyclical *Pacem in Terris*, because of its threefold stress on "communication, relevance, and love." Quinn understood the church as basically a house. But he was also inclined to think that the questions about parish places and house churches were "stop-gaps" and "temporary measures to allow a maximum of environmental and communal relevance within our anachronistic parish structures." To really build the church of the future would require the total "rewriting of the architectural program, the redefinition of the shape, nature, and purpose of the Christian community. . . .

A real liturgical brief must extend beyond the boundaries of the sanctuary and the chancery office into the life of the urban community." This work had only begun, but would eventually lead to "the abandonment of the church building as we know it, the parish structure as we know it, the church administration as we know it, and to a reorganization on lines that are relevant to life in the future urban community."[153] Quinn's meditation recognized that the problems of the church building, of the Christian community's self-organization, and of its relationship to the rest of creation were indissolubly linked. And he believed this theological insight would lead to the "abandonment" of church-building in the future, rather than its rethinking.

While Quinn's rejection of "the church building as we know it" was indeed radical, he was not a lone voice drawing this conclusion in the later 1960s. Shaped by their interpretation of Vatican II in the light of writings by Teilhard, Cox, and other theologians, American Catholic futurists' evolutionary desires led to proposals not only for new architectural forms, but for the near-total elimination of church buildings. To the frustration of bishops and architects, the key insight about the nature of liturgical space that made home masses and mall chapels seem possible and desirable also threatened to undermine the role of buildings and centralized institutions. Robert Hovda and Gabe Huck articulated the the implications of a renewed sacramental theology: "It is the people and their liturgical deed, it is the action of the celebrating community, which *creates the place*. . . . Bricks and mortar became sacred historically only as the result of their use by a celebrating people."[154] The walls of the church building became a "skin" against and within which the core architectural elements were not brick, stone, wood, or even concrete, but the dynamically active people.[155] Almost any place that was not "sufficient unto itself and proud of its own completeness" could be "a place that offers itself to people and their appropriate activity, a place that is incomplete without . . . people and human activity," and, therefore, a "church building."[156]

Postconciliar futurists called for action they knew would destabilize well-worn patterns of parochial life, relocating "beauty" from a church's architecture and decoration into its inhabitants. G. R. Bullock, OSB, a graduate student at Notre Dame, argued that by fully renovating the Basilica of the Sacred Heart, the university could provide an example. "The hemisphere includes thousands of churches like this one," he lamented, "where the liturgy is failing to come to life because some of the men in charge naturally hesitate to shelve the old concepts of space and furniture for the new and unexpected needs of the People of God."[157] But these suggestions relied on the belief that the destruction of preexisting architectural and aesthetic elements would become ecclesiologically productive if it drew the community's focus beyond even the altar. In the debates over the design and location of liturgical space in the 1960s, the wide-ranging eschatology of Teilhard, Cox, and Vatican II came home, turning questions about the future, the far reaches of the universe, the redemptive presence of God in the city and in the Church as a whole, into the framework within which Catholics debated the minutiae of folding walls, new carpets, portable furniture, and laypeople's distance from the altar. A new church architecture—whether or not it abandoned anything recognizable as "architecture"—would have to respond to a series of cultural changes identified by Hovda and Huck as "a new personalism, a new concern for social justice as an eschatological reality related to the coming kingdom, a new sense of man's mastery and co-creatorship, a new attitude toward 'the world,' a new unity with nature and with human beings everywhere."[158] In the church of tomorrow, spatial and aesthetic change would be limited only by the Church's capacity to envision its own journey in the direction of God's kingdom.

CONCLUSION

Dennis Howard's 1965 interview with the liturgical movement leader Godfrey Diekmann, OSB, titled "The Church of the Future," opened with an extended description of the two churches of St. John's Abbey in Collegeville, Minnesota. The new concrete and glass church, designed by Marcel Breuer, helped the liturgy to "come alive as an active experience, an expression of the Church living here and now—in this place, among these people, in a unique way," while the former abbey church was characterized as "a brick structure in mixed Gothic and Romanesque styles that is typical of nineteenth-century church structures, lacking any genuine style of its own and encrusted with the vestiges of a past already long dead when the first bricks were laid." Howard's tale of two churches stood, not at all subtly, as a metaphor for two kinds of Church folk: those like Diekmann who had correctly predicted the future once (and should now be consulted further); and those who held to the past "tenaciously despite the fantastic changes taking place in the world around us." The liturgical movement's organic ecclesiology had evolutionary implications: "This concept of the Church in incarnational terms calls for a continual process of transformation." Diekmann saw the recent Vatican Council as the chance for this idea to take root against four centuries of anti-Protestant rhetoric about the unchanging Church. "If the Council is successful," he told Howard, "the principle of adaptation will be accepted."[1]

This kind of absolute openness to the future, structured by the biological paradigm, marked one aspect of the postconciliar period. If, as many American Catholics now believed, "theology grows out of reflection upon actual human experience in the world," then, as the layman Michael Novak wrote in 1967, "the experience which captivates the imagination of our age is the experience of change, the move toward further frontiers, the hope of a human brotherly world civilization."[2] Evolutionary convictions caused ecclesiological upheaval. It was "overwhelming," Daniel Callahan remarked, to "constantly encounter" questions like "What should the Church be doing? Where is the Church going? What is the Church?"[3] The uncertainties embedded in this line of thought flowed into the creation of multipurpose, flexible worship spaces. But during the 1960s they also led both Catholics and Protestants to call for a moratorium on all church-building.[4] Perhaps, some predicted, a study of "basic questions" over five or ten years might conclude that no dedicated churches should be built ever again. Existing ones might even be pulled down, where they were no longer needed, or drastically renovated in light of future needs. "*Coragio!*" Msgr. Frank Rodimer, the diocesan chancellor of Paterson, New Jersey, suggested. "What we need are pastors who are Joshuas—courageous and strong enough to bring [the old decoration] tumbling down."[5]

They might or might not have agreed that no churches should be built for the present, but most architects, naturally, did not think the "moratorium" should continue forever. Clovis Heimsath continued to believe in the need for "a place apart, God-centered, to worship in," although he was less concerned with architectural grandeur than with simple separation from the "dreary" suburban world of the parking lot.[6] Maurice Lavanoux, despite championing small, flexible spaces, dismissed as "nonsense" the idea "that [dedicated] places of worship are not needed."[7] He asserted that church buildings would not be "an anachronism in the next decade" and that what was needed was not the "radical solution" of having no churches at all but rather a reliance on "talented, competent, and imaginative architects" who could produce work of "living, dynamic continuity" appropriate to local means and needs.[8] What kinds of churches would these architects build?

Although many tried—both by allowing their imaginations free rein and through sober attempts at accurate analysis—to understand the future of the church and the Church, their prophecies were frequently wrong. By 1961 Lavanoux was writing confidently that "the nostalgic age of the gothic 'revival' is safely buried."[9] In the immediate postconciliar period, it seemed inconceivable that anyone would ever seriously argue again for the use of historic styles, or for liturgical "regression" to the stylistically baroque Tridentine rite. And yet, one contribution to the moratorium debate became a harbinger of the neohistoricism that would indeed revive several decades later. Philip Johnson noted angrily at the first International Congress on Religion, Architecture, and the Visual Arts, "If you don't want to build great and lasting buildings, you don't need me and I don't need you. . . . Now [Americans have no one] who will build grand spaces for the future. I want great structures again. For whom is it worth building a great and holy place, if not for God?" Johnson concluded his defense of much-maligned "monumentality" by challenging the idea that "it's not buildings that are holy, but people," stating flatly, "I think that rules me out to design your church."[10]

The *New York Times* reported Johnson's speech under the headline "Architect Sees Need for Great Religious Edifices." Although these controversies were never entirely quiescent, beginning in the 1990s the heirs of modernist architects and critics began a pitched battle with a neotraditionalist school of architects and theorists that argues for the use of forms associated with a particular set of historical memories (roughly, medieval through baroque).[11] Like Johnson, the members of this school are more postmodern than conservative in their insistent historical eclecticism.[12] The proponents of the biological paradigm in the mid-twentieth century utterly failed to anticipate either the reemergence of neohistoricist design interests, or the extent to which "traditionalists" would continue to agitate for a decidedly unevolved liturgy. But the future has a way of surprising us all.

The track record of mid-twentieth-century prognostication about American Catholic churches thus seems rather poor. Even at the time, some realized futurist visions were technical or liturgical failures, producing nightmares rather than dreams.[13] Why, then, did so many midcentury architects, liturgists, and congregations value futurist speculation? Since they saw reality as fundamentally evolving, sheer curiosity about what was coming next provided sufficient motive. Practical considerations, too, drove speculation: no building committee that understood the direction of the liturgical winds wanted to immediately renovate a brand-new church to accommodate a freestanding altar or declutter a devotional area. But it is clear—especially in the elaborate speculations of the 1950s and passionate visions of the 1960s—that something more was driving American Catholics' need to envision the future. Consider Donald Thorman's 1968 justification of his book-length attempt to do just that:

> The future is now. We are in large part determining how the future of the Church will look by what we do—or don't do—now, with the opportunities available to us. . . . Most of all, like Martin Luther King, we too must have a dream of the future. A dream of an open, honest, humble, and sincere Church, a Church which puts the needs of the person above the rigidity of the institution, a Church which attempts to be a mature community of loving human beings—men and women together, a People of God which reconciles the alienated, which seeks out the lowly, the minorities, the poor, the outcasts of an impersonal technological society. . . . A Church which courageously preaches and practices the words of Jesus Christ, and which from Pope to priest and from Knight of St. Gregory to Knight of Columbus is a Pilgrim Church built on love and service to men and God. This is my dream, this is my prayer, this is the Church I want in my future.[14]

Futurist projection like Thorman's envisioned a transformation of the present. And as the science fiction critic Fredric Jameson observes, the act of imagining a future different from the present is fundamentally political.[15] Whether the fantasized future is dark or bright, it creates otherwise unavailable possibilities for change. While visions of the future can seem fantastical in hindsight, most secular mid-twentieth-century attempts to predict and realize the future were not intended to be unrealistic. American Catholics, too, attempted to realistically predict the future of the church building and of the Church, often with the purpose of inspiring the pursuit of particular futures.[16] Revamped nave floor plans look prosaic next to visionary projections of alien architectures, and deep fissures appeared to separate those who wanted to build "house churches" on dedicated land, and those who sought to abandon the ownership of buildings. But these disparate projections shared a common interest in creating environments to help the people of God participate in the creation of a new world. Catholic futurists would have agreed with—and some of them may have been in the audience for—a comment made by Robert Scholes at the University of Notre Dame in 1974: "To live well in the present . . . *we must see into the future*."[17]

It is not so surprising that so many midcentury American Catholics saw the reconstruction of their physical environment, and especially the settings for their liturgies, as vital to the task of making a redeemed world. As geographers and spatial theorists have long pointed out, the act of making places gives shape both to the power to control the future and the desires of those making it.[18] Places and buildings are not constituted simply by their material form, but come into being when the financial and cultural power to make a space intersects with the desire to embody a particular kind of future.[19] The work of American Catholic modernists emphasizes that making places is a way of intervening in the flow of time—both envisioning temporality and shaping it through a dialectical process.[20] They saw churches as, in David Harvey's eschatological phrase, "spaces of hope."[21] In the early twenty-first century, the physical form of American Catholic building is again in doubt under new sets of financial pressures, population shifts, and theological and moral challenges. As we make and remake today's churches of the future, it is good to remember, in all its complexity, this period in which so many American Catholics felt called to envision themselves as fundamentally oriented, along with the rest of creation, in the direction of God's future.

ABBREVIATIONS

AAB/AASMSU	Archives of the Archdiocese of Baltimore, Associated Archives at St. Mary's Seminary & University, Baltimore, MD
AANY	Archives of the Archdiocese of New York, St. Joseph's Seminary, Dunwoodie
AASF	Archives of the Archdiocese of San Francisco, Menlo Park, CA
AASL	Archives of the Archdiocese of St. Louis, St. Louis, MO
AASP	Archives of the Archdiocese of St. Paul, St. Paul, MN
ACUA	American Catholic History Research Center and University Archives, Catholic University of America, Washington, DC
AR	*Architectural Record*
ASLA	Abbey of St. Louis Archives, Creve Coeur, MO
BRAA	Boston Redevelopment Authority Archives, Boston, MA
CA	Columbia Archives, Columbia, MD

CAA	Conception Abbey Archives, Conception, MO
CAP	Carolyn Arena Papers, RGXXIV Columbia Religious Facilities Corporation, Columbia Archives, Columbia, MD
CBLP	Clare Boothe Luce Papers, Manuscript Division, Library of Congress, Washington, DC
C+CC	Chapel + Cultural Center Parish Archives, Troy, NY
CLAV	Maurice Lavanoux Papers, University of Notre Dame Archives, Notre Dame, IN
CLIT	Liturgical Arts Society Records, Manuscripts, University of Notre Dame Archives, Notre Dame, IN
EFJP	Emil Frei Jr. Papers, Missouri History Museum, St. Louis, MO
EOSP	Eloise and Otto Spaeth Papers, 1937–83, Archives of American Art, Washington, DC
FRMP	Monsignor Frederick Richard McManus Papers, American Catholic History Research Center and University Archives, Catholic University of America, Washington, DC
GLIT	Liturgical Arts Society Photograph Collection, Liturgical Arts Society Records, University of Notre Dame Archives, Notre Dame, IN
HARVARD GSD	Harvard University Graduate School of Design Archives, Cambridge, MA
JPSP	James P. Shannon Papers, Minnesota Historical Society, St. Paul, MN
LA	*Liturgical Arts*
ML	Maurice Lavanoux
NCR	*National Catholic Reporter*
NYT	*New York Times*
PAA	Portsmouth Abbey Archives, Portsmouth, RI
RCA	Society for the Renewal of Christian Art Papers, University of Notre Dame Archives, Notre Dame, IN
RLJ	Robert Lawton Jones, personal archives
RP	Raymond Pavia, personal archives
SJEPA	St. John the Evangelist Parish Archives, Hopkins, MN

NOTES

INTRODUCTION

1. ML, "Never a Dull Moment," 24–25, CLAV, 3/2. Lavanoux retold this story often.

2. Susan J. White, *Art, Architecture, and Liturgical Reform: The Liturgical Arts Society (1928–1972)* (New York: Pueblo, 1990); Keith F. Pecklers, *The Unread Vision: The Liturgical Movement in the United States of America, 1926–1955* (Collegeville: Liturgical Press, 1998), 226–55; Catherine R. Osborne, "American Catholics and the Art of the Future, 1930–1975" (PhD diss., Fordham University, 2013).

3. Jay P. Dolan, *The American Catholic Experience: A History from Colonial Times to the Present* (Notre Dame, IN: University of Notre Dame Press, 1992), 349–83. Sacred spaces remain a highly charged aspect of American Catholicism (John Seitz, *No Closure: Catholic Practice and Boston's Parish Shutdowns* [Cambridge, MA: Harvard University Press, 2011]).

Historical literature on American Catholic church architecture has been limited until very recently. Some older studies were written from a particular theological perspective (e.g., R. Kevin R. Seasoltz, OSB, *A Sense of the Sacred: Theological Foundations of Christian Architecture and Art* [New York: Bloomsbury Academic, 2005], 221–322). Others (e.g., Jeanne Halgren Kilde, *Sacred Power, Sacred Space: An Introduction to Christian Architecture and Worship* [Oxford: Oxford University Press, 2008], 161–98) offer only a brief overview of the twentieth century, while general studies of American worship space often focus on Protestant architecture (e.g.,

Peter W. Williams, *Houses of God: Region, Religion, and Architecture in the United States* [Urbana: University of Illinois Press, 1997]). Recent work has more closely analyzed the intellectual context of modernist church architecture in the United States, Britain, and Europe: Jay M. Price, *Temples for a Modern God: Religious Architecture in Postwar America* (New York: Oxford University Press, 2013); Robert Proctor, *Building the Modern Church: Roman Catholic Church Architecture in Britain, 1955–1975* (London: Ashgate, 2014); Gretchen Buggeln, *The Suburban Church: Modernism and Community in Postwar America* (Minneapolis: University of Minnesota Press, 2015). Studies of individual buildings and architects also reflect a less polemical analysis.; see, e.g., Victoria M. Young, *Marcel Breuer's Saint John's Abbey Church: A New Vision for Liturgical Architecture* (Minneapolis: University of Minnesota Press, 2014); Vincent L. Michael, *The Architecture of Barry Byrne: Taking the Prairie School to Europe* (Urbana: University of Illinois Press, 2013); and Meredith L. Clausen, *Spiritual Space: The Religious Architecture of Pietro Belluschi* (Seattle: University of Washington Press, 1992).

4. Charles Morris, *American Catholic: The Saints and Sinners Who Built America's Most Powerful Church* (New York: Vintage, 1998), 165–95.

5. See Sarah Williams Goldhagen, "Something to Talk About: Modernism, Discourse, Style," *Journal of the Society of Architectural Historians* 64, no. 2 (2005): 144–67.

6. E.g., ML, "Modernistic Art—A Misnomer," *Catholic Daily Tribune*, November 25, 1930, CLIT, 4/10. On the modernist crisis, see R. Scott Appleby, *"Church and Age Unite!": The Modernist Impulse in American Catholicism* (Notre Dame, IN: University of Notre Dame Press, 1992).

7. Una M. Cadegan, *All Good Books Are Catholic Books: Print Culture, Censorship, and Modernity in Twentieth-Century America* (Ithaca, NY: Cornell University Press, 2013).

8. *Futurism* here refers to the larger cultural practice, not to the Italian artistic movement.

9. See Robert Heilbroner, *Visions of the Future: The Distant Past, Yesterday, Today, and Tomorrow* (New York: Oxford University Press, 1996); Reinhart Koselleck, *Futures Past: On the Semantics of Historical Time*, trans. Keith Tribe (New York: Columbia University Press, 2004); and J. B. Bury, *The Idea of Progress: An Inquiry into Its Origin and Growth* (Dodo Press, [1921] 2008).

10. Paula Kane, "Is That a Beer Vat under the Baldochino? From Antimodernism to Postmodernism in Catholic Church Architecture," *U.S. Catholic Historian* 15, no. 1 (1997): 2. Sacred space, in Louis P. Nelson's phrase, often "enlists memory in the construction and reconstruction of identity" (introduction to *American Sanctuary: Understanding Sacred Spaces*, ed. Nelson [Bloomington: Indiana University Press, 2006], 9).

11. Patrick J. Quinn and Richard Perry, eds., *Architecture and Religion in the Future City: A Study Presented at the 27th National Conference on Church Architecture, San Francisco, April 1966*, Berkeley, CA, 1966, iii.

12. For a broader exploration of this phenomenon, see Eugene D. McCarraher, "The Saint in the Gray Flannel Suit: The Professional-Managerial Class, 'The Layman,' and American-Catholic-Religious Culture, 1945–1965," *U.S. Catholic Historian* 15, no. 3 (1997): 99–118.

13. Louis Bouyer, *Liturgy and Architecture* (Notre Dame, IN: University of Notre Dame Press, 1967), 6.

14. On the concept of progress, see William M. Halsey, *The Survival of American Innocence: Catholicism in an Era of Disillusionment, 1920–1940* (Notre Dame, IN: University of Notre Dame Press, 1980). On American Catholic medievalism, see Eugene McCarraher, "American Gothic: Sacramental Radicalism and the Neo-medievalist Cultural Gospel, 1928–1948," *Records of the American Catholic Historical Society of Philadelphia* 106, no. 1/2 (1995): 3–23; and Philip Gleason,

"American Catholics and the Mythic Middle Ages," in *Keeping the Faith: American Catholicism, Past and Present* (Notre Dame, IN: University of Notre Dame Press, 1987), 11–34.

15. On the modernist crisis and developmentalism, see Appleby, *Church and Age Unite*. On antimodernism and evolutionary theory, see Appleby, "Exposing Darwin's 'Hidden Agenda': Roman Catholic Responses to Evolution, 1875–1925," in *Disseminating Darwinism: The Role of Place, Race, Religion, and Gender*, ed. Ronald L. Numbers and John Stenhouse (New York: Cambridge University Press, 2001), 173–208.

16. §26. See John W. O'Malley, *What Happened at Vatican II* (Cambridge, MA: Belknap Press of Harvard University Press, 2008), 53–71.

17. Pre-1960s Catholic views of biological evolution varied, but tended toward nonfundamentalist conservatism and "theistic evolution." See Don O'Leary, *Roman Catholicism and Modern Science: A History* (New York: Continuum, 2006), 108–28; and Appleby, *Church and Age Unite*, 13–52. Recent work based on newly opened archives suggests that early Vatican policy on evolution was ad hoc, not ideological (e.g., Mariano Artigas, Thomas F. Glick, and Rafael A. Martínez, *Negotiating Darwin: The Vatican Confronts Evolution, 1877–1902* [Baltimore: Johns Hopkins University Press, 2006]). David Mislin shows that evolution inspired relatively little controversy among nineteenth-century American Catholics ("'According to His Own Judgment': The American Catholic Encounter with Organic Evolution, 1875–1896," *Religion and American Culture* 22, no. 2 [2012]: 133–62). Some theories allowed for the evolution of the human body while positing that God created the soul ex nihilo.

18. Gillian Beers, *Darwin's Plots: Evolutionary Narrative in Darwin, George Eliot and Nineteenth-Century Fiction*, 2nd ed. (Cambridge: Cambridge University Press, 2000), 13.

19. Suzanne Guerlac, *Thinking in Time: An Introduction to Henri Bergson* (Ithaca, NY: Cornell University Press, 2006).

20. Meriol Trevor, *Newman* (Garden City, NY: Doubleday, 1963), 1:3.

21. Stephen Schloesser, *Jazz Age Catholicism: Mystic Modernism in Postwar Paris, 1919–1933* (Toronto: University of Toronto Press, 2005), 142, 72; on the Maritains' theory of art, see 41–209. Jacques Maritain's *Art et scholastique* was first published in French in 1920 and in English by Eric Gill's press in 1923, highlighting its fundamental importance for the Christian branch of the Arts and Crafts movement, which increasingly diverged from modernist futurism.

22. Robert Smithson, "Quasi-infinities and the Waning of Space," *Arts Magazine*, November 1966, 29. On the tendency to "equate 'Darwinism' with the broader theory of organic evolution rather than with Darwin's (changing) interpretation of the mechanics of that process," see Jon H. Roberts, *Darwinism and the Divine in America: Protestant Intellectuals and Organic Evolution, 1859–1900*, 2nd ed. (Notre Dame, IN: University of Notre Dame Press, 2001), x.

23. "The Reaches of History," *Commonweal*, August 15, 1958, 487.

24. Hyungmin Pai, *The Portfolio and the Diagram: Architecture, Discourse, and Modernity in America* (Cambridge, MA: MIT Press, 2002). American architects also have a powerful professional organization: the American Institute of Architects (AIA). Nearly all the architects I discuss were members, although at least one (Mark Mills) refused to join.

25. Until the 1960s, there was ongoing tension in Catholic artistic circles over whether good work came from faithful commitment or from professional, often non-Catholic, training. On Bethune and the deliberately "amateur" artists at Grailville, see Katharine E. Harmon, *There Were Also Many Women There: Lay Women in the Liturgical Movement in the United States, 1926–59* (Collegeville, MN: Liturgical Press, 2013), 188–241. Bethune, Kacmarcik, and Schickel

made the financial sacrifices to prove their vocational commitment, living attached to remote religious communities; but Kacmarcik trained at the Minneapolis School of Art and Schickel's grandfather was a New York architect (Charlotte Anne Zalot, "Revisioning Liturgical Space and Furnishings in American Roman Catholic Churches, 1947–2002: The Pioneering Role of Frank Kacmarcik, Artist-Designer and Consultant in the Sacred Arts" (PhD diss., Drew University, 2004); Pecklers, *The Unread Vision*; Gregory Wolfe, *Sacred Passion: The Art of William Schickel* (Notre Dame, IN: University of Notre Dame Press, 2010).

26. See Richard Chafee, "The Teaching of Architecture at the Ecole des Beaux-Arts," in *The Architecture of the Ecole des Beaux-Arts*, ed. Arthur Drexler (Cambridge, MA: MIT Press, 1977); and Harry Francis Mallgrave, *Modern Architectural Theory: A Historical Survey, 1673–1968* (Cambridge: Cambridge University Press, 2009), 13–43, 67–90.

27. Heinrich Hübsch, *In welchem Style sollen wir bauen?* (Karlsruhe: C. F. Müller, [1828] 1984). See Wolfgang Herrmann, *In What Style Should We Build? The German Debate on Architectural Style* (Santa Monica, CA: Getty Center for the History of Art and the Humanities, 1992); Calder Loth, Julius Sadler, and Trousdale Sadler Jr., *The Only Proper Style: Gothic Architecture in America* (Boston: New York Graphic Society, 1986); Kathleen Curran, *The Romanesque Revival: Religion, Politics, and Transnational Exchange* (University Park: Pennsylvania State University Press, 2003); and Richard Kieckhefer, *Theology in Stone: Church Architecture from Byzantium to Berkeley* (New York: Oxford University Press, 2008), 196–211.

28. Oliver A. I. Botar and Isabel Wünsche, "Introduction: Biocentrism as a Constituent Element of Modernism," in *Biocentrism and Modernism*, ed. Botar and Wünsche (London: Ashgate, 2011), 1–14; and Botar, "Defining Biocentrism," in *Biocentrism and Modernism*, 15–46.

29. The best general introduction is O'Malley, *What Happened at Vatican II*. See also Stephen Schloesser, "Against Forgetting: Memory, History, Vatican II," in *Vatican II: Did Anything Happen?*, ed. David G. Schultenover (New York: Continuum, 2007), 92–152.

30. See Annibale Bugnini, *The Reform of the Liturgy, 1948–1975*, trans. Matthew J. O'Connell (Collegeville, MN: Liturgical Press, 1990); and Archbishop Piero Marini, *A Challenging Reform: Realizing the Vision of the Liturgical Renewal, 1963–1975*, ed. Mark R. Francis, CSV, John R. Page, and Keith F. Pecklers, SJ (Collegeville, MN: Liturgical Press, 2007).

31. See Colleen McDannell, *The Spirit of Vatican II: A History of Catholic Reform in America* (New York: Basic Books, 2011).

32. On floor plans, see Kieckhefer, *Theology in Stone*. Long, narrow basilican plans with a clear distinction between nave and sanctuary or chancel are a subset of Kieckhefer's "classic sacramental church" (11).

33. See O'Malley, *What Happened at Vatican II*.

34. At a later date, Proctor, *Building the Modern Church*, notes a similar alliance between liturgists and architects in Britain (142–66). See also Young, *Marcel Breuer's Saint John's Abbey Church*.

35. See Pecklers, *The Unread Vision*, especially 235–55; and Harmon, *There Were Also Many Women There*.

36. For more common, and more individualistic, contemporary views of the Eucharist, see Margaret M. McGuinness, "Let Us Go to the Altar: American Catholics and the Eucharist, 1926–1976," in *Habits of Devotion: Catholic Religious Practice in Twentieth-Century America*, ed. James M. O'Toole (Ithaca, NY: Cornell University Press, 2004), 186–235.

37. H. A. Reinhold, *Bringing the Mass to the People* (Baltimore: Helicon, 1960), 5.

38. Pierre Teilhard de Chardin, SJ, "Mass on the World." Teilhard dated the "official"

published version "Ordos [Desert], 1923." However, he worked on similar texts throughout his adult life. Thomas King, SJ, *Teilhard's Mass: Approaches to "The Mass on the World"* (Mahwah, NJ: Paulist Press, 2005) untangles some textual history; see especially 1–36.

39. White, *Art, Architecture, and Liturgical Reform*; Pecklers, *The Unread Vision*, 226–29; and Price, *Temples for a Modern God*, 39 and passim.

40. Aaron Godfrey, interview by the author, Port Jefferson, NY, September 11, 2011. For Lavanoux's diary, 1950–1974, see CLAV, boxes 2 and 3. (Much, though not all, of this material was subsequently published in the regular feature "The Editor's Diary" in *Liturgical Arts*; where possible I cite the published version.) For correspondence, see CLIT, boxes 1–56; he regularly described his meetings and suggested that various friends, acquaintances, and correspondents write to or visit one another. For an example of *Liturgical Arts*' outsized readership versus its circulation, see E. J. Mattimoe, SJ, to ML, March 28, 1973, RCA 01/04.

41. Pai, *The Portfolio and the Diagram*, 13.

42. Jones and Heimsath both told me that during European tours they visited and sketched medieval, Renaissance, and Baroque churches, but did not seek out well-known modernist churches.

43. *America*, October 12, 1935, 6.

44. Michael Novak, "The Absolute Future," *Commonweal*, January 13, 1967, 402.

45. Alvin Toffler, *Future Shock* (New York: Random House, 1970), 14–15.

46. Toffler, 20–22. On the history of this feeling, see Koselleck, *Futures Past*.

47. Michael Christopher, "Maybe the Catholic Novel Isn't Dead," *U.S. Catholic & Jubilee*, February 1971, 51.

48. Editorial, *LA* 30, no. 4 (1962): 117. The editorial opening each issue of *Liturgical Arts* was always unsigned. After Henry Lorin Binsse left his position as editor in 1937, they were written entirely by Maurice Lavanoux. From 1931 to 1936, authorship is less clear, but generally they were written by Binsse, sometimes with participation from Lavanoux.

49. "The Church in the Year 2000," advertisement, *NCR*, October 8, 1969.

50. William Keady to Joseph McGucken, February 27, 1967, AASF.

51. Jean Daniélou, "Hope and the Christian," *Commonweal*, April 1, 1960, 7.

52. Daniélou, 7.

53. Donald J. Thorman, *American Catholics Face the Future* (Wilkes-Barre, PA: Dimension Books, 1968); Mario von Galli and Bernard Moosbrugger, *The Council and the Future* (New York: McGraw-Hill, 1966); Thomas F. O'Meara and Donald M. Weisser, eds., *Projections: Shaping an American Theology for the Future* (Garden City: Doubleday, 1970); George Tavard, *The Church Tomorrow* (New York: Herder and Herder, 1965). This is not to mention countless magazine articles—e.g., Dennis Howard, "The Church of the Future: An Interview with Godfrey Diekmann," *U.S. Catholic*, October 1965, 6–12.

54. On futurology, see Jenny Andersson, "The Great Future Debate and the Struggle for the World," *American Historical Review* 117, no. 5 (2012): 1411–30; David C. Engerman, "Introduction: Histories of the Future and the Futures of History," *American Historical Review* 117, no. 5 (2012): 1402–10; Donna Goodman, *A History of the Future* (New York: Monacelli, 2008); Robert Bundy, preface to *Images of the Future: The Twenty-First Century and Beyond*, ed. Bundy (Buffalo, NY: Prometheus Books, 1976), 1–5; I. F. Clarke, *The Pattern of Expectation, 1644–2001* (New York: Basic Books, 1979); and Joseph J. Corn and Brian Horrigan, *Yesterday's Tomorrows: Past Visions of the American Future* (New York: Summit Books, 1984). American Catholic

considerations of futurology include Neil Hurley, SJ, "The Futurists: '. . . I Dream Things That Never Were,'" *Ave Maria*, January 4, 1969, 8–12.

55. Bouyer, *Liturgy and Architecture*, 8.

56. Bouyer, 9.

57. The reemergence of eschatological theology—distinct from popular millenarianism or apocalypticism—began with nineteenth-century liberal Protestants (Hans Schwarz, *Eschatology* [Grand Rapids, MI: Eerdmans, 2000], 107–51). Modern Christian eschatology emerged concurrently, and sometimes in dialogue, with scientific materialism and evolutionary theory (ibid., 185–94). Catholic interest developed later but played a prominent role in Vatican II, and was subsequently influenced strongly by Teilhard and, later, by the German Protestant Jürgen Moltmann and the Catholics Johann Baptist Metz and Edward Schillebeeckx.

58. Response to Hurley, "The Futurists," 12.

CHAPTER ONE

1. Pietro Belluschi, "Some Thoughts on the Architecture of Portsmouth Abbey," *Portsmouth Abbey Bulletin*, Fall 1971, PAA. As an adult, Belluschi did not identify as Catholic; see Meredith L. Clausen, *Spiritual Space: The Religious Architecture of Pietro Belluschi* (Seattle: University of Washington Press, 1992), and *Pietro Belluschi: Modern American Architect* (Cambridge, MA: MIT Press, 1994).

2. Meredith L. Clausen, "Transparent Structure: Belluschi Churches of the 1950s," *Journal of the Interfaith Forum on Religion, Art, & Architecture*, Fall 1990, 10–14; anonymous sermon ca. 1984, PAA.

3. "In order that any style of Architecture should exactly suit the living ritual of the nineteenth century, it should be the living architecture of the nineteenth century—it should never have died—else, while the ritual has changed, the architecture has not kept pace with it. . . . Gothic is like an old dress which fitted a man well twenty years back but must be altered to fit him now" (quoted in Meriol Trevor, *Newman* [Garden City, NY: Doubleday, 1963], 1:435). The phrase "living architecture" derived from John Ruskin.

4. Walter Rüegg, ed., *A History of the University in Europe: Universities in the Nineteenth and Early Twentieth Centuries (1800–1945)*, vol. 3 (Cambridge: Cambridge University Press, 2004); Chad Wellmon, *Organizing Enlightenment: Information Overload and the Invention of the Modern Research University* (Baltimore: Johns Hopkins University Press, 2015).

5. Elizabeth Mansfield, "Art History and Modernism," in *Art History and Its Institutions: Foundations of a Discipline*, ed. Mansfield (London: Routledge, 2002), 11.

6. Robert O. Bork, "Art, Science, and Evolution," in *Making Art History: A Changing Discipline and Its Institutions*, ed. Elizabeth Mansfield (London: Routledge, 2007), 188. See also Lauren Golden, "Science, Darwin, and Art History," in *Raising the Eyebrow: John Onians and World Art Studies*, ed. Golden (Oxford: Archaeopress, 2001), 79–90; Kathryn Brush, *The Shaping of Art History: Wilhelm Vöge, Adolph Goldschmidt, and the Study of Medieval Art* (New York: Cambridge University Press, 1996); Mansfield, *Art History and Its Institutions*; and Craig Hugh Smyth and Peter M. Lukehart, eds., *The Early Years of Art History in the United States: Notes and Essays on Departments, Teaching, and Scholars* (Princeton, NJ: Department of Art and Archaeology, Princeton University, 1993).

7. Kathryn Brush, *Vastly More Than Brick & Mortar: Reinventing the Fogg Art Museum in the 1920s* (Cambridge, MA: Harvard University Art Museums, 2003); Charles Rufus Morey, "A Humanistic Laboratory," *Bulletin of the Department of Art and Archaeology of Princeton University*, October 1929, 5–9; David Van Zanten, "Formulating Art History at Princeton and the 'Humanistic Laboratory,'" in Smyth and Lukehart, *Early Years of Art History*, 174–82.

8. C. R. Morey, "The Sources of Mediaeval Style," *Art Bulletin* 7, no. 2 (1924), 50.

9. Sybil Gordon Kantor, *Alfred H. Barr, Jr., and the Intellectual Origins of the Museum of Modern Art* (Cambridge, MA: MIT Press, 2001), 21–22.

10. Kantor identifies at least four similar enterprises, beginning with a 1925 genealogy of European printmaking (*Alfred H. Barr, Jr.*, 22–26, 325–28).

11. The Avery Index to Architectural Periodicals lists ninety-nine articles with "evolution" in the title between 1900 and 1940.

12. While dynamic evolutionary models were native to the nineteenth century, the idea of comparing a building to an organism was not. See Philip Steadman, *The Evolution of Designs: Biological Analogy in Architecture and the Applied Arts* (Cambridge: Cambridge University Press, 1979).

13. Viollet-le-Duc was an atheist with an at best tense relationship with local Catholic clergy at his major restoration sites (Kevin D. Murphy, *Memory and Modernity: Viollet-Le-Duc at Vézelay* [University Park: Pennsylvania State University Press, 2000]). His claims about rational and scientific medieval builders were meant to distance them from the Church, not celebrate it—a point lost on twentieth-century American Catholics who primarily knew his ideas at third- or fourthhand.

14. K. D. Murphy, *Memory and Modernity*, 32–33; Martin Bressani, *Architecture and the Historical Imagination: Eugène-Emmanuel Viollet-Le-Duc, 1814–1879* (London: Routledge, 2016); Caroline van Eck, *Organicism in Nineteenth-Century Architecture: An Inquiry into Its Theoretical and Philosophical Background* (Amsterdam: Architectura & Natura Press, 1994).

15. M. F. Hearn, ed., *The Architectural Theory of Viollet-Le-Duc: Readings and Commentary* (Cambridge, MA: MIT Press, 1990), 14; K. D. Murphy, *Memory and Modernity*, 8–9; Donald Hoffmann, "Frank Lloyd Wright and Viollet-Le-Duc," *Journal of the Society of Architectural Historians* 28, no. 3 (1969): 173–83. Viollet-le-Duc's reputation as a pure protorationalist has been persuasively questioned by K. D. Murphy, *Memory and Modernity*, and Michael Camille, *The Gargoyles of Notre-Dame: Medievalism and the Monsters of Modernity* (Chicago: University of Chicago Press, 2009).

16. Louis H. Sullivan, "The Tall Office Building Artistically Considered," *Lippincott's Magazine*, March 1896, 408.

17. See Van Eck, *Organicism in Nineteenth-Century Architecture*, 268–78. Of three premodern architectural analogies—mechanical, moral, and organic—only the organic remained "a major concern after the establishment of the modern movement," with the term *organic* used by architects like Mies often contrasted with Wright (Larry L. Ligo, *The Concept of Function in Twentieth-Century Architectural Criticism* [Ann Arbor, MI: UMI Research Press, 1984], 12). See also Rosalind Williams on Lewis Mumford and Patrick Geddes: "Lewis Mumford as a Historian of Technology in *Technics and Civilization*," in *Lewis Mumford: Public Intellectual*, ed. Thomas P. Hughes and Agatha C. Hughes (New York: Oxford University Press, 1990), 43–65.

18. Moholy-Nagy cited in Peder Anker, *From Bauhaus to Ecohouse: A History of Ecological Design* (Baton Rouge: Louisiana State University Press, 2010), 2.

19. Donald Drew Egbert, "The Idea of Organic Expression and American Architecture," in *Evolutionary Thought in America*, ed. Stow Persons (New Haven, CT: Yale University Press, 1950), 336–96.

20. Frank Lloyd Wright, "In the Cause of Architecture" (1914), *Frank Lloyd Wright Collected Writings*, 1:127n. Peter Collins comments that for Wright, "organic architecture" primarily meant "an architecture in which useless forms were sloughed off as part of the process of a nation's growth, and in which every composition, every element, and every detail was deliberately shaped for the job it had to perform" (*Changing Ideals in Modern Architecture, 1750–1950* [Montreal: McGill University Press, 1965], 156).

21. Wright, *Collected Writings*, 1:127n.

22. Frank Brannach, in *Church Architecture: Building for a Living Faith* (Milwaukee: Bruce Publishing, 1933), balanced the two imperatives by noting that while Americans should not "copy in our own land the work of another country," nevertheless "we may have something to learn by the study of what others are at present doing" (200).

23. Anker, *From Bauhaus to Ecohouse*, 9–36. The Olgyays' American careers included research on what we would now call environmental or ecological design.

24. On the transformation of architectural education, see Hyungmin Pai, *The Portfolio and the Diagram: Architecture, Discourse, and Modernity in America* (Cambridge, MA: MIT Press, 2002); Joan Ockman, ed., *Architecture School: Three Centuries of Educating Architects in North America* (Cambridge, MA: MIT Press, 2012); Jill Pearlman, *Inventing American Modernism: Joseph Hudnut, Walter Gropius, and the Bauhaus Legacy at Harvard* (Charlottesville: University of Virginia Press, 2007); Anthony Alofsin, *The Struggle for Modernism: Architecture, Landscape Architecture, and City Planning at Harvard* (New York: W. W. Norton, 2002); and Eric Mumford, "Triumph and Eclipse: Modern Architecture in St. Louis and the School of Architecture," in *Modern Architecture in St. Louis: Washington University and Postwar American Architecture, 1948–1973*, ed. E. Mumford (St. Louis: Washington University School of Architecture, 2004), 42–69.

25. J. B. O'Connell, *Church Building and Furnishing: The Church's Way, A Study in Liturgical Law* (Notre Dame, IN: University of Notre Dame Press, 1955), 32.

26. Vincent L. Michael, *The Architecture of Barry Byrne: Taking the Prairie School to Europe* (Urbana: University of Illinois Press, 2013), 82–83.

27. Byrne worked for Wright from 1902 to 1908.

28. The full details of this trip are recounted in Michael, *The Architecture of Barry Byrne*, 67–81.

29. Barry Byrne, "The Gesture of Impotence," *Commonweal*, February 25, 1925, 436. On concepts of "natural," "original," and "authentic" in this period, see Miles Orvell, *The Real Thing: Imitation and Authenticity in American Culture, 1880–1940* (Chapel Hill: University of North Carolina Press, 1989), 157–97.

30. [Rev.] Thomas F. Coakley, "For Better Church Art," *Commonweal*, March 4, 1925, 465.

31. Coakley, "For Better Church Art," 465.

32. Oliver Reagan, "Building the House of God," *Commonweal*, March 11, 1925, 491.

33. Reagan, 491.

34. Ralph Adams Cram, "Why a New Architecture?," *Commonweal*, December 16, 1925, 151.

35. Cram, 152.

36. Walter Copeland, "This Talk about Art," *Commonweal*, September 25, 1929, 535; Harold Rambusch, "This Talk about Art," *Commonweal*, October 2, 1929, 561.

37. Lewis Mumford, "Decoration and Structure," *Commonweal*, October 7, 1925, 532–33.

38. L. Mumford, 532–33; Barry Byrne, "A New Architecture," *Commonweal*, November 25, 1925, 73.

39. Byrne, "A New Architecture," 74. He cited Sullivan as well.

40. Byrne, 74.

41. Byrne, 74.

42. Barry Byrne, "Why an Old Architecture?," *Commonweal*, January 13, 1926, 272.

43. E.g., H. A. Reinhold, "Styles Do Not Make a Church," *Orate Fratres* 17, no. 9 (August 8, 1943): 414–18.

44. Lewis Mumford, "Architecture and Catholicism," *Commonweal*, April 15, 1925, 623.

45. L. Mumford, 624. Mumford also agreed with the modernists that modeling and mass, the "manner of enclosing space," were far more important markers of the architect's talent than decoration.

46. Lewis Mumford, "A Modern Catholic Architect," *Commonweal*, March 2, 1927, 458.

47. Barry Byrne, "The Orthodoxy of Columns," *Commonweal*, March 25, 1925, 551.

48. ML, "Observations . . . ," *LA* 5, no. 1 (1936): 24.

49. Barry Byrne, "Tangled Thinkers of Today," *Commonweal*, June 3, 1931, 131.

50. Byrne, 131. This letter responded to a *Commonweal* editorial ("The Tangled Towers of Today," April 22, 1931, 673–74) describing modernism as "the denial of tradition and of all doctrine handed down from the past," and supporting Cram over Joseph Hudnut.

51. Susan J. White, *Art, Architecture, and Liturgical Reform: The Liturgical Arts Society (1928–1972)* (New York: Pueblo, 1990), 2–10.

52. John LaFarge, SJ, "The Liturgical Arts Society," *America*, December 6, 1930, 204.

53. John LaFarge, SJ, to ML, April 11, 1930, CLIT, 7/03.

54. C. R. Morey, "The Genesis of Christian Art," *LA* 1, no. 1 (1931): 7–17; "Byzantine Art," *LA* 1, no. 2 (1932): 67–77; "Romanesque Art," *LA* 1, no. 3 (1932): 101–12; "Gothic Style," *LA* 1, no. 4 (1932): 175–80. Lavanoux, who during the early 1930s was suspicious of collaboration with Protestants, commented that "it does seem a shame that we can't have someone of our own to write the articles" (ML to Harry Lorin Binsse, July 4, 1931, CLIT, 7/13). But he shortly ceased to worry about the faith of an artist, architect, or critic, as long as he or she was willing to understand the "requirements" of Catholic liturgy.

55. In this limited way they did, as Eugene McCarraher suggests, wield the past as a critique of present systems of production ("American Gothic: Sacramental Radicalism and the Neo-medievalist Cultural Gospel, 1928–1948," *Records of the American Catholic Historical Society of Philadelphia* 106, no. 1 [1995]: 8).

56. Rev. Edward J. Sutfin and Maurice Lavanoux, "Contemporary Catholic Architecture," in *Modern Church Architecture: A Guide to the Form and Spirit of Twentieth Century Religious Building*, by Albert Christ-Janer and Mary Mix Foley (New York: McGraw-Hill, 1962), 1–3.

57. E.g., George W. Eggers to ML, September 19, 1945, CLIT, 22/02; H. A. Reinhold, "Thoughts on Church Planning," *Orate Fratres* 23, no. 11 (1949): 509–14.

58. Byrne, "A New Architecture," 75.

59. John Walter Wood to Harry Lorin Binsse, December 1, 1931, CLIT, 16/37. See Pierre de la Ruffinière du Prey, ed., *The House That Jack Built* (Kingston, Ontario: Queen's University Archives, 2010).

60. Leopold Arnaud, "Modernism in Church Architecture," *Summary of Proceedings: The*

North American Conference of Church Architecture and Allied Arts, October 9, 1936, CLIT, 3/10. See Richard Oliver, ed., *The Making of an Architect, 1881–1981: Columbia University in the City of New York* (New York: Rizzoli, 1981), 139–45.

61. Talbot Hamlin, "A Modern Gothic Church," *LA* 3, no. 1 (1934): 30.

62. Hamlin, 30.

63. ML to Paul J. Decker, OMI, May 24, 1955, CLIT, 31/04. Priests and lay experts routinely urged Catholics to visit art museums in order to get a more current, professionalized understanding of art; e.g., Herbert G. Kramer, SM, correspondence, *LA* 8, no. 3 (1940): 78–79; editorial, *LA* 11, no. 2 (1943): 23; and Henry Clifford and C. V. Higgins, correspondence, *LA* 11, no. 3 (1943): 92–93.

64. There are hundreds of examples both in *Liturgical Arts* and Lavanoux's letters, but he also took opportunities to use them in lectures and remarks wherever possible—e.g., as a member of a jury for New York's Beaux-Arts Institute of Design in 1949 (ML, "A Stained Glass Window," jury report, May 4, 1949, CLIT, 25/01).

65. Rev. Anthony Jacobs to ML, April 15, 1945, CLIT, 22/03.

66. Paul Thiry, Richard M. Bennett, and Henry L. Kamphoefner, *Churches & Temples* (New York: Reinhold, 1953), 12. This was also cited as a Hudnut story by the Catholic architect Charles Hannan of Michigan in *Church Property Administration*, September–October 1952, 100.

67. E.g., ML to Willis P. Gerhart, April 9, 1945, CLIT, 22/02; ML to Rev. Anthony Jacobs, July 26, 1945, CLIT, 22/03; Richard McMonigal to ML, February 22, 1947, and ML to McMonigal, February 24, 1947, CLIT, 24/01.

68. Rev. John L. Walch to ML, September 30, 1949, CLIT, 26/02.

69. José de Vinck to ML, March 15, 1956, CLIT, 33/01.

70. John Walsh to ML, December 19, 1944, CLIT, 21/07.

71. G. W. Lancer, "Why Not Skyscrapers?" letter to the editor, *America*, February 25, 1928, 496.

72. Lancer, 496. This tribal motivation was especially strong during the 1920s through the '40s. In 1937, Lavanoux wrote sharply to Francis Kervick at Notre Dame that he "would like to see the Catholic institutions taking the lead in the solution of these problems rather than to wait until the other schools have done the experimenting" (September 15, 1937, CLIT, 6/43).

73. Albert Christ-Janer and Mary Mix Foley, *Modern Church Architecture: A Guide to the Form and Spirit of Twentieth-Century Religious Building* (New York: McGraw-Hill, 1962), 14. Antonin Raymond and Ladislav Rado, both originally from Eastern Europe, immigrated to the United States (Raymond in 1910, where he shortly began working for Frank Lloyd Wright, and Rado immediately prior to World War II). They formed a partnership in 1945, with Raymond living much of the time in Japan, while Rado's office was in New York. See Kurt Helfrich and William Whittaker, *Crafting a Modern World: The Architecture and Design of Antonin and Noemi Raymond* (Princeton, NJ: Princeton Architectural Press, 2006).

74. Christ-Janer and Foley, *Modern Church Architecture*, 14.

75. "A Panel Discussion at the National Catholic Building Convention," *LA* 17, no. 2 (1949): 31.

76. Correspondence, *LA* 18, no. 4 (1950): 110.

77. E.g., ML to Vincent Holden, SSP, November 5, 1941, CLIT, 22/02; to Hugh Farrington, OSB, September 21, 1944, CLIT, 21/01; to Rev. Victor F. Ciciarelli, n.d., 1945, CLIT,

22/01; to Rev. Augustine Murray, November 2, 1945, CLIT, 22/04; to Mary Louise Garrity, March 24, 1963, CLIT, 41/01.

78. "Small Churches in the Kansas City Diocese," *LA* 15, no. 1 (1946): 13.

79. ML, "A Diocesan Building Project," *LA* 12, no. 4 (1944): 86.

80. ML, 86.

81. Julian Whittlesey to Rev. George Smith, May 10, 1944, CLIT, 21/5.

82. On this point, modernists overlapped and collaborated with Arts and Crafts theorists like Eric Gill and Ralph Adams Cram, who insisted on the use of medieval building techniques and materials as well as on medieval forms.

83. Joseph Salerno, "Louis Sullivan—Return to Principle," *LA* 16, no. 2 (1948): 49–50.

84. Salerno, 49.

85. Salerno, 49.

86. John Keegan, "Beauty through Simplicity," *LA* 25, no. 2 (1957): 51.

87. Keegan, 51–52.

88. Editorial, *LA* 2, no. 2 (1932): 49.

89. ML to Francis Kervick, September 15, 1937, and September 9, 1937, CLIT, 6/43.

90. Christ-Janer and Foley, *Modern Church Architecture*, 295.

91. Christ-Janer and Foley, 295.

92. Thiry, Bennett, and Kamphoefner, *Churches & Temples*, 12.

93. Thiry, Bennett, and Kamphoefner, 12.

94. Jean Labatut, "An Approach to Architectural Composition," November 4, 1955, CLIT, 40/02.

95. Brochure, ca. 1958, CLIT, 96/19.

96. "Curent Ordinarii, audito etiam, si opus fuerit, peritorum consilio, ut in ecclesiarum aedificatione vel refectione serventur formae a traditione christiana receptae et artis sacrae leges" (1164, §1).

97. ML, "The Authentic Tradition in Art," *LA* 22, no. 4 (1954): 122–25.

98. ML, 122–25.

99. ML, 122–25.

100. ML, "More Observations . . . European and Otherwise," *LA* 8, no. 1 (1939): 15–17 Liturgical circles emphasized the phrase *living tradition* in the decade surrounding Vatican II. See Giacomo Lercaro, "The True Sense of Tradition in Sacred Art," *LA* 25, no. 1 (1956): 7–8; Benjamin P. Javier, "Living Tradition," *LA* 27, no. 2 (1959): 30–32; Kilian McDonnell, "The Meaning of Tradition," *Worship* 32, no. 3 (1958): 149–58; William Schickel and James Rogan, "The Cultural Importance of the Liturgy," *LA* 28, no. 3 (1960): 66–67; and Thomas F. Mathews, SJ, "Toward an Adequate Notion of Tradition in Sacred Art," *LA* 32, no. 2 (1964): 43–49.

101. John Walsh to ML, December 19, 1944, CLIT, 21/07.

102. Walsh to ML.

103. Pietro Belluschi, "Eloquent Simplicity in Architecture," *AR*, July 1963, 132–34.

104. Yves Congar, OP, *The Meaning of Tradition*, trans. A. N. Woodrow [San Francisco: Ignatius Press, 2004], 2. See also Congar, *La tradition et les traditions: Essai historique* (Paris: Fayard, 1960); and Congar, *La tradition et les traditions: Essai théologique* (Paris: Fayard, 1963).

105. Congar, *The Meaning of Tradition*, 2–3.

106. Congar, 3.

107. Christ-Janer and Foley, *Modern Church Architecture*, 293.

108. This pattern began with a 1932 editorial explaining that press coverage of Vatican objections to an exhibition of modern liturgical arts in Germany did not mean that modern art was officially condemned (*LA* 1, no. 4 [1932]: 128–29).

109. E.g., ML to Amleto Cicognani, March 29, 1937, CLIT, 2/32; ML to Jacques Maritain, June 3, 1947, CLIT, 24/01; Joachim Nabuco to ML, February 18, 1948, and ML to Nabuco, February 26, 1948, CLIT, 24/06; Melville Steinfels to ML, May 28, 1953, CLIT, 29/05.

110. H. A. Reinhold, "'Liturgical' Art," *LA* 21, no. 2 (1953): 33.

111. See Françoise Caussé, *La revue "L'art sacré": Le débat en France sur l'art et la religion (1945–1954)* (Paris: Cerf, 2010), and related material in CLIT, 63/16.

112. Quoted in O'Connell, *Church Building and Furnishing*, 40–41.

113. Leo Dworschak to ML, May 30, 1953, CLIT, 28/05.

114. Philip Johnson to ML, April 20, 1953, CLIT, 29/01. See Frank D. Welch, *Philip Johnson & Texas* (University of Texas Press, 2000), 57.

115. Edward Schuster, PhD, to Fr. Alphonse Westhof, Archbishop Joseph Ritter, and Amleto Cicognani, September 2, 1952, AASL, Parish File–Kirkwood, St. Peter's.

116. Schuster to Westhof, Ritter, and Cicognani. Having also received several letters of less-learned complaint, Ritter—who had not been in the church since the crucifix was installed—ordered Westhof to "refrain from introducing anything unusual or novel in the new church" and to remove the crucifix in favor of "a more moderate and traditional design" (September 9, 1952, AASL, Parish File–Kirkwood, St. Peter's). Westhof replied defending his practices in general and the crucifix in particular; he promised to submit to Ritter's authority, but asked him to see the piece first, citing Lavanoux, Frei, and Murphy as experts who thought highly of it (September 10, 1952, AASL, Parish File–Kirkwood, St. Peter's). The crucifix was ultimately allowed to remain. However, the affair demonstrates the pressure on priests and bishops interested in "forward-looking" art and architecture.

117. ML, "The Authentic Tradition in Art," 123. Sometimes, as in Paul Thiry's essay in *Churches & Temples*, it was more convenient to include the statement approving "modern art" and exclude, through the artful use of ellipses, the condemnation of "distortion and perversion" (81C).

118. ML, "The Authentic Tradition in Art," 124.

119. Jesuit Josef Jungmann's research was available in English as *The Mass of the Roman Rite: Its Origins and Development* (New York: Benziger, 1951). The subtitle of Jungmann's majestic two-volume work in German (Vienna: 1948–49)—*Eine genetische Erklärung der römischen Messe*—clarifies its biological analogy. For a similar argument by an American, see Gerald Ellard, SJ, *The Mass of the Future* (Milwaukee: Bruce Publishing, 1948).

120. See Andrew Meszaros, *The Prophetic Church: History and Doctrinal Development in John Henry Newman and Yves Congar* (Oxford: Oxford University Press, 2016); Jürgen Mettepenningen, *Nouvelle Théologie—New Theology: Inheritor of Modernism, Precursor of Vatican II* (London: T & T Clark, 2010); and John W. O'Malley, *What Happened at Vatican II* (Cambridge, MA: Belknap Press of Harvard University Press, 2008), 75–80.

121. Joseph P. Chinnici, OFM, *Living Stones: The History and Structure of Catholic Spiritual Life in the United States* (Maryknoll, NY: Orbis Books, 1996), 120.

122. Pecklers, *The Unread Vision*, 27–29.

123. *Mediator dei*, §59. While Pius also warned against "the temerity and daring of those who introduce novel liturgical practices," liturgical movement circles generally regarded it as favorable.

124. Cajetan Baumann, "Some Trends in Church Design," *AR*, September 1944, 95.

125. John Walter Wood, "Ferro-Concrete as a Building Material," *LA* 2, no. 2 (1933): 69.

126. Leopold Arnaud, "The Living Tradition in Christian Art," *LA* 9, no. 3 (1941): 47–48.

127. Thiry, Bennett, and Kamphoefner, *Churches & Temples*, 5.

128. Thiry, Bennett, and Kamphoefner, 13.

129. Thiry, Bennett, and Kamphoefner, 29.

130. Otto Spaeth to John McNicholas, April 17, 1944, CLIT, 21/07.

131. Spaeth to McNicholas.

132. "A Panel Discussion at the National Catholic Building Convention," 30.

133. "A Panel Discussion at the National Catholic Building Convention," 30.

134. "Architecture To-Day: A Symposium," *LA* 19, no. 1 (1950): 22.

135. Rev. Michael Gillgannon, "Position Paper: On Some Possible Directions for Liturgical Renewal in the Diocese of Kansas City–St. Joseph," December 1, 1966, FRMP. I consulted the McManus papers prior to their recent reorganization, and therefore do not cite box and folder numbers for this collection.

136. "Renewal and Future Development of the Liturgy," Frederick McManus to Bishop Victor J. Reed, January 14, 1965, FRMP.

137. John Cogley, "The Future of an Illusion," *Commonweal*, June 2, 1967, 312.

138. Daniel Berrigan, SJ, to ML, September 28, 1955, CLIT, 31/03.

139. Nogar, *The Lord of the Absurd*, 17.

140. William Birmingham, "Evolution in Theology," *Jubilee*, March 1966, 50.

141. George Tavard, *The Church Tomorrow* (New York: Herder and Herder, 1965), 40.

142. Walter Ong, *Knowledge and the Future of Man* (New York, 1968), 24–25, cited in *Projections: Shaping an American Theology for the Future*, ed. Thomas F. O'Meara and Donald M. Weisser (Garden City, NY: Doubleday, 1970), 1–2.

143. O'Meara and Weisser, *Projections*, 2.

144. O'Meara and Weisser, 5.

145. Quoted in Donald J. Thorman, *American Catholics Face the Future* (Wilkes-Barre, PA: Dimension Books, 1968), 9.

CHAPTER TWO

1. Joseph D. Murphy, "Meeting with Archbishop Ritter," March 14, 1947, EFJP, 26/4.

2. It was preceded by at least one Episcopalian church and one synagogue; see Kathleen James-Chakraborty, "Moderate Modernism: Sacred Architecture in St. Louis and Its Suburbs," in *Modern Architecture in St. Louis: Washington University and Postwar American Architecture, 1948–1973*, ed. Eric Mumford (St. Louis: Washington University School of Architecture, 2004), 26–40. For national context, see Gretchen Buggeln, *The Suburban Church: Modernism and Community in Postwar America* (Minneapolis: University of Minnesota Press, 2015).

3. Murphy, "Meeting with Archbishop Ritter."

4. Joseph E. Ritter, "Towards a Living Climate of Religious Art," *LA* 23, no. 1 (1954): 3–4. The archbishop later approved two more parish churches by Murphy and Mackey, in addition to a modernist chancery and the Benedictine foundation in nearby Creve Coeur (see chap. 3).

5. See Richard Kieckhefer, *Theology in Stone: Church Architecture from Byzantium to Berkeley* (New York: Oxford University Press, 2008); and Joseph P. Chinnici, OFM, *Living Stones: The History and Structure of Catholic Spiritual Life in the United States* (Maryknoll, NY: Orbis Books, 1996).

6. Scholars have recently argued for attention to a discourse carried out through objects and images rather than words. See, e.g., David Morgan, ed., *Religion and Material Culture: The Matter of Belief* (London: Routledge, 2009); Colleen McDannell, *Material Christianity: Religion and Popular Culture in America* (New Haven, CT: Yale University Press, 1995); and Sarah Williams Goldhagen, "Something to Talk About: Modernism, Discourse, Style," *Journal of the Society of Architectural Historians* 64, no. 2 (2005): 144–67.

7. Andrew M. Shanken, *194X: Architecture, Planning, and Consumer Culture on the American Home Front* (Minneapolis: University of Minnesota Press, 2009), vii.

8. Shanken, 156–58.

9. Cited in Richard Pommer, introduction to *Idea as Model*, ed. Kenneth Frampton and Silvia Kolbowski (New York: Rizzoli International, 1981), 1.

10. Karen Moon, *Modeling Messages: The Architect and the Model* (New York: Monacelli, 2005), 28.

11. Robin Evans, "Architectural Projections," in *Architecture and Its Image: Four Centuries of Architectural Representation*, ed. Eve Blau and Edward Kaufman (Montreal: Canadian Center for Architecture, 1989), 19.

12. Evans, 19.

13. Cited in Moon, *Modeling Messages*, 109.

14. James Cardinal McGuigan, preface to Gerald Ellard, SJ, *The Mass of the Future* (Milwaukee: Bruce Publishing, 1948), viii.

15. Ellard, foreword to *The Mass of the Future*, xi.

16. Ellard, xi, xii.

17. Ellard, xii, xiii; and 345.

18. Eames's Catholicism has not been much noted; however, his first major commission was St. Mary's, Arkansas (1936). For Ellard's friendship with Frei and Eames, see Gerald Ellard, SJ, to ML, November 6, 1937, CLIT, 4/02. Eames stayed friendly with the *Liturgical Arts* circle; Lavanoux first met him on a 1935 tour of the Midwest and later saw him on the West Coast ("Observations," *LA* 5, no. 1 (1936): 24; "Editor's Diary," *LA* 21, no. 4 (1953): 1).

19. Gerald Ellard, SJ, to ML, April 21, 1947, CLIT, 23/04. For his seeking help with architectural journals, see Gerald Ellard, SJ, to ML, January 21, 1947, CLIT, 23/04. Ellard again requested bibliographies of recent articles from *Architectural Record* and *Architectural Forum* in 1954 (CLIT, 30/02).

20. Frederick McManus quoted Pius X on the "squalor" of the contemporary liturgy due to the "dirt and neglect" of the centuries since the Council of Trent in his introduction to H. A. Reinhold, *Bringing the Mass to the People* (Baltimore: Helicon, 1960), 3.

21. Jay M. Price, *Temples for a Modern God: Religious Architecture in Postwar America* (New York: Oxford University Press, 2013).

22. Moon, *Modeling Messages*, 104; John Kelly to ML, August 4, 1955, CLIT, 32/02.

23. Barry Byrne, "Plan for a Church," *LA* 10, no. 3 (1942): 58–60.

24. Byrne, 59.

25. Mark Morris, *Models: Architecture and the Miniature* (Chichester: Wiley-Academy, 2006), 19–23.

26. E.g., Philip Cotton and Nelson Garmendia, *LA* 28 (1960): 48–49. Lavanoux frequently saw student work in the New York area (e.g., Yale theses at the Architectural League [ML to T. Lawrason Riggs, December 23, 1938, CLIT, 17/05]; and Cooper Union theses at MoMA [ML to John Hejdek, November 17, 1971, CLIT, 51/04]). He also advised Columbia and Princeton students, especially during the 1950s.

27. James A. Holt Jr., "The Religious Space," *LA* 37, no. 1 (1968): 8–9.

28. Holt, 8.

29. See also Clovis Heimsath, *Behavioral Architecture: Towards an Accountable Design Process* (New York: McGraw-Hill, 1977).

30. Ray Pavia, interview by the author, Staten Island, NY, 2012.

31. Emily Genauer, "Matisse Chapel, Modern Church Project Both Applauded by Catholic Clergymen," *New York Herald Tribune*, December 23, 1951.

32. For Smith's model, funded by Ossorio, see Robert Storr, "A Man of Parts," in *Tony Smith: Architect, Painter, Sculptor* (New York: Museum of Modern Art, 1998), 10–35. Generally, the secondary literature on this meeting relies on problematic later interviews with Ossorio; unfortunately, the relevant volume of Maurice Lavanoux's diary is missing.

33. Genauer, "Matisse Chapel, Modern Church Project Applauded." The exhibit attracted other media comment: "A Church for Lent," *Interiors*, February 1952; James Fitzsimmons, "Prototype of an Organic Modern Church," *Art Digest*, December 15, 1951, 11, 23; Paul Thiry, Richard M. Bennett, and Henry L. Kamphoefner, *Churches & Temples* (New York: Reinhold, 1953), 108–9.

34. Jean Labatut and André Girard, "Adventure in Light-Color Polychromy: A Church Prototype," *LA* 20, no. 1 (1951): 2–8.

35. A few years later, Girard's windows for the Chapel of St. Ann in Palo Alto, California, painted directly on clear glass, became the defining element of the interior. Changing light conditions were a common concern in modernist architecture. Joseph Murphy's design for St. Ann's included a massive apse window; the Emil Frei Company created a mural in stained glass and painted wood. In bright sunlight and under artificial interior light at night, the apse wall looks dramatically different as, in turn, the glass and the wood become the focus of attention. Changing light was also a major aspect of, e.g., Gyo Obata's design for St. Louis Priory church (chap. 3) and José Luis Sert's design for the Chapel of St. Botolph, Boston (chap. 5).

36. Celia Hubbard to ML, June 14, 1956, CLIT, 34/01.

37. Thomas F. McNulty and Mary S. Fawcett, "Proposed Catholic Church for the Boston Archdiocese," *LA* 25, no. 4 (1957): 110–12. McNulty probably met Fawcett—a protégée of Walter Gropius who briefly worked at The Architects Collective—through those circles. Fawcett, the former Mary Otis Stevens, divorced William Fawcett in 1958 and married McNulty shortly thereafter. The two formed a professional partnership; both the marriage and the design firm lasted for twenty years. See Susana Torre, "Building Utopia: Mary Otis Stevens and the Lincoln, Massachusetts, House," in *Impossible to Hold: Women and Culture in the 1960s*, ed. Avital H. Bloch and Lauri Umanky (New York: NYU Press, 2005), 29–42.

38. Philip Cotton to ML, January 19, 1960, CLIT, 63/17; competition: Fr. Patrick O'Donnell, ed., *Churches for Tomorrow: Thirty-Three Designs from the Cardinal Lercaro Prize-Spaeth*

Competition Sponsored by the North American Liturgical Conference 1961 (Cincinnati: F&W Publishing, 1961).

39. "Notes for the Subcommission on Sacred Art—Preparatory Ecumenical Council II," April 7, 1961, CLAV, 3/10.

40. Jeanne Heiberg to ML, September 29, 1966, CLIT, 45/02.

41. Holt, "The Religious Space," 8.

42. Holt, 8.

43. Mary Rose Shaughnessy, email messages to the author, March 9, 2010, and March 26, 2010. Joe Shaughnessy frequently worked with Barry Byrne.

44. Albert C. Smith, *Architectural Model as Machine: A New View of Models from Antiquity to the Present Day* (Oxford: Elsevier, 2004), xvi.

45. Hélène Lipstadt, "Architectural Publications, Competitions, and Exhibitions," in *Architecture and Its Image*, ed. Blau and Kaufman, 109–37, explores the relationship between publications and exhibitions on the one hand, and the "social status, reception, and, eventually, meaning" of architectural works on the other (109).

46. Editorial, *LA* 12, no. 1 (1943): 1.

47. Editorial, *LA* 12, no. 1 (1943): 1.

48. Leopold Arnaud, "The Living Tradition in Christian Art," *LA* 9, no. 3 (1941): 48.

49. Howard Dearstyne, "Basic Teaching of Architecture," *LA* 12, no. 3 (1944): 56–60; Barry Byrne, "On Training for Architecture," *LA* 13, no. 3 (1945): 56–62. Dearstyne, the only American to graduate from the Bauhaus, soon became head of design at Cranbrook. On postwar planning, see also Rev. Robert Brennan, "Sumer is icumen in," *LA* 13, no. 1 (1944): 4–7, originally titled "Looking to the Future" (CLIT, 21/01).

50. Rev. Raymond J. Morrison to ML, November 26, 1944, CLIT, 21/4.

51. Hyungmin Pai, *The Portfolio and the Diagram: Architecture, Discourse, and Modernity in America* (Cambridge, MA: MIT Press, 2002), 258. Eve Blau and Edward Kaufman comment that "architectural representations [frequently] structure their subjects through groups of interrelated images" and highlight the role played by selection, sequencing/compositioning, cropping, and other kinds of editing in producing an "image" of a building for a viewer (Blau and Kaufman, introduction to *Architecture and Its Image*, 13–15).

52. "Three Churches in the Mid-West," *LA* 18, no. 4 (1950): 91–93.

53. *LA* 25, no. 4 (1957), 109.

54. E.g., John Jakob of Columbia University, *LA* 27, no. 2 (1959): 49.

55. Frank Kacmarcik to ML, Feast of St. Ephrem, 1947, CLIT, 23/05.

56. ML to Rev. J. G. McGarry, August 1, 1955, CLIT, 32/02. As *Liturgical Arts*' first editor wrote, it "would serve as a medium for acquainting the clergy, the professions, and the laity with good modern work and with the historic monuments of Christian art. To make these better known is, after all, the central educational purpose of the society" (Henry Lorin Binsse to ML, March 15, 1931, CLIT, 7/13).

57. ML to Paul Douglas Roller, September 3, 1963, CLIT, 86/15. See also Paul Douglas Roller, "An Ecumenical Council Center for the Christian Churches," *LA* 32, no. 3 (1964): 75–86. Other imagined ecumenical spaces in *LA* include Walter Abbott, SJ, "Church of the Encounter," *LA* 37, no. 2 (1969): 42–49.

58. Lavanoux visited the Whitney in August 1970 (ML to Robert Howes, August 13, 1970, CLIT, 50/01). See Sarah Deyong, "Memories of the Urban Future: The Rise and Fall of the

Megastructure," in *The Changing of the Avant-Garde: Visionary Architectural Drawings from the Howard Gilman Collection*, ed. Terence Riley (New York: Museum of Modern Art, 2002), 23–35; Matilda McQuaid, *Envisioning Architecture: Drawings from the Museum of Modern Art* (New York: Museum of Modern Art, 2002); and Peter Cook, *Experimental Architecture* (New York: Universe Books, 1970).

59. ML to Thomas Burns, February 29, 1972, CLIT, 54/02.

60. ML to James F. Johnson, July 24, 1944, CLIT, 21/05.

61. J. B. O'Connell, *Church Building and Furnishing: The Church's Way, A Study in Liturgical Law* (Notre Dame, IN: University of Notre Dame Press, 1955).

62. "Editor's Diary," *LA* 22, no. 1 (1953): 31; Michael Mathis, CSC, preface to O'Connell, *Church Building and Furnishing*, ix–x, x. Mathis welcomed modernist architects to his summer workshops in liturgy at Notre Dame.

63. "Montana Society: Mission Statement: Frank Montana's Biography," accessed December 16, 2012, http://montanasociety.nd.edu/about/; O'Connell, *Church Building and Furnishing*, "Illustrations." The essays in the official history of Notre Dame's School of Architecture also downplay Montana's, and the school's, midcentury ties to modernism (Jane A. Devine, ed., *100 Years of Architecture at Notre Dame: A History of the School of Architecture, 1898–1998* [Notre Dame: University of Notre Dame School of Architecture, 1999]).

64. The plates also included several sanctuaries in historicist styles, but these were chosen by O'Connell.

65. Mathis, preface to O'Connell, *Church Building and Furnishing*, x.

66. J. B. O'Connell, *Church Building and Furnishing: The Church's Way* (London: Burns & Oates, 1955).

67. "[Church Architecture]," *Architectural Forum* 91 (December 1949): 58, 63.

68. Catherine R. Osborne, "Anarchy in Our Churches? The American Architectural Press, 1944–65," *European Legacy* 22, no. 3 (2017): 278–92. For the context of these "tri-faith" features, see Kevin M. Schultz, *Tri-Faith America: How Catholics and Jews Held Postwar America to Its Protestant Promise* (New York: Oxford University Press, 2011).

69. Mildred Schmertz to ML, August 15, 1967, CLIT, 47/01. Lavanoux must have been especially delighted with Schmertz's praise of his recent printing of the model and plans for José Luis Sert's never-built Boston chapel (see chap. 5): "You scooped us after all," she wrote, and "must have some more new projects which would do nicely [in *AR*]." Lavanoux enjoyed "scooping" the larger magazines, but he also had a friendly relationship with them that frequently went in the other direction, with their editors offering him access to plates and photos (e.g., James Burns Jr. [of *Progressive Architecture*] to ML, August 3, 1954, CLIT, 31/01).

70. E.g., ML to Marguerite Brunswig Staude, February 4, 1939, CLIT, 17/05; and to Ferdinando Zobel, 1953, CLIT, 29/04.

71. Swati Chattopadhyay, "Architectural Representations, Changing Technologies, and Conceptual Extensions," *Journal of the Society of Architectural Historians* 71, no. 3 (2012): 271.

72. "Church of Christ the King, Seattle, Washington," *LA* 18, no. 2 (1950): 38–39.

73. [Rev.] Thomas F. Coakley, correspondence, *LA* 2, no. 3 (1933): 159–60. Sacred Heart is a beautifully detailed neohistoricist church; Coakley was one of Barry Byrne's antagonists in the *Commonweal* debates (see chap. 1). His use of models for study, publicity, and fundraising was, however, a classic modernist move.

74. Moon, *Modeling Messages*, 111–13.

75. George N. Shuster, *Notre Dame*, Spring 1964, 5 (University of Notre Dame Archives, PNDP 83-Nd-3s).

76. M. Morris, *Models*, 13.

77. Joseph Salerno, "The Life and Death of a Church," n.d. [1958], CLIT, 35/03. Salerno published an account of the affair anonymously, as well: "The Church That Never Was," *Voice of St. Jude*, March 1958, 13–15, 34, including a photograph of the rejected model. The article that so annoyed the building commission was "Religious Buildings," *AR*, June 1956, 202–5.

78. Salerno, "The Life and Death of a Church."

79. Salerno, "The Life and Death of a Church."

80. E.g., Fr. Athanasius, OSCO, to ML, September 3, 1962, CLIT, 39/03.

81. Philip Johnson to ML, April 20, 1953, CLIT, 29/01; Donald Bartheleme to ML, December 16, 1953, CLIT, 28/03.

82. On modernist exhibits, see McQuaid, *Envisioning Architecture*, 21–22.

83. September 5, 1950, CBLP, 734/9.

84. Penn State: "Editor's Diary," *LA* 24, no. 3 (1956): 64. Other non-Catholic venues included a 1949 talk in Chicago sponsored by the American Federation of Arts (ML to Henry D. Ellis, June 22, 1949, CLIT, 25/02). Lavanoux gave nationally broadcast radio lectures on NBC's *Catholic Hour* August 22 and 29, 1948, receiving a letter from a California architect who "trusted that enough of our clergymen were listening to benefit from it" (George J. Adams to ML, August 26, 1948, CLIT, 24/04). He also appeared on CBS TV's *Look Up and Live* on June 19 1955 and November 22 1956.

85. Mary Fay to ML, February 4, 1948, CLIT, 25/05.

86. ML to Ellard, July 9, 1948, CLIT, 24/04.

87. Richard Timm, CSC, to ML, November 17, 1948, CLIT, 25/05.

88. E.g., "Editor's Diary," *LA* 22, no. 2 (1954): 64.

89. C. D. Innes, *Designing Modern America: Broadway to Main Street* (New Haven, CT: Yale University Press, 2005), 120.

90. ML, "Art at the Liturgical Week," *LA* 26 (1957): 2.

91. ML, 2.

92. On the role of exhibitions in promoting modernist religious art and architecture see John Dillenberger, *The Visual Arts and Christianity in America* (New York: Crossroad, 1989), 174–77. On laywomen, see Katharine E. Harmon, *There Were Also Many Women There: Lay Women in the Liturgical Movement in the United States, 1926–59* (Collegeville, MN: Liturgical Press, 2013), especially 147–60. The very determined proprietors—often converts—of these gallery/bookshops included Sara B. O'Neill and Nina Polcyn Moore of St. Benet's, Chicago; Celia Hubbard of Botolph Group Gallery, Boston; Elizabeth Sullivan of Paraclete Bookshop, New York City; Emily Bouchard of Contemporary Christian Art, New York City; Kyra Kuhar of Parnassus, Charleston, South Carolina; and, in England, Iris Conlay of the Ashley Gallery, London.

93. Spaeth cited in Clement J. Lambert, SM, "Religious Art of Today," *Marianist*, July 1944, 14.

94. Spaeth cited in Lambert, "Religious Art of Today," 14.

95. "Religious Art in Dayton," *Dayton Herald*, April 13, 1944, EOSP.

96. The catalogue is available in EOSP. Three of Barry Byrne's churches (Christ the King, Cork, Ireland; SS. Peter and Paul, Pierre, South Dakota; and St. Anthony of Padua, Hartford,

Connecticut); Freeman, French, & Freeman's St. Mark's, Burlington, Vermont; and Paul C. Reilly's St. Peter Claver Chapel, Montclair, New Jersey, made up the Catholic contribution.

97. Maurice Lavanoux was a member of the jury, along with architects Marcel Breuer and Percival Goodman and with Jan Rowan, the editor of *Progressive Architecture* ("Editor's Diary," *LA* 32, no. 3 [1964]: 98).

98. Lambert, "Religious Art of Today," 18.

99. "Interest Piqued by Exhibit of 'Religious Art of Today,'" clipping in EOSP.

100. James McConnaughey, OWI, to Eloise Spaeth, April 10, 1944, EOSP; "File Request for Catalogs on Art Show" and "Art Catalogs Will Combat Nazi Slurs," clippings in EOSP.

101. For Eloise Spaeth's promotion of American modern art, see Michael L. Krenn, *Fall-Out Shelters for the Human Spirit: American Art and the Cold War* (Durham: University of North Carolina Press, 2006).

102. Stephen P. Dorsey to ML, November 10, 1953, CLIT, 28/04.

103. Eloise Spaeth to Percival Goodman, June 16, 1954, EOSP.

104. Eloise Spaeth to Gerard Carroll, August 29, 1956, EOSP.

105. Smaller-scale exhibition activity increased in the late 1950s, as measured by Maurice Lavanoux's correspondence; e.g., organized by Catholic Conference of College Alumnae of Staten Island ("Editor's Diary," *LA* 26, no. 1 [1957]: 14); St. Joseph's College for Women, Brooklyn ("Editor's Diary," *LA* 26, no. 2 [1958]: 47); Conception Seminary, Missouri, February 1958 (Roger Mollison, correspondence, *LA* 26, no. 2 [1958]: 68).

106. Mrs. Parker Hall, correspondence, *LA* 27, no. 1 (1958): 24–25.

107. Newman Club of Washington University St. Louis, "Ars Sacra 1951: The 1st Annual Showing of Contemporary Religious Art," June 1951, CLIT, 27/4.

108. Press release, December 1955, CLIT, 30/03.

109. Celia Hubbard, "Catalogue Introduction to 'Religious Art Today' Exhibition," CLIT, 30/03.

110. Jack Harwell, "Are Traditions Fading? New Trend for Churches Depicted," *Houston Post*, 1953, CLIT, 28/03.

111. Harwell, "Are Traditions Fading?"

112. Celia Hubbard to ML, October 15, 1954, CLIT, 30/03.

113. Avery Dulles, SJ, *Models of the Church* (Garden City, NY: Doubleday, 1974), 15.

114. Dulles, 8.

115. Dulles, 8.

116. Dulles, 21.

117. Peter Hammond, ed., *Towards a Church Architecture* (London: Architectural Press, 1962). See also Peter Hammond, *Liturgy and Architecture* (New York: Columbia University Press, 1961). Hammond was an Anglican, but his work was respected by American Catholic modernists, and his New Churches Research Group included Catholics from its inception in 1957.

118. Kieckhefer, *Theology in Stone*, analyzes this type of plan as the "modern communal church" (12).

119. Gabriel M. Weber, OSM, to ML, n.d. [May 1967], CLIT, 47/02.

120. Robert Bundy, preface to *Images of the Future: The Twenty-First Century and Beyond*, ed. Bundy (Buffalo, NY: Prometheus Books, 1976), 2, referencing Frederik Polak, *The Image of the Future: Enlightening the Past, Orientating the Present, Forecasting the Future* (New York: Oceana, 1961).

CHAPTER THREE

1. John Toomey, SJ, "The First Zeppelin Mass," *America*, May 23, 1936, 153. Schulte, a German pilot during World War I, also founded the Missionalium Vehiculorum Associatio, an organization providing planes, boats, and cars to remote missions. Its motto, *Obviam Christo terra marique et in aera*, translates to "Toward Christ by land, sea, and air."

2. "Ideas Aerial," *America*, January 20, 1934, 369; "Sky and Underseas," *America*, February 3, 1934, 416. When *America* first heard of the *Hindenburg* Mass, they commented on "this idea of Mass a-wing, of Christ being offered high over the waters of the sea" ("Super Pennas Ventorum," *America*, May 16, 1936, 125).

3. Leopold Arnaud, "Concrete in Architectural Service," *Journal of the American Concrete Institute* 10 (1939): 355. Arnaud was indebted to Lewis Mumford, *Technics and Civilization* (New York: Hartford, Brace, 1934). The argument that modern building technologies were cost-effective was significant, but not absolute; see Robert Proctor, *Building the Modern Church: Roman Catholic Church Architecture in Britain, 1955–1975* (London: Ashgate, 2014), 62–64; Gretchen Buggeln, *The Suburban Church: Modernism and Community in Postwar America* (Minneapolis: University of Minnesota Press, 2015); and Jay M. Price, *Temples for a Modern God: Religious Architecture in Postwar America* (New York: Oxford University Press, 2013), 44–45.

4. "Some Thoughts on the Architecture of Portsmouth Abbey," 35.

5. Concept statement for SS. Peter and Paul Church, Tulsa, Oklahoma, ca. 1960, RLJ.

6. Concept statement for SS. Peter and Paul Church.

7. "Some Thoughts on the Architecture of Portsmouth Abbey," 35.

8. Walter Behrendt, *Modern Building: Its Nature, Problems, and Forms* (New York: Harcourt, Brace, 1937).

9. See Reyner Banham, *A Concrete Atlantis: U.S. Industrial Building and European Modern Architecture* (Cambridge, MA: MIT Press, 1986).

10. Frank Brannach, *Church Architecture: Building for a Living Faith* (Milwaukee: Bruce Publishing, 1933), 167. Brannach illustrated the complexity of early Catholic modernism; while arguing for adoption of American norms and praising "a new admiration of material in its natural state," he also warned against "modernistic" architecture and art as irreverent and unfitted (189).

11. Correspondence, *LA* 5, no. 2 (1936): 71.

12. See Sidney Castle to ML, November 2, 1931, CLIT, 2/12; and John Walsh to ML, December 19, 1944, CLIT, 21/07.

13. Otto Spaeth, "Worship and the Arts," *AR* 118 (December 1955): 162–67.

14. Meta-Mold: CLIT, 93/10. Compare Mary Chomeau's remark that if a church was to "express this civilization's attitude of worship" and hold "the public official prayer of the Church," it could not be a "Gothic type of church" because "people no longer possess[ed] medieval minds" (Mary Broderick Chomeau, *One Hundred and Twenty Five Years: A History of St. Peter's Parish, Kirkwood, Missouri, 1832–1957* [Kirkwood, MO: St. Peter's Parish, 1957], 112).

15. John Paul Harding to ML, n.d. [January 1945], CLIT, 21/02.

16. Cited in Vincent L. Michael, *The Architecture of Barry Byrne: Taking the Prairie School to Europe* (Urbana: University of Illinois Press, 2013), 5.

17. This phrasing is from "How the Chapel Came into Being," written in the mid-1950s. However, it echoes statements Staude made in the 1930s, e.g., to ML, March 4, 1939, CLIT, 17/05.

18. Cited in NCWC News Service, "U.S. Girl's Inspiration May Bring Erection of Basilica at Budapest," January 30, 1939, CLIT, 17/05, in the brief period during which Staude flirted with building the design abroad. Staude later embellished her account, focusing less on the final building and more on the internal structure, which may reflect the increasing penetration of modernist ideas about exterior form exposing structural support. "How the Chapel Came into Being" claimed that "when viewed from a certain angle, a cross seemed to impose itself through the very core of the structure," so that the idea of a church that would take on that structural shape "for days it haunted and obsessed me." By the time of her death, the account had mutated further: "As her eyes absorbed all the new structures which she passed, suddenly there was the Empire State Building, then under construction. Emerging from its scaffolding, she saw a cross taking its form where the major vertical beam deliberately crossed the horizontal. Ah, she thought. Just as the Gothic spirit overrides matter. . . . This is the hidden strength it carries behind its own structure" (Kate Ruland Thorne, *Upon This Rock: Marguerite Brunswig Staude and Her Sedona Chapel* (Sedona, AZ: Chapel of the Holy Cross, 1995), 2).

19. Lloyd Wright to ML, May 10, 1939, CLIT, 17/06. See also David Gebhard and Harriette Von Breton, *Lloyd Wright, Architect* (Santa Monica: Hennessey + Ingalls, 1998).

20. Lloyd Wright to ML, May 10, 1939; Gebhard and Von Breton, *Lloyd Wright, Architect*, 52–53.

21. Marguerite Brunswig to ML, March 4, 1939, CLIT, 17/05.

22. Françoise Caussé, *La revue "L'art sacré": Le débat en France sur l'art et la religion (1945–1954)* (Paris: Cerf, 2010). See also William Rubin, *Modern Sacred Art and the Church at Assy* (New York: Columbia University Press, 1961).

23. Staude claimed decades later that she "urged and pleaded with" Wright "to work with us on our new idea," but he "refused, and clung to the original plans" (Ruland Thorne, *Upon This Rock*, 7). However, Staude's stories about other artists often make them seem unreasonable; it is unclear what exactly happened. A photograph of Wright's model was included in a 1971 retrospective of his work, under the title *Catholic Cathedral, Los Angeles*; the description made no mention of Staude (Gebhard and Von Breton, *Lloyd Wright, Architect*, 52–53, 60).

24. Monica Michelle Penick, "The Pace Setter Houses: Livable Modernism in Postwar America" (PhD diss, University of Texas, 2007), 97–98.

25. Ruland Thorne, *Upon This Rock*, 8. Espelage thought the money would be better spent on local missions, but ultimately agreed to provide sacramental support.

26. Dave Weinstein, "Eichler Architect, Bob Anshen: Self-Made Man," accessed January 9, 2012, http://www.eichlernetwork.com/article/eichler-architect-bob-anshen-self-made-man; "magnificently simple . . . challenge": Ruland Thorne, *Upon This Rock*, 15–33.

27. Staude, "How the Chapel Came into Being." A decade later, Staude had Monroe's corpus removed.

28. Glenn Fowler, "New Churches Are Anticipating the Future Instead of Reflecting the Past," *NYT*, August 25, 1957.

29. Staude, "How the Chapel Came into Being." For the National Shrine, see Thomas A. Tweed, *America's Church: The National Shrine and Catholic Presence in the Nation's Capital* (New York: Oxford University Press, 2011). The shrine, designed by Charles Maginnis but delayed during the Depression and World War II before being built to its original plans during the 1950s, caused heartburn in Catholic modernist circles. A number of artists, architects, and concerned laypeople wrote to Maurice Lavanoux to see "what could be done" about it (e.g., Clare Fontanini

to ML, December 2, 1952, CLIT, 28/05). He mostly tried to avoid public condemnation, preferring to concentrate on a "positive" vision of the future. This strategy fell apart when Maginnis died and *Liturgical Arts* had to run a tribute to the society's first president, including drawings for the Shrine (Charles D. Maginnis, "Shrine of the Immaculate Conception, Washington, D.C.," *LA* 23, no. 4 [1955]: 162). A sharp exchange ensued: William Justema wrote that he was "heartily sorry to see, once again, that the channels of the present can continue to inflict such pretentious monstrosities on the Catholics of tomorrow"; Lavanoux clarified that he was not a fan of the design; and the neohistoricist architect Richard Shaw wrote in enraged condemnation of this dismissal (correspondence, *LA* 24, no. 1 [1955]: 20; correspondence, *LA* 24 , no. 1 [1956]: 45.

30. Timothy Horner, OSB, *In Good Soil: The Founding of St. Louis Priory and School, 1954–1973* (Creve Coeur, MO: Saint Louis Abbey Press, 2001), 12–46.

31. Patrick J. Holloran, SJ, to Fred Switzer, March 30, 1955, ASLA.

32. Horner, *In Good Soil*, 52.

33. Horner, 52–53.

34. "Basic Ideas for the Architect When Planning the Building of St. Louis Priory and School" (n.d. [1955]), ASLA; reprinted in *In Good Soil*, 450–53. Horner suggests (132) that it may have been composed over a period of time, extending across both the Maritz and HOK periods. It seems to me, however, to be internally consistent with a date prior to the Maritz bids of January 1956.

35. [Columba Cary-Elwes, OSB] to [Abbot Herbert Byrne, OSB], December 30, 1955, ASLA.

36. Doubts: [Columba Cary-Elwes, OSB] to [Timothy Horner, OSB, and Luke Rigby, OSB], January 3, 1956, ASLA. Maritz plan bids: Horner, *In Good Soil*, 53.

37. Horner, *In Good Soil*, 86.

38. For American Benedictine architecture, see Catherine R. Osborne, "American Catholics and the Art of the Future, 1930–1975" (PhD diss., Fordham University, 2013), 105–27. Most American Benedictine houses, including St. John's, are descended from St. Vincent Archabbey, Latrobe, Pennsylvania, established by German immigrants. As such they were direct inheritors of the German Benedictine liturgical movement. Portsmouth and St. Louis are both foundations of English Benedictine houses. Despite their different lineages, in the United States the two groups developed similar architectural and liturgical interests.

39. Victoria M. Young, *Marcel Breuer's Saint John's Abbey Church: A New Vision for Liturgical Architecture* (Minneapolis: University of Minnesota Press, 2014).

40. Hamilton Smith, "The Buildings at St. John's Abbey, Collegeville, Minnesota," *Design Quarterly* 53 (1961): 19.

41. Timothy Horner, OSB, interview by the author, Creve Coeur, MO, January 4, 2011.

42. Horner, *In Good Soil*, 80–81.

43. George F. Hellmuth to Columba Cary-Elwes, OSB, March 22, 1956, ASLA.

44. Obata and Yamasaki, who had worked together earlier, both avoided internment during World War II by leaving the West Coast for architectural study.

45. Columba Cary-Elwes, OSB, "Planning a Monastery and Monastic School: Saint Louis Priory, Crève Coeur, Missouri," *LA* 26, no. 2 (1958): 48–50.

46. Gyo Obata, "Design of the St. Louis Priory," typescript, January 1958, CLIT, 88/19.

47. Timothy Horner, OSB, planning document for the school, 1956 (Horner, *In Good Soil*, 134).

48. Horner, *In Good Soil*, 144.

49. The models divided the monks two against two; Obata broke the tie in favor of the pyramid, which the monks called the "artichoke."

50. Horner, *In Good Soil*, 146–47.

51. Building committee minutes, June 24, 1957, ASLA.

52. Gyo Obata, program notes, n.d., CLIT, 88/19.

53. Gyo Obata, "Design of the St. Louis Priory," January 1958, CLIT, 88/19.

54. Obata, program notes.

55. Luke Rigby, OSB, "Progress Report," January 1961, ASLA, indicates that the construction process was being closely watched by builders; the Portland Cement Association was having its annual convention in St. Louis and was "intensely interested in this new use of cement." See Joseph M. Siry, "Seamless Continuity versus the Nature of Materials: Gunite and Frank Lloyd Wright's Guggenheim Museum," *Journal of the Society of Architectural Historians* 71, no. 1 (2012): 78–108.

56. "St. Louis Priory Church—A Design Triumph in Plastic and Concrete," n.d., CLIT, 88/19.

57. "St. Louis Priory Church—A Design Triumph in Plastic and Concrete."

58. Obata compared the effect to "an alabaster or shoji wall" (comments, n.d., CLIT, 88/19).

59. James Marston Fitch concluded the second edition of *American Building: The Historical Forces That Shaped It* (New York: Schocken Books, 1966) with a photo of the Chapel of the Holy Cross (317).

60. H. A. Reinhold, *The Dynamics of Liturgy* (New York: Macmillan Company, 1961), 83.

61. Paulist Fathers, Tennessee, "Mission Trailer," *LA* 6, no. 2 (1937): 68–69; "Saint Mary of the Highways Chapel: Trailer Equipment for Missionary Priests of the Diocese of Richmond, Virginia," *LA* 7, no. 2 (1939): 27. For "motor missions," see Jeffrey D. Marlett, *Saving the Heartland: Catholic Missionaries in Rural America, 1920–1960* (Dekalb: Northern Illinois University Press, 2002), 133–61.

62. See Sarah Williams Goldhagen, *Louis Kahn's Situated Modernism* (New Haven, CT: Yale University Press, 2001), 12. For related discussions in Britain after 1955, see Proctor, *Building the Modern Church*, 78–103 and 134–35, and in the United States, Buggeln, *The Suburban Church*, especially 85–123.

63. ML to Illtud Evans, OP, January 16, 1961, CLIT, 39/01.

64. Albert Christ-Janer and Mary Mix Foley, *Modern Church Architecture: A Guide to the Form and Spirit of Twentieth-Century Religious Building* (New York: McGraw-Hill, 1962), 45.

65. Brannach, *Church Architecture: Building for a Living Faith*, 195.

66. Editorial, *LA* 2, no. 2 (1933): 49. See Amy E. Slaton, *Reinforced Concrete and the Modernization of American Building, 1900–1930* (Baltimore: Johns Hopkins University Press, 2001).

67. John Walter Wood, "Ferro-Concrete as a Building Material," *LA* 2, no. 2 (1933): 69; Arnaud, "Concrete in Architectural Service," 356.

68. This letter was released under Abbot Baldwin Dworschak's signature on March 7, 1953, and is reprinted in Whitney S. Stoddard, *Adventure in Architecture: Building the New Saint John's* (New York: Longmans, Green, 1958), 23–24.

69. Engineering and technology go entirely unmentioned in, e.g., Louis Bouyer, *Liturgy and Architecture* (Notre Dame, IN: University of Notre Dame Press, 1967), one of the most widely read postconciliar works on the subject.

70. The terms "efficiency, economy, and elegance" are borrowed from Maria E. Moreyra Garlock and David P. Billington, *Félix Candela: Engineer, Builder, Structural Artist* (Princeton: Princeton University Art Museum, 2008).

71. Behrendt, *Modern Building*, 167–68; James Marston Fitch, *American Building: The Historical Forces That Shaped It*, 2nd ed. (New York: Schocken Books, 1966; first published 1947).

72. Editorial, *LA* 2, no. 2 (1933): 49–50.

73. "The Slow Evolution of Religious Buildings," *AR* 106 (December 1949): 121.

74. Editorial, *LA* 2, no. 2 (1933): 49–50.

75. Christ-Janer and Foley, *Modern Church Architecture*, 4.

76. Paul Thiry, Richard M. Bennett, and Henry L. Kamphoefner, *Churches & Temples* (New York: Reinhold, 1953), 18.

77. See Brannach, *Church Architecture*, 195. Many of the churches in this book have had at least one significant problem in the course of their construction or maintenance. Marcel Breuer's St. John's Abbey developed serious cracking during construction, requiring swift and inventive intervention from the structural engineers Paul Weidlinger and Matthys Levy (see "Two Churches by Breuer," The Restless Hungarian: Dispatches on the Life and Times of Paul Weidlinger, September 12, 2014, http://restlesshungarian.com/two-churches-by-breuer/); Robert Lawton Jones's St. Patrick's had leaking problems with the skylights linking the concrete umbrellas; the first generation Kal-Wall at St. Louis Abbey had to be replaced with a later and stronger variant; the Chapel of the Holy Cross had its roof replaced due to serious structural issues. A leaking roof in Lisle, Illinois's St. Procopius almost caused a total breakdown in the relationship between architect Ed Dart and Abbot Daniel Kucera. Contractor Richard Pepper recalls watching water pour onto the new pipe organ while Kucera pointed his umbrella threateningly in Dart's direction (Ann B. McGowan, *Pepper Construction: Beyond Bricks and Mortar* [Chicago: Pepper Construction Company, 2003], 100). While most problems were eventually resolved, Mario Ciampi's St. Peter's, Pacifica, California (fig. 4.8) had to be demolished when the experimental pressed plywood he used became infected with dry rot.

78. See Aly Ahmed Raafat, *Reinforced Concrete in Architecture* (New York: Reinhold, 1958), Mario Salvadori and Robert Heller, *Structure in Architecture: The Building of Buildings*, 2nd ed. (Englewood Cliffs, NJ: Prentice-Hall, 1975), and the polemical but informative Peter Collins, *Concrete: The Vision of a New Architecture*, 2nd ed. (Toronto: McGill-Queen's University Press, 2004).

79. Raafat, *Reinforced Concrete in Architecture*, 229.

80. Young, *Marcel Breuer's Saint John's Abbey Church*; Stoddard, *Adventure in Architecture.*

81. J. W. Wood, "Ferro-Concrete as a Building Material."

82. Christ-Janer and Foley, *Modern Church Architecture*, 30.

83. Raafat, *Reinforced Concrete in Architecture*, 50–51.

84. Siry, "Seamless Continuity versus the Nature of Materials," 104, citing Wright, "In the Cause of Architecture" (1908). For an extended analysis of Wright's approach to concrete as an organic material, see Siry, *Unity Temple: Frank Lloyd Wright and Architecture for Liberal Religion* (Cambridge: MIT Press, 1996), 108–15.

85. Garlock and Billington, *Félix Candela*, 120–21.

86. See also Proctor, *Building the Modern Church*, 80–83.

87. Garlock and Billington, *Félix Candela*, 98–113. For a particularly helpful exploration of

hyperbolic paraboloids, with a variety of diagrams and construction photographs, see Colin Faber, *Candela the Shell Builder* (New York: Reinhold, 1963).

88. David P. Billington, *Thin Shell Concrete Structures* (New York: McGraw-Hill, 1966).

89. Wright quoted in Janey Bennett, "Work of Mark Mills: Structural Elegance and a Sense of Reverent Space," *Journal of the Taliesin Fellows* 10 (Spring 1993): 19.

90. Quoted in Faber, *Candela the Shell Builder*, 59.

91. Christ-Janer and Foley, *Modern Church Architecture*, 23.

92. Fr. Patrick O'Donnell, ed., *Churches for Tomorrow: Thirty-Three Designs from the Cardinal Lercaro Prize-Spaeth Competition Sponsored by the North American Liturgical Conference 1961* (Cincinnati: F&W Publishing, 1961).

93. Vera Graham, "Easter in a New Church," *San Mateo Times and Daily News Leader*, April 9, 1966.

94. William Schickel to ML, September 21, 1962, CLIT, 88/19.

95. Brannach, *Church Architecture*, 195.

96. Barry Byrne, "The Orthodoxy of Columns," *Commonweal*, March 25, 1925, 551.

97. Byrne, 551. Byrne, like other modernist architects, thus dodged the aesthetic issues around concrete.

98. Byrne, 551. See also Brannach, *Church Architecture*, 207.

99. Jim Ringrose, "Church of Future," *Catholic Voice* (Oakland, CA), February 1, 1967, 9.

100. The suggested church's other furnishings would be movable, and allowance would be made for "occasional and removable banners." On the same page, Lavanoux printed photographs of the Oakland, California, cathedral, which had introduced "freedom of action" as well as a projection screen; he felt it was a good effort but observed that these elements were not really "*at home* in this neo-gothic interior" ("Freedom of Action—a Suggestion," *LA* 38, no. 2 [1970]: 54). Projection screens for the incorporation of slides or filmstrips were a popular suggestion; as early as 1945, Drew Johnston proposed their use during Mass, writing, "It might be said then that the modern sciences and techniques could be enlisted much as the different arts and crafts of the Middle Ages were utilized in glorifying the medieval cathedral" (correspondence, *LA* 13, no. 4 [1945]: 89–90).

101. "Dedication of the New St. Mary's Church, Storm Lake, Iowa, April 28, 1954," CLIT, 30/3.

102. Correspondence, *LA* 26, no. 1 (1957): 39–40.

103. Thomas F. McNulty and Mary S. Fawcett, "Proposed Catholic Church for the Boston Archdiocese," *LA* 25, no. 4 (1957): 110–12.

104. "Religious Buildings," *AR*, June 1956, 204.

105. "Dedication Address: Why Our Building Now," *St. Procopius Abbey News Quarterly*, August 1970, 1, 4, CLIT, 89/20.

106. Robert Lawton Jones, lecture at the University of Dallas, June 17, 1965, RLJ.

107. Jones's father, a building contractor, received a free subscription to the *Forum* (Robert Lawton Jones, interview by the author, Santa Fe, NM, January 30, 2011).

108. Robert Lawton Jones, "Historical Summary of the International Style," ca. 2001, RLJ; "the tradition of architecture," etc.: Jones, lecture at the University of Dallas.

109. Jones, interview.

110. See "Work of Felix Candela," *Progressive Architecture* 36 (July 1955): 106–15; and "Wizard of the Shells," *Architectural Forum* 111 (November 1959): 154–59.

111. The skylights which originally seamed the umbrellas were roofed over during the 1970s.

112. "Early Christian simplicity": "Medieval Forms Transformed," *Progressive Architecture*, November 1963, 139. Other quotations, Jones, lecture at the University of Dallas.

113. Jones, lecture at the University of Dallas.

114. The elimination of the choir became a topic of sustained debate in the later 1960s (see, e.g., Patrick J. Quinn, "The Architectural Implications of the Choir in the Worshipping Community," *LA* 34, no. 2 [1966]: 38–46). A later renovation of St. Patrick's introduced an area for a small choir near the sanctuary. At Jones's SS. Peter and Paul, the choir was located immediately adjacent to the sanctuary so that it could respond directly to the celebrant—a favored location for pre–Vatican II liturgists. SS. Peter and Paul also had a chapel adjacent to the church intended specifically to separate private devotions from communal space.

115. Charles Maginnis, "Architecture and Religious Tradition," *AR*, September 1944, 90.

116. See "Electric Demolition, a Milestone in Church Art: St. Francis de Sales, Philadelphia," *Progressive Architecture* 51 (September 1970): 92–95; and John T. McGreevy, *Parish Boundaries: The Catholic Encounter with Race in the Twentieth-Century Urban North* (Chicago: University of Chicago Press, 1996), 207.

117. ML, "Saint Francis de Sales Church," *LA* 38, no. 4 (1970): 126.

118. ML, 126.

119. O'Donnell, *Churches for Tomorrow*, n.p.

120. See, e.g., David Sutor, "Secular Campus Catholics: Who Cares about Them?, *U.S. Catholic,* May 1965, 41–46. For Newman clubs generally, see John Whitney Evans, *The Newman Movement: Roman Catholics in American Higher Education, 1883–1971* (Notre Dame, IN: University of Notre Dame Press, 1980).

121. Shields Remine, "A Catholic Center for New York University," *U.S. Catholic*, May 1966, 46.

122. Jean Daniélou, "Christianity and the Machine-Age World," *Jubilee*, February 1963, 17.

123. Daniélou, 17.

124. William Wilson, OCSO, to Frederick McManus, February 9, 1968; Donald J. Hamilton, OSCO, to Frederick McManus, February 10, 1968, FRMP.

125. Wilson to McManus. Wilson had received "technical advice that A.I.S.I. No. 303 Stainless Steel would never lose its original polished surface even though subjected to the chemical action of altar wine, water, and perspiration from hands." He hoped the pre–Vatican II requirement of interior gold plating was no longer in force.

126. Justus George Lawler, "Transfigured Universe," in *The Christian Imagination: Studies in Religious Thought* (Westminster, MD: Newman Press, 1955), 54. See James O'Mahony, "The Sacramental Principle," *Orate Fratres* 3, no. 1 (1928): 7–9; Josef Pieper, "Of the Goodness of the World: The Sacramental Principle," *Orate Fratres* 25, no. 10 (1951): 433–37; and Niels J. Andersen, SJ, "The Creator of Heaven and Earth," *Worship* 37, no. 7 (1963): 398–405.

127. Lawler, "Transfigured Universe," 56.

128. Illtud Evans, OP, "St. John's Abbey Church: An Appraisal," *Worship* 35, no. 8 (1961): 521, 516.

129. Aelred Tegels, OSB, "The Church: House of God's People," *Worship* 35, no. 8 (1961): 500. See also Columba Cary-Elwes, OSB, "The Theology of the Church and the Architect," *LA* 31, no. 1 (1962): 28.

130. Tegels, "The Church: House of God's People," 500.

131. Tegels, 500.

132. September 14, 1962, 54–66.

133. See James Gilbert, *Redeeming Culture: American Religion in an Age of Science* (Chicago: University of Chicago Press, 1997).

134. Eugene C. Kennedy, M.M., "The Mythology of Modern Renewal," *U.S. Catholic*, March 1967, 52.

135. Kennedy, "The Mythology of Modern Renewal," 8.

136. "A Highway to Space," *Life*, August 3, 1962, 55.

137. Kennedy, "The Mythology of Modern Renewal," 11.

138. Kennedy, 11.

CHAPTER FOUR

1. Michael Dvortcsak, "The Artist/Scientist in the Twentieth Century," *Harvard Art Review* 2, no. 2 (1967): 9; Dvortcsak, telephone interview by the author, August 15, 2011.

2. Linda Sargent Wood, *A More Perfect Union: Holistic Worldviews and the Transformation of American Culture After World War II* (New York: Oxford University Press, 2010), vii.

3. L. S. Wood, 6.

4. Dvortcsak, "The Artist/Scientist in the Twentieth Century," 10.

5. Dvortcsak, interview; Pierre Teilhard de Chardin, *The Phenomenon of Man*, trans. Bernard Wall (New York: Harper & Brothers, 1959), 257.

6. UCSB Newman Center pamphlet, n.d. [late 1960s or early 1970s].

7. Dvortcsak, interview. See György Kepes, *The New Landscape in Art and Science* (Chicago: Paul Theobold, 1956), 260); Elizabeth Finch, "Languages of Vision: Gyorgy Kepes and the 'New Landscape' of Art and Science" (PhD diss., CUNY Graduate Center, 2005); and Edward A. Fischer, "Design as Worship," *Worship* 48, no. 10 (1974): 601–12.

8. Dvortcsak, interview.

9. Bernard G. Murchland, CSC, "The Prophetic Principle," *Commonweal*, April 1966, 171–72.

10. The description is Andrei Codrescu's; see "Whose Worlds Are These?," in Martin A. Lee and Bruce Shlain, *Acid Dreams: The Complete Social History of LSD: The CIA, the Sixties, and Beyond*, 2nd ed. (New York: Grove Press, 1994), xiii–xv, xiii. On LSD as a transformation of vision and experience of space, see Alastair Gordon, *Spaced Out: Radical Environments of the Psychedelic Sixties* (New York: Rizzoli, 2008), 17–31. See also Jay Stevens, *Storming Heaven: LSD and the American Dream* (New York: Atlantic Monthly Press, 1987).

11. Noel Keith Roberts, *From Piltdown Man to Point Omega: The Evolutionary Theory of Teilhard de Chardin* (New York: Peter Lang, 2000).

12. Trans. Bernard Wall (New York: Harper & Brothers, 1959).

13. For Ong, see, e.g., his "Reaches of History," *Commonweal*, August 15, 1958, 487–490; *Darwin's Vision and Christian Perspectives* (New York: Macmillan, 1960); and "The Renaissance Myth and the American Catholic Mind," in *Frontiers of American Catholicism* (New York: Macmillan, 1957), 52–85. See also, e.g., Dorothy Poulain, "Christ and the Universe," *Commonweal*, January 30, 1959, 461–64.

14. Robert Francoeur, "A Call to Greatness," *Commonweal*, September 2, 1960, 441.

15. See Tom Wolfe, "McLuhan's New World," *Wilson Quarterly* 28, no. 2 (Spring 2004): 18–25.

16. Patricia Malarcher, interview by the author, Englewood, N.J., August 22, 2011.

17. By 1981, a bibliography of European and American scholarship and popular articles listed 4,317 works *about* Teilhard, in addition to 600 items *by* him (Joseph M. McCarthy, *Pierre Teilhard de Chardin: A Comprehensive Bibliography* [New York: Garland, 1981]). During the 1960s a number of academics became instant specialists. For one list, see Robert J. O'Connell, SJ, introduction to *Proceedings of the Teilhard Conference 1964* (New York: Human Energetics Research Institute, Fordham University, 1964), vii–x.

18. Madeleva Wolff, CSC, to Mr. and Mrs. Henry R. Luce, December 16, 1960, CBLP, 766/12.

19. Patrick Quinn, email to the author, July 8, 2011.

20. Wolff to Mr. and Mrs. Luce.

21. Pieter Frans Smulders, *The Design of Teilhard De Chardin: An Essay in Theological Reflection*, trans. Arthur Gibson (Westminster, MD: Newman Press, 1967), v.

22. E.g., "Critics' Choices for Christmas," *Commonweal*, December 2, 1966, 264–69.

23. Advertisement for *The Appearance of Man* in *Jubilee*, March 1966.

24. Sister Agnes, CSJ, "For Père Teilhard de Chardin at My Father's Grave," *Commonweal*, January 22, 1960, 461; Sister Mary Aquin, BVM, "Teilhard de Chardin," *Commonweal*, June 21, 1963, 353; Sebastian Temple, *The Universe Is Singing: 12 Songs in the Spirit of Teilhard de Chardin* (Chicago: Ephram/GIA, 1969).

25. Hugh McElwain, "Teilhard and John Stewart: A Metaphysics of the Future," in *Rediscovering Teilhard's Fire*, ed. Kathleen Duffy, SSJ (Philadelphia: Saint Joseph's University Press, 2010), 147–48.

26. Gregory McAllister, telephone interview by author, July 15, 2011.

27. "Père Teilhard de Chardin," *Jubilee*, September 1959, 22.

28. *Jubilee*, March, 1963, 3. *Commonweal*'s editors were torn. Acknowledging that Teilhard was not a model of orthodoxy, they nevertheless worried that the Holy Office was overreacting and refusing to give "full credit" to Teilhard's "good intentions" ("The Monitum on Teilhard," *Commonweal*, July 27, 1962, 422–23). They knew the monitum was a "warning" not to the deceased Teilhard, but to "the volcanic forces stirring below the surface in the Church" and "awaiting action by the Council Fathers" ("The Council and the Future," *Commonweal*, October 4, 1963, 27–29).

29. The most helpful secondary sources on Teilhard are L. S. Wood, *A More Perfect Union*, 111–37; Henri de Lubac, SJ, *The Religion of Teilhard de Chardin*, trans. René Hague (New York: Desclee, 1967); Roberts, *From Piltdown Man to Point Omega*; Robert T. Francoeur, "The Cosmic Piety of Teilhard de Chardin," in *Cosmic Piety: Modern Man and the Meaning of the Universe*, ed. Christopher Derrick (New York: P. J. Kenedy, 1965), 99–118; Neville Braybrooke, ed., *Teilhard De Chardin: Pilgrim of the Future* (New York: Seabury, 1964); and Siôn Cowell, *The Teilhard Lexicon: Understanding the Language, Terminology, and Vision of the Writings of Pierre Teilhard de Chardin* (Portland: Sussex Academic Press, 2001). Cowell's *Lexicon* is especially helpful on the definitions of Teilhardian coinages like those mentioned in this paragraph.

30. L. S. Wood, *A More Perfect Union*, 10.

31. Pierre Teilhard de Chardin, *The Future of Man*, trans. Norman Denny (New York:

Harper & Row, 1964), 306, quoted in I. F. Clarke, *The Pattern of Expectation, 1644–2001* (New York: Basic Books, 1979), 316.

32. Clarke, *The Pattern of Expectation,* 316.

33. Thomas Merton, characteristically sharp, pointed out that Teilhard had "regarded the dead and wounded of Hiroshima with a certain equanimity as inevitable by-products of scientific and evolutionary progress" ("The Plague of Camus," in *The Literary Essays of Thomas Merton*, ed. Patrick Hart [New York: New Directions Publishing, 1985], 216).

34. Teilhard de Chardin, *The Phenomenon of Man*, 31–36.

35. Teilhard de Chardin, 31.

36. Teilhard de Chardin, 34.

37. "The Art of Rose H. Sulymoss: Statement by the Artist," *LA* 34, no. 1 (1965): 18. Among other Teilhardian works sharing the formal strategy of semiabstraction are Claude Ponsot, *The Divine Milieu*, *LA* 32, no. 4 (1964): 124; Willet Studios, *Noogenesis*, Riverside Park Methodist Church, Jacksonville, FL, 1969; Henry Setter, *The Omega Point*, University of Dayton, Dayton, OH, 1973; Louisa Jenkins, works on paper; and Michael Dvortcsak's mural.

38. E.g., Pierre Teilhard de Chardin, SJ, "The Meaning and Constructive Value of Suffering," trans. Noel Lindsey, *Jubilee*, June 1962, 21–23; Teilhard de Chardin, "Building the Earth," *Jubilee*, December 1965, 8–11.

39. Peder Anker, *From Bauhaus to Ecohouse: A History of Ecological Design* (Baton Rouge: Louisiana State University Press, 2010).

40. Raymond Pavia, review of *Survival through Design*, by Richard Neutra, *LA* 35, no. 3 (1967): 133.

41. Flora Samuel, "Le Corbusier, Teilhard de Chardin, and 'The Planetisation of Mankind,'" *Journal of Architecture* 4 (Summer 1999): 153. Le Corbusier may have come into early contact with Teilhard's writings through his many Jesuit connections or through his friendship with Marie-Alain Couturier.

42. William Schickel, "Unifying the Old and the New," *LA* 36, no. 4 (1968): 99–100.

43. Raymond Pavia, "Modern Church Building: Problems of Sacred Space," *LA* 31, no. 3 (1963): 74.

44. Pavia, 75.

45. Pavia, 76.

46. Catherine R. Osborne, "From Sputnik to Spaceship Earth: American Catholics in the Space Age," *Religion & American Culture* 25, no. 2 (2015): 218–63.

47. See L. S. Wood, *A More Perfect Union.*

48. Daniel Berrigan, SJ, *They Call Us Dead Men: Reflections on Life and Conscience* (New York: Macmillan Company, 1962), 15.

49. Berrigan, 15.

50. Moltmann's speech "Bringing Peace to a Divided World" (Webster College, St. Louis, MO, September 28, 1972) is reprinted in his *Experiment Hope* (Fortress Press, 1975), 172–85.

51. Cited in Murchland, "The Prophetic Principle," 172.

52. Justus George Lawler, "Catholics and the Arms Race," *Commonweal*, May 18, 1962, 199. On the IGY, see Paul Allen Carter, *Another Part of the Fifties* (New York: Columbia University Press, 1983), 277–79; and Paul Dickson, *Sputnik: The Shock of the Century* (New York: Walker, 2001), 76–79, 101–4.

53. Walter J. Ong, SJ, "The Reaches of History," *Commonweal*, August 15, 1958, 488–90.

54. Aaron W. Godfrey, "The Reality of Dreams," 1972, CLIT, 55/01.

55. Editorial note, *Jubilee*, December 1965, n.p.; Pierre Teilhard de Chardin, SJ, "In Expectation of the Parousia: The Second Coming," *Jubilee*, December 1960, 37–41. The association of evolution, Christmas, and Teilhard dated to at least 1952: see H. A. Reinhold, "Father of the World to Come," *Worship* 26, no. 2 (1952): 74–81.

56. James V. Schall, "Christmas and the World," *Commonweal*, December 27, 1963, 390.

57. Schall, 392.

58. Teilhard de Chardin, *The Future of Man*, 140.

59. Dennis Howard, "The Church of the Future: An Interview with Godfrey Diekmann," *U.S. Catholic*, October 1965, 15.

60. Howard, "The Church of the Future," 15.

61. Maritain was more concerned with "*Teilhardism*, the ideology fabricated by the initiates and given circulation by the popular press" ("Teilhard de Chardin and Teilhardism," *U.S. Catholic*, November 1967, 7). He cited Étienne Gilson, another doyen of Thomism, to the effect that "scientific illumination and the cult of evolution, in a manner somewhat similar to the confused evolutionism of Julian Huxley, invited him to conceptualize . . . a religious experience of whose depth there can be no doubt" (ibid.). Maritain believed, not incorrectly, that "Teilhardism" was not "a Christianity . . . rooted in the Trinity and the Redemption, but in the evolving Cosmos," and hoped it would soon die out (ibid.).

62. ML to Robert Bonnette, July 26, 1972, CLIT, 54/02.

63. William R. Sims, "Ecosynthesis in Architecture, Genesis, Sinus Medii, The Moon," June 7, 1963, CLIT, 42/01. Lavanoux's handwritten note reads: "Would this involve a lunar liturgy? What a problem for the S. Congregation of Rites!"

64. Daniel Bell, ed., *Toward the Year 2000: Work in Progress* (Boston: Houghton Mifflin, 1967). Lavanoux sent copies to several friends and collaborators, e.g., ML to Edward Sutfin, October 20, 1967, CLIT, 47/01. Lavanoux's first reference to his own reading of Teilhard is in his diary for May 6–7, 1964, where he cited *Letters from a Traveler*. Probably he had read *The Phenomenon of Man* and *The Divine Milieu* earlier.

65. Editorial, *LA* 36, no. 1 (1967): 1.

66. Mark Mills oral history, interview by Indira Berndtson, July 6–8, 1994, Frank Lloyd Wright Foundation Archives, Taliesin West, Scottsdale, AZ.

67. Barbara Mills, interview by author, Carmel, CA, February 21, 2011.

68. See Janey Bennett, *The Fantastic Seashell of the Mind: The Architecture of Mark Mills* (ORO Editions, 2017).

69. There are no extant Catholic churches designed by Mills. However, there is a church at New Camaldoli monastery, south of Carmel. According to Barbara Mills, when the first abbot was making plans to build, he asked Mills for a sketch and Mills gave it to him—only to find later that the architect of record had appropriated it. I have not been able to confirm this, but the church at New Camaldoli does look like a Mills design, if perhaps a little less graceful.

70. Cited in Janey Bennett, "Work of Mark Mills: Structural Elegance and a Sense of Reverent Space," *Journal of the Taliesin Fellows* 10 (Spring 1993): 25.

71. Aside from Wright, the architect Mills admired most was Santiago Calatrava—especially Calatrava's bridges (Barbara Mills, interview).

72. ML to Mark Mills, May 10, 1967, CLIT, 46/04.

73. Mills rarely sketched, but he mulled ideas over while performing other work until he was

ready to commit to paper (Barbara Mills, interview). Mark Mills to ML, May 21, 1967, CLIT, 46/04, indicates that "many dreams are passing through my mind" but "right now I don't have time to get them on paper. . . . Let me know if I may go on 'dreaming' for a while."

74. ML to Mark Mills, June 26, 1967, CLIT, 46/04.

75. Isaac Asimov, "After Apollo, A Colony on the Moon," *NYT*, May 28, 1967.

76. Terence J. Mangan, CO, "The Doman Moon Chapel," *LA* 36, no. 1 (1967): 3.

77. One of the articles accompanying the plans, by the Lutheran Constance Parvey, did envision such a future, where denominational boundaries and the borderline between worship space and other kinds of space had dissolved, along with other artificial divisions ("Moon People's Liturgy," *LA* 36, no. 1 (1967): 11–12).

78. Regional Oral History Office, the Bancroft Library, *Renaissance of Religious Art and Architecture in the San Francisco Bay Area, 1946–1968* (Berkeley: University of California, 1985), 13.

79. Mangan, "The Doman Moon Chapel," 3.

80. Neil Hurley, SJ, "Liturgy and Play in Our Expanding Tele-civilization," *LA* 40, no. 1 (1971): 6–8.

81. Clement McNaspy, SJ, "Man, the Sea, and Peace," *LA* 40, no. 1 (1971): 4.

82. Mark Mills, "A 'Batoid' Peace Ship," *LA* 40, no. 1 (1971): 10–13. See also ML to Rev. Robert Howes, July 9, 1971, CLIT, 52/01.

83. ML to Brenda Bettinson, August 19, 1969, CLIT, 48/04.

84. ML to Bettinson.

85. *Oculus*, *LA* 40, no. 1 (1971): back cover.

86. CLIT 232 contains correspondence, research, and draft articles.

87. Diary entry, July 3, 1972, CLAV, 3/31.

88. Diary entry, August 4, 1972, CLAV, 3/31.

89. Diary entry, August 29, 1973, CLAV, 3/31.

90. Diary entries, May 10, 11, 12, 13, 1973, CLAV, 3/31.

91. Diary entry, July [*sic*], 1973, CLAV, 3/31.

92. ML, "Editor's Diary," *LA* 40, no. 2 (1972): 65. See also, for variations on this theme, ML to Robert Bonnette, July 26, 1972, CLIT, 54/02; and to Paul Bourne, OSCO, May 12, 1972, CLIT, 54/02.

93. Hurley, "Liturgy and Play in Our Expanding Tele-civilization," 7–8.

94. Rev. Clifford Stevens, "The Cosmic Adventure: A Challenge to Theology," *LA* 36, no. 1 (1967): 10.

95. Mangan, "The Doman Moon Chapel."

96. Quoted in David Seed, *American Science Fiction and the Cold War: Literature and Film* (Chicago: Fitzroy Dearborn, 1999), 8.

97. Katharine Way and Dexter Masters, eds., *One World or None* (New York: McGraw-Hill, 1946).

98. The classic exemplars of these two positions in American sci-fi are, respectively, Robert Heinlein and Asimov.

99. ML to Brenda Bettinson, August 19, 1969, CLIT, 48/04.

100. Editorial, *LA* 40, no. 1 (1971): 3.

101. Hurley, "Liturgy and Play in Our Expanding Tele-civilization." This was obviously a McLuhanite/Teilhardian idea.

102. Editorial, *LA* 37, no. 3 (1969): 69.

103. James Nisbet, *Ecologies, Environments, and Energy Systems in Art of the 1960s and 1970s* (Cambridge, MA: MIT Press, 2014), 2.

104. Nisbet, *Ecologies, Environments, and Energy Systems*, 3.

105. L. S. Wood, *A More Perfect Union*.

106. William Lynch, SJ, "Creativity and Autonomy: A Christian Theory," ca. 1963–64, CLIT, 43/04.

107. Nisbet, *Ecologies, Environments, and Energy Systems*, 19.

108. It also appeared in quasi-educational spaces like the World's Fair; see James Gilbert, *Redeeming Culture: American Religion in an Age of Science* (Chicago: University of Chicago Press, 1997), especially 297–320.

109. Fr. Henry Fehren, essay in "Living Stones of the New Jerusalem," dedication booklet for St. Bede's Priory, Eau Claire, WI, 1967 (St. Bede's Archives); Dom Philip Verhaegen, OSB, prior, St. Andrew's Priory newsletter, Valyermo, CA, July–August 1965 (St. Andrew's Abbey Archives). St. Andrew's hired Kahn the same year to design a monastery, although this was never built (Robert McCarter, *Louis I. Kahn* [London: Phaidon, 2005], 295–96). See also Lyle Terhune, "Atomic Bombs and Trappist Monks," *Ave Maria*, July 22, 1950, 103–5, commenting on the proximity of the new Trappist foundation at Valley Ranch, New Mexico, to Los Alamos.

110. Nisbet, *Ecologies, Environments, and Energy Systems*, 50–60; on "LSDesign" generally, see Gordon, *Spaced Out*, 87–123.

111. Alan Watts, *The Joyous Cosmology: Adventures in the Chemistry of Consciousness* (New York: Vintage Books, 1965), 19. See Monica Furlong, *Zen Effects: The Life of Alan Watts* (Boston: Houghton Mifflin, 1986).

112. J. Stevens, *Storming Heaven*, 38–41.

113. Huxley's letter is cited in J. Stevens, *Storming Heaven*, 71. For Hubbard's psychedelic Catholic crusade, see ibid., 53–72.

114. Murray: "The Mystical World of Louisa Jenkins," *Community Spirit* (Carmel, CA), March/April 1981, clipping in CBLP, 239/3; see also Jeffrey J. Kripal, *Esalen: America and the Religion of No Religion* (Chicago: University of Chicago Press, 2008), 225–26. For a more cautious Jesuit analysis of LSD, see George B. Murray, SJ, "Pharmacological Mysticism," *Jubilee*, June 1967, 8–13.

115. Louisa Jenkins to Clare Boothe Luce, February 26, 1959, CBLP, 766/4. See Stephen Siff, "Henry Luce's Strange Trip," *Journalism History* 34, no. 3 (2008): 126–34.

116. Louisa Jenkins to Clare Boothe Luce, December 4, 1959, CBLP, 766/4.

117. Louisa Jenkins to "Tony" (Clare Boothe Luce), June 16, 1971, CBLP, 231/14.

118. Louisa Jenkins to Clare Boothe Luce, June 16, 1971, CBLP, 231/14.

119. See Gordon, *Spaced Out*, 125–281; and Nisbet, *Ecologies, Environments, and Energy Systems*.

120. On geodesic domes as countercultural spatial practice, see L. S. Wood, *A More Perfect Union*, 53–81; Gordon, *Spaced Out*, 127–219; and Christine Macy and Sarah Bonnemaison, *Architecture and Nature: Creating the American Landscape* (London: Routledge, 2003), 293–346. See also Scott Eastham, *American Dreamer: Bucky Fuller and the Sacred Geometry of Nature* (Cambridge: Lutterworth Press, 2007); and Anker, *From Bauhaus to Ecohouse*, 68–82.

121. "Editor's Diary," *LA* 37, no. 4 (1969): 126–28.

122. Andrew Greeley, *Religion in the Year 2000* (New York: Sheed and Ward, 1969), 126. See

also Walter Houston Clark, "Psychadelics: A Function in the Church of the Future?," *Jubilee*, November, 1967, 31–39.

123. Harvey Cox, "McLuhanite Christianity at Expo 67," *Commonweal*, May 26, 1967, 277–79.

124. On the conference, see Rolfe Lanier Hunt, ed., *Revolution, Place, and Symbol: Journal of the First International Congress on Religion, Architecture, and the Visual Arts, New York City and Montreal, August 26 through September 4, 1967* (New York: Benziger, 1969); on the "happening" or "be-in" (called "Ordeals"), see especially Harvey Cox's review, "Kinesthetic Happening: Art or Atrocity? Interpretation of 'Ordeals,'" reprinted in ibid., 216–19.

125. Robert Frei to Don Shepherd (Jonynas & Shepherd Art Studio), September 1, 1966, Frei 43/2.

126. Frei to Shepherd.

127. Roman J. Verostko, OSB, "Abstract Art and the Liturgy," *LA* 30, no. 4 (1962): 132.

128. Verostko, 132.

129. Verostko, 132.

130. See Martin Filler, "Building Organic Form: Architecture, Ceramics, Glass, and Metal in the 1940s and 1950s," in *Vital Forms: American Art and Design in the Atomic Age, 1940–1960*, ed. Brooke Kamin Rapaport and Kevin L. Stayton (Brooklyn: Brooklyn Museum of Art, 2001), 122–61; and Nisbet, *Ecologies, Environments, and Energy Systems*. "Land art" is related; Robert Smithson, the creator of *Spiral Jetty*, was raised Catholic and made explicitly religious art during his early career (Jennifer L. Roberts, *Mirror-Travels: Robert Smithson and History* [New Haven, CT: Yale University Press, 2004], 12–35).

131. ML, "An Exercise in Architectural Humanism," *LA* 33, no. 2 (1965): 38–47.

132. William Granger Ryan and Gary Jurysta, "Alive and Unfinished," *LA* 38, no. 1 (1969): 7.

133. E.g., Robert Hovda, ed., *Manual of Celebration* (Washington, DC: Liturgical Conference, 1970), 6/16–21.

134. See photos in Lucien Deiss and Gloria Gabriel Weyman, *Dance for the Lord* (Cincinnati: World Library Publications, 1975).

135. Some Catholics were concerned: Illtud Evans, OP, worried that clear glass at the San Francisco cathedral would be "betraying that sense of *enclosure* that a sacred building should have" and "turning the whole thing into a super-market display" (to Msgr. Thomas Bowe, January 9, 1965, AASF).

136. "Two Chapels on the Campus of the University of St. Thomas, Houston," *LA* 35, no. 1 (1966): 34–35.

137. Rapson, dean of architecture at the University of Minnesota from 1954 to 1984, studied under Eliel Saarinen at Cranbrook. He taught for Mies at IIT from 1942 to 1946. See Robin Pogrebin, "Ralph Rapson, Modernist Architect, Is Dead at 93," *NYT*, April 3, 2008.

138. "Church-in-the-round has a view all around," advertisement for Starlux plate glass, *AR* (November 1967): 26–27.

139. "Editor's Diary," *LA* 38, no. 1 (1969): 17. For complete plans and photos, see "Newman Hall, Texas Southern University, Houston, Texas," *LA* 38, no. 1 (1969): 18–20.

140. Rev. Jim Nielsen, "James Bond: My Country Right or Wrong," in *And the Voz de la Tortuga Shall Be Heard in Our Land: The Newman Center of St. Albert the Great*, New Mexico State University newsletter, February 26, 1967, CLIT, 46/04.

141. *God's People on Man's Journey: Proceedings of the Third World Congress for the Lay Apostolate* (Rome: Permanent Committee for International Congresses of the Lay Apostolate, 1961), 78.

142. See Paolo Soleri, *The Bridge between Matter and Spirit Is Matter Becoming Spirit: The Arcology of Paolo Soleri* (Garden City, NY: Anchor Books, 1973); Soleri, *Technology and Cosmogenesis* (New York: Paragon House, 1985); Donald Wall, *Visionary Cities: The Arcology of Paolo Soleri* (New York: Praeger, 1971); and Gordon, *Spaced Out*, 232–62.

143. GLIT 32.

144. Paolo Soleri, "Religion as Simulation," 1972 typescript, Arcosanti Archives. A later version was published in Soleri, *The Omega Seed: An Eschatological Hypothesis* (Garden City, NY: Anchor/Doubleday, 1981).

145. "Fantastic": ML to Mary Vance, July 31, 1970, CLIT, 92/16; "several hours": ML to Mark Mills, July 27, 1970, CLIT, 92/16. See also "Editor's Diary," *LA* 39, no. 1 (1970): 13–14.

146. "The Cosanti Foundation and Arcosanti," 1970, CLIT, 92/16.

147. The Millses visited often (Barbara Mills, interview). The Heimsaths recall being so excited by news of Arcosanti that they drove there from Texas in the early 1970s (Clovis and Maryann Heimsath, interview by the author, Fayetteville, TX, January 19, 2011).

148. Supported by the sale of Soleri's signature ceramic bells, tourism, and workshops on sustainable design and construction, Arcosanti houses a permanent group of 100 to 150 residents.

149. March 15, 1970.

150. Murchland, "The Prophetic Principle"; John XXIII: "profeti di sventura," "Discorso del Santo Padre Giovanni XXIII, Solenne Apertura del Concilio Ecumenico Vaticano II," October 11, 1962.

CHAPTER FIVE

1. Richard Cardinal Cushing, "The Servant Church: A Beginning and a Blueprint," *Boston Globe*, December 11, 1966.

2. Cushing, "The Servant Church."

3. Cushing, "The Servant Church."

4. Harvey Cox, *The Secular City: Secularization and Urbanization in Theological Perspective* (New York: Macmillan, 1965). The quotation is from the preface to the revised 1966 edition.

5. Robert A. Orsi, "Introduction: Crossing the City Line," in *Gods of the City: Religion and the Urban American Landscape*, ed. Robert A. Orsi (Bloomington: Indiana University Press, 1999), 6.

6. Patrick J. Quinn, "Is There a Place for the Church in the Future City?," *Churchbuilding* 4 [1968]: 6.

7. On de Hueck Doherty, see Katharine E. Harmon, *There Were Also Many Women There: Lay Women in the Liturgical Movement in the United States, 1926–59* (Collegeville, MN: Liturgical Press, 2013), 180–86.

8. See, e.g., William Issel, *Church and State in the City: Catholics and Politics in Twentieth-Century San Francisco* (Philadelphia: Temple University Press, 2013); Gerald H. Gamm, *Urban Exodus: Why the Jews Left Boston and the Catholics Stayed* (Cambridge, MA: Harvard University Press, 1999); John T. McGreevy, *Parish Boundaries: The Catholic Encounter with Race in*

the Twentieth-Century Urban North (Chicago: University of Chicago Press, 1996); Steven M. Avella, *This Confident Church: Catholic Leadership and Life in Chicago, 1940–1965* (Notre Dame, IN: University of Notre Dame Press, 1992); and Paula M. Kane, *Separatism and Subculture: Boston Catholicism, 1900–1920* (Chapel Hill: University of North Carolina Press, 1989).

9. Dennis Clark, *Cities in Crisis* (New York: Sheed & Ward, 1960). See also Eugene J. Halus Jr., "The Difficult Ethnic and Religious Mind of Dennis Clark," *U.S. Catholic Historian* 27, no. 4 (Fall 2009): 45–57.

10. Robert G. Howes, *The Church and the Change: An Initial Study of the Role of the Roman Catholic Church in the Changing American Community* (Boston: St. Paul Editions, 1961), 163–66.

11. E.g., Robert Howes wrote Higgins for career advice; Higgins suggested that he make contact with Dennis Clark—which he evidently did, as the two convened the NCSAC's Workshop on Housing and Planning the following year (George G. Higgins to Robert G. Howes, January 29, 1959, George G. Higgins Papers, Collection 129, 29/11, ACUA).

12. Howard Gillette Jr., *Between Justice and Beauty: Race, Planning, and the Failure of Urban Policy in Washington, D.C.* (Baltimore: Johns Hopkins University Press, 1995), 151–69; Richard Longstreth, "Brave New World: Southwest Washington and the Promise of Urban Renewal," in *Housing Washington: Two Centuries of Residential Development and Planning in the National Capitol Area*, ed. Richard Longstreth (Chicago: Center for American Places at Columbia College Chicago, 2010), 255–80; Margaret E. Farrar, *Building the Body Politic: Power and Urban Space in Washington, D.C.* (Urbana: University of Illinois Press, 2008), 58–74.

13. Howes's report was published as *Crisis Downtown: A Church Eye-View of Urban Renewal* (Washington, DC: National Conference of Catholic Charities, 1959). In a July 29, 1959, summary of his recommendations, he concluded that the black community was watching the Church closely on this issue—with the implication that it should not neglect conversion opportunities (NCCC Catholic Charities USA, M41/2, ACUA).

14. Howes's testimony: Representative Thompson of New Jersey, speaking on Urban Renewal in the District of Columbia, on September 1, 1960, to the House of Representatives, 86th Cong., 2d Sess., Cong. Rec. 17549–54.

15. "Catholic Group Hears Attack on SW Renewal," *Washington Post*, February 13, 1961, B7. The delegates also heard Archbishop Patrick O'Boyle's call to support better-housing legislation and to "see to it that colored people can get jobs to provide themselves with decent housing" (ibid.).

16. For diocesan policy on public housing in Pittsburgh in the 1950s, see Timothy I. Kelly, *The Transformation of American Catholicism: The Pittsburgh Laity and the Second Vatican Council, 1950–1972* (Notre Dame, IN: University of Notre Dame Press, 2009), 115–16. For several other late 1950s/early 1960s Catholic efforts, see Howes, *The Church and the Change*, 31–35.

17. Kane, *Separatism and Subculture*; McGreevy, *Parish Boundaries*; Gamm, *Urban Exodus*.

18. Cited in "The Curious Island," *Jubilee*, January 1962, 8. The poet Ned O'Gorman responded that New York was "the city of the incarnation," even "the most incarnate of cities" and therefore "an experience—if a man were equal to it—of the highest and holiest kind" (ibid., 16).

19. David S. Bovée, *The Church & the Land: The National Catholic Rural Life Conference and American Society, 1923–2007* (Washington, DC: Catholic University of America Press, 2010).

20. "The Terrible Super-City," *Commonweal*, May 13, 1925, 1–2.

21. Harmon, *There Were Also Many Women There*, 224. See James Terence Fisher, *The*

Catholic Counterculture in America, 1933–1962 (Chapel Hill: University of North Carolina Press, 1989); Bovée, *The Church & the Land*; and Jeffrey D. Marlett, *Saving the Heartland: Catholic Missionaries in Rural America, 1920–1960* (Dekalb: Northern Illinois University Press, 2002).

22. Fisher, *The Catholic Counterculture in America*, 121–29.

23. Merton himself came early to the incarnational mysticism reported by many Catholics in the later 1960s. In 1958, after more than a decade in the monastery, he was visiting Louisville when, in the middle of "the shopping district," at Fourth and Walnut he "was suddenly overwhelmed with the realization that I loved all these people, that they were mine and I theirs, that we could not be alien to one another even though we were total strangers. It was like waking from a dream of separateness. . . . I have the immense joy of being . . . a member of a race in which God Himself became incarnate" (*Conjectures of a Guilty Bystander* [New York: Doubleday, 1968], 156–57).

24. Aelred Wall, OSB, Chrismas circular 1964, CLIT, 44/04.

25. Wall, Christmas circular. On desert communes, see Alastair Gordon, *Spaced Out: Radical Environments of the Psychedelic Sixties* (New York: Rizzoli, 2008), 125–281.

26. See, e.g., Amy L. Koehlinger, *The New Nuns: Racial Justice and Religious Reform in the 1960s* (Cambridge, MA: Harvard University Press, 2007), 176–97.

27. Orsi, "Crossing the City Line," 2.

28. Woodstock College: Edward B. Fiske, "Jesuit Seminary from Maryland to Move to Morningside Heights," *NYT*, February 28, 1968. See also Koehlinger, *The New Nuns*, 176–97.

29. Donald R. Campion, SJ, "Church and City," in *The Church in the Changing City*, ed. Louis J. Luzbetak, SVD (Techny, IL: Divine Word Publications, 1966), 13–14.

30. "NBC-TV presents *The Catholic Hour-TV: Images of Hope: Show #1, May 9, 1965 'The City of Man',*" written by Rev. William F. Lynch, SJ, produced in association with the National Council of Catholic Men," National Council of Catholic Men Records, 46/6, ACUA.

31. Daniel Callahan, ed., *The Secular City Debate* (New York: Macmillan, 1966), 97.

32. Martin Marty, *The Search for a Usable Future* (New York: Harper & Row, 1969), 50. On Catholic spirituality and "secularity" in the 1960s, see James P. McCartin, *Prayers of the Faithful: The Shifting Spiritual Life of American Catholics* (Cambridge, MA: Harvard University Press, 2010), 100–38.

33. Callahan, *The Secular City Debate*, 92. Both Cox (in the preface to the revised edition of 1966 and in his 1990 recollections) and Callahan emphasized Catholics' love for *The Secular City*. This interest was not limited to the United States; Cox was invited a number of times to Latin America to meet incipient liberation theologians (Harvey Cox, "The Secular City 25 Years Later," *Christian Century*, November 7, 1990, 1025–29).

34. *Worship in the City of Man: Twenty-Seventh North American Liturgical Week, Houston, Texas, August 22–25, 1966* (Washington, DC: Liturgical Conference, 1966).

35. Cox, *The Secular City*, 1.

36. As Cox wrote later, he had "portrayed [the death-of-God theologians] as remaining obsessed . . . with the classical god of metaphysical theism, while I was talking about Someone Else, the mysterious and elusive Other of the prophets and Jesus, who—like Jacques Brel—was very much alive although living in unexpected quarters" (Cox, "The Secular City 25 Years Later.") Leo Cardinal Suenens, speaking at Graduate Theological Union in Berkeley in February 1968, made a similar claim (cited in Quinn, "Is There a Place for the Church," 5).

37. Quoted in Donald J. Thorman, *American Catholics Face the Future* (Wilkes-Barre, PA: Dimension Books, 1968), 106.

38. Cox, *The Secular City*, 94.

39. Cox cited Teilhard as "summing up" Cox's "affirmation of Christian secularity" in Callahan, *The Secular City Debate*, 118.

40. Cox, *The Secular City*, 114–28.

41. Cox, 91, 108–9, 91, 141.

42. Harvey Cox, "On Columns and Cities," *Commonweal*, November 4, 1966, 134.

43. E.g., Marie Augusta Neal, SNDdeN, "Parish Structures," in Luzbetak, *The Church in the Changing City*, 64.

44. Clarence Rivers, *Celebration* (New York: Herder and Herder, 1969), 52.

45. *Baltimore Urban Parish Study* (Baltimore: Archdiocese of Baltimore, 1967). See Catherine R. Osborne, "Managing and Quantifying Grace? Rev. Robert G. Howes, the Archdiocese of Baltimore, and the Origins of 'Pastoral Planning,'" *American Catholic Studies* 125, no. 1 (2014): 1–23.

46. McGreevy, *Parish Boundaries*; Gamm, *Urban Exodus*.

47. Luzbetak, introduction to *The Church in the Changing City*, 1.

48. Neal, "Parish Structures," in Luzbetak, *The Church in the Changing City*, 66. Neal picked up the theme not just of presence but of permanent commitment that figured prominently in a number of midcentury Catholic contexts: e.g., the highly influential French worker-priest movement and the writing of Ivan Illich.

49. Daniel Callahan, "Creating a Community," in *The Postconciliar Parish*, ed. James O'Gara (New York: P. J. Kenedy & Sons, 1967), 109.

50. John J. Hill, "Presentation Parish," in O'Gara, *The Postconciliar Parish*, 85. On priests' approach to parish plants in this period, see R. Scott Appleby, "Present to the People of God: The Transformation of the Roman Catholic Parish Priesthood," in *Transforming Parish Ministry: The Changing Roles of Catholic Clergy, Laity, and Women Religious*, ed. Jay Dolan (New York: Crossroad, 1989), 79–88.

51. Ruth Rejnis, "Catholics Update Church Design," *NYT*, July 23, 1972.

52. Norman Laliberté, "Explanation of the Symbols of St. James Banner, Jamesburg, N.J," May 1, 1967, St. James the Less parish archives.

53. Notes on Marymount [Manhattan] College chapel, n.d. (probably 1966), RP.

54. Robert Hovda, *Dry Bones: Living Worship Guides to Good Liturgy* (Washington, DC: Liturgical Conference, 1973), 115.

55. Hovda, 115.

56. Quoted in Robert Taylor, "Shapes of Worship . . . In a Changing World," *Boston Globe*, December 22, 1968, A4.

57. "St. Christopher's Chapel," n.d. [November 1965], CLIT, 87/25.

58. Rejnis, "Catholics Update Church Design"; Rambusch Company Records, Dept. of Drawings & Archives, Avery Architectural and Fine Arts Library, Columbia University, New York, NY, box 22, "Chapel of St. Christopher." Records indicate a steady attendance of five hundred to seven hundred a day (rising to four thousand to five thousand on holy days of obligation) from at least 1965 to 1971 (*Status Animarium*, AANY).

59. Felix Miritello, OFMCap, to Francis J. Spellman, August 7, 1945, AANY; announcement of plans for St. John's Friary, Province of St. Mary of the Capuchin Order, *Bulletin*, November 1972, AANY.

60. Although the intention was to begin construction by August 1964, a series of delays ensued, some due to construction details, some to Cushing's declining health. Finally, an

October 31, 1968 memo authorized closing on the land parcel, with construction to begin imminently—but it never did (Hale Champion to BRA, BRAA, 380/1). The archdiocese was granted a postponement on closing, and the project faded out of the record. Around 1980 the site became a small park dedicated to Cushing.

61. Thomas H. O'Connor, *Building a New Boston: Politics and Urban Renewal, 1950–1970* (Boston: Northeastern University Press, 1995).

62. Pete Riemer to Edward J. Logue, November 6, 1961, BRAA, 380/2. Logue, the BRA director, wrote on this memo that he also preferred a freestanding chapel to a room "on the ground floor of a large building," the other available option.

63. Martin Adler to Peter Riemer, April 30, 1962, BRAA, 380/2.

64. Jose Luis Sert, "A Lively and Human City," *Boston Globe*, March 15, 1964, C12. See Eric Mumford and Hakim Sarkis, eds., *Josep Lluís Sert: The Architect of Urban Design, 1953–1959* (New Haven, CT: Yale University Press, 2008); and Eric Mumford, *Defining Urban Design: CIAM Architects and the Formation of a Discipline, 1937–69* (New Haven, CT: Yale University Press, 2009).

65. Archdiocesan News Bureau press release, May 14, 1965, CLIT, 44/04.

66. Archdiocesan News Bureau press release.

67. "Preview: Church and State in Boston," n.d., clipping in Sert B23A, Harvard GSD.

68. ML to José Luis Sert, November 4, 1965, CLIT, 44/04; "Saint Botolph's Chapel," *LA* 35, no. 2 (1967): 98–99.

69. Taylor, "Shapes of Worship," A4.

70. James P. Gaffey, "The Anatomy of Transition: Cathedral-Building and Social Justice in San Francisco, 1962–1971," *Catholic Historical Review* LXX, no. 1 (1984): 45–73.

71. Joseph McGucken to Angus McSweeney, October 4, 1965, hoping for windows that would have a "symbol, representative scene, or figure speaking of the Sacred Mysteries," AASF.

72. A. Richard Gemperle Jr., "The Design of a New Catholic Cathedral for Houston, Texas, in Accordance with the Form Determinants Proper to the Second Half of the Twentieth Century," *LA* 35, no. 4 (1967): 154–55.

73. Gemperle, "The Design of a New Catholic Cathedral for Houston," 154.

74. Gemperle, "The Design of a New Catholic Cathedral for Houston," 154.

75. "Proposed Cathedral of Rockford, Rockford, Illinois," *LA* 34, no. 2 (1966): 53–55.

76. John M. Cates Jr., "The Steeple Goes to Ground," *LA* 37, no. 4 (1969): 108.

77. Cates also suggested using air rights to build an office building that would fund the operation of the church, a plan actually implemented by the Protestant church of St. Luke on East 63rd Street, New York City. Fascinatingly, the first suggestion for an underground urban church may have been made by Paul Claudel in the 1920s: "Projet d'une église souterraine à Chicago," in *Positions et propositions* (Paris: Gallimard, 1934), 228–42.

78. Syllabus for "Religion and Architecture in the Future City," CAP.

79. Robert E. Park, "The City: Suggestions for the Investigations of Human Behavior in the City Environment," *American Journal of Sociology* 20, no. 5 (1915): 577–612.

80. Patrick Quinn, "Religion on the Campus: The Contemporary Architectural Response," speech given at Rensselaer Polytechnic Institute, Troy, New York, November 1, 1968 (C+CC).

81. Quinn, "Religion on the Campus."

82. Gregory McAllister, "Finding the Sacred in the Profane," in *Architecture and Religion in the Future City: A Study Presented at the 27th National Conference on Church Architecture, San Francisco, April 1966*, ed. Patrick J. Quinn and Richard Perry (Berkeley, CA, 1966), 18, 21–22.

83. ML to Bob Rambusch, September 1, 1966, CLIT, 45/04.

84. "On Tape with the Editor," *Your Church*, September/October 1970, 11. *Bauen für die Kirche in der Welt* (Zurich, 1966) was published in English as *New Trends in Church Architecture* (New York: Universe Books, 1967).

85. E.g., Richard H. Guerrette, "Experiments in Parish Community," *Homiletic and Pastoral Review* XLVIII (1968): 1029–36; Landon G. Dowdey, "Communities of Interest in the Modern City: A Challenge to Form New Kinds of Worship Groups," in *Worship in the City of Man*, 162–71; Neal, "Parish Structures." *Commonweal*'s March 25, 1966, issue included "Reforming the Parish"; "The Parish—1980"; James O'Gara, "Laymen in the Parish"; Joseph E. Cunneen, "The Servant Parish"; Doris Grumbach, "Parish Organizations"; Michael E. Schiltz, "Facing Outward"; Daniel J. Mallette, "In the Inner City"; Gerald S. Sloyan, "The Parish as Educator"; Daniel Callahan, "Creating a Community"; and Leonard Swidler, "Ecumenism in the Parish?"

86. Editorial, *LA* 36, no. 4 (1968): 97. See, e.g., ML to Br. James Blacker, April 11, 1966, CLIT, 45/01, inquiring about storefront chapels in Rome and Paris.

87. Neal, "Parish Structures," 74.

88. Neal, 64.

89. Joseph T. Nolan, "What Can You Say about the Priesthood at a Time like This?," *U.S. Catholic*, May 1968, 18.

90. Quoted in Ann-Mary Currier, "Cardinal Cushing Opens 'Ecumenical' Pru Chapel," *Boston Globe*, November 12, 1969, 17.

91. E.g., Paul Douglas Roller, "An Ecumenical Council Center for the Christian Churches," *LA* 32, no. 3 (1964): 75–86

92. Editorial, *LA* 38, no. 4 (1970): 111. For Lavanoux's earlier positive comment on the Air Force Academy Chapel, see "Editor's Diary," *LA* 26, no. 1 (1957): 14.

93. "Ecumenism: Four for St. Mark's," *Time*, July 22, 1966, 65–66.

94. Helmsing, who became bishop of Kansas City in 1962, had a long-standing interest in ecumenical collaboration, having suggested inviting Protestant observers to Vatican II. He was a major player in the US bishops' Committee on Ecumenism (Joseph P. Chinnici, OFM, "Ecumenism, Civil Rights, and the Second Vatican Council: The American Experience," *U.S. Catholic Historian* 30, no. 3 [2012]: 28–29).

95. Tom Blackburn, "St. Mark's: Where the Mission Built a Bridge," in "The Story of St. Mark's Church: A New Christian Community to Begin in 1968," CAA.

96. Fundraising brochure, n.d., CAA.

97. "Progress Report on the 'Wayne Miner Project,'" CAA.

98. The building reveals the difficulty of creating a consistently "secularist" message: as James S. Tinney pointed out in *Christianity Today*, the "practically windowless sanctuary" operated to "hide 227 worshippers from the sights outside"—namely "a high-rise project . . . an assortment of bars, street missions," and the like ("Kansas City Happening," December 6, 1968, 38). So much for total engagement of church and city.

99. Rev. William A. Hayes, "St. Mark's Church," clipping, CAA. Hayes was the only black clergyman on opening day; he succeeded Rev. Archie Allen III, also of the UCC, who had been the sole black clergyman on the initial organizing team.

100. Edwin Lynn, *Tired Dragons: Adapting Church Architecture to Changing Needs* (Boston: Beacon Press, 1972), 232–35.

101. Thorman, *American Catholics Face the Future*, 165.

102. Frank Spurlock, "A Church to Serve 4 Faiths," *Kansas City Star*, n.d. [1967], CAA.

103. Donald Janson, "Protestants and Catholics Join to Build a Church," *NYT*, July 31, 1966, CAA.

104. David O. Shipley, "St. Mark's Church," January 1970, Archives of the Diocese of Kansas City, Kansas City, MO.

105. Hayes, "St. Mark's Church."

106. Rev. Robert Ready, "New Outlook: Inner City," *Kansas City Star*, January 12, 1969, CAA.

107. Austin Healy to Lawrence Cardinal Shehan, August 26, 1966, St. John the Evangelist, Columbia, 1963–(Restricted), AAB/AASMSU.

108. Cited in Jack Ladd Carr to John Walsh, November 8, 1972, RG XXIV 1/8, CA. For a Protestant statement of the same idea, see James W. Hoffman, "New Model for City Living," *Presbyterian Life*, November 1, 1971, 5–7, 28–34.

109. Village Religious Center: Paul L. Gaudreau to the Columbia Committee, March 20, 1967, St. John the Evangelist, Columbia, 1963–(Restricted), AAB/AASMSU.

110. "All Faiths under One Roof," press release, n.d. [c. 1969], RG XXIV 1/8, CA.

111. "All Faiths under One Roof."

112. For a full account, see Catherine R. Osborne, "'So That One Day We May Be One': The Interfaith Center at Columbia, Maryland," *U.S. Catholic Historian* 35, no. 3 (2017): 76–104.

113. S. T. Ritenour to James Rouse, August 5, 1968, James W. Rouse Papers, RG 1, Series III (Columbia, MD), 12/1, CA.

114. Thomas F. Mathews, SJ, "New City, New Church," *Commonweal*, August 25, 1967, 519.

115. CAP.

116. Mathews, "New City, New Church," 521.

117. Anthony Tappé, "Architecture of Involvement in Columbia, Maryland," n.d. [1970?], CAP.

118. Tappé, "Architecture of Involvement in Columbia, Maryland."

119. Tappé, "Architecture of Involvement in Columbia, Maryland."

120. John Walsh, "Prayer for the Dedication of the Village of Wilde Lake," June 21, 1967, RGXXIV 2/8, CA.

121. Michael Barnes, "Man-Centered Churches," *Commonweal*, December 9, 1966, 279, 303.

122. "Demonstration and Arrests in St. Patrick's Cathedral," AANY, St. Patrick's Cathedral 15/D-1h. The report named twenty-three demonstrators, including each's "prior subversive record." The archdiocese claimed the action violated "the constitutional right of peaceful assembly" and "freedom of worship" (NC News Service, "Denounces Peace Demonstration during Cathedral Mass," January 23, 1967). See Will Lissner, "23 War Protestors Arrested in St. Patrick's after Disrupting a Mass," *NYT*, January 23, 1967.

123. "The Words of a Cardinal," *New York Times*, December 29, 1966.

124. Gary Youree to Cardinal Spellman, February 6, 1967, AANY, St. Patrick's Cathedral 15/D-1h.

125. Clark Whelton to Msgr. McGovern, January 26, 1967, AANY, St. Patrick's Cathedral 15/D-1h.

126. "Nab 23 Vietniks in St. Pat's," *New York Daily News*, January 23, 1967.

127. E.g., "Viet Protestors Parade in Aisle as Mass Is Said," *Chicago Tribune*, February 13, 1967.

128. "Militants Enter, Mass Is Canceled," *NCR*, July 9, 1969.

129. "Militants Enter, Mass Is Canceled."

130. Photo caption, *NCR*, July 16, 1969.

131. James Forman issued the manifesto from the pulpit of Riverside Church in New York on May 4, 1969. See Robert S. Lecky and H. Elliott Wright, eds., *Black Manifesto: Religion, Racism, and Reparations* (New York: Sheed and Ward, 1969); Keith Dye, "The Black Manifesto for Reparations in Detroit: Challenge and Response, 1969," *Michigan Historical Review* 35, no. 2 (2009): 53–83; and, for a sample of Catholic reaction, Robert Bauman, "'Kind of a Secular Sacrament': Father Geno Baroni, Monsignor John J. Egan, and the Catholic War on Poverty," *Catholic Historical Review* 99, no. 2 (2013): 298–317.

132. "Dearden Urges Courtesy for Black Spokesmen," *NCR*, August 6, 1969.

133. "200 Walk Out in Race Protest," *NCR*, August 6, 1969.

134. "Militants Enter, Mass Is Canceled."

135. "'Black Sunday' Given a Hearing," *NCR*, August 6, 1969.

136. "Black Given Pulpit to Ask 'Reparations,'" *NCR*, May 15, 1969.

137. Quinn, "Is There a Place for the Church," 6.

CHAPTER SIX

1. Program script, June 21, 1968, JPSP, 143.E.4.1B. Incensed by Shannon's appearance on a program featuring the IHM sisters, with whom he was embroiled in a battle over postconciliar reform, James Cardinal McIntyre of Los Angeles objected strongly to his participation. Hounded by McIntyre and dismayed by the appearance of the "birth control encyclical" *Humanae vitae* in July 1968, Shannon resigned from the episcopacy in November 1968. The title of his memoir gives the flavor of his public version of events: James P. Shannon, *Reluctant Dissenter* (New York: Crossroads, 1998).

2. "A Disgusted Catholic" to James P. Shannon, June 26, 1968, JPSP, 143.E.4.1B.

3. Mrs. M. Fink to James P. Shannon, June 24, 1968, JPSP, 143.E.4.1B.

4. Sr. M. Paulissa, SSND, to James P. Shannon, June 25, 1968, JPSP, 143.E.4.1B.

5. See Colleen McDannell, *The Spirit of Vatican II: A History of Catholic Reform in America* (New York: Basic Books, 2011), especially 151–76. The pastor of St. Jude's, a suburban church near Denver, Colorado, opened in 1969, specifically said he was "building a church 'with no pillars,'" harking back to the *Commonweal* debates of the 1920s (ibid., 153).

6. Fr. Leo Howley, dedication program for St. John the Evangelist parish church, Hopkins, Minnesota, 1969, AASP.

7. "The Liturgy of the Future," March 2, 1966, 25/15, FRMP.

8. Editorial, *LA* 1, no. 1 (1931): 1–2. Early articles in *Liturgical Arts* often focused on how to meet rubrical requirements, e.g., Edwin Ryan, DD, "The Liturgical Construction of the Altar," *LA* 1, no. 1 (1931): 28–33.

9. H. A. Reinhold, *The Dynamics of Liturgy* (New York: Macmillan Company, 1961), 80.

10. Reinhold, 88.

11. Reinhold, 83.

12. Reinhold, 80.

13. Gerald Ellard, SJ, to ML, January 21, 1947, CLIT, 23/04.

14. Kilian McDonnell, OSB, and Cloud Meinberg, OSB, "Architecture and the Constitution on the Sacred Liturgy," *LA* 34, no. 1 (1963): 2.

15. "Report on the One Day Conference Entitled 'Liturgical Renewal Now,' Sponsored by the Regional Committee of the National Liturgical Conference and the Boston Sacramental Apostolate, on Jan. 25, 1969," RP.

16. Robert Lawton Jones, lecture at the University of Dallas, June 17, 1965, RLJ.

17. Willy J. Malarcher, interview by the author, Englewood, NJ, August 22, 2011.

18. Parish council notes, September 20, 1966, and October 25, 1966, St. James the Less parish archives.

19. Sacred Congregation of Rites, *Instruction on Eucharistic Worship* (Washington, DC: United States Catholic Conference, 1967).

20. "Barry Byrne: Architect, Critic, Writer, Lecturer," August 1945, CLIT, 22/01.

21. Rev. Joseph Champlin, "Church Architecture in the Space Age," *American Ecclesiastical Review*, March 1969, 170–78.

22. On the first Sunday of Advent 1964, see Mark S. Massa, SJ, *The American Catholic Revolution: How the Sixties Changed the Church Forever* (New York: Oxford University Press, 2010), 1–5.

23. Ruth Rejnis, "Catholics Update Church Design," *NYT*, July 23, 1972.

24. Roger M. Jacobs to Anthony G. Gerst, June 28, 1967, Conrad Schmitt Studios Archives.

25. "How Cathedral Plan Developed," *Monitor*, January 31, 1964.

26. James P. McCartin, *Prayers of the Faithful: The Shifting Spiritual Life of American Catholics* (Cambridge, MA: Harvard University Press, 2010), 117–19.

27. Dennis Howard, "The Church of the Future: An Interview with Godfrey Diekmann," *U.S. Catholic*, October 1965, 11.

28. Frederick McManus, "Renewal and Future Development of the Liturgy," January 14, 1965, FRMP.

29. "The New Liturgy," *Progressive Architecture*, March 1965, 135.

30. "Frank Kacmarcik and the Church of Tomorrow," *Sign*, November 1968, 21–28.

31. "The Renovation of the Sanctuary in the Church of Saint Therese," *LA* 34, no. 1 (1965): 17.

32. Adé Bethune, correspondence, *LA* 35, no. 4 (1967): 156.

33. "An Appraisal of Problems Confronted in Applying the Directives of the Constitution on the Sacred Liturgy," *LA* 34, no. 3 (1966): 103.

34. "An Appraisal of Problems," 103.

35. Champlin, "Church Architecture in the Space Age," 172.

36. Adé Bethune and Thomas A. Drain, "Some Plans on Renovating the Sanctuary for the Renewed Liturgy," *LA* 33, no. 4 (1965): 106–18.

37. Patrick J. Quinn, "The Architectural Implications of the Choir in the Worshipping Community," *LA* 34, no. 2 (1966): 44.

38. Sacred Congregation of Rites, "Instruction on Implementing the Constitution on the Sacred Liturgy," §91.

39. ML, "Editor's Diary," *LA* 37, no. 2 (1968): 51.

40. "To Update a Large Church Built in the 1920s Is a Problem," *LA* 38, no. 2 (1970): 52.

41. See Catherine R. Osborne, "Renovating for the New Liturgy: The Boston College Students' Chapel," *American Catholic Studies* 125, no. 3 (2014): 93–104. This solution was also used in several churches built on preexisting sites. Epiphany, on 2nd Avenue in Manhattan, burned down in 1963 and was rebuilt with the interior rotated ("The Church That Turned a Corner," *Architectural Forum* 127 [1967]: 82–87). St. John the Baptist in New Brighton, Minnesota, opened in 1968 on a long-planned site as part of a twenty-year-old parish group (interior layout in *St. John the Baptist Catholic Parish: Building on a Century of Faith*, AASP).

42. See Matthew J. Cressler, "Black Power, Vatican II, and the Emergence of Black Catholic Liturgies," *U.S. Catholic Historian* 32 (2014): 99–119.

43. Quoted in Mary J. Henold, "Breaking the Boundaries of Renewal: The American Catholic Underground, 1966–1970," *U.S. Catholic Historian* 19 (2001): 111.

44. Protestants, too, had generally been barred from the sanctuary—a major issue for interfaith couples who had been married outside the sanctuary, as Colleen McDannell points out (*The Spirit of Vatican II*, 155).

45. They might also, of course, have pointed to recent American Catholic precedent; many churches built in the previous hundred years had been constructed largely with volunteer parishioner labor. As building codes became more rigorous and equipment more complex and specialized, this had become impractical. Gretchen Buggeln, in *The Suburban Church: Modernism and Community in Postwar America* (Minneapolis: University of Minnesota Press, 2015, 71–73), describes the limited though meaningful work church members could typically undertake by the 1950s: painting the interior or laying carpet, for example. Mandating congregational labor in the late 1960s primarily meant decorating a preexisting building, with the occasional exception, such as the small stone-and-mortar chapels built by a lay community at the Abbey of Regina Laudis, Bethlehem, Connecticut, and by the student group at New Mexico State–Las Cruces, New Mexico.

46. "Editor's Diary," *LA* 36, no. 1 (1967): 12.

47. "Art 1964: A Discussion between Sister Corita, I.H.M., & Adolph Gottlieb," *Jubilee*, December 1964, 21.

48. Robert Hovda and Gabe Huck, *There's No Place Like People: Liturgical Celebration in Home and Small-Group Situations* (Washington, DC: Liturgical Conference, 1969), 81.

49. Willy Malarcher, "Art and the Liturgy since Vatican II," *Catholic Market*, October 1967, 26–29.

50. A concern over "mobile" populations appears in liturgists' notes with some frequency; a conference of diocesan liturgists meeting at Notre Dame in June 1967, for example, recommended that bishops make provision for "the fact that our Catholic people are highly mobile—not only changing residence often, but even more so, traveling widely across diocesan boundaries on vacation trips, etc" (FRMP, 12/39). Concern for business travelers and airline employees whose travel might prevent them from association with a parish sparked a suggestion for a "parish" located in airports across the country ("Seminarian Envisions Coast-to-Coast Parish," *Boston Pilot*, May 13, 1967).

51. John King Mussio, "Bishop: Parish Form Revolution Ahead," *Boston Globe*, March 22, 1964.

52. Commission for Sacred Liturgy, Archdiocese of Hartford (Connecticut), "Guidelines for Masses in Homes and Neighborhoods," ca. 1966–67, FRMP.

53. "Mass in the Home," *Sign*, August 1966.

54. Henold, "Breaking the Boundaries of Renewal," 112.

55. Jerome Stowell, CP, "Is There a Future for the Neighborhood Mass?," *Homiletic and Pastoral Review* LXVIII (1967): 225.

56. Bishops' Commission on the Liturgical Apostolate, "Statement," February 17, 1967, reprinted in *Thirty Years of Liturgical Renewal: Statements of the Bishops' Committee on the Liturgy*, ed. Frederick McManus (Washington, DC: United States Catholic Conference, 1987), 69. For an example of one Colorado priest who did just this, see McDannell, *The Spirit of Vatican II*, 166–68.

57. Stowell, "Is There a Future for the Neighborhood Mass?," 227.

58. Stowell, 228–29. Middle-class norms of dress and hygiene were, however, not to be violated: "No frilly, feminine lace albs! No rustling silken chasubles! . . . It can be very disgusting for the people to see the celebrant leaning directly over the altar breads and breathily vocalizing the words of consecration on what they will be given to eat. Stand erect" (ibid., 231).

59. " 'Auto Mass' Scheduled in Portage," *Chicago Tribune*, April 30, 1964.

60. Cynthia Placek, "The Little Chapel in the Mall," *Sign*, April 1974, 19. For another example, this one an ecumenical operation, see Clifford Yudell, "Ministry in the Market Place," *U.S. Catholic & Jubilee*, November 1970, 23, 30.

61. Placek, "The Little Chapel in the Mall," 20.

62. Placek, 20.

63. Placek, 21.

64. Quoted in Jasper Chiodini, "Vatican II in Suburbia," in *The Postconciliar Parish*, ed. James O'Gara (New York: P. J. Kenedy & Sons, 1967), 75.

65. Quinn, "The Architectural Implications of the Choir," 46.

66. Gerald Ellard, SJ, *The Mass of the Future* (Milwaukee: Bruce Publishing, 1948); Josef A. Jungmann, *The Mass of the Roman Rite: Its Origins and Development* (New York: Benziger, 1951); Hans Küng, "The Mass of the Future," *Sign*, September 1963, 18–21; David Meade, "The Evolution of the Mass," *U.S. Catholic*, February 1965, 28–33.

67. Rev. John E. Corrigan, "Understanding the Changes in the Mass," *U.S. Catholic*, July 1965, 11.

68. Frédéric Debuyst, OSB, "Church Architecture and Christian Celebration," *LA* 32, no. 1 (1963): 2–9; Debuyst, "Problems of Modern Church Architecture," *LA* 34, no. 3 (1966): 92–97, 102; Debuyst, *Modern Architecture and Christian Celebration* (Richmond, VA: John Knox Press, 1968). For Debuyst and house churches, see Richard Kieckhefer, *Theology in Stone: Church Architecture from Byzantium to Berkeley* (New York: Oxford University Press, 2008), 52–53, 124–26.

69. Adé Bethune, "Report of the National Committee on Catholic Concerns," enclosed in Robert Rambusch to ML, November 11, 1968, CLIT, 48/01. Many liturgists suggested variations on this phrasing at about this time; e.g., *Church Architecture: The Shape of Reform* (Washington, DC: Liturgical Conference, 1965), 19.

70. Bethune, "Report of the National Committee on Catholic Concerns." As John Seitz demonstrates in his ethnographic work among early twenty-first-century Boston Catholics, many of whom had lived through this transition, over time many laypeople developed a hybrid concept in which the church was, on different registers of understanding, both the House of God and the house of God's people (*No Closure: Catholic Practice and Boston's Parish Shutdowns* [Cambridge, MA: Harvard University Press, 2011]).

71. *Church Architecture: The Shape of Reform*, 29, 20. On Sövik's importance to both Catholic and Protestant modernism, see Buggeln, *The Suburban Church*; and Jay M. Price, *Temples for a Modern God: Religious Architecture in Postwar America* (New York: Oxford University Press, 2013).

72. Joseph Diviney, "Christian Community—Today and Tomorrow," *LA* 37, no. 1 (1968): 17.

73. *Our Legacy of Faith: The History of a Living Parish: The Church of St. John the Evangelist, 1950–2000*, n.d., AASP.

74. Notes on conversation with Fr. W. Leo Howley, September 23, 1998, SJEPA.

75. "Basic Philosophy Required for Building a Church," n.d. [mid-1960s], SJEPA.

76. "Basic Philosophy Required for Building a Church."

77. "The Church of St. John the Evangelist, Hopkins, Minnesota, Dedication, May 11, 1969," AASP.

78. Mrs. Robert (Patricia) Witte, typescript, 1970, SJEPA; W. Leo Howley to Most Rev. Leo Byrne, November, 1969, AASP.

79. Quoted in "Fifteenth Annual Design Awards Program," *Progressive Architecture* 49, no. 1 (1968): 88–133.

80. "Basic Philosophy Required for Building a Church." Howley commented that the "large, roomy corridors" connecting front door, baptistery, and church were spaces "where God's People have space to meet one another, to know, to share one another because this is the first step in preparation for the Eucharist" ("House of God's People," *Our Sunday Visitor*, August 31, 1969).

81. Witte typescript, SJEPA.

82. "The New Church Architecture: The Passing of Sacred Space?," *Progressive Architecture*, December 1968, 92.

83. "The New Church Architecture," 92.

84. Desmond O'Grady, "Liturgy: Medium or Message?," *U.S. Catholic*, June 1970, 22–23.

85. "Church Destined for Dual Roles: Norwalk Parish to Dedicate It to Alternate Religious and Secular Uses," *NYT*, September 19, 1960.

86. "The New Church Architecture."

87. "Newman Student Center, University of Maine Orono, Architect Willoughby Marshall," RCA, 01/01; Rev. Clifford Stevens, "The Las Cruces Experiment," *LA* 34, no. 4 (1966): 142–43.

88. E.g., St. Thomas Center, University of Oklahoma, Norman (Robert Rambusch to ML, April 3, 1967, CLIT, 47/01).

89. "Minutes of Special Meeting of Troy Trustees," January 19, 1966, C+CC.

90. "A Program for a Catholic Chapel Building for Rensselaer Polytechnic Institute," 1966, C+CC.

91. "A Program for a Catholic Chapel Building."

92. "Revolution on the Secular Campus," *Jubilee*, April 1967, 16–23.

93. "To Serve Many," *Troy Record*, July 28, 1966.

94. Maureen Murphy, "The Search for Right Reason in an Unreasonable World: A History of the Catholic Art Association, 1937–1970" (PhD diss., University of Notre Dame, 1975).

95. Thomas Phelan, "25 Chapel + Cultural Center," *Sun & Balance*, March 1989, C+CC.

96. "Troy Priest's Talk at Houston Urges Multi Purpose Church," *Times Union*, August 21, 1966, C+CC.

97. This was the title of his Houston lecture.

98. Thomas Phelan, "A Chapel and Cultural Center to Serve Rensselaer Polytechnic Institute: Needs and Purposes," lecture at "Architecture and the College" symposium, University of Illinois, April 1968, C+CC.

99. Phelan, "A Chapel and Cultural Center."

100. Phelan, "A Chapel and Cultural Center." For the C+CC's contemporaneous use of its space, see Myron B. Bloy Jr., ed., *Community on Campus: Its Formation and Function* (New York: Seabury Press, 1971), especially 65–88.

101. ML, editorial, *LA* 39, no. 4 (1971): 97.

102. ML, 97.

103. Edward Anders Sövik, "Consensus," *LA* 38, no. 3 (1970): 97.

104. Patrick J. Quinn, "Church of Our Divine Savior, Chico, California," *LA* 38, no. 2 (1970): 50–51.

105. Clovis Heimsath, "A Catholic Student Center for a University in Texas," CLIT, 47/04.

106. Robert H. Mutrux, "A Post-Vatican Perspective," *Progressive Architecture*, December 1971, 46–53.

107. "A Church for the Revised Catholic Liturgy," *AR*, February 1970, 119.

108. Peter McLaughlin, "The Form of the Church Building," *Mediator*, Lent/Easter 1967, 5. A lengthy period of questioning the placement and design of almost every element ensued, which McLaughlin summed up as "the evolution of the form for this chapel" (ibid., 7).

109. Msgr. George W. Casey, "The Same Always, Please: Evelyn Waugh's Hopes for the Council," *Commonweal*, February 1, 1963, 487.

110. Hovda and Huck, *There's No Place Like People*, 52.

111. ML, "Editor's Diary," *LA* 36, no. 1 (1967): 24.

112. Louis J. Luzbetak, SVD, ed., *The Church in the Changing City* (Techny, IL: Divine Word Publications, 1966), 86–90.

113. Thomas E. Ambrogi, SJ, "A Mass of the Future," in *Experiments in Community: Twenty-Eighth North American Liturgical Week, Kansas City, Missouri, August 12–24, 1967* (Washington, DC: Liturgical Conference, 1967), 42.

114. Ambrogi, "A Mass of the Future," 42. For other suggestions along the same lines, see, e.g., Hovda and Huck, *There's No Place Like People*, 53; and Robert Hovda, *Dry Bones: Living Worship Guides to Good Liturgy* (Washington, DC: Liturgical Conference, 1973), 26.

115. See, e.g., Fr. John J. Ryan, "Post-Tribal Worship," in O'Gara, *The Postconciliar Parish*, 172. Archbishop Hallinan's less scientific phrasing, "responsible" experimentation, is cited in Henold, "Breaking the Boundaries of Renewal," 114.

116. See, e.g., Robert F. Hoey, SJ, *The Experimental Liturgy Book* (New York: Herder and Herder, 1969); John Gallen, SJ, ed., *Eucharistic Liturgies: Studies in American Pastoral Liturgy* (Paramus, NJ: Newman Press, 1969); Stephen W. McNierney, ed., *The Underground Mass Book* (Baltimore: Helicon, 1968).

117. Henold, "Breaking the Boundaries of Renewal," 114.

118. Hovda and Huck, *There's No Place Like People*, 49.

119. Donald J. Thorman, *American Catholics Face the Future* (Wilkes-Barre, PA: Dimension Books, 1968), 208.

120. Cressler, "Black Power, Vatican II, and Black Catholic Liturgies."

121. Malarcher, interview.

122. "St. Louis Liturgy Group Told to Go," *NCR*, August 13, 1969.

123. "New Pastor Restores St. Louis Basement Mass," *NCR*, September 17, 1969.

124. "Liturgical Orgy," *Catholic Herald*, September 15, 1966.

125. Donald A. Abramo, "Religious Educators' Liturgies Suppressed," *NCR*, September 10, 1969.

126. Thorman, *American Catholics Face the Future*, 208.

127. James M. O'Brien, "A Place to Put the Liturgy In," *NCR*, August 20, 1969, 4.

128. Abramo, "Religious Educators' Liturgies Suppressed."

129. "36 Arrested for Having Mass at the Pentagon," *NCR*, August 27, 1969; Marian Mollin, "Communities of Resistance: Women and the Catholic Left of the Late 1960s," *Oral History Review* 31 (2004): 45. Two days before the massive November 15 anti-Vietnam demonstration on the Mall, three hundred Episcopalians and Catholics joined South African Episcopalian Bishop Edward Crowther to attempt to repeat the Pentagon Mass. One hundred and eighty-six protestors, including twelve from the University of Notre Dame and Saint Mary's College, were arrested ("186 Arrested at Peace Mass Resistance," *Observer*, November 14, 1969).

130. "Floating parishes" also drew on historical research by liturgists like Josef Jungmann, who claimed that "the departure from a cultus of place-worship connected with certain localities" was "one of the most revolutionary innovations which Christianity produced" in the ancient world (*The Mass of the Roman Rite*, 253).

131. Luzbetak, *The Church in the Changing City*, 86–90.

132. Michael E. Schiltz, "We Need Some Parishes without Boundaries," *U.S. Catholic & Jubilee*, September 1970, 17.

133. More typical parishes shared these financial concerns as well, of course; Good Shepherd in Holbrook, New York, for example, chose modular construction and multipurpose space for their "sharp and necessary economies of time and cost" ("Holbrook Church Pioneers Modular Construction Methods," *Long Island Catholic*, January 20, 1972).

134. Donald Foust, "Parish without Bounds," *Commonweal*, August 25, 1967, 514. For the history of Christ Our Brother, see Andrew S. Moore, "Christian Unity, Lay Authority, and the People of God: The Community of Christ Our Brother in the Archdiocese of Atlanta, 1967–1969," in *Empowering the People of God: Catholic Action Before and After Vatican II*, ed. Jeremy Bonner, Mary Beth Fraser Connolly, and Christopher Denny (Fordham University Press, 2013), 274–97.

135. This lay-led group significantly outlasted the Woodstock experiment, meeting until the 1990s. Their experience of liturgy-planning highlights why it was so difficult for groups of laypeople to maintain their commitment; John Gallen, SJ, hosted a two-hour liturgy planning session on Tuesday nights, to which all were welcome to read the scriptures for the following Sunday and discuss them (Malarcher, interview). While this was exhilarating, it was also, over time, exhausting.

136. Francine du Plessix Gray, *Divine Disobedience: Profiles in Catholic Radicalism* (New York: Alfred A. Knopf, 1970), 9.

137. Thorman, *American Catholics Face the Future*, 202. Thorman, not incidentally, was a member of "an experimental kind of parish community" in Kansas City. Contemporary news articles were often based on Jesuit sociologist Rocco Caporale's unpublished report "The

Underground Church: Its Pastoral and Liturgical Significance" (NCCB Committee on the Liturgy, 1968); e.g., Kevin H. Axe, "The Underground Parishes," *U.S. Catholic*, June, 1969, 6–11. See Henold, "Breaking the Boundaries of Renewal."

138. Robert E. Moran, CSP, *The Community of John XXIII, Oklahoma City, Oklahoma, and the Community of the Living Christ, Tulsa, Oklahoma: An Evaluative Study* (Washington, DC: Center for Applied Research in the Apostolate, 1973), 15. See Jeremy Bonner, *The Road to Renewal: Victor Joseph Reed & Oklahoma Catholicism, 1905–1971* (Washington, DC: Catholic University of America Press, 2008), especially 148–180.

139. "A Declaration of the Commitment of the Community of John XIII," November 6, 1966, reprinted in Moran, *Community of John XXIII and Community of the Living Christ*, 38.

140. Moran, *Community of John XXIII and Community of the Living Christ*, 16.

141. Reed carefully noted to a fellow bishop, "I insisted that there be no liturgical 'aberrations' and that all experimentation be confined to the form and style of community life" (Moran, *Community of John XXIII and Community of the Living Christ*, 19).

142. Community of John XIII brochure, n.d. [probably 1969], reprinted in Moran, *Community of John XXIII and Community of the Living Christ*, 34. Reed also authorized Fr. William Skeehan to organize Resurrection, a buildingless territorial parish of three hundred families, which met for a number of years in rented space.

143. Community of John XIII brochure.

144. Community of John XIII brochure.

145. Moran, *Community of John XXIII and Community of the Living Christ*, 21.

146. Moran, 66.

147. Moran, 70.

148. Moran, 70–72.

149. Moran, 81. CARA's researchers concluded that helping mobile professionals acclimate to new cities was an important function of experimental communities.

150. Typescript report of the National Committee on Catholic Concerns, ca. 1968, CLIT, 48/01.

151. "Parish Center, St. Rita's Church, Cottage Grove, Minnesota," April 25, 1971, St. Rita's parish archives.

152. Robert Walcott to Fr. Leo R. Hubert, October 1, 1979, AASP.

153. Patrick J. Quinn, "The Church in the Future City: House-Church or Parish Place?," *LA* 35, no. 2 (1967): 88–90.

154. Hovda and Huck, *There's No Place Like People*, 5.

155. Hovda and Huck, 11.

156. Hovda, *Dry Bones*, 85.

157. G. R. Bullock, "The Updated Church?," *Scholastic*, November 17, 1967.

158. Hovda and Huck, *There's No Place Like People*, 72.

CONCLUSION

1. Dennis Howard, "The Church of the Future: An Interview with Godfrey Diekmann," *U.S. Catholic*, October 1965, 6–12.

2. Michael Novak, "The Absolute Future," *Commonweal*, January 13, 1967, 402.

3. "Fortieth Anniversary Symposium," *Commonweal*, November 20, 1964, 278.

4. Jay M. Price, *Temples for a Modern God: Religious Architecture in Postwar America* (New York: Oxford University Press, 2013), 162–64.

5. Quoted in Willy Malarcher, "Art and the Liturgy since Vatican II," *Catholic Market*, October 1967, 29.

6. Clovis Heimsath, "Holy-Card Architecture," *Commonweal*, November 4, 1966, 133.

7. ML, editorial, *LA* 38, no. 4 (1970): 111.

8. ML, editorial, *LA* 36, no. 2 (1968): 33. Lavanoux's correspondence reflected this turn as well; e.g., Anthony Lauck of Notre Dame wrote him that "we have got to remake our 'rooms' and 'cubes' into churches again" (n.d. [July 1971], CLIT, 52/02).

9. ML, editorial, *LA* 30, no. 1 (1961): 1.

10. Rolfe Lanier Hunt, ed., *Revolution, Place, and Symbol: Journal of the First International Conference on Religion, Architecture, and the Visual Arts, New York City and Montreal, August 26 through September 4, 1967* (New York: Benziger, 1969), 273; Steven V. Roberts, "Architect Sees Need for Great Religious Edifices," *NYT*, September 1, 1967.

11. See Steven J. Schloeder, *Architecture in Communion: Implementing the Second Vatican Council Through Liturgy and Architecture* (San Francisco: Ignatius Press, 1998); Michael S. Rose, *Ugly as Sin: Why They Changed Our Churches from Sacred Places to Meeting Spaces—And How We Can Change Them Back Again* (Manchester, N.H.: Sophia Institute Press, 2001); and Duncan G. Stroik, "Environment and Art in Catholic Worship: A Critique," *Sacred Architecture* 2, no. 1 (Summer 1999). For the prehistory of the "look like a church" phrasing, see Price, *Temples for a Modern God*, 119–45. For a contrasting contemporary argument to Schloeder, etc., see Richard S. Vosko, *God's House Is Our House: Re-imagining the Environment for Worship* (Collegeville, MN: Liturgical Press, 2006). The debate about these ideas often runs on rather vague accusations about "ugliness" and "beauty," with occasional detours into somewhat more theological arguments about "transcendence" and "immanence." I, however, agree with Kieckhefer's critique of the grounds on which this discussion unfolds: there are no specific architectural forms that always, in all times and places and for all people, represent transcendence or immanence, let alone ugliness or beauty. See Richard Kieckhefer, "Immanence and Transcendence in Church Architecture," *Koinonia: The Journal of the Anglican & Eastern Churches Association* 54 (All Saintstide 2008): 29–40.

12. Richard Kieckhefer, *Theology in Stone: Church Architecture from Byzantium to Berkeley* (New York: Oxford University Press, 2008), 266–67, 275–78; Mark Allen Torgerson, *An Architecture of Immanence: Architecture for Worship and Ministry Today* (Grand Rapids, MI: Eerdmans, 2007), 200–204. For a critique of the school on different grounds, see Paula Kane, "Is That a Beer Vat under the Baldochino? From Antimodernism to Postmodernism in Catholic Church Architecture," *U.S. Catholic Historian* 15 (1997): 14–15.

13. On "nightmares," see Yi-Fu Tuan, *Space and Place: The Perspective of Experience* (Minneapolis: University of Minnesota Press, 1977), 197.

14. Donald J. Thorman, *American Catholics Face the Future* (Wilkes-Barre, PA: Dimension Books, 1968), 299.

15. Fredric Jameson, "Progress versus Utopia; or, Can We Imagine the Future?," *Science-Fiction Studies* 9 (July 1982): 147–58. Eschatology's reemergence as a major theological paradigm only clarifies the usefulness of science fiction criticism in understanding Catholic

futurism; for, as Frederick Kreuziger argues, science fiction is itself a basically apocalyptic literature, "involving an intense longing for a new age and a new world . . . a literature of hope" that "views the present-time as a time of crisis, and concurrently a time of great expectation, indeed imminent expectation" (*Apocalypse and Science Fiction: A Dialectic of Religious and Secular Soteriologies* [Chico, CA: Scholars Press, 1982], 49).

16. Thomas M. Disch, *The Dreams Our Stuff Is Made Of: How Science Fiction Conquered the World* (New York: Free Press, 1998), 218. I. F. Clarke dates this core technique of science fiction to the late eighteenth century (*The Pattern of Expectation, 1644–2001* [New York: Basic Books, 1979], 31).

17. Robert E. Scholes, *Structural Fabulation: An Essay on Fiction of the Future* (Notre Dame, IN: University of Notre Dame Press, 1975), 75, a lightly edited version of his 1974 Ward-Phillips Lectures.

18. As Kevin Lynch, one of the first generation of space-and-place theorists, a Catholic from Newark, New Jersey, noted, "We reach out to [the] world to preserve or to change it and so to make visible our desire" (*What Time Is This Place?* [Cambridge, MA: MIT Press, 1972], 1).

19. Doreen Massey, *Space, Place, and Gender* (London: Polity Press/Blackwell, 1994), 154.

20. See Edward W. Soja, *Postmodern Geographies: The Reassertion of Space in Critical Social Theory* (London: Verso, 1989), 79–93.

21. David Harvey, *Spaces of Hope* (Berkeley: University of California Press, 2000).

SELECTED BIBLIOGRAPHY

Abbott, Walter, SJ. "Church of the Encounter." *Liturgical Arts* 37, no. 2 (1969): 42–49.

Alofsin, Anthony. *The Struggle for Modernism: Architecture, Landscape Architecture, and City Planning at Harvard*. New York: W. W. Norton, 2002.

Anker, Peder. *From Bauhaus to Ecohouse: A History of Ecological Design*. Baton Rouge: Louisiana State University Press, 2010.

Appleby, R. Scott. *"Church and Age Unite!": The Modernist Impulse in American Catholicism*. Notre Dame, IN: University of Notre Dame Press, 1992.

Arnaud, Leopold. "Concrete in Architectural Service." *Journal of the American Concrete Institute* 10 (April 1939): 355–58.

———. "The Living Tradition in Christian Art." *Liturgical Arts* 9, no 3 (1941): 47–48.

Baltimore Urban Parish Study. Baltimore: Archdiocese of Baltimore, 1967.

Banham, Reyner. *A Concrete Atlantis: U.S. Industrial Building and European Modern Architecture*. Cambridge, MA: MIT Press, 1986.

Baumann, Cajetan. "Some Trends in Church Design." *Architectural Record*, September 1944, 95–97.

Beers, Gillian. *Darwin's Plots: Evolutionary Narrative in Darwin, George Eliot and Nineteenth-Century Fiction*. 2nd ed. Cambridge: Cambridge University Press, 2000.

Behrendt, Walter. *Modern Building: Its Nature, Problems, and Forms*. New York: Harcourt, Brace, 1937.

Bell, Daniel, ed. *Toward the Year 2000: Work in Progress*. Boston: Houghton Mifflin, 1967.

Belluschi, Pietro. "Eloquent Simplicity in Architecture." *Architectural Record*, July 1963, 131–35.

Bennett, Janey. *The Fantastic Seashell of the Mind: The Architecture of Mark Mills*. Novato, CA: ORO Editions, 2017.

———. "Work of Mark Mills: Structural Elegance and a Sense of Reverent Space." *Journal of the Taliesin Fellows* 10 (Spring 1993): 18–29.

Bethune, Adé, and Thomas A. Drain. "Some Plans on Renovating the Sanctuary for the Renewed Liturgy." *Liturgical Arts* 33, no. 4 (1965): 106–18.

Billington, David P. *Thin Shell Concrete Structures*. New York: McGraw-Hill, 1966.

Blau, Eve, and Edward Kaufman, eds. *Architecture and Its Image: Four Centuries of Architectural Representation*. Montreal: Canadian Center for Architecture, 1989.

Bonner, Jeremy. *The Road to Renewal: Victor Joseph Reed & Oklahoma Catholicism, 1905–1971*. Washington, DC: Catholic University of America Press, 2008.

Bouyer, Louis. *Liturgy and Architecture*. Notre Dame, IN: University of Notre Dame Press, 1967.

Bovée, David S. *The Church & the Land: The National Catholic Rural Life Conference and American Society, 1923–2007*. Washington, DC: Catholic University of America Press, 2010.

Brannach, Frank. *Church Architecture: Building for a Living Faith*. Milwaukee: Bruce Publishing, 1933.

Braybrooke, Neville, ed. *Teilhard De Chardin: Pilgrim of the Future*. New York: Seabury, 1964.

Brennan, Rev. Robert. "Sumer is icumen in." *Liturgical Arts* 13, no. 1 (1944): 4–7.

Bressani, Martin. *Architecture and the Historical Imagination: Eugène-Emmanuel Viollet-Le-Duc, 1814–1879*. London: Routledge, 2016.

Brush, Kathryn. *The Shaping of Art History: Wilhelm Vöge, Adolph Goldschmidt, and the Study of Medieval Art*. New York: Cambridge University Press, 1996.

———. *Vastly More Than Brick & Mortar: Reinventing the Fogg Art Museum in the 1920s*. Cambridge, MA: Harvard University Art Museums, 2003.

Buggeln, Gretchen. *The Suburban Church: Modernism and Community in Postwar America*. Minneapolis: University of Minnesota Press, 2015.

Bugnini, Annibale. *The Reform of the Liturgy, 1948–1975*. Translated by Matthew J. O'Connell. Collegeville, MN: Liturgical Press, 1990.

Bundy, Robert, ed. *Images of the Future: The Twenty-First Century and Beyond*. Buffalo, NY: Prometheus Books, 1976.

Bury, J. B. *The Idea of Progress: An Inquiry into Its Origin and Growth*. Dodo Press, (1921) 2008.

Byrne, Barry. "A New Architecture." *Commonweal*, November 25, 1925, 73–75.

———. "Plan for a Church." *Liturgical Arts* 10, no. 3 (1942): 58–60.

———. "Tangled Thinkers of Today." *Commonweal*, June 3, 1931, 131–32.

———. "The Gesture of Impotence." *Commonweal*, February 25, 1925, 436.

———. "The Orthodoxy of Columns." *Commonweal*, March 25, 1925, 551.

———. "Why an Old Architecture?" *Commonweal*, January 13, 1926, 272.

Cadegan, Una M. *All Good Books Are Catholic Books: Print Culture, Censorship, and Modernity in Twentieth-Century America*. Ithaca, NY: Cornell University Press, 2013.

Callahan, Daniel, ed. *The Secular City Debate*. New York: Macmillan, 1966.

Carter, Paul Allen. *Another Part of the Fifties*. New York: Columbia University Press, 1983.

Cary-Elwes, Columba, OSB. "Planning a Monastery and Monastic School: Saint Louis Priory, Crève Coeur, Missouri." *Liturgical Arts* 26, no. 2 (1958): 48–50.

———. "The Theology of the Church and the Architect." *Liturgical Arts* 31, no. 1 (1962): 9, 28.

Cates, John M., Jr. "The Steeple Goes to Ground." *Liturgical Arts* 37, no. 4 (1969): 108–11.

Caussé, Françoise. *La revue "L'Art sacré": Le débat en France sur l'art et la religion (1945–1954)*. Paris: Cerf, 2010.

Champlin, Rev. Joseph. "Church Architecture in the Space Age." *American Ecclesiastical Review*, March 1969, 170–78.

Chinnici, Joseph P., OFM. "Ecumenism, Civil Rights, and the Second Vatican Council: The American Experience." *U.S. Catholic Historian* 30 (2012): 21–49.

———. *Living Stones: The History and Structure of Catholic Spiritual Life in the United States*. Maryknoll, NY: Orbis Books, 1996.

Christ-Janer, Albert, and Mary Mix Foley. *Modern Church Architecture: A Guide to the Form and Spirit of Twentieth-Century Religious Building*. New York: McGraw-Hill, 1962.

"[Church Architecture]." *Architectural Forum* 91 (December 1949): 57–73.

Church Architecture: The Shape of Reform. Washington, DC: Liturgical Conference, 1965.

"A Church for the Revised Catholic Liturgy." *Architectural Record*, February 1970, 119–22.

"Church of Christ the King, Seattle, Washington." *Liturgical Arts* 18, no. 2 (1950): 38–39.

Clark, Dennis. *Cities in Crisis*. New York: Sheed & Ward, 1960.

Clarke, I. F. *The Pattern of Expectation, 1644–2001*. New York: Basic Books, 1979.

Clausen, Meredith L. *Pietro Belluschi: Modern American Architect*. Cambridge, MA: MIT Press, 1994.

———. *Spiritual Space: The Religious Architecture of Pietro Belluschi*. Seattle: University of Washington Press, 1992.

———. "Transparent Structure: Belluschi Churches of the 1950s." *Journal of the Interfaith Forum on Religion, Art, & Architecture*, Fall 1990, 10–14.

Collins, Peter. *Changing Ideals in Modern Architecture, 1750–1950*. Montreal: McGill University Press, 1965.

———. *Concrete: The Vision of a New Architecture*. 2nd ed. Toronto: McGill-Queen's University Press, 2004.

Cook, Peter. *Experimental Architecture*. New York: Universe Books, 1970.

Cowell, Siôn. *The Teilhard Lexicon: Understanding the Language, Terminology, and Vision of the Writings of Pierre Teilhard De Chardin*. Portland: Sussex Academic Press, 2001.

Cox, Harvey. *The Secular City: Secularization and Urbanization in Theological Perspective*. New York: Macmillan, 1965.

Cram, Ralph Adams. "Why a New Architecture?" *Commonweal*, December 16, 1925, 151–52.

Cressler, Matthew J. "Black Power, Vatican II, and the Emergence of Black Catholic Liturgies." *U.S. Catholic Historian* 32 (2014): 99–119.

Curran, Kathleen. *The Romanesque Revival: Religion, Politics, and Transnational Exchange*. University Park: Pennsylvania State University Press, 2003.

Danielou, Jean. "Christianity and the Machine-Age World." *Jubilee*, February 1963, 14–17.

———. "Hope and the Christian." *Commonweal*, April 1, 1960, 7–9.

Davies, J. G. *The Secular Use of Church Buildings*. New York: Seabury, 1968.

Dearstyne, Howard. "Basic Teaching of Architecture." *Liturgical Arts* 12, no. 3 (1944): 56–60.

Debuyst, Frédéric, OSB. *Modern Architecture and Christian Celebration*. Richmond, VA: John Knox Press, 1968.

———. "Church Architecture and Christian Celebration." *Liturgical Arts* 32, no. 1 (1963): 2–9.

———. "Problems of Modern Church Architecture." *Liturgical Arts* 34, no. 3 (1966): 92–97, 102.

Deiss, Lucien, and Gloria Gabriel Weyman. *Dance for the Lord*. Cincinnati: World Library Publications, 1975.

De Lubac, SJ, Henri. *The Religion of Teilhard De Chardin*. Translated by René Hague. New York: Desclee, 1967.

Deyong, Sarah. "Memories of the Urban Future: The Rise and Fall of the Megastructure." In *The Changing of the Avant-Garde: Visionary Architectural Drawings from the Howard Gilman Collection*, edited by Terence Riley, 23–35. New York: Museum of Modern Art, 2002.

Dickson, Paul. *Sputnik: The Shock of the Century*. New York: Walker, 2001.

Dillenberger, John. *The Visual Arts and Christianity in America*. New York: Crossroad, 1989.

Disch, Thomas M. *The Dreams Our Stuff Is Made Of: How Science Fiction Conquered the World*. New York: Free Press, 1998.

Diviney, Joseph. "Christian Community—Today and Tomorrow." *Liturgical Arts* 37, no. 1 (1968): 17–19.

Dolan, Jay P. *The American Catholic Experience: A History from Colonial Times to the Present*. Notre Dame, IN: University of Notre Dame Press, 1992.

Dulles, Avery, SJ. *Models of the Church*. Garden City, NY: Doubleday, 1974.

Eastham, Scott. *American Dreamer: Bucky Fuller and the Sacred Geometry of Nature*. Cambridge: Lutterworth Press, 2007.

Ellard, Gerald, SJ. *The Mass of the Future*. Milwaukee: Bruce Publishing, 1948.

Evans, John Whitney. *The Newman Movement: Roman Catholics in American Higher Education, 1883–1971*. Notre Dame, IN: University of Notre Dame Press, 1980.

Experiments in Community: Twenty-Eighth North American Liturgical Week, Kansas City, Missouri, August 12–24, 1967. Washington, DC: Liturgical Conference, 1967.

Fisher, James Terence. *The Catholic Counterculture in America, 1933–1962*. Chapel Hill: University of North Carolina Press, 1989.

Fitch, James Marston. *American Building: The Historical Forces That Shaped It*. 2nd ed. New York: Schocken Books, 1966. First published 1947.

Foust, Conald. "Parish without Bounds." *Commonweal*, August 25, 1967, 514–15.

Fowler, Glenn. "New Churches Are Anticipating the Future Instead of Reflecting the Past." *New York Times*, August 25, 1957.

Francoeur, Robert T. "The Cosmic Piety of Teilhard de Chardin." In *Cosmic Piety: Modern Man and the Meaning of the Universe*, edited by Christopher Derrick, 99–118. New York: P. J. Kenedy, 1965.

"Frank Kacmarcik and the Church of Tomorrow." *Sign*, November 1968, 21–28.

Gallen, John, SJ, ed. *Eucharistic Liturgies: Studies in American Pastoral Liturgy*. Paramus, NJ: Newman, 1969.

Gamm, Gerald H. *Urban Exodus: Why the Jews Left Boston and the Catholics Stayed*. Cambridge, MA: Harvard University Press, 1999.

Garlock, Maria E. Moreyra, and David P. Billington. *Félix Candela: Engineer, Builder, Structural Artist*. Princeton, NJ: Princeton University Art Museum, 2008.

Gebhard, David, and Harriette Von Breton. *Lloyd Wright, Architect: 20th Century Architecture in an Organic Exhibition*. Santa Monica, CA: Hennessey + Ingalls, 1998.

Gleason, Philip. "American Catholics and the Mythic Middle Ages." In *Keeping the Faith: American Catholicism, Past and Present*, 11–34. Notre Dame, IN: University of Notre Dame Press, 1987.

Golden, Lauren. "Science, Darwin, and Art History." In *Raising the Eyebrow: John Onians and World Art Studies*, edited by Lauren Golden, 79–90. Oxford: Archaeopress, 2001.

Goldhagen, Sarah Williams. *Louis Kahn's Situated Modernism*. New Haven, CT: Yale University Press, 2001.

———. "Something to Talk About: Modernism, Discourse, Style." *Journal of the Society of Architectural Historians* 64 (2005): 144–67.

Goodman, Donna. *A History of the Future*. New York: Monacelli, 2008.

Gordon, Alastair. *Spaced Out: Radical Environments of the Psychedelic Sixties*. New York: Rizzoli, 2008.

Gray, Francine du Plessix. *Divine Disobedience: Profiles in Catholic Radicalism*. New York: Alfred A. Knopf, 1970.

Greeley, Andrew. *Religion in the Year 2000*. New York: Sheed and Ward, 1969.

Guerlac, Suzanne. *Thinking in Time: An Introduction to Henri Bergson*. Ithaca, NY: Cornell University Press, 2006.

Guerrette, Richard H. "Experiments in Parish Community." *Homiletic and Pastoral Review* XLVIII (1968): 1029–36.

Halsey, William M. *The Survival of American Innocence: Catholicism in an Era of Disillusionment, 1920–1940*. Notre Dame, IN: University of Notre Dame Press, 1980.

Hammond, Peter. *Liturgy and Architecture*. New York: Columbia University Press, 1961.

———, ed. *Towards a Church Architecture*. London: Architectural Press, 1962.

Harmon, Katharine E. *There Were Also Many Women There: Lay Women in the Liturgical Movement in the United States, 1926–59*. Collegeville, MN: Liturgical Press, 2013.

Harvey, David. *Spaces of Hope*. Berkeley: University of California Press, 2000.

Hearn, M. F., ed. *The Architectural Theory of Viollet-Le Duc: Readings and Commentary*. Cambridge, MA: MIT Press, 1990.

Heilbroner, Robert. *Visions of the Future: The Distant Past, Yesterday, Today, and Tomorrow*. New York: Oxford University Press, 1996.

Heimsath, Clovis. "Holy-Card Architecture." *Commonweal*, November 4, 1966, 132–34.

Henold, Mary J. "Breaking the Boundaries of Renewal: The American Catholic Underground, 1966–1970." *U.S. Catholic Historian* 19 (2001): 97–118.

Herrmann, Wolfgang. *In What Style Should We Build? The German Debate on Architectural Style*. Santa Monica, CA: Getty Center for the History of Art and the Humanities, 1992.

Hoey, Robert F., SJ. *The Experimental Liturgy Book*. New York: Herder and Herder, 1969.

Hoffmann, Donald. "Frank Lloyd Wright and Viollet-Le-Duc." *Journal of the Society of Architectural Historians* 28 (1969): 173–83.

Holt, James A., Jr. "The Religious Space." *Liturgical Arts* 37, no. 1 (1968): 8–9.

Horner, Timothy, OSB. *In Good Soil: The Founding of St. Louis Priory and School, 1954–1973*. Creve Coeur, MO: Saint Louis Abbey Press, 2001.

Hovda, Robert. *Dry Bones: Living Worship Guides to Good Liturgy*. Washington, DC: Liturgical Conference, 1973.

———, ed. *Manual of Celebration*. Washington, DC: Liturgical Conference, 1970.

Hovda, Robert, and Gabe Huck. *There's No Place Like People: Liturgical Celebration in Home and Small-Group Situations*. Washington, DC: Liturgical Conference, 1969.

Howard, Dennis. "The Church of the Future: An Interview with Godfrey Diekmann." *U.S. Catholic*, October 1965, 6–15.

Howes, Robert G. *Crisis Downtown: A Church Eye-View of Urban Renewal*. Washington, DC: National Conference of Catholic Charities, 1959.

———. *The Church and the Change: An Initial Study of the Role of the Roman Catholic Church in the Changing American Community*. Boston: St. Paul Editions, 1961.

Hunt, Rolfe Lanier, ed. *Revolution, Place, and Symbol: Journal of the First International Conference on Religion, Architecture, and the Visual Arts*. New York: Benziger, 1969.

Hurley, Neil, SJ. "Liturgy and Play in Our Expanding Tele-Civilization." *Liturgical Arts* 40, no. 1 (1971): 6–8.

———. "The Futurists: '. . . I Dream Things That Never Were.'" *Ave Maria*, January 4, 1969, 8–12.

Innes, C. D. *Designing Modern America: Broadway to Main Street*. New Haven, CT: Yale University Press, 2005.

Issel, William. *Church and State in the City: Catholics and Politics in Twentieth-Century San Francisco*. Philadelphia: Temple University Press, 2013.

Jameson, Fredric. "Progress versus Utopia; Or, Can We Imagine the Future?" *Science-Fiction Studies* 9 (July 1982): 147–58.

Javier, Benjamin P. "Living Tradition." *Liturgical Arts* 27, no. 2 (1959): 30–32.

Jungmann, Josef A. *The Mass of the Roman Rite: Its Origins and Development*. New York: Benziger, 1951.

Kane, Paula. "Is That a Beer Vat under the Baldochino? From Antimodernism to Postmodernism in Catholic Church Architecture." *U.S. Catholic Historian* 15 (1997): 1–32.

———. *Separatism and Subculture: Boston Catholicism, 1900–1920*. Chapel Hill: University of North Carolina Press, 1989.

Kantor, Sybil Gordon. *Alfred H. Barr, Jr., and the Intellectual Origins of the Museum of Modern Art*. Cambridge, MA: MIT Press, 2001.

Kelly, Timothy I. *The Transformation of American Catholicism: The Pittsburgh Laity and the Second Vatican Council, 1950–1972*. Notre Dame, IN: University of Notre Dame Press, 2009.

Kennedy, Eugene C., MM. "The Mythology of Modern Renewal." *U.S. Catholic*, March 1967, 6–11.

Kieckhefer, Richard. "Immanence and Transcendence in Church Architecture." *Koinonia: The Journal of the Anglican & Eastern Churches Association*, no. 54 (All Saintstide 2008): 29–40.

———. *Theology in Stone: Church Architecture from Byzantium to Berkeley*. New York: Oxford University Press, 2008.

Kilde, Jeanne Halgren. *Sacred Power, Sacred Space: An Introduction to Christian Architecture and Worship*. Oxford: Oxford University Press, 2008.

King, Thomas, SJ. *Teilhard's Mass: Approaches to "The Mass on the World."* Mahwah, NJ: Paulist Press, 2005.

Koehlinger, Amy L. *The New Nuns: Racial Justice and Religious Reform in the 1960s*. Cambridge, MA: Harvard University Press, 2007.

Koselleck, Reinhart. *Futures Past: On the Semantics of Historical Time*. Translated by Keith Tribe. New York: Columbia University Press, 2004.

Krenn, Michael L. *Fall-Out Shelters for the Human Spirit: American Art and the Cold War*. Durham: University of North Carolina Press, 2006.

Kreuziger, Frederick A. *Apocalypse and Science Fiction: A Dialectic of Religious and Secular Soteriologies*. Chico, CA: Scholars Press, 1982.

Kripal, Jeffrey J. *Esalen: America and the Religion of No Religion*. Chicago: University of Chicago Press, 2008.
Küng, Hans. "The Mass of the Future." *Sign*, September 1963, 18–21.
Labatut, Jean, and André Girard. "Adventure in Light-Color-Polychromy: A Church Prototype." *Liturgical Arts* 20, no. 1 (1951): 2–8.
Lambert, Clement J., SM. "Religious Art of Today." *Marianist*, July 1944, 14–18, 45–46.
Lavanoux, Maurice. "A Diocesan Building Project." *Liturgical Arts* 12, no. 4 (1944): 85–86.
———. "The Authentic Tradition in Art." *Liturgical Arts* 22, no. 4 (1954): 123–25.
Lawler, Justus George. "Catholics and the Arms Race." *Commonweal*, May 18, 1962, 199–200.
———. "Transfigured Universe." In *The Christian Imagination: Studies in Religious Thought*, 53–66. Westminster, MD: Newman, 1955.
Lecky, Robert S., and H. Elliott Wright, eds. *Black Manifesto: Religion, Racism, and Reparations*. New York: Sheed and Ward, 1969.
Lee, Martin A., and Bruce Shlain. *Acid Dreams: The Complete Social History of LSD: The CIA, the Sixties, and Beyond*. 2nd ed. New York: Grove Press, 1994.
Lercaro, Giacomo. "The True Sense of Tradition in Sacred Art." *Liturgical Arts* 25, no. 1 (1956): 7–8.
Ligo, Larry L. *The Concept of Function in Twentieth-Century Architectural Criticism*. Ann Arbor, MI: UMI Research Press, 1984.
Luzbetak, Louis J., SVD, ed. *The Church in the Changing City*. Techny, IL: Divine Word Publications, 1966.
Lynch, Kevin. *What Time Is This Place?* Cambridge, MA: MIT Press, 1972.
Lynn, Edwin. *Tired Dragons: Adapting Church Architecture to Changing Needs*. Boston: Beacon Press, 1972.
Macy, Christine, and Sarah Bonnemaison. *Architecture and Nature: Creating the American Landscape*. London: Routledge, 2003.
Maginnis, Charles Donagh. "Architecture and Religious Tradition." *Architectural Record*, September 1944, 89–91.
Malarcher, Willy. "Art and the Liturgy since Vatican II." *Catholic Market*, October 1967, 26–29.
Mallgrave, Harry Francis. *Modern Architectural Theory: A Historical Survey, 1673–1968*. Cambridge: Cambridge University Press, 2009.
Mangan, Terence J., CO. "The Doman Moon Chapel." *Liturgical Arts* 36, no. 1 (1967): 3.
Mansfield, Elizabeth, ed. *Art History and Its Institutions: Foundations of a Discipline*. London: Routledge, 2002.
Marini, Archbishop Piero. *A Challenging Reform: Realizing the Vision of the Liturgical Renewal, 1963–1975*. Edited by Mark R. Francis, CSV, John R. Page, and Keith F. Pecklers, SJ. Collegeville, MN: Liturgical Press, 2007.
Maritain, Jacques. "Teilhard de Chardin and Teilhardism." *U.S. Catholic*, November 1967, 6–10.
Marlett, Jeffrey D. *Saving the Heartland: Catholic Missionaries in Rural America, 1920–1960*. Dekalb: Northern Illinois University Press, 2002.
Massa, Mark S., SJ. *The American Catholic Revolution: How the Sixties Changed the Church Forever*. New York: Oxford University Press, 2010.
Massey, Doreen. *Space, Place, and Gender*. London: Polity Press/Blackwell, 1994.
Mathews, Thomas F., SJ. "New City, New Church." *Commonweal*, August 25, 1967, 518–21.

———. "Toward an Adequate Notion of Tradition in Sacred Art." *Liturgical Arts* 32, no. 2 (1964): 43–49.

McCarraher, Eugene. "American Gothic: Sacramental Radicalism and the Neo-medievalist Cultural Gospel, 1928–1948." *Records of the American Catholic Historical Society of Philadelphia* 106 (1995): 3–23.

McCartin, James P. *Prayers of the Faithful: The Shifting Spiritual Life of American Catholics*. Cambridge, MA: Harvard University Press, 2010.

McDannell, Colleen. *Material Christianity: Religion and Popular Culture in America*. New Haven, CT: Yale University Press, 1995.

———. *The Spirit of Vatican II: A History of Catholic Reform in America*. New York: Basic Books, 2011.

McDonnell, Kilian, OSB, and Cloud Meinberg, OSB. "Architecture and the Constitution on the Sacred Liturgy." *Liturgical Arts* 34, no. 1 (1963): 2–6.

McGreevy, John T. *Parish Boundaries: The Catholic Encounter with Race in the Twentieth-Century Urban North*. Chicago: University of Chicago Press, 1996.

McGuinness, Margaret M. "Let Us Go to the Altar: American Catholics and the Eucharist, 1926–1976." In *Habits of Devotion: Catholic Religious Practice in Twentieth-Century America*, edited by James M. O'Toole, 186–235. Ithaca, NY: Cornell University Press, 2004.

McNulty, Thomas F., and Mary S. Fawcett. "Proposed Catholic Church for the Boston Archdiocese." *Liturgical Arts* 25, no. 4 (1957): 110–12.

McQuaid, Matilda. *Envisioning Architecture: Drawings from the Museum of Modern Art*. New York: Museum of Modern Art, 2002.

Mettepenningen, Jürgen. *Nouvelle Théologie—New Theology: Inheritor of Modernism, Precursor of Vatican II*. London: T&T Clark, 2010.

Michael, Vincent L. *The Architecture of Barry Byrne: Taking the Prairie School to Europe*. Urbana: University of Illinois Press, 2013.

Michel, Virgil, OSB. "The Liturgical Movement and the Future." *America*, October 12, 1935, 6–7.

Mills, Mark. "A 'Batoid' Peace Ship." *Liturgical Arts* 40, no. 1 (1971): 10–13.

Mislin, David. "'According to His Own Judgment': The American Catholic Encounter with Organic Evolution, 1875–1896." *Religion and American Culture* 22 (2012): 133–62.

Mollin, Marian. "Communities of Resistance: Women and the Catholic Left of the Late 1960s." *Oral History Review* 31 (2004): 29–51.

Moon, Karen. *Modeling Messages: The Architect and the Model*. New York: Monacelli, 2005.

Moran, Robert E., CSP. *The Community of John XXIII, Oklahoma City, Oklahoma, and the Community of the Living Christ, Tulsa, Oklahoma: An Evaluative Study*. Washington, DC: Center for Applied Research in the Apostolate, 1973.

Morey, Charles Rufus. "A Humanistic Laboratory." *Bulletin of the Department of Art and Archaeology of Princeton University*, October 1929, 5–9.

Morgan, David, ed. *Religion and Material Culture: The Matter of Belief*. London: Routledge, 2009.

Morris, Charles. *American Catholic: The Saints and Sinners Who Built America's Most Powerful Church*. New York: Vintage, 1998.

Morris, Mark. *Models: Architecture and the Miniature*. Chichester: Wiley-Academy, 2006.

Mumford, Eric. *Defining Urban Design: CIAM Architects and the Formation of a Discipline, 1937–69*. New Haven, CT: Yale University Press, 2009.

———, ed. *Modern Architecture in St. Louis: Washington University and Postwar American Architecture, 1948–1973*. St. Louis: Washington University School of Architecture, 2004.
Mumford, Eric, and Hashim Sarkis, eds. *Josep Lluís Sert: The Architect of Urban Design, 1953–1959*. New Haven, CT: Yale University Press, 2008.
Mumford, Lewis. "A Modern Catholic Architect." *Commonweal*, March 2, 1927, 458–59.
———. "Architecture and Catholicism." *Commonweal*, April 15, 1925, 623–25.
———. "Decoration and Structure." *Commonweal*, October 7, 1925, 532–33.
———. *Technics and Civilization*. New York: Hartford, Brace, 1934.
Murchland, Bernard G., CSC. "The Prophetic Principle." *Commonweal*, April 1966, 171–75.
Murphy, Kevin D. *Memory and Modernity: Viollet-Le-Duc at Vézelay*. University Park: Pennsylvania State University Press, 2000.
Murphy, Maureen. "The Search for Right Reason in an Unreasonable World: A History of the Catholic Art Association, 1937–1970." PhD diss., University of Notre Dame, 1975.
Mutrux, Robert H. "A Post-Vatican Perspective." *Progressive Architecture*, December 1971, 46–53.
Nelson, Louis P., ed. *American Sanctuary: Understanding Sacred Spaces*. Bloomington: Indiana University Press, 2006.
"The New Church Architecture: The Passing of Sacred Space?" *Progressive Architecture*, December 1968, 92–107.
"The New Liturgy." *Progressive Architecture*, March 1965, 134–37.
Nisbet, James. *Ecologies, Environments, and Energy Systems in Art of the 1960s and 1970s*. Cambridge, MA: MIT Press, 2014.
Nogar, Raymond J., OP. *The Lord of the Absurd*. Notre Dame, IN: University of Notre Dame Press, 1998.
Nolan, Joseph T. "What Can You Say about the Priesthood at a Time Like This?" *U.S. Catholic*, May 1968, 14–18.
Novak, Michael. "The Absolute Future." *Commonweal*, January 13, 1967, 400–402.
O'Brien, James M. "A Place to Put the Liturgy In." *National Catholic Reporter*, August 20, 1969, 4.
Ockman, Joan, ed. *Architecture School: Three Centuries of Educating Architects in North America*. Cambridge, MA: MIT Press, 2012.
O'Connell, J. B. *Church Building and Furnishing: The Church's Way, A Study in Liturgical Law*. Notre Dame, IN: University of Notre Dame Press, 1955.
O'Connor, Thomas H. *Building a New Boston: Politics and Urban Renewal, 1950–1970*. Boston: Northeastern University Press, 1995.
O'Donnell, Fr. Patrick, ed. *Churches for Tomorrow: Thirty-Three Designs from the Cardinal Lercaro Prize-Spaeth Competition Sponsored by the North American Liturgical Conference 1961*. Cincinnati: F&W Publishing, 1961.
O'Gara, James, ed. *The Postconciliar Parish*. New York: P. J. Kenedy & Sons, 1967.
O'Grady, Desmond. "Liturgy: Medium or Message?" *U.S. Catholic*, June 1970, 21–25.
O'Leary, Don. *Roman Catholicism and Modern Science: A History*. New York: Continuum, 2006.
Oliver, Richard, ed. *The Making of an Architect, 1881–1981: Columbia University in the City of New York*. New York: Rizzoli, 1981.
O'Malley, John W. *What Happened at Vatican II*. Cambridge, MA: Belknap Press of Harvard University Press, 2008.
O'Meara, Thomas F., and Donald M. Weisser, eds. *Projections: Shaping an American Theology for the Future*. Garden City, NY: Doubleday, 1970.

Ong, Walter J., SJ. *Darwin's Vision and Christian Perspectives*. New York: Macmillan, 1960.
———. *Frontiers of American Catholicism*. New York: Macmillan, 1957.
———. "The Reaches of History." *Commonweal*, August 15, 1958, 487–90.
Orsi, Robert A. "Introduction: Crossing the City Line." In *Gods of the City: Religion and the Urban American Landscape*, edited by Robert A. Orsi, 1–78. Bloomington: Indiana University Press, 1999.
Orvell, Miles. *The Real Thing: Imitation and Authenticity in American Culture, 1880–1940*. Chapel Hill: University of North Carolina Press, 1989.
Osborne, Catherine R. "American Catholics and the Art of the Future, 1930–1975." PhD diss., Fordham University, 2013.
———. "Anarchy in Our Churches? The American Architectural Press, 1944–65." *European Legacy* 22, no. 3 (2017): 278–92.
———. "From Sputnik to Spaceship Earth: American Catholics in the Space Age." *Religion & American Culture* 25, no. 2 (2015): 218–63.
———. "Managing and Quantifying Grace? Rev. Robert G. Howes, the Archdiocese of Baltimore, and the Origins of 'Pastoral Planning.'" *American Catholic Studies* 125, no. 1 (2014): 1–23.
———. "Renovating for the New Liturgy: The Boston College Students' Chapel." *American Catholic Studies* 125, no. 3 (2014): 93–104.
Pai, Hyungmin. *The Portfolio and the Diagram: Architecture, Discourse, and Modernity in America*. Cambridge, MA: MIT Press, 2002.
"A Panel Discussion at the National Catholic Building Convention." *Liturgical Arts* 17, no. 2 (1949): 29–33.
Pavia, Raymond. "Modern Church Building: Problems of Sacred Space." *Liturgical Arts* 31, no 3 (1963): 74–76.
Pearlman, Jill. *Inventing American Modernism: Joseph Hudnut, Walter Gropius, and the Bauhaus Legacy at Harvard*. Charlottesville: University of Virginia Press, 2007.
Pecklers, Keith F. *The Unread Vision: The Liturgical Movement in the United States of America, 1926–1955*. Collegeville, MN: Liturgical Press, 1998.
Polak, Frederik. *The Image of the Future: Enlightening the Past, Orientating the Present, Forecasting the Future*. New York: Oceana, 1961.
Pommer, Richard. *Idea as Model*. New York: Rizzoli International, 1981.
Price, Jay M. *Temples for a Modern God: Religious Architecture in Postwar America*. New York: Oxford University Press, 2013.
Proctor, Robert. *Building the Modern Church: Roman Catholic Church Architecture in Britain, 1955–1975*. London: Ashgate, 2014.
Quinn, Patrick J. "Church of Our Divine Savior, Chico, California." *Liturgical Arts* 38, no. 2 (1970): 50–51.
———. "Is There a Place for the Church in the Future City?" *Churchbuilding* 4 (1968): 3–6.
———. "The Architectural Implications of the Choir in the Worshipping Community." *Liturgical Arts* 34, no. 2 (1966): 38–46.
———. "The Church in the Future City: House-Church or Parish Place?" *Liturgical Arts* 35, no. 2 (1967): 88–90.
Quinn, Patrick J., and Richard Perry, eds. *Architecture and Religion in the Future City: A Study Presented at the 27th National Conference on Church Architecture, San Francisco, April 1966*. Berkeley, CA, 1966.

Raafat, Aly Ahmed. *Reinforced Concrete in Architecture*. New York: Reinhold, 1958.
Rambusch, Harold William. "This Talk about Art." *Commonweal*, October 2, 1929, 561.
Reagan, Oliver. "Building the House of God." *Commonweal*, March 11, 1925, 491–92.
Regional Oral History Office, the Bancroft Library. "Renaissance of Religious Art and Architecture in the San Francisco Bay Area, 1946–1968." Berkeley: University of California, 1985. Available at http://digitalassets.lib.berkeley.edu/roho/ucb/text/renaissance_v1.pdf.
Reinhold, H. A. "Father of the World to Come." *Worship* 26 (1952): 74–81.
———. *Bringing the Mass to the People*. Baltimore: Helicon, 1960.
———. "Styles Do Not Make a Church." *Orate Fratres* 17, no. 9 (1943): 414–18.
———. *The Dynamics of Liturgy*. New York: Macmillan, 1961.
———. "Thoughts on Church Planning." *Orate Fratres* 23 (1949): 509–14.
Rejnis, Ruth. "Catholics Update Church Design." *New York Times*, July 23, 1972.
"Religious Buildings." *Architectural Record*, June 1956, 183–213.
Remine, Shields. "A Catholic Center for New York University." *U.S. Catholic*, May 1966, 44–48.
"Revolution on the Secular Campus." *Jubilee*, April 1967, 16–23.
Ritter, Joseph E. "Towards a Living Climate of Religious Art." *Liturgical Arts* 23, no. 1 (1954): 3–4.
Rivers, Clarence. *Celebration*. New York: Herder and Herder, 1969.
Roberts, Jennifer L. *Mirror-Travels: Robert Smithson and History*. New Haven, CT: Yale University Press, 2004.
Roberts, Noel Keith. *From Piltdown Man to Point Omega: The Evolutionary Theory of Teilhard de Chardin*. New York: Peter Lang, 2000.
Roller, Paul Douglas. "An Ecumenical Council Center for the Christian Churches." *Liturgical Arts* 32, no. 3 (1964): 75–86.
Rubin, William. *Modern Sacred Art and the Church at Assy*. New York: Columbia University Press, 1961.
Rüegg, Walter, ed. *A History of the University in Europe: Universities in the Nineteenth and Early Twentieth Centuries (1800–1945)*. Vol. 3. Cambridge: Cambridge University Press, 2004.
Ruland Thorne, Kate. *Upon This Rock: Marguerite Brunswig Staude and Her Sedona Chapel*. Sedona, AZ: Chapel of the Holy Cross, 1995.
Sacred Congregation of Rites. *Instruction on Eucharistic Worship*. Washington, DC: United States Catholic Conference, 1967.
"Saint Botolph's Chapel." *Liturgical Arts* 35, no. 2 (1967): 98–99.
Salerno, Joseph. "Louis Sullivan—Return to Principle." *Liturgical Arts* 16, no. 2 (1948): 49–50.
Salvadori, Mario, and Robert Heller. *Structure in Architecture: The Building of Buildings*. 2nd ed. Englewood Cliffs, NJ: Prentice-Hall, 1975.
Schickel, William. "Unifying the Old and the New." *Liturgical Arts* 36, no. 4 (1968): 99–100.
Schickel, William, and James Rogan. "The Cultural Importance of the Liturgy." *Liturgical Arts* 28, no. 3 (1960): 66–67.
Schiltz, Michael E. "We Need Some Parishes without Boundaries." *U.S. Catholic & Jubilee*, September 1970, 14–18.
Schloesser, Stephen, SJ. "Against Forgetting: Memory, History, Vatican II." In *Vatican II: Did Anything Happen?* edited by David G. Schultenover, 92–152. New York: Continuum, 2007.
———. *Jazz Age Catholicism: Mystic Modernism in Postwar Paris, 1919–1933*. Toronto: University of Toronto Press, 2005.

Scholes, Robert E. *Structural Fabulation: An Essay on Fiction of the Future*. Notre Dame, IN: University of Notre Dame Press, 1975.

Schultz, Kevin M. *Tri-Faith America: How Catholics and Jews Held Postwar America to Its Protestant Promise*. New York: Oxford University Press, 2011.

Schwarz, Hans. *Eschatology*. Grand Rapids, MI: Eerdmans, 2000.

Seasoltz, R. Kevin, OSB. "From the Bauhaus to the House of God's People: Frank Kacmarcik's Contribution to Church Architecture and Art." *U.S. Catholic Historian* 15 (1997): 105–22.

———. *A Sense of the Sacred: Theological Foundations of Christian Architecture and Art*. New York: Bloomsbury Academic, 2005.

Seitz, John. *No Closure: Catholic Practice and Boston's Parish Shutdowns*. Cambridge, MA: Harvard University Press, 2011.

Shanken, Andrew M. *194X: Architecture, Planning, and Consumer Culture on the American Home Front*. Minneapolis: University of Minnesota Press, 2009.

Siff, Stephen. "Henry Luce's Strange Trip." *Journalism History* 34 (2008): 126–34.

Siry, Joseph M. *Unity Temple: Frank Lloyd Wright and Architecture for Liberal Religion*. Cambridge, MA: MIT Press, 1996.

Slaton, Amy E. *Reinforced Concrete and the Modernization of American Building, 1900–1930*. Baltimore: Johns Hopkins University Press, 2001.

"The Slow Evolution of Religious Buildings." *Architectural Record*, December 1949, 121–28.

"Small Churches in the Kansas City Diocese." *Liturgical Arts* 15, no. 1 (1946): 13.

Smith, Earl Baldwin. *The Study of the History of Art in the Colleges and Universities of the United States*. Princeton, NJ: Princeton University Press, 1912.

Smith, Hamilton. "The Buildings at St. John's Abbey, Collegeville, Minnesota." *Design Quarterly* 53 (1961): 1–31.

Smithson, Robert. "Quasi-infinities and the Waning of Space." *Arts Magazine*, November 1966, 28–31.

Smyth, Craig Hugh, and Peter M. Lukehart, eds. *The Early Years of Art History in the United States: Notes and Essays on Departments, Teaching, and Scholars*. Princeton, NJ: Department of Art and Archaeology, Princeton University, 1993.

Soja, Edward W. *Postmodern Geographies: The Reassertion of Space in Critical Social Theory*. London: Verso, 1989.

Soleri, Paolo. *The Bridge between Matter and Spirit Is Matter Becoming Spirit: The Arcology of Paolo Soleri*. Garden City, NY: Anchor Books, 1973.

———. *The Omega Seed: An Eschatological Hypothesis*. Garden City, NY: Anchor /Doubleday, 1981.

———. *Technology and Cosmogenesis*. New York: Paragon House, 1985.

Spaeth, Otto. "Worship and the Arts." *Architectural Record*, December 1955, 162–67.

Steadman, Philip. *The Evolution of Designs: Biological Analogy in Architecture and the Applied Arts*. Cambridge: Cambridge University Press, 1979.

Stevens, Jay. *Storming Heaven: LSD and the American Dream*. New York: Atlantic Monthly Press, 1987.

Stevens, Rev. Clifford. "The Cosmic Adventure: A Challenge to Theology." *Liturgical Arts* 36, no. 1 (1967): 10.

———. "The Las Cruces Experiment." *Liturgical Arts* 34, no. 4 (1966): 142–43.

Stoddard, Whitney S. *Adventure in Architecture: Building the New Saint John's*. New York: Longmans, Green, 1958.
Storr, Robert. "A Man of Parts." In *Tony Smith: Architect, Painter, Sculptor*, 10–35. New York: Museum of Modern Art, 1998.
Stowell, Jerome, CP. "Is There a Future for the Neighborhood Mass?" *Homiletic and Pastoral Review* LXVIII (1967): 225–31.
Tavard, George. *The Church Tomorrow*. New York: Herder and Herder, 1965.
Teilhard de Chardin, Pierre, SJ. *The Future of Man*. Translated by Norman Denny. New York: Harper & Row, 1964.
Thiry, Paul, Richard M. Bennett, and Henry L. Kamphoefner. *Churches & Temples*. New York: Reinhold, 1953.
Thorman, Donald J. *American Catholics Face the Future*. Wilkes-Barre, PA: Dimension Books, 1968.
"Three Churches in the Mid-West." *Liturgical Arts* 18, no. 4 (1950): 91–93.
"To Update a Large Church Built in the 1920s Is a Problem." *Liturgical Arts* 38, no. 2 (1970): 52.
Toffler, Alvin. *Future Shock*. New York: Random House, 1970.
Torgerson, Mark Allen. *An Architecture of Immanence: Architecture for Worship and Ministry Today*. Grand Rapids, MI: Eerdmans, 2007.
Trevor, Meriol. *Newman*. 2 vols. Garden City, NY: Doubleday, 1963.
Tuan, Yi-Fu. *Space and Place: The Perspective of Experience*. Minneapolis: University of Minnesota Press, 1977.
Tweed, Thomas A. *America's Church: The National Shrine and Catholic Presence in the Nation's Capital*. New York: Oxford University Press, 2011.
Van Eck, Caroline. *Organicism in Nineteenth-Century Architecture: An Inquiry into Its Theoretical and Philosophical Background*. Amsterdam: Architectura & Natura Press, 1994.
Wall, Donald. *Visionary Cities: The Arcology of Paolo Soleri*. New York: Praeger, 1971.
Watts, Alan. *The Joyous Cosmology: Adventures in the Chemistry of Consciousness*. New York: Vintage Books, 1965.
White, Susan J. *Art, Architecture, and Liturgical Reform: The Liturgical Arts Society (1928–1972)*. New York: Pueblo, 1990.
Williams, Peter W. *Houses of God: Region, Religion, and Architecture in the United States*. Urbana: University of Illinois Press, 1997.
"Wizard of the Shells." *Architectural Forum* 111 (1959): 154–59.
Wolfe, Gregory. *Sacred Passion: The Art of William Schickel*. Notre Dame, IN: University of Notre Dame Press, 2010.
Wolfe, Tom. "McLuhan's New World." *Wilson Quarterly* 28, no. 2 (Spring 2004): 18–25.
Wood, John Walter. "Ferro-Concrete as a Building Material." *Liturgical Arts* 2, no. 2 (1933): 68–79.
Wood, Linda Sargent. *A More Perfect Union: Holistic Worldviews and the Transformation of American Culture after World War II*. New York: Oxford University Press, 2010.
Worship in the City of Man: Twenty-Seventh North American Liturgical Week, Houston, Texas, August 22–25, 1966. Washington, DC: Liturgical Conference, 1966.
Young, Victoria M. *Marcel Breuer's Saint John's Abbey Church: A New Vision for Liturgical Architecture*. Minneapolis: University of Minnesota Press, 2014.

INDEX